WORKING LIVES & WORKER MILITANCY

The Politics of Labour in Colonial India

WORKING LIVES & WORKER MILITANCY

The Politics of Labour in Colonial India

Edited by RAVI AHUJA

Tulika Books

Published by
Tulika Books
35 A/1, Shahpur Jat, New Delhi 110 049, India
tulikabooks.wordpress.com

First edition (hardback) 2013

ISBN: 978-93-82381-21-1

Printed at Chaman Offset, Delhi 110 002

Contents

Acknowledgments

Earlier versions of all but one of the essays in this volume (Ahmad Azhar, Shahana Bhattacharya, Anna Sailer, Aditya Sarkar, Tanika Sarkar) were originally presented at an international workshop on 'The Politics of Poverty and the Politics of the Poor in Modern South Asia' that was held at the Centre for Modern Indian Studies in Göttingen, in 2011. A first draft of the remaining essay (Ravi Ahuja) was first discussed at an international workshop on 'The Boundaries of "Free" Labor: XIX and XX Century Perspectives', convened by Henrique Espada Lima in 2012 at the IGK 'Work and Human Lifecycle in Global History' at Humboldt University, Berlin. Engaging discussions at both workshops helped to improve the original texts and we thank all who contributed to them.

We are also indebted to our friends of the Association of Indian Labour Historians, particularly to Sabyasachi Bhattacharya, Rana Behal, Chitra Joshi and Prabhu Mohapatra, for creating extraordinarily lively and egalitarian forums of debate on Indian labour history over many years – forums that have created an environment conducive to the development of new ideas and approaches, including some that are central to this book.

Research for Ravi Ahuja's and Ahmad Azhar's contributions, and the translation of Bashir Ahmed Bakhtiar's memoirs, were generously funded by the German Research Council (DFG). In the process of preparing the book manuscript, Anja Collazo's assistance has been extremely valuable. We also thank Maya John and others at Tulika Books for their committed work.

Preface

'Labour', as a political category, has been subjected to severe depreciation in South Asia since the 1980s – a dramatic reversal of a process that had set in during the deep global as well as regional crisis following the First World War. The intensity of worker militancy in the 1920s and 1930s had pushed the 'labour problem' squarely on to the stage of Indian politics. Whether in search of an anti-colonial and/or anti-capitalist revolutionary force, of a newly emerging and as yet untapped electoral constituency, or of a condition of social peace and trusteeship conducive to nation-building, diverse Indian political forces 'discovered' (mainly urban and industrial) working classes in these decades as a source of political energy to reckon with, like it or not. The brief period of Congress provincial rule in the late 1930s, the following years of a late-colonial war administration, as well as the first decade of political independence saw the emergence of a state-centred labour regime that sought to contain and control this source of political energy by enforcing 'industrial peace', fostering 'responsible trade unions' and developing a social policy focused on workers in the 'organized sector', thereby separating them from the majority of the workforce. In Pakistan, with a divergent political trajectory, the social policy component was less pronounced and state repression so prominent as to confine labour militancy largely to the narrow chronological window of 1968–72. In India, however, labour militancy certainly did not freeze as the state assumed the role of a supreme regulatory agency with regard to industrial relations. In fact, worker participation in industrial conflicts expanded considerably in the two decades after the Second World War, and reached new heights between the late 1960s and mid-1980s. Even so, the state-centred, corporativist labour regime that began to take shape in the last decade of colonial rule persisted as the main frame of reference for India's politics of labour until the 1980s: legal rights, though often unimplemented and granted only to a minuscule proportion of the workforce, generated horizons of expectation and helped to formulate and substantiate more far-reaching political demands.

By then, however, the utility of this labour regime was questioned more insistently by corporate spokesmen and other influential constituents of India's ruling bloc, and a new hegemonic consensus emerged that the 'liberalization' of India's economy required to put to rest the old labour policy. This objective was subsequently achieved, in the main, by way of systematic non-implementation and circumvention, rather than by formally abolishing the legal framework. What amounted to a major policy change became possible in a situation when industrial restructuring offered, as an important side-effect, an opportunity to do away altogether with those cores of labour militancy the old regime had failed to rein in. If industrial labour up to the 1980s had received official and public attention to a degree out of all proportion with the consistently small share of factory workers in India's workforce, 'labour' has now all but ceased to be a useable category in Indian politics. Whereas leading politicians from S.A. Dange to Jagjivan Ram and V.V. Giri to George Fernandes gained their clout by engaging with issues of 'labour', present-day union leaders complain of political marginalization even if their own party is in power. 'Labour', accordingly, is no longer 'good copy' and most Indian dailies have got rid of their labour correspondents. By the same token, 'labour' has lost much of its earlier attraction for the lower classes and their movements as a conceptual tool of self-assertion; its ambit has narrowed down considerably. While caste issues could at one time be expressed, for instance, with reasonable hope of success in the political language of 'labour' (just think of Ambedkar's Independent Labour Party), the progressive political invisibilization of workers in recent decades has rendered it more promising to address 'traditional' labour issues in 'identitarian' political languages of 'caste' or of minority rights.

The story, though interpreted in various ways, has been told many times – nor is it unique, in its broad features, to the Indian subcontinent. Moreover, the postcolonial half of this account does not seem to be, at first sight, centrally relevant to the subject of a book focusing on the period between the late 1890s and the 1950s. But I think it is, for the political and social climate of the last three decades has had its impact on the angles researchers chose when they approached the history of South Asian labour. The present enabled them to ask new and important historical questions; it overshadowed, simultaneously, other (at times) no less critical ones and could even encourage to read history backwards. The result was a new, inventive, argumentative, intellectually attractive historiography of South Asian labour, to which Dipesh Chakrabarty, Rajnarayan Chandavarkar, Ranajit Das Gupta, Chitra Joshi, Samita Sen and many others have made significant contributions.[1] This variegated corpus of writings is distinguishable from earlier studies of the history of Indian labour in that it refused to equate the history of workers with labour movement history, or, even more narrowly, with the history of trade unions and their top-level leadership. This was an extremely productive move as it permitted a much broader perspective on working lives, working households, bonds of community and on the so far neglected majority of labour relations outside large industrial units. This discrimination between the history of workers and labour movement history was facilitated by a social climate where, on the one hand, the decline of 'labour' *as a political category* implied the decay of key labour organizations across the political spectrum, while, on the other hand, wage labour persisted and even expanded *as a mode of subsistence*, though subjected to important processes of restructuring (including relocation, 'informalization', deindustrialization, the rise of new industries and unheard-of levels of international labour migration).

Yet, laying emphasis on the non-identity of the histories of labour and of the labour movement begged the question of how exactly they (and their protagonists) related to each other. The political and social dynamics unfolding before the eyes of historians implied that the simplistic, linear narrative of a coming into its own of the working classes by way of a steadily growing class consciousness, resulting in a progressively unified labour movement, was irretrievably refuted by life itself. There was thus a strong backlash among academics against such labourist modernization narratives. The boldest counter-narrative was that of Dipesh Chakrabarty, who proclaimed that 'the class identity of the worker could never be distilled out of the precapitalist identities that arose from the relationships he had been born into'. Sustained class-based mentalities and self-organization among Indian workers were thus impossible on the grounds of their inescapable imprisonment in a hierarchical, inegalitarian culture, or, in other words, because of unbridgeable cultural difference.[2] This argument was received with much interest. It even commanded a certain degree of intuitive plausibility as it resonated with the decline of labour as a political category that was so conspicuous by the late 1980s. However, it eventually found few takers in the emerging new historiography of Indian labour – perhaps an upshot of most historians' distrust in deterministic models. For, if the now-implausible labourist narrative had been based on a comprehensively deterministic model of history (with social practice only having the tasks of following a set track and of filling the gaps of the model with random detail), the counter-narrative was based on a comprehensively deterministic model of culture (with social practice only having the tasks of turning the treadmill and, again, of filling the gaps).

Most labour historians of India chose not to opt for either of the models and focused instead on the 'gaps', which were no gaps after all but concrete historical situations, each bearing the potential to unfold in more than one way. These concrete historical situations, comprising *inter alia* the structures of everyday working-class life and events of worker militancy, needed to be understood on their own terms and as *actively experienced*. Workers needed to be understood, accordingly, not as comprehensively and exclusively subsumed under fully predetermined structures of either economic class or community culture, but as actively inhabiting (and thereby reproducing as well as reshaping) various fields of social practice (e.g., as wage workers, rural tenants and urban petty commodity producers), including forms of self-identification (such as gender, caste, nation, class or religion).

The result of this theoretically often more reticent and at times even agnostic scholarship was a series of highly nuanced, rich and sophisticated social and cultural histories of concrete *situations* of working life, and of *moments* of social mobilization involving workers.

Much of this writing self-consciously sought to keep a distance from the old labourist modernization narrative with two, in some cases perhaps inadvertent, side-effects: first, there was some aversion, as one wished to avoid hackneyed teleologies, to move beyond a particular historical situation in order to contextualize it in a longer, possibly complex historical tendency; second, though workers' militancy and involvement with social and political movements were at the centre of this new historiography, a reluctance still prevailed to investigate the connections of the local 'politics of the poor' that one analysed painstakingly with larger political processes and, particularly for the twentieth century, with the politics of the labour movement. These drawbacks are important, but should not be exaggerated. If labour historians may now attempt to overcome them by examining the *history of labour as a political history rooted in particular local situations but extending beyond them*, they can draw upon significant exceptions to the above-mentioned historiographical pattern. The late writings of Raj Chandavarkar, in particular, appear to have strained against the limitations of an earlier, to some extent de-processualized, high-resolution photographic approach, which he himself had co-authored.[3] Moreover, the contributors to this volume, like most historians exploring this field, do not show any inclination to disregard or overturn the micro-historical approach that has proved so productive in South Asia's post-1980s' labour historiography. Rather, they have explored various possibilities of further developing this approach in order to sharpen its critical edge.

The papers gathered in this volume were not written as contributions to a coordinated project or in fulfilment of any overarching agenda, though most were presented and discussed, in earlier versions, at an international workshop in 2011. While all of them are indebted to the lively culture of debate that has attracted many younger scholars to South Asian (and especially Indian) labour history in recent years, each of the essays is grounded in thorough archival research and/or fieldwork conducted by an individual researcher, and shaped by distinct theoretical outlooks and historiographical concerns. All of the articles are, according to the ruthlessly commercialized standards of Anglo-American academic publishers, excessively long – and they ought to be, in order to give space to a careful exposition and analysis of hitherto unused historical material. We appreciate our publisher's irreligious resistance to 'market pressures' that gave us the intellectual freedom to opt for what we think is a more useful format for purposes of developing new themes and approaches. Yet, if the generous space allotted to the authors has allowed for richer texts, one of the consequences is that a preface can hardly do justice to them by way of introduction and, much less, spare the reader the effort of discovering for her/himself the arguments each of these texts has to offer. I will thus confine myself in this preface to pointing out resonances between the essays.

What holds this volume together, it may be said, is an implicit methodological consensus of using the close-up analysis of *modalities* of labour protest for the purpose of making sense of the prevalence of worker militancy in late-colonial India, and for re-examining long-held, seemingly commonsensical assumptions about the politics of labour in that period. Several of the articles look into these modalities by focusing on specific *events* involving large numbers of workers – plague riots in turn-of-the-century Bombay (Aditya Sarkar), a railway strike following the Rowlatt Satyagraha and Khilafat agitation in Lahore (Ahmad Azhar), the 1928 municipal sweepers' strike in Calcutta (Tanika Sarkar) and the famous jute workers' 'general strike' in the following year (Anna Sailer). Some of these events are well known and have been explored before, but the present essays differ from earlier writings in several ways. Crucially, they give more attention to the *unfolding of the event*. Aditya Sarkar and Anna Sailer trace the unfolding of the respective event *in space* – space in a material, social–geographic and non-metaphorical sense. Resulting from this approach, the crucial role of 'circulatory labour' in facilitating the rapid spread of riots and strikes across urban space, or the complex relationships between the townships of an extensive industrial belt that conditioned the spatial, temporal and political pattern of a 'general strike', are brought out clearly – concrete modalities of the unfolding of 'crowd events' which are, in more conventional accounts, often lazily disposed of with naturalizing images (the rising tide, the wildfire and what have you) that obscure the social forces at work. Tracing specific modalities of crowd mobilization is no mean achievement because, by the usually illegal nature of this mobilization in late-colonial India, much social energy went into concealing the forces behind it.

To the extent that painstaking historical reconstruction succeeds in revealing these forces, it will be more difficult to hold up the conventional image of the upper-caste/middle-class leader who, as a social outsider, almost single-handedly, and solely relying on charisma and a culturally determined '*ma–bap*' status, sparks off crowd action and controls the 'masses' (if only fleetingly) in periods of upheaval. The limitedness of caste/class-based hegemony is brought out in Tanika Sarkar's account of a head-on collision between the aspirations of low-caste municipal sweepers and Calcutta's nationalist leadership. According to Ahmad Azhar's analysis of a labour movement that emerged in Lahore from the broader 'plebeian' anti-Rowlatt and Khilafat movements under upper-class hegemony, workers used the forms of protest shaped in the course of these movements, but gained relative autonomy by generating their own more radical agenda and leadership.

Further perspectives on the modalities of labour protest and on the unfolding of events are offered by essays exploring what might be called the 'prehistory of events': the *political* tensions that were embedded in the texture of working lives and in everyday social relations of 'labour'. Shahana Bhattacharya demonstrates accordingly how, in an essentially micro-political way, specific renderings of norms of caste status were used to create what amounted to a new workforce of 'untouchable' industrial leather workers. Moreover, she brings out clearly the politically charged character of quotidian conflicts over 'customary gifts' or casteist verbal abuse. My own contribution (Ravi Ahuja) argues that the highly political notions of 'freedom' and 'slavery' regularly cropped up in and resonated with quotidian 'micro-events', namely, conflicts over the temporal limits of the wage labour relationship at the shop-floor or, in this case, shipboard level.

The careful analysis of events or 'micro-events' of labour protest also calls into question an implicitly held or explicitly formulated hypothesis that has prevailed for long with regard to South Asian labour history: labour leaders were necessarily 'outsiders' in terms of class and often caste, since illiteracy, cultural barriers and the linguistic requirement of negotiating with political authorities in English impeded the rise of 'organic intellectuals' from among the working classes. However, several contributions to this volume (especially Azhar, but also Ahuja, Bhattacharya and Sailer) indicate that the importance of local or shopfloor-level leadership in the unfolding of incidents of labour militancy may have been seriously underrated. This 'lower' but crucial level of leadership was forced, at least as long as the protagonists had to rely on wage labour themselves, to minimize its visibility since the coercive powers of employers and the state came down far more heavily on the worker-militant ('victimization' of so-called 'ringleaders' is a permanent issue in early trade union documents) than on the middle-class 'outsider' (the latter was certainly being frowned upon by the authorities but, as Tanika Sarkar points out in her essay, was also protected to some extent by partaking in powerful social networks). Worker-militants are also less visible for the historian since they were less likely to leave behind memoirs or other published traces of their activities than English-educated, high-caste trade union leaders. This explains, to some extent, why we have several historical analyses of the figure of the 'outsider', but virtually none of the 'ringleader' who, being a part as well as the leader of a 'ring' or 'illicit combination', was an 'insider' by definition. Yet limitations of historical evidence should not be exaggerated: influential labour leaders did rise from the ranks of the worker-militants during the interwar period, and some of them did actually write their memoirs or had them tape-recorded, though usually in their own languages rather than in English. Bashir Ahmed Bakhtiar, a powerful labour organizer in pre-independence Amritsar and later an influential trade union leader in Pakistan, is a fascinating but surely not a unique case in point. His memoirs, published and severally reissued by his Lahore-based trade union, have been translated from the Urdu and are made available in this volume for the first time to an English-language readership, together with an introduction by Ahmad Azhar. We hope this will encourage a more serious engagement with the rich but neglected literature created by South Asian workers (ego documents of various kinds, but more frequently poetry), to reflect upon both working lives and worker militancy in their own languages.

While Bashir Ahmed Bakhtiar's memoirs can be read in many ways, they certainly do call into question two further widespread assumptions about South Asian labour movement history. First, the relationship between militant, even violent, labour movements on the one hand, and on the other, the legally formalized, 'responsible' or, as Bakhtiar puts it, 'genuine' trade unionism emerging from the late 1930s onwards appears highly ambivalent. The latter form of labour politics hence appears to emerge from the former in Bakhtiar's life story without being distinguished as an altogether different approach or phase. Similarly, the tacit combination of highly confrontational, militarized or openly violent forms of protest with politics of formalized bargaining looms large in several of the contributions to this volume (Azhar, Bhattacharya, Tanika Sarkar). A deeper analysis of this ambivalence or tension between militant and pacified, unregulated and regulated forms of labour protest may help us to better understand even more recent developments in South Asia's world of labour, including the dramatic contemporary history of conflict in Manesar.

A second question foregrounded by Bakhtiar's account is the following. The bulk of relevant historical writings has focused on the history of workers and labour movements in large industrial units, mainly factories, which has created the impression that South Asia's trade union movement has been solely confined from its inception to what would figure later as the 'organized' or 'formal sector'. Bakhtiar's proud enumeration of the trade unions he claims to have founded in Amritsar before India's partition and independence demonstrates, however, the total and unwitting indifference of the author to the formal/informal divide, at least at the time he refers to in this account: they included unions for gutter sweepers, cow-herders, cloth hawkers, lorry drivers, '*tandoor* workers' (who prepared bread in restaurants and hotels) and various kinds of artisans employed in small workshops, as much as the more likely textile mill workers' unions. The same preparedness of trade union organizers of the 1930s to 1950s to work indiscriminately among workers employed in many distinct labour forms, including what today is understood as the archetypal 'informal sector' worker, is particularly evident in Shahana Bhattacharya's and Tanika Sarkar's essays on tanners and sweepers who were not only employed outside the space of the large factory, but also subjected to particularly fierce stigmatization as 'untouchables'. In his recent book on *Small Town Capitalism in Western India*, Douglas Haynes has similarly pointed out intense union activities among workers in small weaving workshops or *karkhanas* in the 1940s and 50s.[4] Even for the period preceding the large-scale emergence of trade unions, Aditya Sarkar's contribution to this volume hints at the crucial importance of non-factory-employed, 'circulatory' labour such as construction workers, for the spread of labour militancy across larger spaces. Yet again we are confronted with a specific modality of unfolding labour movements that requires further examination.

On the basis of the joint achievement of many scholars since the 1990s towards reframing South Asian labour history as a social and cultural history, it may now be possible to reclaim labour history as an explicitly political history that is deeply rooted in quotidian social relations of labour, and in the accumulated and active experiences of working lives. The contributions to this volume explore this possibility, each in its own way. If they provoke further discussion and prompt younger scholars to engage historically with the politics of labour well into the postcolonial and contemporary periods, the book will have served its purpose.

Notes and References

1 For a recent, comprehensive and critical survey of Indian labour historiography, see Chitra Joshi, 'Histories of Indian Labour: Predicaments and Possibilities', *History Compass*, 6 (2), 2008: 439–54.

2 Dipesh Chakrabarty, *Rethinking Working-Class History: Bengal 1890–1940*, Princeton: Princeton University Press, 1989: 218, 229 and *passim*.

3 See especially Raj Chandarvarkar, 'From Neighbourhood to Nation: The Rise and Fall of the Left in Bombay's Girangaon in the Twentieth Century', in M. Menon and N. Adarkar (eds), *One Hundred Years, One Hundred Voices: The Mill Workers of Girangaon: An Oral History*, Calcutta: Seagull Books, 2004; and Raj Chandavarkar, 'The Decline and Fall of the Jobber System in the Bombay Cotton Textile Industry, 1870–1955', *Modern Asian Studies*, 42 (1), 2008: 117–210.

4 Douglas Haynes, *Small Town Capitalism in Western India: Artisans, Merchants, and the Making of the Informal Economy, 1870–1960*, Cambridge: Cambridge University Press, 2012.

February 2013 RAVI AHUJA

Contributors

RAVI AHUJA is Professor of Modern Indian History at the Centre for Modern Indian Studies, University of Göttingen, Germany. He works on various problems of social history, including labour, urbanism, infrastructure and war.

AHMAD AZHAR is a Ph.D. student of South Asian History at the Centre for Modern Indian Studies, University of Göttingen, Germany. He investigates the history of plebeian and labour movements in pre-partition Lahore.

BASHIR AHMED BAKHTIAR (1909–1993) established himself as a militant labour organizer in Amritsar in the 1930s, was an official of the 'Royist' Indian Federation of Labour during World War II, and emerged, after partition, as one of Pakistan's most influential trade union leaders with strong links to the International Confederation of Free Trade Unions (ICFTU).

SHAHANA BHATTACHARYA is Associate Professor of History at Kirori Mal College, University of Delhi, India. Her research explores the interdependence of caste and labour relationships.

ANNA SAILER is a Ph.D. student of South Asian History at the Centre for Modern Indian Studies, University of Göttingen, Germany. She works on a reappraisal of the history of labour in Kolkata's jute industry.

ADITYA SARKAR is Assistant Professor of Modern Indian History at the University of Warwick, Coventry, United Kingdom. His research interests include the history of labour, the social history of Bombay and the political history of post-independence India.

TANIKA SARKAR is Professor of History at Jawaharlal Nehru University, New Delhi, India. She has published widely on various aspects of India's political and intellectual history, on gender history, and on the history of social reform movements.

The City, Its Streets and Its Workers

The Plague Crisis in Bombay, 1896–98

Aditya Sarkar

Between the concluding years of the nineteenth century and the first quarter of the twentieth, colonial India was recurrently struck by bubonic plague. The infected rat flea (which was very belatedly recognized by official medical opinion as the principal vector of the disease) began to make its presence felt in Bombay in mid-1896. India's principal port and central commercial artery thus swiftly appeared in another incarnation, as one of the nodal points of the third – and last – global plague pandemic, which spread from Hong Kong, left its most legible imprints upon China and India, and in large part journeyed through the maritime networks of European colonialism. Historians of the pandemic have considered Bombay's crisis within a global narrative of epidemic catastrophe and its consequences. Bombay, it has been demonstrated, exhibited many of the historical regularities that underpinned the global spread of the epidemic. These included the practices of inoculation (after Yersin developed the serum in 1894); governmental and medical obsessions with contagion (and residual preoccupations with miasma); a close correlation between social class and plague mortality; episodes of panic-driven flight and migration, and widespread urban chaos dovetailing with projects of city renewal in the wake of the disease.[1]

This essay is concerned with the early years of the epidemic in Bombay – to be precise, the year and a half following the initial outbreak of the disease in September 1896 – and the crisis of urban social control that attended it. Bombay's plague *crisis*, in the fullest sense, was played out in these years. To make this claim is not to refute the fact that many of the consequences of the plague, its demographic effects (the increase in mortality rates and the recurrence of panic-driven flight from the city) in particular, fully unfolded in the medium rather than in the short term. However, the middle of 1898 did mark a sharp shift, ushering in a significantly new – and, in comparison with its predecessors, less invasive – system of plague control which rested largely on inoculation rather than on widespread inspection, confinement, destruction of dwellings, and compulsory segregation and hospitalization of the sick, measures which had defined early experiments in plague policy.

The outbreak of plague in Bombay, as its historians have observed, was characterized above all by intense conflicts between the city's rulers and its urban working classes. An unprecedented crisis of authority took shape, principally over attempts to impose authoritarian systems of plague control upon working-class neighbourhoods and the often violent resistance that these provoked. The arguments developed in this essay seek to identify, at the base of these tensions, a serious *crisis of labour relations*. To this end, the essay surveys different episodes of urban unrest provoked by policies of plague control and in each case relates them to the threat of a withdrawal of labour – a threat that acquired a new salience in these years since it appeared to menace the very survival of the city, and forced new priorities and policy choices upon the colonial and municipal administration.

The other vector of argument developed here concerns the spatial configuration of class relations in late nineteenth-century Bombay. The urban unrest attendant upon the plague crisis, it is suggested, invested the ways in which social space came to be composed in the city, with new tensions. Bombay's rapid industrialization in the closing decades of the nineteenth century produced sharp socio-spatial polarizations between an affluent south and a predominantly working-class north, buffered by a mostly plebeian 'native town' in between. As systems of public order and labour control broke down at critical junctures during the plague crisis, this disposition of spatial relations revealed latent social tensions that were hitherto submerged, for the most part, by the rhythms of everyday life.

The architecture of the argument merits some explanation. The essay begins with a detailed narrative reconstruction of an event often identified as a turning-point in strategies of plague control – a riot in the working-class locality of Madanpura in March 1898. The themes that run through the essay – the confrontation between state authorities and the city's working classes; the spatial dimensions of this conflict; the labour relations, now threatened, that sustained social order in the city – are all present in this section. However, these themes are not analysed separately but introduced as they flow through the event, and into each other. The choice is deliberate: only an extended narrative account can adequately render the dynamism and the shifts in the relationships between supervening structures and the events that confirm and disturb them.

Having introduced the principal elements of analysis through this narrative, the essay works backwards as it were, to the history of urban socio-spatial relations in the age of capitalist industrialization in Bombay. This culminates in an analysis of two other episodes of social unrest that prefigured the riot of 1898 that the essay begins with. Then, the story moves back to the riot and its repercussions – a week-long strike that paralysed the rhythms that urban order was built on, and the historical shifts this sequence of events heralded.

The Riot

'What is the object of streets?' asked Barker.

'What is the object of supper?' cried Buck, furiously. 'Isn't it obvious? This

> military science is mere common sense. The object of a street is to lead from one place to another; therefore all streets join; therefore street fighting is quite a peculiar thing. You advanced into that hive of streets as though you were advancing into an open plain where you could see everything. Instead of that, you were advancing into the bowels of a fortress, with streets pointing at you, streets turning on you, streets jumping out at you, and all in the hands of the enemy.'
>
> – G.K. Chesterton, *The Napoleon of Notting Hill*

On the morning of 9 March 1898, with bubonic plague raging all round Bombay, a nervous team of temporary government employees arrived at No. 33-A, Ripon Cross Lane, to search it for people whom the colonial administration charmingly described as 'plague suspects'.[2] The lane was part of a cluster of winding lanes and back streets enclosed by two larger roads on their west and east flanks – Ripon Road and Morland Road – and bounded by Bellasis Road on their south. Ripon Road stretched northwards till Jacob's Circle, popularly known as *Saat Rasta* (Seven Roads), where seven of the roads at the heart of Bombay's working-class district met.[3] The small stretch of land between Ripon Road and Morland Road comprised Madanpura, a distinctive locality of the poor and the very poor, populated largely by Muslim weavers and their families.[4] Most of these families were made up of migrants from eastern Uttar Pradesh belonging to the Julaha (or, in colonial parlance, 'Jhulai') caste, as did the eponymous Madan who had given his name to the locality – a name, curiously, that appears to have attached itself to many places in northern and western India where members of this community chose to settle down.[5] Over 2,000 people from such families were, in the time-honoured custom of Bombay, packed into a large chawl located on Ripon Cross Lane, a small lane that forked off Ripon Road into the heart of Madanpura (see map on p. 12).

The search party was led by D.R. Gilder, a Parsi medical student, and comprised M.S. Ruknuddin, a Muslim sub-inspector, and three other employees hastily drafted into plague duty by the British administration. It was one of many that scoured the city in the closing years of the nineteenth century, inspecting houses and localities mainly inhabited by the city's labouring poor where the existence of 'plague suspects' was considered a probability. The outbreak of the epidemic in September 1896 had stretched the resources and imagination of the city's thinly 'representative' municipal executive beyond its powers, and the Presidency administration stepped in by appointing a series of Plague Committees – consisting of doctors, 'respected members of communities', Indian policemen, European police officers and, periodically, European soldiers – to do the work of inspection, identification, segregation and hospitalization. A posse of municipal servants at the bottom of Bombay's caste hierarchy generally accompanied or followed such teams to perform the riskier and more fatiguing labour of conservancy and sanitation. Such incursions of state authority into Indian households and neighbourhoods, as Jim Masselos has observed, broke down the boundaries established by law and social custom between public and private space, and exposed the 'sovereign' domain of the Indian household to external scrutiny. Much like the epidemic itself, the work of scrutiny, to borrow Masselos' evocative phrase, 'leapfrogged barriers and hierarchies'.[6]

Such barriers, according to official gossip, had been most effectively put up by the Julaha community of Madanpura in Bombay. J.M. Campbell, scholar–administrator and head of the Plague Committee in 1898, summed up official opinion well: 'The Jhulais of Madanpura have for years been known to be excitable and somewhat disaffected.'[7] The reference was both general and particular: it attested the fear of 'Mahomedan discontent' that had held much of the British-Indian administration in its grip ever since the Mutiny of 1857, but also invoked memories of a more recent event, the communal riots of 1893 in Bombay where Muslim weavers and Hindu mill-hands had been the most violent and visible antagonists.[8] R.H. Vincent, the Commissioner of Police who had handled that confrontation, appended his own, slightly more elaborate sociology to the interpretation of the Julaha mind. The jumble of castes, races and sects in Bombay, he asserted, made 'a certain contingent of bad characters inevitable'. The 'Jhulais' exemplified this, being 'a sect of fanatical, turbulent and bigoted Musalmans'.[9]

Such fears helped to generate a situation where the weavers of Madanpura were, on the whole, more lightly policed under plague regulations than most other working-class communities in the city. At several junctures in 1897 and 1898 military search parties were deployed to help with plague investigation. They were kept away from Madanpura, however, which was serviced instead by medical officers, Justices of the Peace and other 'men of position'.[10] Nor were Julaha houses vacated with the casual brutality suffered by many other working-class inhabitants of the city. Instead, following a long-standing principle of colonial administration, the Bombay government made use of designated/recognized 'community headmen', in this case Sardar Umar Jamal and the 'Jhulai Chaudhuri' Nur Ali, to help them with the work of identifying plague victims and removing them to hospital. The hospital in question had been specifically set up to treat Julahas and was managed 'by their own *Hakim*, who has lived in Madanpura for years'.[11] No plague hospital, declared Campbell, 'has been more successful or popular'.[12] As so often with colonial policy, an available explanatory sociology of the potential 'source of disturbance' was mapped on to the relevant strategy of control. In this case, the 'community leadership' was identified as an adequate suturing agent for the grievances of a homogeneous, undifferentiated and 'fanatical' community.[13]

At the beginning of March 1898, however, suspicion within the weavers' community appeared to be mounting. This may have had something to do with the rising death toll at the Madanpura hospital: one person died of plague on 7th March, eight on the 8th and two on the 9th, at a time when plague mortality was reaching its annual peak.[14] In keeping with the pattern of 1896–97, when the epidemic first broke out, 1898 witnessed a spike in deaths recorded during the first three months of the year. As compared to 95 deaths recorded in the first week of December 1897, 302 deaths were registered in the first week of January 1898. The corresponding figure for the first week of February was 927, and a month later the weekly mortality had risen to 1,097.[15] On the morning of 8 March, search parties in Madanpura were confronted with a 'point-blank refusal by Jhulais to allow removal of a suspicious case'.[16]

Other sources of dissatisfaction can be adduced from the tensions of the plague crisis. Rumour, as officials and journalists never tired of pointing out, was rife. So, while house-to-house inspections ('visitations', as the Plague Committee quaintly labelled them) leading to eviction and destruction of working-class property may not have affected the weavers as directly as others, there was never a guarantee that such benevolence would last. Levels of strictness in government scrutiny had been ratcheted up at the beginning of 1898 with the recrudescence of plague in its most virulent form. Hesther Mary Dowson, a nurse working at the time in the government-run Infectious Diseases Hospital on Arthur Road, and one of the more sensitive observers of the social and racial tensions arising from arbitrary plague control measures, noted the latency of violent unrest. 'There are a great many native soldiers in Bombay just now,' she wrote a month before the riot,

> as they are afraid of rioting, owing to the very strict house to house visitation that is now going forward, in fruitless hope of stopping the ravages of the plague. And I really should not be surprised if the natives did rise; I think it awfully hard on them, all these regulations being enforced, simply because we have the power.[17]

The inspection of corpses for traces of bubonic plague, frequently threatened though rarely practised, promised another, even more objectionable invasion of intimate space. For the city's Muslim communities this meant not only arbitrary interference with religious practice, but also intolerable delays in burial of the dead. Given the government's anxiety about 'fanatical' Muslim rioters, this was a policy that was usually eschewed. The Plague Committee had reintroduced the idea in January 1898 but, confronted with strong opposition from Muslim opinion across classes and most of all from the Madanpura weavers, it had to be summarily abandoned.[18] On Tuesday, 8 March, a day before the riot, however, there were rumours that corpse inspection had actually been carried out. Writing in her diary two days later, on Thursday, Hesther Mary Dowson saw an immediate correlation:

> It is the order that 'all dead bodies are to be inspected to see if they died from plague', which was carried out for the first time on Tuesday night, that has caused the Mahomedans to rise; they had always threatened to do so, if such an order were enforced.[19]

The vagaries of employment were another source of discontent.

Weavers who worked in northern Bombay's cotton mills, who constituted a substantial minority of Madanpura's population, had suffered through much of 1897 from enforced unemployment as the city's limited export trade in piece-goods ground to a virtual halt. During the summer and monsoon of 1897 these weavers had been at the forefront of strikes that had shaken the textile industry to its foundations. These and other latent flashpoints exploded on the morning of 9 March 1898.

Dhanjibhai Ratanji Gilder, the medical student who led the expedition into Madanpura, decided, in what appears to have been an excessive display of zeal (given the explicit and silent prohibition on over-interference with the Julahas), to inspect the entire chawl at 33-A, Ripon Cross Lane. In a tantalizing aside in his report to the District Plague Officer, R.B. Stewart of the Indian Civil Service, Gilder mentioned having 'received some private information about a case being concealed in that chawl'.[20] How he came by this information cannot be determined with any precision, but it seems not unreasonable to speculate that one of the Julaha headmen employed as a mediator by the Plague Committee, possibly Nur Ali or even the redoubtable Hakim, acted as informer – or at least as conduit. Gilder, Ruknuddin and the other Plague Committee employees made a beeline for the dwelling of a weaver named Anudin-Badal, whose twelve-year-old daughter Masuma had been reported to be suffering from plague-like symptoms by Gilder's mysterious informant. Ruknuddin reported the initial confrontation as follows:

> At house no. 33 A off Ripon Road we went into the outer room and looked around, and we saw somebody lying on the bed in the inner room. We asked the owner of the house, who said that that was her daughter, and that she would not allow us to see her without a Lady Doctor. Then Mr Gilder wrote a note for the nurse, but she was away on duty. Then Mr Gilder himself returned to the office and reported the case to Lieutenant Warneford [a military officer of the 44th Gurkha Regiment, in charge of house-to-house visitation in Byculla district], who ordered the Hakim to accompany us to the house. The parents refused to allow the Hakim to see the girl and told him to go away. Then Lt Warneford and the Nurse Mrs Murfoy came to the house. Mrs Murfoy saw the girl lying on her bed and said that it was a case of plague, after which the parents said that they would not allow their child to be removed, and that we could kill them first.[21]

Gilder's own gloss on this visit effectively reveals the strategy that the plague operations in this opaque neighbourhood were founded on. They thought, he wrote, 'that the Hakim being a Mahomedan, the father will allow the Hakim to examine the girl'.[22] Clearly, however, the rules of gendered seclusion trumped those of racial or religious identity. Mrs Murfoy was the only employee of the Plague Committee in the district who could legitimately examine the girl, and by the time she arrived it was 10 o'clock. Gilder and his men whiled away the time 'at the end of the bye-lane', while a crowd rapidly swelled around and within the house.[23] Within minutes of the incursion by

Gilder and his team, 'nearly 500 people surrounded us inside and outside the house'.[24] The numbers may have been exaggerated, for Lieutenant Warneford reported that 'a large number, probably from 60 to 100 Mahomedans, collected in and about the house'.[25] Regardless of the number, people who had in all likelihood been drawn to the scene of the confrontation by raised voices and what Vincent was later to ruefully describe as 'protracted wrangling', had within an hour organized into a formidable collective, consciously acting as a barricade against the intrusion of the Plague Committee authorities.[26] When Warneford reiterated the search party's intention to take Masuma away, her father refused and 'the crowd in and about the house shouted their approval, saying, I think, "*Hum usko le jane nahin denge*" ["We won't let her be taken away"]'.[27]

Gilder and Warneford, perhaps anticipating that a more or less spontaneous and immediate act of collective refusal (the Police Commissioner searched in vain afterwards for evidence of premeditation) was about to turn into something more ominous and precise, decided to beat a retreat. Warneford later took up the story in vivid detail in his account to Stewart, Gilder apparently having decided that he had done his bit for the cause and that it was time to retire gracefully.[28]

> I then went out of the house, and we walked down the lane followed by a large crowd, who began shouting and hooting. As we reached the main road the first stone was thrown, hitting me on the back of my neck. I stopped and turned around, saying that we did not want conduct of that sort. . . . The older men in the crowd there told the others to be quiet and not throw stones, on which they calmed down for a bit. We then started on again, walking slowly down Ripon Road followed by the crowd, which had now considerably increased. They soon started hooting again, and a few more stones were thrown, one of which hit Mrs Murfoy on the back. Walking slowly on, we reached the office, into which I sent Mrs Murfoy. We stood on the road opposite the office for some time, the crowd passing around and hooting, but not throwing stones. As they seemed fairly quiet for the moment, I went up to the office and telephoned to the Crawford Market and Ripon Road for the police.[29]

Several small batches of policemen arrived in a trickle. Inspector Coxon, in charge of Jacob's Circle, led the first contingent and Superintendent Nolan, in command of the E Division of the City Police, led the second. The District Plague Officer, R.B. Stewart, arrived shortly afterwards, followed by Inspector Sheehy who commanded a regiment of mounted police or *sowars*. By 11.30 a handful of officers and less than a dozen armed sepoys had formed a bloc in Madanpura.[30] This was the point at which the tensions that underwrote the relations of force in plague-struck Bombay were revealed at their starkest. The inherent *weakness* of readily available state power, camouflaged behind the persistent everyday terror and harassment of plague regulations, was momentarily exposed. Vincent wrote of this later in his report to the Bombay government: plague duty had depleted his reserves of police to the point of crisis. Of 167 native police officers and 1,985 native police constables, only 78 of the former and 805 of the latter were available for day duty at that time; 116 policemen had died of plague and another 100 had been given over to the Plague Committee, leaving him with 'inefficient substitutes'. Such police reinforcements as were available were distributed across the 22 square miles that made up Bombay, including the harbour and the docks. Policemen lived scattered all over the island-city, often in chawls and cheek-by-jowl with people very like those they had been called out to confront that day.[31] Inquiries into the health of the native police force in 1895 had revealed a high degree of sickness among them, ascribed chiefly to overcrowding in squalid tenements. Semi-official watchmen and guards who were frequently pressed into night duty died with corresponding frequency.[32]

A police force stretched thin across the city and unable to respond with 'massive force' when required owing to its scattered nature: such spatio-temporal tensions produced a situation of barely disguised panic among the mounted *sowars*, European officers and the sprinkling of constables who confronted a seething and apparently implacable crowd in Madanpura. Nor was there a sufficient supply of ammunition at hand. After the Bombay riots of 1893 all police officers had been granted ammunition, but a new regulation, instituted after an officer's suicide, stipulated that ammunition would be granted only upon application to the Superintendent – itself an oblique acknowledgment of how small the everyday resources of coercive force were.[33]

A *Times of India* journalist who arrived on the scene shortly afterwards reported as follows:

> It still wanted ten minutes before noon when I arrived at the open space formed by the junction of Duncan and Ripon Roads with Bellasis Road. The Native Town wore its usual aspect save that here and there one came across ominous signs of the severity of the present visitation of plague in the spectacle of here and there three, four and even five successive shops were closed, barred and bolted, their owners having fled the stricken city. In Duncan Road and Two Tanks there was no sign of any unwanted stir, and not until Ripon Road was entered was evidence encountered that trouble was in the air. The first two hundred yards or so of the broad thoroughfare were deserted, but every window and balcony was crowded with women-folk, whose eager expectant glances were directed to the small knot of police about a third of the way down.[34]

Ten armed police sepoys barricaded the road, eight mounted *sowars* faced the west side of the street, and, completing the bloc, Superintendents Nolan and Brewin faced Jacob's Circle, presumably awaiting reinforcement. The northern portion of the road, however, was blocked solidly by '700–1000 *badmashes*', wrote the journalist (apparently having succumbed to the temptation of preposterously precise numbers amidst collective tumult),

> armed with *lathis* . . . [and] literally lashing themselves into a fury. . . . Now they would rush forward shouting and yelling, some frantically beating the ground with their sticks, now they would dash back, and flight after flight of brickbats, stones and missiles of every sort would hurtle through the air. Some of the bolder spirits could be seen urging the more timorous to cast aside their hesitancy, and indeed had the rush come to close quarters with the police the scanty force of sepoys would have been tossed aside like leaves before the north-east wind.[35]

These images metonymically condense the shape of the initial confrontation between the plague authorities and the weavers' families of Madanpura. If Anudin-Badal asserted his claims over his sick daughter (who, as it later turned out, was indeed not suffering from plague but from an ordinary fever), the gendered division of functions on the narrow lane may have borne witness to some of the libidinal investments at stake in the street battle. The women watched from upstairs as their men fought off the intruders who threatened the privacy of their cramped domestic spaces and familial arrangements. So far, Masselos' observation, that 'the plague, as illness, put the home under siege and, because it did so, provides illustrations of what the home represented and what it constituted', appears apt.[36] So does his more precise assertion that the plague represented 'two incursions: one from the bacilli which attacked the individual; the other from a government which . . . instituted measures equally invasive of the individual's personal and domestic space'.[37] This insight into the constitutive spatial mechanics of plague regulation does not, however, adequately describe the forms of resistance that made up the other side of the equation of forces on Bombay's streets, as exemplified most strongly by the Madanpura riot.

A quarrel over the proper disposition of gendered domestic space snowballed into a 'public' conflagration where the effects of the initial showdown rippled beyond its normal frontiers. A conflict forged in the inner sanctum of a cramped tenement was driven, by the force of neighbourhood solidarities and networks whose precise contours remain elusive, into the realm of the street beyond the house. The seamlessness of this movement is attested by the reports of Gilder and Warneford, which speak of crowds almost magically appearing 'inside and outside the house' as Gilder and Masuma's family wrestled over her removal. This is a description that makes considerable sense if we remember that the conflict originated in a chawl with its distinctive spatial character. No descriptions survive of the chawl in question but there is a vivid journalistic account of the disposition of space in a nearby street, one whose social composition and density bear important clues to the contours of working-class life in Madanpura and neighbouring areas:

> Nagpada is an essentially poor quarter, largely occupied by weavers, and contains several very queer little *gulleys*. Turning off Tank Street, for instance, some of the search parties found themselves in Kazeepura, a neighbourhood which must be almost unique even in Bombay. Here an irregular narrow

> unpaved street, a few yards wide, is lined by two rows of houses, so closely placed together that scarcely an interval separates them, and giving shelter to a population which must reach almost the maximum limit of density. Upper and lower stories are almost completely separate, the upper floors are edged with verandahs, and two light wooden gangways run from side to side, allowing the recipients of these upper stories to communicate without coming to the ground. This is essentially a place for home industries. At the north end the weavers ply their craft . . . and the dull roar of bellows, the ringing of the hammer on the anvil, and showers of sparks flying from glowing metal indicate the presence of a blacksmith's shop or two. Each family occupies but a single room, at most a few yards square, which is at once the dwelling room, kitchen and workshop of the family. Here the weaver erects his loom, sitting on the ground, and stowing away his feet in a hole made for the purpose, and with his apparently ramshackle but really very effective little machine in which the shuttle is thrown from hand to hand, turns out his daily quota of *saree* cloth or 'trouserings', whose bright colours contrast strangely with the dingy character of the surroundings. Here the whole family were at work, the head of the household at the loom, the housewife busily cooking the morning meal, and preternaturally grave *chokra*, and staid little maid, gravely fill bobbin after bobbin with thread from a reeling machine so *cutcha* that one wondered how it hung together.[38]

This is a description that renders, quite precisely, the opacity of dwellings and neighbourhoods like these to the external observer. As such, it also furnishes a clue to the terror this apparently enclosed community of weavers and other workers evidently posed to officials like the Plague Committee members and the Police Commissioner. Tenements like these were characterized both by material poverty and by a distinct sphere of economic activity subsisting beyond the control of state agencies. These spaces could only be made intelligible through invocations of a stereotypically oriental stasis where the dynamics of everyday life appeared self-perpetuating and motionless even though perpetually in motion. Behind the staid quality of work-rhythms and domestic routine conjured by such a description, however, it is not difficult to see the glimmers of community networks and forms of co-dependency made necessary by the cramped quarters of domestic life and workplace, and the built spaces of communication between families and individuals. When the plague officials and the police confronted Ripon Cross Lane, they confronted these networks in a winding maze of back streets, alleys and hideouts that they had no way of controlling. Small wonder, then, that Vincent rendered the escalation of conflict on 9 March as an 'uproar' that 'spread with the usual Oriental rapidity to the adjoining streets' – what presented itself to him as an irrational velocity of conflict was the necessary obverse of the stasis depicted five days later by the *Times of India* journalist in a very similar neighbourhood.[39]

If the assertion of community solidarity against police action was one prong of the confrontation on Ripon Cross Lane, another dimension was made visible when Nur Ali, the Julaha headman who had made a favourable impression upon the Plague Committee, appeared on the scene. Nur Ali and a 'subordinate headman' came to Stewart's office shortly after Madanpura erupted. 'I asked them what the people's complaint was,' wrote Stewart, 'and whether they could not quiet the mob. They could not state any definite complaint, but merely said that the people's heads were turned, and that they would not listen to them, their own *Sirdars*, or any one else.'[40] Though the exact sequence of events after the arrival of the police is understandably confused by the agitation of their chroniclers, it is clear that Nur Ali's arrival before the crowd, which the Plague Committee must have hoped would help pacify them, was like fire set to a tinderbox. At the subsequent trial of the rioters Superintendent Nolan mentioned having heard several men calling out for Nur Ali and Sardar Karim, another headman. They shouted: 'Give these two men in our charge; they get Rs 200 a month from the *sarkar*, it will be seen how long they remain alive to enjoy that!'[41] At that moment, with the legitimacy of the principal mediators – who subsequently had to go into hiding – broken, any hegemony exercised by the state over Madanpura vanished completely.

This was exemplified by what followed. R.H. Dastur, Presidency Magistrate and city notable, was hurriedly pressed into service by Stewart to stem the anger of the crowd. Dastur, in a speech cautioning the men, chose his words ill-advisedly: '*Tum log police ke saamne fasad mat karo, tum tumhare ghar ko gup-chup chale jao*' ('Don't create a ruckus before the police, go back quietly to your homes'). Unsurprisingly, this was greeted with hooting, further shouts demanding Nur Ali's life, and eventually a stone that flew through the air and struck the Magistrate on the nose. Dastur instructed the police to fire as he began to bleed and, driven to panic, they did so. Instantly the crowd broke up. 'Some dashed into a big bungalow near the corner of the street, others dashed for the open ground on to which Mahomedan Street debouches, the remainder fled for Jacob's Circle. Seven bodies were stretched on the ground', wrote the *Times of India* correspondent.[42] A temporary 'lull' followed as the police took over the street.

The riot was only 'dispersed', though, in the sense that it spread. Onlookers from adjacent streets who had been drawn out of their homes, shops and workplaces by the tumult now added their weight to the temporary inversion of authority. Swelling crowds gathered south, west and east of Madanpura, and apparently innocuous spaces of residence and work assumed menacing shape as a violent game of hide-and-seek was played out between the police and the people incensed by the firing.

Police Commissioner Vincent, fortunately for historians, sketched out a rough but revealing map of the riot (see p. 12) after its eventual pacification. The temporal sequence of events is unclear since the police inevitably lagged behind the rioters, but their *spatial* sequence is much more visible. It appears that a large number of people fled into the immediately adjacent Ripon Road,

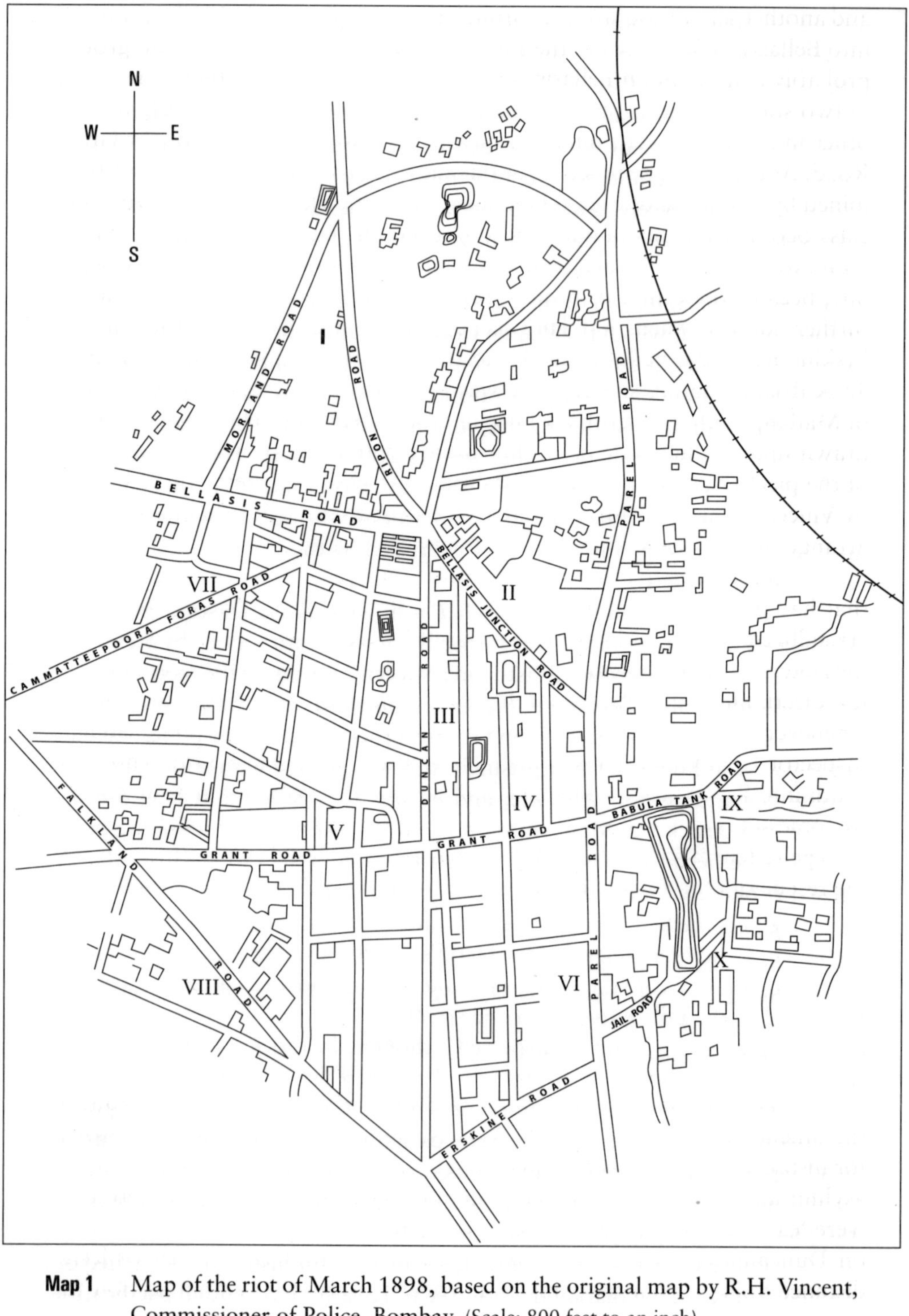

Map 1 Map of the riot of March 1898, based on the original map by R.H. Vincent, Commissioner of Police, Bombay. (Scale: 800 feet to an inch)

and another set ran southwards through the twisting lanes of Madanpura and into Bellasis Road. South of the former and east of the latter, the two groups probably converged on Bellasis Junction Road, from where they fanned out in two southern directions: one directly south down Duncan Road, and the other in a south-eastern direction down Parel Road till where it met Grant Road. At each of these junction-points the original rioters seem to have been joined by – or perhaps even replaced by – large numbers of mainly working-class people from surrounding neighbourhoods. During the mid-afternoon Grant Road, which bisected these different directions in a more or less straight line, became the centre of prolonged street battles. The 'mobs' also moved further south towards Falkland Road, South Parel Road, Mazagaon and Erskine Road, towards Arthur Road to the north, and eastward to Babula Tank Road. Another site of battle was Foras Road, immediately south-west of Madanpura, where groups of fleeing Madanpura residents appear to have drawn upon a thick matrix of immediate neighbourhood solidarities. Most of the places that became major flashpoints in the clash were marked in red by Vincent in his map as he tried to make sense of the sequence of events and arrange them in some kind of logical/temporal order.[43]

It seems evident that at each junction riot fanned riot, as grievances that had accumulated during many months of arbitrary plague inspection crystallized into an outburst with precise forms. The most obvious targets of the rioters were symbols and practices of state authority, and also, apparently less discriminatingly, Europeans in general. European officers 'were attacked whenever the rioters saw them singly or in twos or threes'.[44] For instance, Inspector Coady and Constable de Burg of the Mounted Police, who rode south into Ripon Road from Sankli Street, were at their destination 'chased by some six hundred Jhulais' (the exactitude of the terrified observer again) who pelted them with stones and beat a passing constable with sticks.[45] Upon the rescue of this constable, the

> *budmashes* then gave chase to Coady . . . hot on his heels, [they] ran shouting, '*mardalo goreku, mardalo goreku, mat jaane do*' ['kill the whitey, don't let him go'] and it was not until he quitted the road for the boggy ground and made his way to the Byculla segregation camp that he managed to shake off his pursuers.[46]

The built spaces of the working-class localities of Bombay, opaque to the official gaze, became a major resource for the rioters. On Bellasis Road, for instance, large numbers of people hid behind the low walls of the lunatic asylum and threw stones at the police from behind this shelter. Here they were 'easily dispersed', but the crowds were larger and 'more pertinacious' on Duncan Road where they had to be driven back by a series of long-distance volleys from the guns of European officers. The ammunition for these volleys was contingent upon the proximity of a firearms shop run by Treacher's, a British firm, since the officers who arrived on the scene were, as a consequence of the regulations mentioned above, short of ammunition.

In what must have looked to passers-by like a curious juxtaposition of chaos and order, Treacher's, guarded no doubt by policemen and soldiers, carried on brisk business through much of the evidently profitable day, while all the Hindu and Muslim shops around, either from fear or solidarity (or possibly both), hastily downed their shutters as the crowd and the police approached.[47]

Race, class and, more specifically, any association with plague control seem to have determined the targets of the rioters to an overwhelming extent. The riots, understandably, seemed maniacal and irrational to Vincent and other observers, but in retrospect they seem to have had a fairly precise rationality. On Bellasis Road plague hospitals – more accurately, makeshift huts erected for victims – were set on fire and a segregation camp was attacked. The Municipality appears to have been a particular target of hatred. On Jail Road at Umarkhadi, which was adjacent to Babula Tank Road and a fair distance south-east of the original site of the riot, according to the description of a witness testifying during the trials of prisoners held for rioting, a 'mob of 100–125 people' armed with sticks and stones attacked, shouting '*maro municipal-wala ko*' ('kill/beat the municipal officers'), while hammering and breaking plague ambulance carriages, and burning the municipal shed that served as the local Plague Office. On Duncan Road, Arthur Road, Grant Road and elsewhere there was a relentless series of attacks on carriages or '*gharries*' carrying European police officers, state officials and, not infrequently, civilians as well. The Municipal Commissioner of Bombay, Snow, and the Health Officer, Weir, suffered near-fatal stoning. The Grant Road hospital was attacked by a crowd of '400–500 people', and was saved only by the fortuitous presence of an armed person inside whose firing scared off the attackers.[48]

Another dramatic event summoned a broader articulation of popular grievance. The crowd who had burned down the Plague Office at Umarkhadi Jail Road, after attacking the standing symbol of the authority of the Plague Committee, turned their attention to the jail the road was named after. A gallows-screen had been set up there for an execution scheduled for that day. The crowd splashed oil on the screen and set it on fire, threatening – though not harming – a policeman who stood in their way. As the fire blazed, in a richly symbolic gesture, they threw into it broken pieces of the ambulance carriages they had earlier destroyed.[49]

The spatial trajectory of the riot seems to have had another consequence: the temporary dissolution of physical and political barriers that may have existed between communities. The Julahas had been marked out by Vincent and other British administrators in Bombay – as also by colonial officials across the country in general – as irremediably bigoted, 'fanatical Mahomedans'. The riots of 1893, which saw simultaneous attacks on Hindus by Julahas and attacks on Muslims by thousands of Hindu mill-hands, had inscribed upon the minds of observers like Vincent the image of apparently implacably opposed, homogeneous communities who could be kept away from each other's throats only by wise and firm ruling-class intervention. This in part explains the immense faith that colonial officials and Plague Committees seem to have invested in the mediatory powers of community 'headmen' like Nur Ali: the troubles of working-class Bombay, this implied, could be satisfactorily resolved within the boundaries of community. An understanding between the state and the leaders of putatively bounded communities, then, could found the effective execution of state policy.

Now, as crowds of Julahas moved beyond the frontiers of Madanpura, an area tightly enclosed by overlapping boundaries of space and religion, they were joined by large groups of (chiefly) Hindu mill-hands. We do not have adequate accounts of the kinds of relations formed between Muslim weavers and Hindu factory workers, though many in both categories may have shared the solidarities – and the tensions – of work in the same mills. Be that as it may, the numbers of the Julahas, according to Vincent and other observers, were swollen by Hindu mill-hands who were celebrating *Holi*.[50] Normally, these workers would have been back in their homes on the occasion of the festival, in Ratnagiri and other districts of the Konkan, but plague restrictions – which had imposed severe limits upon exit from the city – made sure they were present, gathered along the tracks of those suddenly dangerous streets. Within moments of the angry jeers that marked the Madanpura weavers' break with their community headman, a violent articulation of solidarity with the Hindu workers seems to have been reached. The boundaries of space and community, however weak or strong their overlap may have been, were no longer coextensive in any effective sense.

An incident on Foras Road, a few streets south of Madanpura, throws a faint light upon the hidden injuries of class that made the riot, in one of its dimensions at least, a specifically proletarian event. It also exemplifies, again, the ways in which built space could be deployed as a weapon at explosive moments. Foras Road, which was populated largely by mill workers, also contained the Byculla Cottages, a set of dwellings built for poor Europeans and Eurasians. Several rows of chawls occupied by Julahas and other workers adjoined these cottages. At one of the entrances to these chawls which stood at the south-west corner of the wall enclosing the cottages, reported the *Times of India*, one of two 'notorious scoundrels' among the Julahas took up his position. The 'blind passage' behind him housed the 'main body of Jhulai rioters'. His partner stood at a lamp-post on the south side of the road and the two communicated with each other by means of hand signals.[51]

At about 1.45 in the afternoon Jacob Sassoon, one of Bombay's wealthiest and most politically influential mill owners, passed by with his secretary in a brougham carriage. Mrs Hudson, a resident of the Byculla Cottages and a witness at the trials after the riot, told the police that she heard one of the accused shout, '*Bara Sahib ka gharry ko maro!*' ('Strike, it's the big sahib's carriage!').[52] Men attacked the carriage with sticks and stones. Sassoon escaped unhurt but his coachman suffered a heavy beating. Reporting the incident, the *Times of India* correspondent put it querulously:

> It is strange that these Mahomedan weavers should not have recognized

> Mr Sassoon's liveries, as they are well known to all natives, and Mr Jacob Sassoon is probably the largest employer of native labour in his mills, and it seems a poor way of thanking him for his support of many families.[53]

The reverse speculation – that the weavers did indeed recognize Sassoon's liveries and that the attack was a deliberate one – seems to have been too unsettling for the reporter to entertain.

The incident signals grievances wider than the plague regulations themselves: an Indian mill owner, by virtue of his position as a city notable and an employer of labour, could become as pronounced a target of the animosities of the poor as the colonial state. A disparate set of antipathies, clearly, were mapped on to the confrontations in the streets on 9 March, as a riot that began over a very specific disagreement spiralled into a broader matrix of meanings and resonances.

Vincent eventually had to call in a number of military detachments – well over a hundred heavily armed soldiers from the 8th Native Infantry, the Shropshire Regiment and the Defence Squadron – to bring matters under control. Thirty men from the Shropshire Regiment were strategically stationed near Treacher's so that revolvers and ammunition could be sold to Europeans in safety. As the riot simmered down and the state authorities slowly took control of the situation, much of the city became a bristling armed camp: men of the Arsenal and Garrison Artillery Companies, with 'special cars' and massive four-pounder field guns, were drafted to patrol Jacob's Circle, the docks and various other parts of the city that were either affected or threatened.[54]

Effective military force displayed so conspicuously could signal contradictory things. On the one hand, the deployment of heavy artillery to cow down a population that, however turbulent, could boast few implements more threatening than knives, sticks and stones, signified the readiness of the plague control authorities to effectively declare war upon people it claimed to be protecting from the epidemic. Correspondingly, the riot was quelled within minutes of the troops' arrival and the threat of violent civil mutiny abated for the time being. On the other hand, the steps taken by the state to quell the riot embodied, as the *Times of India* perspicuously observed,

> the concentration of a force of cavalry, artillery and infantry, the proportions of which were more consistent with an important military operation than with the turning out of their houses of sick and dying people. *The inherent and normal power of an authority is weakened by every demonstration of military force that is largely disproportionate to the end proposed.* When people see an imposing array of military force brought out for accomplishing work of this sort they will ask if the Government are as confident in the strength of their own civil agencies as they ought to be.[55] [Emphasis added.]

This was an insight that summed up well the shifting balance of power in the prolonged war of position between the plague authorities and the urban poor. The massive display of military force against a civilian population was much more a declaration of available and deployable strength than it was a product of necessity. However, if the effectiveness of this assertion rested on the symbolic power it could command, this very power was clearly undercut by a deep anxiety about the possible consequences of a real and prolonged confrontation; and, while the troops fulfilled their immediate purpose, they did nothing to allay this anxiety. Letters in the press bear this out: frequently, correspondents to the *Times of India* suggested the 'cat' (flogging, or the 'cat-o'-nine-tails') as a punishment for suspects in the riot. One of these letters, from a person who styled himself 'J.P.', suggested the cat, in addition to a term of imprisonment, for anyone who owned or lived in a house or room where *lathis* were found.[56] As another, saner letter pointed out in response, this would effectively make criminals of more or less the entire working-class population of the city.[57]

Events like the Madanpura riot and its repercussions – which are discussed at the end of this essay – had a very distinctive shape, which can only be elucidated by careful contextualization. In the sections that follow a brief outline sketch is given, first, of the long socio-spatial transformation of Bombay in the nineteenth century which provided the structural underpinnings for confrontations like this. This is followed by a detailed, micro-historical account of a more immediately relevant development: the assault of plague upon Bombay in the closing years of the nineteenth century, and the shape of the relationships between the colonial administration and the city's urban poor that were forged in this period.

Class and the City: Urban Transformation, Plague and Other Crises

Through the nineteenth century, Bombay's social geography underwent a continuous transformation as the city not only expanded within the cramped and unfavourable space it inhabited (through reclamation of land from the sea and frenetic construction), but also witnessed precise articulations of urban space and social relationships. In 1803, following a major fire, an attempt was made for the first time to fully formalize the division of social space along racial lines as the European 'Fort' in the south of the city was separated from the native 'Town' to its north. Racial segregation, however, increasingly came to be trumped by social fraternities in a city where British rulers and Indian business elites were more closely co-dependent than in any other. From the mid-nineteenth century, Indian magnates began to move out of the native 'Town' to areas like Malabar Hill, Cumballa Hill, Breach Candy and Mahalakshmi, setting up a strong base in the south-western corner of the island, and segregating themselves from a much poorer population of small traders and labourers. The latter, left with no option due to the colonization of the southern part of the city, increasingly shifted northwards to the swampy, inhospitable land of 'the Flats'.[58]

In the 1860s the Municipal Commissioner of Bombay, Arthur Crawford, further clarified the city's socio-spatial structure by 'cleansing' the Fort area of 'offensive trades' – tanners, indigo dyers, catgut makers and butchers – and ejecting them north of the native Town. It was in this period too that the northern extremities of the island began to be reclaimed: the Municipality, for instance, reclaimed 86 acres of swampland in Tardeo by filling it with town-sweepings. Road construction and drainage made the north-western part of Bombay habitable in an elementary sense.[59]

From the 1850s, an even more profound transformation of Bombay's social geography began: this was the development of an indigenous cotton textile industry, whose rhythms and uncertainties were to define much of the social and political life of the city for well over a century. The first spinning mill was set up in 1854, the first weaving mill in 1857, and by 1865 ten mills employing 6,600 people were scattered across the native Town. At the beginning of 1875 there were fifteen cotton mills in Bombay city, employing a little over 5,000 workers. By the end of 1890 there were 67, employing over 70,000.[60] Building of mills, in common with the general tempo of industrial growth in the city, developed in sudden, dramatic bursts. Thus, of the forty-one new mills set up between 1874 and 1888, as many as thirty-four were constructed in just three years – eleven in 1874, thirteen in 1883 and ten in 1888.[61] As early as 1891 mill workers constituted over 7.5 per cent of a rapidly growing population; ten years later they would constitute over 10 per cent.[62]

In his nostalgic evocation of nineteenth-century Bombay, Dinshaw E. Wacha, a fairly representative member of Bombay's commercial elite, wrote about the radical transformation of Bombay in the 1880s:

> Industrialism came to stay in Bombay and vie with the spindles and looms of proud Lancashire. Suburbs which were dedicated to the ruling hierarchy of Governors, Members of Council, Judges and high State functionaries, for purposes of villa residences, were slowly appropriated by the new hierarchy devoted to the worship of King Cotton. . . . Industrial capitalism drove out Civilianism who [*sic*], therefore, planted itself thickly on the breezy Malabar and Cumballa Hills. The suburbs were appropriated by the cotton mills and jerrybuilders of the day found chawls, now reduced to slums, for the accommodation of the growing industrial population.[63]

Wacha's memoir attests a very precise metamorphosis; prominent buildings, as Preeti Chopra observes, changed hands in these years. Elphinstone College moved from Parel in the north to Fort in the south-west; Parel Government House was eventually converted into a plague hospital in the late 1890s; access to the eastern foreshore of Bombay was blocked by trade and industry, forcing the city's propertied elites to virtually flee south-westwards. The north-eastern and south-western tips of the island, therefore, acquired utterly distinct morphologies, the one being an obverse of the other. Places like Byculla and Parel, formerly affluent and sparsely populated, were transformed into a continuous industrial landscape characterized by massive horizontal factory buildings and towering chimneys.[64] In May 1880, early in the city's industrial growth, the *Times of India* observed:

> Bombay has of late years witnessed the erection and starting of so many spinning and weaving mills, and other concerns of a similar nature, that it has come to be called the 'Manchester of India'. Tall chimney shafts show above the surrounding buildings on every side and give to the city, when viewed from a distance, an appearance of manufacturing activity which justifies the term which has been applied to it. This state of things must be a matter of congratulation to all those who have the progress and welfare of the Presidency city at heart; but private individuals, who are not directly interested in the mills, will come to look upon these concerns as unmitigated nuisances, if something is not done to prevent the nuisance arising from the smoke which issues from the chimneys. Those who have lived any time in Bombay must have noticed the thick black clouds of smoke which belch forth from the mill chimneys, and even to some extent darken the intense brightness of a tropical sky. The nuisance is most noticeable in early morning, when the mills are starting work, and when, presumably, fires are being stoked for the day's work.[65]

The article went on to stress the need for a Smoke Prevention Act that would compel mill owners to fit their boilers with smoke-preventing apparatuses, along the lines of large manufacturing towns in northern England. It also wistfully expressed the desire for an inspector modelled on similar precedent, someone who 'has the eye of an eagle and can tell amidst a forest of chimneys to whose mill any particular shaft belongs. He is no respecter of persons, and it is not an unusual thing to see a magistrate, or the mayor of a town, sum-moned for a smoke nuisance.'[66] This desire was met, but not in the form of a specialist inspector to seek out and punish the excessive use of fuel. Instead, the internal rhythms of the factory became, increasingly, the province of inspection under the Factory Acts of 1881, 1891 and 1911.

The complaints by 'private individuals' anticipated by the *Times of India* came soon enough, in 1881 and 1884.[67] A memorial to the Town Council from people living on Duncan Road, in the heart of the town, put the matter most eloquently. Writing of the deleterious effects upon the city of smaller enterprises, specifically corn mills and wool-cleaning factories, the memorialists complained:

> Hitherto the authorities concerned – the guardians of the public health – who ought to move in the matter, have not as yet raised their voice against this nuisance, while the evil has been growing prodigiously . . . the chimney shafts of these Mills and Factories are considerably lower than the height provided for in the Smoke Nuisance Act, the smoke besides being dangerous to health, fills the houses of neighbours and gives their walls a smoky and dingy appearance, while the dust of the wool-cleaning factories is a much greater nuisance than anything the smoke may possibly do. The neighbours cannot open their windows without getting their houses filled with dust, dust on their furniture, dust on their clothes, papers and books, and wherever they turn, they seem to be moving in a poisonous atmosphere of dust. . . .

> Nor is this all. The sufferings to which the neighbours are subjected during the day are continued even at night. They are denied even the refreshment of sleep by the incessant whirl of the machinery which keeps working till that late hour, and the volumes of mingled smoke and dust entering their sleeping apartments.[68]

Proto-ecological campaigns of this sort had a precise effect for they increasingly made the erection of new factories in the south of the city untenable. A suit brought against the Nicol Mill in Colaba in southern Bombay succeeded, for instance, in compelling the mill owner to 'keep the windows on the north side permanently closed so as to palliate as far as possible the noise of the machinery and the dust arising from the mill'.[69] In 1884 the Sanitary Commissioner of Bombay, Thomas Hewlett, observed:

> it is . . . satisfactory to notice that all the new mills are being erected on such open situations . . . where there is a free perflation of air and where plenty of space can be obtained for . . . the provision in the vicinity of each group of mills of proper habitations for the operatives.[70]

This change was accompanied by an intensification of existing patterns of migration from the Konkan coast and the Deccan into Bombay, and the beginning of similar inflows of migrant labour from the north, as population expanded on a scale hitherto unimaginable. It was in this period that the basic pattern of land use, which was to characterize Bombay till well into the twentieth century, was concretized. The city came to acquire precise socio-spatial divisions: an elite composed of Europeans and rich Indians in the south-west of the island; a 'native town' where busy local markets and shops twisted into narrow, crowded and socially diverse residential alleys and streets; and a large industrial district ('Girangaon' or the 'mill village', as it was locally known) spreading north and east from the heart of the town. It was the spurt in mill-building from the mid-1870s that set this pattern, quite literally, in stone.[71] The development of 'Bombay the Beautiful' in the south ('the second city of the empire', as it was often called), with its magnificent Victorian public architecture, its fountains and open spaces, was coextensive with the very differently built space of 'Girangaon' in the north, with its uncontrolled expansion of mill construction, jerry-built chawls and densely packed neighbourhoods that wound round each other in a labyrinth of back-streets and lanes. Two radically opposed socio-spatial experiences crystallized simultaneously within a small and narrow island, and this could have explosive political consequences.

As Chandavarkar has noted, the constraints of physical geography and the priorities of class power resulted in an effective apartheid in the disposition of municipal finances in nineteenth-century Bombay.[72] The seven islands that were finally linked in 1838 lay, for the most part, beneath the mean level of the sea. The reclamation of land and the arduous processes of landfill that raised the city to safety were expensive operations in a situation where resources were stringent. Thus the work of municipal 'improvement' posed a stark choice before the rulers of Bombay. 'To pay for these improvements through taxation,' Chandavarkar observes, 'the British would have to lean heavily upon their most favoured collaborators: the city's sheikhs, merchant princes, and mill owners.'[73]

The compromise chosen was to effect such forms of 'improvement' as dovetailed with the city's mercantile and industrial-capitalist interests. To put it baldly: roads were preferred to drains. Drains and sewers were limited to the city's richer quarters; as late as 1925, 'when Bombay had more sewers than any other city in the East, the city's poorer quarters had none'.[74] Similarly, the city's water supply, managed under equally severe constraints, was lavished upon the residential areas where European and Indian elites lived, and distributed with chilling parsimony to the working-class neighbourhoods. Sanitation was organized in a corresponding manner: narrow gullies separated dwellings, acting as informal drains for waste water and excretions, which were carried away by municipal scavengers in open baskets that were often, not unreasonably, deposited in the nearest open space.[75] While the writings of colonial officials – notably in the Sanitary Reports for the city – lamented this state of affairs, more often than not such horrors were explained away by 'the habits of the poor', the commonest rhetorical device in the colonial arsenal.

The disposition of social space in Bombay, then, was governed by an effective *laissez-faire* when it came to the homes and streets of the poor. The costs of social reproduction of the multiple forms of labour that kept the city running – from mill workers to scavengers, from cart drivers to washermen, from wives to coolies – were entirely borne by working-class neighbourhoods and families. This pattern, with some variations, has lasted to the present day. What it also meant, ironically, was a certain autonomy of action: neighbourhoods that were largely left to themselves experienced only sporadic state intrusion and policing. Vincent's description of the limited resources of the city police, cited above, is a case in point.

This was the grim social compact that was interrupted, and made momentarily impossible, by the advent of plague in 1896. The boundaries of social space suddenly made no sense as officials, soldiers, policemen, doctors, nurses and municipal workers descended upon the families, houses and streets of the city's poor. If this constituted several more or less precise forms of transgression, so too, as argued in the sections that follow, did the public response of Bombay's working classes, i.e. in terms of collective assertions of power experienced at points of absolute desperation and crisis.

Apprehensions of Contagion

Plague began to lay claim to Bombay as early as August 1896, but it was only in the winter of that year that genuine panic began to emerge. By the end of 1896, 2,544 plague cases had been reported and 1,936 deaths, of which 1,271 occured in December alone. In January 1897 the number of deaths outstripped the total plague mortality of the preceding year, the toll for the month being 2,110. February claimed 3,349 lives and in March there were 2,424 deaths. It was not till the summer months that the toll slipped significantly.[76]

Correspondingly a popular panic gripped the city, in response as much to the administration's attempts to survey, control and attack the bodies and congested neighbourhoods of the city's working poor, as to the fact of the epidemic itself. By the spring of 1897, Bombay was a city near collapse. The contagion of plague appeared to be travelling the streets hand in hand with the contagion of urban breakdown. The most visible signifier of this was the devastating flight from the city. People began to escape Bombay in droves in the winter of 1896: in October, an estimated 20,000 people fled the city; in November and December, 171,500 were added to that number.[77] By the end of January 1897, roughly 400,000 people, or a little under half of Bombay's population, had fled to the countryside which itself was ravaged by famine. It was indeed the grimly Malthusian balance between famine and plague that lay at the root of Bombay's survival as a city, as flight to the countryside was balanced, in the medium term, by flight *from* the countryside. Had it not been for the famine, Bombay quite possibly would not have outlasted the plague.

Plague mortality peaked in March 1897, and receded over the spring and summer months. People started drifting back to the city in the summer, but the flow was reversed as the toll began to rise again during and after the monsoon.[78] This, broadly, was the pattern for several years to come: ferocious epidemic attacks at the end of the year, with a slackening of the virulence over the spring and summer. The popular panic of the first year and a half was never quite replicated, however, and plague gradually took its place as one of many killers that stalked a city racked by many crises.

A verse account from 1899 by B.F. Patell, a teacher at Elphinstone High School, evokes the sense of colossal calamity produced by the plague. The verse is less than inspired, but Patell's description of a deserted, crumbling city is nonetheless eloquent:

> Now, silent as the grave these streets
> A straggler here and there one meets.
> And where is gone the surging crowd
> That made the city look so proud?
> A part unto that dismal bourne
> From which no traveler may return:
> But most have fled to distant parts,
> Sad fugitives with bleeding hearts.[79]

The epidemic seemed to bear mortal consequences not only for the individuals who encountered it, but for the city as a whole. The sense of helplessness was accentuated by the fact that the aetiology of bubonic plague was only very dimly understood in the late nineteenth century.[80] Miasmatic schemes of explanation, linking plague to 'emanations' from stores of decaying grain, described one vector of understanding that associated the epidemic with local sanitary conditions. Over the months, officials and experts repeated their apprehension that the plague was 'in the soil', and that the ground itself needed to be broken up and disinfected. A telegram from the Secretary of State to the Governor on 22 January 1897 attests the urgency of this apprehension: 'Experts lay stress on importance, in addition to general disinfection, of casting away and burning earth of floors to depth of four inches.'[81]

'Pythogenetic' explanatory schemes, on the other hand, identified the cramped and insanitary living conditions of the city as a sort of meta-vector of the disease, while contagionist understandings targeted the human body as the prime vector.[82] These schemes provided the prime scientific bedrock for state-imposed measures of plague control. In the absence of a reliable consensus, and given the relative newness of voluntary inoculation and vaccination as a solution, the measures initiated by the city's Municipality and, subsequently, the government-appointed Plague Committees, necessarily bore the marks of other anxieties about the industrial transformation of the city and its social consequences. Health officials' reports and medical testimonies from the 1860s and the 1870s had warned, though very intermittently, of the possible consequences of such uncontrolled urban expansion: population overload, overburdened drainage and sewage networks, insanitary concentrations of poverty behind fortresses of dirt and disease.[83]

Shortly after the outbreak of plague, Bombay was threatened with an international trading embargo. While the British kept their ports open throughout the decades of the global pandemic, their trading partners were quick to impose regimes of surveillance and regulation upon all ships from India. The French, for instance, intimated the possibility of riots in Marseilles, the site of Europe's last major plague attack in 1721. They barred South Asian passengers from their Mediterranean ports and issued tight controls on Indian trade, including a ban on raw-hide imports.[84] Such threats were seen as portents of economic death for Bombay, a future that contemporary observers, ranging from officials to visitors, held as all too possible. Global pressures, then, also drove the British response to plague, which was formalized in the Epidemic Diseases Act of 1897, giving the Municipal Commissioner wide-ranging powers of regulation without reference to a magistrate.[85]

As this response indicates, to colonial and municipal legislators, corporators and officials, plague represented both a nightmare of death for Bombay and a ground where fantasies of social control could be enacted. Hotly contested debates over explanations of the plague and the most efficient methods to combat it meant that plague control, of necessity, had to be experimental. The programme of the Bombay Municipality and, subsequently, of a succession of Plague Committees installed by the colonial administration in the period 1896–98, rested, successively or simultaneously, on the following measures: compulsory hospitalization and segregation of plague 'suspects'; disinfection and, if necessary, destruction of homes and buildings labelled 'Unfit for Human Habitation' or U.H.H.; compulsory medical examination; forced entry into homes; projects of sanitation and conservancy.[86]

Between the winter of 1896 and the spring of 1898, plague policy travelled an undecided, shifting road, veering between attempts on the part of Bombay's administration to institute draconian and invasive measures of plague control, on the one hand, and retreats towards a more conciliatory and accommodative path, on the other. This was, as most social historians of the epidemic have recognized, in large part driven by an eruption of popular suspicion and discontent in neighbourhoods of the urban poor. Official thinking at this time largely foregrounded the necessity of laying siege, violently if needed, to the dwellings, neighbourhoods and streets where the poor resided, in order to stamp out the insanitary practices that were widely perceived to produce conditions favourable to plague.[87] Popular resistance, however, urged the strategic necessity of retreat upon the initiators and executors of this policy, and this accounts for the on-again, off-again nature of plague policy in these years.

It is possible to go a step further and specify with some precision, one of the major grounds for the shifts and turns in the government's plague policy: an unfolding crisis, an attendant anxiety to do with the mobilization of *labour*, and the inability of Bombay's masters to effectively control the forms of work urgently needed to keep the city functioning in a time of crisis. Two events – which punctured and ruptured the state's plague control strategy between the pandemic's arrival in 1896 and the riot in Madanpura in 1898 – illustrate this dynamic well. They also enable a deeper understanding of the Madanpura conflict itself, as a part of a wider pattern of 'disruptive' events with their own, very specific texture. As argued, each interruption of plague policy by popular protest between 1896 and 1898 followed a common path. A visible and dramatic demonstration of working-class unrest spiralled into wider and more generalized withdrawals of labour, or at least the threat of such withdrawals, which were apprehended by the state in terms of what would effectively be a general strike.

Arthur Road Hospital, October 1896: Mill-hands and Scavengers

The first of these incidents followed closely upon the heels of the Bombay government's initial attempts to articulate plague control. The responsibility for addressing the epidemic lay, between September 1896 and February 1897, in the hands of the Municipal Corporation and Commissioner rather than the provincial government.[88] Sandhurst, the Governor of Bombay and a liberal, was initially reluctant to interfere with the workings of the Corporation, which was elected by rate payers and was responsible for sanitary policy in the city. It was not till February 1897, at the height of the epidemic-driven exodus from the city, that he authorized a transfer of executive authority in the matter of plague control from the Corporation to a government-appointed Plague Committee.[89] At the outset of the plague, more or less unrestrained powers of plague control were vested in the hands of the Corporation's executive officer, Municipal Commissioner P.C.H. Snow.

As the epidemic rapidly moved through the southern district of

Mandvi and threatened the working-class clusters to its north, Snow was quick to institute a strict policy. In early October 1896, he announced that plague victims and houses were to be isolated and 'segregated', and certified cases removed instantly to the Infectious Diseases Hospital on Arthur Road.[90] Arthur Road was one of seven streets that converged at Jacob's Circle, the intersection itself a very short distance south of the hospital. Mills and workshops to its north, east and south towered over the hospital, and across the road, to the west, was the *dhobikhana* (or *dhobi ghat*, as it is known today), an enormous open-air laundry and 'drying ground' maintained by the Municipality.[91] Throughout the course of the epidemic, the hospital was to be a catalyst of rumour, tension and, not infrequently, violence.[92] Writing in 1898, George Lambert, an American missionary who had visited Bombay the previous year, described the way the working-class areas surrounding 'the dreaded plague hospital' viewed it:

> None who can help it pass by its doors, and those who do, avert their faces and hold their shoulder cloths to their mouths as though to ward off an imaginary evil influence. Nor is this to be wondered at. Have not the majority of the poor sufferers who entered those sad precincts, emerged only when carried out feet foremost . . . ?[93]

The removal of 'plague suspects' to the hospital in October 1896 was often more arbitrary than the regulations prescribed, and the proviso that medical certification was necessary prior to hospitalization was often more honoured in the breach. The cries of pain from plague victims and suspects within the hospital would hardly have contributed towards building trust among Bombay's working classes in the motives of the state, and so rumours abounded that this was effectively a policy to isolate and kill the poor.[94] 'A horrid tale is abroad,' noted Lambert, 'to the effect that the doctors "dispose of" those who do not appear likely to recover.'[95]

Nor were practices inside the hospital, either in October 1896 or in subsequent years, designed to allay suspicions. Over a year after the events described below, Hesther Mary Dowson, at the beginning of her stint as a government nurse in the Arthur Road Hospital, described a pitiful state of affairs: over 150 patients, tended to by no more than a couple of trained nurses and a clutch of 'ward boys' at any given time; the absence of bedding and mattresses; the difficulty of procuring blankets; the refusal of the government to provide language training to facilitate communication between nurses and patients (and Indian hospital subordinates); and the parsimony of municipal funds.[96] 'I feel dreadfully for the poor patients here,' she wrote, 'taken by force, by an alien race, out of their homes, and obliged to enter our Hospitals and be treated and drugged by any young English Doctor who may have only lately come out, and who can try pretty nearly any treatment he chooses.'[97] Such arbitrary procedures – driven both by the inefficacy of institutional provisions and by the inadequacy of medical knowledge – inevitably generated immense social tensions.

In October 1896, a strange and dramatic concatenation of events amplified these tensions, and hostilities burst into the open. The trouble came from mill workers who worked in the factories around Arthur Road, who briefly and menacingly besieged the hospital on 10 October.[98] There was no violence on this occasion, but matters were different at the end of the month, on 28 and 29 October, when tensions escalated beyond control. On the evening of 28 October, another threatening crowd of workers gathered outside the hospital. The following morning, the journey of a hapless Goanese cook from mill to mill, seeking work, fuelled rumours that he was a Municipal Health Department employee who had come to inspect 'plague suspects'. A hand-drawn cart that passed for an 'ambulance' had the misfortune to draw up before the hospital during the workers' lunch hour, and in a matter of minutes they congregated before the hated building, shouting threats, lobbing stones and trying to break into the compound. A crowd of about a hundred reportedly swelled to about a thousand, and the hospital was in serious danger for a while.[99] Mill employers and the state alike might well have regretted their decision, crystallized in the 1880s, to institute and standardize a daily lunch break for mill workers, for a gathering of this size would have been inconceivable without a designated time during the day when the latter had half an hour 'for what they will'. In this case, they willed a demonstration and a riot. The afternoon's drama ended as abruptly as it had begun with the factory siren halting proceedings and drawing workers back to their posts in the mills. But a warning signal had been sounded, and plague policy was to be haunted for a long time by the possibility of recurrence of such violent responses.

The riot seemed to amplify the capacity of mill workers to cause civic instability. Since the early 1890s – marked by a 'strike mania' in 1892–93[100] and a communal riot in 1893, in which Hindu mill-hands participated vigorously[101] – mill workers had been marked out, in the eyes of state and municipal authorities, as a potential motive force in urban unrest and conflict. The Municipal Commissioner instantly issued public notifications, one addressed specifically to the mill workers and the other to the general public, disclaiming any intention of forcibly removing people to hospital.[102] The mill workers were a source of much anxiety although, puzzled the Executive Health Officer, T.S. Weir,

> they had been very considerably dealt with. Whenever a case occurred in mill buildings occupied by mill-hands, or in other buildings, as long as it was fairly isolated, it was left alone. We had also agreed that if the mill-hands gave information of the cases and isolated them, they would not be removed to hospital.[103]

Early in the course of the plague, then, conciliation of potentially turbulent sections of Bombay's working classes was seen as essential to the execution of plague policy.

The officials in charge of plague policy, however, seem to have been driven by a deeper anxiety that had to do less with general, vague apprehensions of chaos and more with specific fears of a cessation of crucial labouring activity in the city. The sanitary staff of the Municipal Department, it appeared, were 'almost in open sympathy with the rioters owing to the fear of forcible segregation'.[104] The mill workers' action was dangerous not so much in itself as in the domino effect it promised to have, which would erode the massive mobilization of labour upon which rested the still fledgling institutions of plague control. The sanitary staff employed by the Municipality were vital agents in the project of cleansing the city that the municipal administrators began, in a frenzied fashion, in September 1896. To take just one example of this sudden, colossal investment of human energy, the Drainage Department, between the end of September and the middle of November, employed as many as 1,337 men *daily* on emergency cleaning and desilting of the Port Trust drains.[105] At the same time men were mobilized to make new openings and manholes, flush the drains with seawater, disinfect manholes, overhaul the connections of individual houses, disinfect rooms and grain godowns (an early source of panic as there was a widespread belief that the plague travelled through grain), limewash infected rooms, deploy large numbers of flushing engines on infected houses, and burn the clothing and bedding of the sick.[106] All this describes a part – not the whole – of the manual labour mobilized and expended upon plague control *before* the epidemic had begun to spiral towards the uncontrollable levels it was to reach between December 1896 and February 1897.

At the time, 2,392 *halalkhores* (sweepers who mainly came from Gujarat) and 3,660 *bigarris* (Mahar scavengers, mostly from the Deccan) comprised the sanitary work force of the Municipality. The former carried away sweepings of refuse and faeces in carts, and the latter removed them by hand, entirely unprotected from the sanitary consequences. In a city by now notorious for its neglect of sanitation, and fostered by its elites' pursuit of wealth and growth, sanitary workers were a body of men despised for their association with human 'filth' and were shunned by the superior castes. But at a time of emergency, when their fullest powers and energies were called upon in the service of a city that had offered them little by way of reward and compensation, their labour became a source of desperate fears. 'These men', observed Snow, 'form the working basis of the sanitary system, and the slightest hitch in their organization, which is a most elaborate one, or depletion in their numbers, would immediately involve a serious danger.'[107] He drew attention to the fact that *halalkhores* and *bigarris* were scattered across the city, that any move towards a strike in their numbers would instantly affect 'other low caste natives, and any development of panic or alarm straightaway spreads to their immediate surroundings'. The large numbers of untouchable labourers recruited by the Executive, Drainage and Water Engineers, 'on whom we were largely dependent on carrying on our struggle with the plague', he lamented, would instantly follow suit if the *halalkhores* struck work, as indeed they had in 1866 and 1889.[108]

The *halalkhores* and *bigarris* of the city had indeed been restless since the beginning of the plague, which began its journey in Mandvi, and had consequently emptied the quarters of that district, which was inhabited by small traders and local shopkeepers who were the chief suppliers of credit and grain to the working classes of Bombay. According to the Health Officer, the sanitary staff and cart drivers of the city openly threatened flight and withdrawal of their services.[109] 'I admitted at once', wrote Weir, 'that if the policy was continued, not only would a riot occur, but that all the sanitary business of the city would stop and that we should not have men either to segregate the sick or to clean the city and that we should be left alone.'[110] Snow, the Municipal Commissioner, spelt out in Cassandra-like tones the apocalyptic consequences of this:

> Bombay would in a few days have become uninhabitable and left to reek in a mass of sewage, sweepings and pollution, with no one at hand to conduct the daily routine of sanitation, much less to adopt a single preventive measure against the plague. The pestilence in such surroundings would have increased a hundredfold, and the remaining inhabitants would have been literally decimated and forced to fly.[111]

Matters were rapidly taken in hand. Snow instantly drafted two proclamations withdrawing the harsher clauses of plague policy, one addressed specifically to the city's mill-hands, and the other to the 'general public'.[112] They both carried reassurances that compulsory hospitalization was not going to be on the agenda of the Municipality. At the same time, stricter measures were needed to enforce discipline among the sanitary staff, and Snow instructed the railway and steamer companies to refuse issue of tickets to scavengers and sweepers trying to escape.[113] A judicious distribution of carrots and sticks was thus deployed: overt conciliation of mill-hands, hasty withdrawal of the most unpopular plague control measures, and an attempt to lock the sanitary staff within the island by cutting off modes of exit. Frequently, though, the Municipality and the Plague Committees – which took over the work of epidemic control from it – continued to express alarm at the prospect of a *halalkhore* mutiny by strike or by flight. Through the plague crisis of 1896–98, Bombay's government and its sanitary workers were to hold each other in this delicate balance of terror.

The Docks and Colaba, April 1897: Cartmen and Dockers

The next instance of a dramatically interwoven series of working-class protests occurred in April 1897. By this time the municipal administration's control over plague policy had been transferred to the authoritarian hands of a Plague Committee headed by an army man, General Gatacre, and endowed with emergency powers of a correspondingly military nature. The escalation of the epidemic over the winter of the previous year had reversed the state's temporary retreat from draconian measures in the wake of the October crisis. Employees of the Plague Committee were instructed to carry out arbitrary house-to-house visitations, to isolate victims and habitations understood to be afflicted or in danger of affliction, and – a major point of social tensions in this time – to designate suspect buildings as 'unfit for human habitation' and destroy them. The death sentence, 'U.H.H.', came to be liberally sprayed across the walls and doors of working-class chawls, which were either congested multistoreyed buildings bereft of light and air or makeshift huts made from coconut palms, both of which were thought to be prime sources of plague.

At the beginning of April 1897, the Plague Committee received a petition on behalf of about 2,000 factory workers, cart drivers and coolies residing in a set of chawls in Colaba marked U.H.H.[114] The Colaba workers, acting as a neighbourhood rather than as distinct segments of the urban labour force, appealed against the proposed destruction of their homes. The petition was ignored and the consequences were dramatic, though short-lived. On 6 April, the area around the Colaba Cotton Green was thronged by over 3,000 casual workers, principally cart drivers (*khattarawalas*) and *toleewalas*, or coolies employed in gangs by the Municipality (as opposed to the regularized municipal staff). The Colaba Causeway was filled with large numbers of workers organized to deter other cartmen and coolies from infringing the strike.[115] A central urban artery – the roads of this part of southern Bombay were characterized in normal times by the flow of goods on carts, and also enabled access to the port and docks – was thus paralysed. It took the efforts of a large police contingent, merchants concerned about the disruption of their business by the cartmen's cessation of labour, as well as carting agents and contractors, to quell the strike.[116]

Official assurances of conciliation were less forthcoming now than they had been in October the previous year, and amounted to little more than a vaguely worded promise of restraint. The cartmen and coolies were conciliated, however, and they returned to work. The very next morning – barely a few hours after an agreement had been brokered between the employers and strikers – another strike rocked south Bombay. The issue was the same: house-to-house visitations and the 'condemnation' of dwellings by the Plague Committee. Day labourers at the Prince's and Victoria Docks – some 8,000 men – struck work, and the import and export trade of the city, which rested on the loading and unloading of cargo from vessels in the port, came to a complete standstill.[117] Many of the cart drivers who had been on strike the previous day but had returned to work, found themselves blocked by another set of strikers who refused to allow the unloading of goods, carried in carts, at the docks. During the morning, the area outside the dock gates was animated and full of people. In surreal contrast, the wharves were all but empty and the docks were deserted. The strike lasted till afternoon, when a verbal agreement was reached between the dockers' *muccadums*, the Port Trust and the police, that house-to-house visitations would continue but gratuitous destruction of workers' possessions would be restrained.[118]

This incident illustrates, once again, the possibility of instances of workers' ferment spilling beyond normal boundaries, and the function of the plague as a catalyst for social confrontations around labour that moved, with alarming rapidity, from one space of work to another and filled the streets with visible demonstrations of working-class discontent. The conciliation of workers was both less and more pronounced than it had been in October. The plague authorities refused to climb down from the current basis of their work, i.e. house-to-house visitations. On the other hand, they paid careful and close attention to the 'religious susceptibilities' of the strikers, which revolved around caste. They were promised that the Plague Committee would consider setting up separate hospitals on the basis of caste, and that 'untouchable' employees of the Municipal Department would not be allowed to enter the homes of higher-caste workers to carry out sanitary work.[119] This concession should instantly alert us against the temptation of positing a model of militant class unity and solidarity to explain the nature of labour discontent at this time. Fragmentations of caste and religion, if anything, were often sharpened in this period, and relations *within* working-class neighbourhoods often bore the burdens of these tensions, as plague, and the practices of hospitalization and sanitary labour attendant upon it, threatened to break down physical distances between workers of different castes.

The Strike

On 11 March 1898, two days after the dramatic events at Madanpura, two batches of prisoners held by the Bombay police in connection with the riot were brought before Justice Sanders, the Chief Presidency Magistrate, who presided over a special court at Byculla Prison. A third batch was scheduled for trial at the Umarkhadi Jail on 16 March. The social composition of the accused provides a useful, if not unexpected insight into the dynamics of the situation that prevailed on the streets on 9 March. Twenty-nine handweavers and twenty-five mill workers, all Muslims, were named among the principal instigators and torchbearers of the violence; three Muslim shopkeepers were also listed. The remaining prisoners, 50 or so to begin with and eventually swelling to over 200, comprised mill-hands, hawkers, cooks, barbers, fitters, embroiderers, cart drivers, carpenters, beggars, washermen, casual labourers, tailors, goldsmiths and masons – a fairly exhaustive cross-section of Bombay's proletarian and plebeian classes.[120]

Grim corroborative testimony can be found in the summary by the *Times of India* of some of the people who died in the rioting. A mendicant was killed on Ripon Road while begging for alms. The remaining deaths are reduced to names and occupations: a mill labourer's brother, a Julaha woman's husband, a Julaha hawker's son, two Julaha weavers, a *ghareewala* or driver, a cloth hawker's brother, and a shopkeeper's servant's brother, all seem to have died in the vicinity of Ripon Road, though it is unknown whether their deaths were caused by the rioting crowd or the police.[121] Whether instigators, participants or victims, the overwhelming majority of the protagonists belonged to the city's labouring poor.

Consider, in juxtaposition with this, Patell's enumeration in verse of the flight from the city in the immediate aftermath of the initial plague crisis of 1896–97:

> . . . menial servants of all grades,
> And votaries of the humbler trades,
> Hamal, masal, cook, ayah, syce,
> Each one with bag and baggage flies ;
> The dhobie, gavlai, butcher, baker,
> The barber, tailor and shoe-maker
> A motley crowd, all fleeing fast,
> They think the town redemption past.[122]

Each instance of labour flight touched upon in Patell's poem suggests a breakdown of the normal configuration of class and labour relations in the city: no one left to cook for those who employed cooks; to clean the houses and look after the children of the rich; to wash other people's clothes; to deliver milk, meat or bread; to cut their hair, tailor their clothes and mend their shoes. The channels of authority and subordination that sustained everyday social relationships in Bombay had been ripped to shreds by the sheer, overwhelming empirical fact of flight. The forms of labour upon which the city was built were now aggregated into a 'motley crowd'.

In Patell's account, the working classes of the city are organized for the purpose of mass desertion. In Madanpura they were organized for civil unrest. In both cases, however, as in the events described in the preceding sections, a new kind of political relationship between rulers and the ruled was beginning to make itself visible. A city hitherto characterized by an abundant, if sectorally wayward, supply of labour was now defined by a pervasive scarcity. Consequently, the centrality of various forms of labour in keeping the city running suddenly became more visible than ever, and – as evidenced by the administration's perennial terror about the disappearance of the city's scavengers and sweepers – menial grades of labour were suddenly invested with a political importance far in excess of their standing in the city's hierarchy. Their mobilization, retention and discipline were recognized, openly, as crucial to the city's survival.

It is possible to look at this dynamic, and this structure of administrative feeling, more precisely – as dimensions of what I choose to term the crisis of *arterial labour*.[123] This designates labour that is deployed to keep the city's normal channels flowing and connect nodal points to one another. Roads, streets and alleys furnish, as a common colonial metaphor put it, the arteries through which human beings and merchandise of various forms travel, and local markets and trade networks are kept running. Railways offer an amplification of the same logic, across greater distances and with greater velocity. Docks connect a port city to channels of para-local trade and exchange. Drains, other channels of waste disposal and water pipes constitute yet another set of arterial connections that keep a city in sanitary order. The flow of people, commodities and waste through these arterial channels is naturalized, for the most part, in the minds of most city dwellers. The cycles of this flow constitute, in a sense, the city's own rhythm. But this is a rhythm built upon specific regimes and practices of labour, and on elaborate regulation of workers engaged in transport, in dock work, and in conservancy and sanitation. It is a rhythm characterized by an immediate relationship with *circulation*, founded on the sustenance of regularized circuits of movement for people, goods, machinery, water and waste. A disturbance of the material conditions and social relations on which this deployment of working bodies is predicated can paralyse the city. The events at Arthur Road and the Colaba Docks, described above, bore this out, but it would be in March 1898, in the immediate aftermath of the Madanpura riot, that the crisis of arterial labour would assume its most threatening shape.

The week that followed was marked by what may well have been recognized as the city's first genuine general strike, were it not for the fact that mill workers, whose practices and antagonisms were shaped more directly by the strategies of their employers and managers than by the supervening colonial state, generally held themselves aloof from the otherwise pervasive stoppage of labour. Mill workers, as this article has already indicated, were no minor figures in the general drama of the period; indeed they were amongst its principal protagonists. In 1897 their flight and subsequent return to the city had marked the most dramatic period of conflict over wage payment in Bombay's history to date, and the fluctuations in the labour market, in the words of a prominent local historian, had snapped 'the tie hitherto binding the employer and employed'.[124] In other words, the balance of power in industrial relations of the cotton mills had swung decisively in favour of labour for the first time, and this was to have consequences perhaps even more far-reaching than those of the latent and open civil conflict over plague regulation. However, to the narrative sketched so far, the dynamics of the mill industry are relevant chiefly as intimations of a general backdrop of simmering labour unrest that worked its way through Bombay's working-class neighbourhoods at multiple levels.[125]

The converse is also true. When the Factory Inspector wrote, in 1897, of the situation in Bombay as 'a Labour Question comparable to those in Europe', he was referring specifically to a world that had turned upside down in Bombay's mills.[126] This worried acknowledgment, however, drew its potency from the more general predicaments of urban labour, as also the specific predicaments of 'arterial' labour, in the shadow of the plague.

This was a worry that had a precise spatial dimension: not only sectorally but geographically, the ferment of Bombay's labouring poor had the capacity, in each of its eventuations, to spill beyond the frontiers designated for it. In the process, the meanings of the event could change, not infrequently, in a matter of hours or even minutes. A mill workers' riot, fuelled by rumours about the practices of plague control, could infect the city's low-caste sweepers and scavengers, as well as evoke worries about the general breakdown of the city's sanitary infrastructure and thereby about what would effectively be the death of the city. A carters' strike could pass into a mutinous situation on the adjacent docks, both grounded in the same oppressive plague operation – the inspection and destruction of working-class dwellings – and, if anything, even more worrying because of the apparent lack of the mediation of organized solidarity. Seemingly, the singular could pass into the general seamlessly, and a precise abstraction – the state's anxiety about the total breakdown of social relations – could be condensed within the thick (and therefore semantically vague) materiality of a more or less bounded event that on its own, in other circumstances, would have been much less resonant.

These tensions were gathered together in a new articulation of unprecedented dramatic magnitude, in the events of March 1898. At 3 in the afternoon on 10 March, the day after the Madanpura riot, an update from Vincent to the Bombay government stated that 'all is quiet so far'. It went on, however, to say that the Hindu and Muslim owners of cloth-shops were closing their establishments across the city.[127] In itself this was not entirely unexpected; rather, it recapitulated a possibility that had been in the air for some time. Two days prior to the riot, for instance, Hindu *mahajans* and Muslim shopkeepers, in separate meetings, had decided to protest against one of the new regulations issued by Campbell's Plague Committee, which required death certificates from medical men before the disposal of corpses – something in contravention to both Hindu custom and the *sharia*.[128]

The working class of Madanpura, in the meantime, appeared to have returned to its habitual opacity, though in an atmosphere of 'suppressed excitement'.[129] Having with difficulty asserted their supremacy on Wednesday, the police on Thursday went through the neighbourhood, followed by the persistent correspondent of the *Times of India*, 'ferreting out' the rioters in their cramped environment:

> Running parallel with Ripon Road, to the east, is a row of exceedingly ill-constructed small huts, bordering an unkempt, unpaved street, and this is entirely inhabited by Jhulais. It was almost amusing to watch the intense preoccupation with which the weavers plied their craft, dexterously handling their curious old-fashioned looms, while the police made their domiciliary visits. One would not be wronging these people if it was asserted that nine men out of every ten were dancing along Ripon Road at noon on Wednesday, brandishing huge sticks and yelling himself hoarse with *Din, Din*, but no one could have looked more innocent than those sturdy *budmashes* when under the eye of the Superintendent.[130]

The amusement in these lines is excessive and laboured, and barely conceals, through insinuation, a worry that could not have been far from the minds of observers sympathetic to the state: the association of the Madanpura troubles with a possible assertion of militant Islam ('yelling himself hoarse with *Din, Din*'). This was an association strengthened by report and rumour. Mrs Hudson, who testified at the trial of prisoners held for the Foras Road affray where Jacob Sassoon was attacked, also said she had heard the rioters say:

'Don't want to see the European's face. The rule of the English is over; that of the Mahomedans has begun.'[131] During the investigations, a labourer who doubled as police informer told Inspector Murfoy of the East Division that the attack was 'premature', and had been planned for Friday after prayers at the city's Jama Masjid. Once again, this was a rumour with strong resonances – the mosque had been the epicentre of the communal riot of 1893.[132] However, notwithstanding the real millenarian investments that some or many of the rioters may have had in the outcome of the Madanpura riot, Vincent, who investigated the matter assiduously and was predisposed by experience to use the 'fanaticism of the Mahomedan' as an all-purpose explanation, was unable to unearth any sort of premeditation. The Julahas, he admitted, 'did not themselves know the riot was going to take place' till it did.[133]

In the event, matters clarified themselves fairly soon; the imprecise and shadowy intimations of continuing unrest crystallized over the week following the riot into a general strike of massive proportions. The closing of shops was followed by signals of mutiny far north as the butchers of the Bandra abattoirs threatened to strike on Thursday night 'in sympathy with Wednesday's rioting' – a threat put down by Douglas Bennett, Superintendent of Markets, only 'with some military assistance' (exactly what the obviously euphemistic phrase connotes is not clear).[134] On the following day, the butchers mutinied again, this time with greater force, and did effect their strike. Bennett was faced with a linked problem at Crawford Market in the heart of the native town, where existing supplies of meat were withheld from their buyers by stall-holders, 'depriving Europeans of their food supply'.[135]

From the outset, this was a strike that rippled across spatial and occupational frontiers, condensing shared grievances into a common mode of protest, but simultaneously multiplying its locations, forms and strategies into a heterogeneous assemblage. On Friday morning, the occupational groups that had been on strike the previous April refused work, alleging plague visits in their absence and the removal of their family members to hospitals and segregation camps, a practice that, besides violating the sanctity of home, also left their residences 'in an unprotected state'.[136] At the Prince's and Victoria Docks, coolies usually involved in the unloading of goods refused to work under the European and Parsi stevedores who supervised them. Steamers plying at the peak of the trading season were unable to depart the harbour. Passenger ships that entered were discommoded as the strike of the cart drivers forced passengers to resort to 'victorias' (cabs) and 'trucks of various descriptions for the conveyance of their heavy packages to their hotels or the railway stations'.[137]

The strike spread to the adjacent railway goods yards of the Great Indian Peninsular (GIP) and Bombay, Baroda and Central India (BB&CI) railway companies, as 15,000 coolies involved in the loading and unloading of goods, and 5,000 cart drivers instrumental in their transport, suspended work. At the Wari Bunder goods station, none of the coolies who loaded and unloaded trains and carts turned up. In a turn of events reminiscent of the strike the previous April, a few cart drivers did turn up to work but were 'waylaid by parties of coolies and persuaded to join the strike'.[138] At the Colaba Goods Depot of the two railway companies, the strike took an even more dramatic form as a gang of 50 or 60 *hamals* engaged in loading wagons, who had begun work at 6 in the morning, abruptly stopped their tasks at 8, followed shortly by the bullock-cart drivers who worked in tandem with them.[139] The effects of the strike dovetailed with those of shop closures across the city. 'Owing to the refusal of the native merchants to take delivery these yards are now absolutely blocked with bales of cotton, and there is hardly room to unload another wagon.'[140]

Added to this was the ever-present source of anxiety that, in distinct ways, seems to have given the entire plague crisis its consistency: a 'serious question was raised when signs of uneasiness were apparent among the *bigharries*' who, as the *Times of India* charmingly put it, around noon, 'evinced a tendency . . . to go out on strike', showing a 'disinclination' to 'continue their somewhat unpleasant but necessary labours'. One of the Municipal Health Officers and the Assistant Health Officer worked together to bring the workers before Superintendent Brewin of the Bombay police, who, probably employing a judicious mixture of threat and blandishment, 'ascertained that pressure had been brought to bear upon them by their fellow-castemen' and 'induced' them to return to work.[141]

The strike was sustained and amplified over the weekend of 12–13 March. There were some significant extensions of discontent as ambulance bearers and 'general labourers' joined in the strike, throwing plague control itself out of gear in areas in and around Second Nagpada.[142] Ten search parties were formed, each protected by a heavy military escort, to forestall the possibility of another Madanpura, but since the 'general factotums' who silently bore the brunt of the real physical labour of inspection refused to work, there was a 'considerable delay' before they could begin.

The main centres of the strike remained the docks, the railways, the markets and the streets – the four 'arteries' that, in different ways, kept the city moving and circulating. Fresh dimensions of the problem, logistical as well as political, were elaborated by '150 Pathans' who were employed as stevedores' labourers on the docks and who were engaged in stowing cargo on board vessels. They put in an appearance but demonstratively refused to work, arguing that the work of carrying cargo from the sheds to the ships' side – preparatory labour that was necessary for their own – could not be carried out by them, 'as their class of work was of a different nature'.[143] Since the Hindu labourers who generally performed the labour of transporting the goods to the ships were absent, the Pathan workers argued that their presence was redundant. Further – and here economic constraints, political choices and religious identity meet – they pointed out that if they returned to work they would be 'offending their co-religionists', and therefore they too joined the strike.

At the railway yards, unclaimed stacks of perishable goods rotted as the *hamals* and cartmen continued their strike. While export firms like Ralli Brothers stopped their requisitions of grain, they still incurred heavy losses since 'about a thousand waggons are now lying in the yard with their contents unloaded'. Heavy policing – the police being the one vital 'artery' of labour still pumping, and pumping overtime – was needed to stave off the threat of robberies.[144]

The strike activity unfolded, it is important to note, in a context of mounting tension and panic, as crowds milled about on the streets, sometimes indifferent, sometimes aggressive, always potentially menacing. On Friday, large crowds, numbering hundreds of people, had gathered around major junction points – Duncan Road, Pydhoni, Nal Bazaar – in the centre of the 'native Town' with an 'air of expectancy'.[145] On Saturday, a rumour circulated that a plague hospital at Narel Wadi, housing 67 plague victims and 'suspects', was going to be attacked. In the evening, a solitary sentry who was standing guard was pelted with stones for half an hour. 'No one could be seen, but brick-bats, road metal, and upon one occasion a big lump of iron were hurled in the direction in which the sentry was known to be standing.'[146] For the plague authorities – and, of course, for the unfortunate sentry – this was resistance at its most malevolent, bereft of name, face and address but at the same time sinister and omnipresent, armed with makeshift but dangerous weapons.

All the strike situations in the city were further elaborated on Monday. Several hundred coolies assembled outside the docks but almost all refused work, even at significantly enhanced wages. Tensions among the stevedores came to the surface as a Parsi managed, with the blandishment of wages four times in excess of their normal rates and what the *Times of India* correspondent mysteriously called 'certain comforts', to induce some men to work for him. European stevedores who paid ordinary wages stood to lose and expressed strong resentment to the journalist:

> While the Parsee as an employer of labour is probably entitled to arrange his own terms with the dissatisfied labourers, it is thought that by his doing so he is encouraging the men to refrain from work, as when they know they can under existing circumstances earn in one day the wages that in the ordinary course of events would require four days' labour, they may see the advantages of remaining on strike...[and] dictating practically their own terms.[147]

The basis of labour discipline on the docks thereby stood undermined.

The situation at the railway goods yard in Colaba was even more extreme as '800 waggons chiefly loaded with grain and a hundred thousand miscellaneous packages of goods' stood forlornly without their habitual tenders, who refused to work despite the persistent offer of higher wages. Here, as on the docks, the refusal of casual labourers to work in their customary occupations – the unloading and transportation of goods – triggered a corresponding refusal by the GIP Railway's regular employees, 'on the grounds that it [the work of *hamals*] is not the class of work to which they have been accustomed'.[148] The line separating a refusal to work based on practical considerations and existing practice cannot be precisely demarcated from the wider politics of the situation, where, regardless of individual motivations, the state of things amounted to an unusual assertion of workers' solidarity across occupational lines.

On Monday, for a brief period of time, the darkest fear of Bombay's administration came true as municipal scavengers and cart drivers attached to the East Division, comprising Grant Road, Byculla, Madanpura and other epicentres of the riot the previous week, went on strike, with the result that 'filth was not removed for a few hours'. The carrot gave way to the stick and the police intervened aggressively, 'advising' the men that they stood to lose their appointments altogether.[149] Catastrophe was narrowly averted, but its amplified proximity seems to have forced an urgent reconsideration of the priorities of the state administration and the plague authorities.

The 'contagion of combination', as a letter to the press pithily put it, finally drew to a close the following day, after a meeting on Monday afternoon involving piece-goods merchants, cotton merchants, Marwari moneylenders, grain and seed merchants, hardware and iron merchants, Police Commissioner Vincent, prominent businessman George Cotton, and representatives of cartmen and labourers. The meeting managed to produce an agreement of sorts. The workers' representatives, fittingly, seem to have dominated proceedings. A strong petition in Gujarati from the striking cart drivers and casual labourers asked for remission of the plague quarantine rules, and relaxation of house-to-house inspections and arbitrary removals to hospital, which were continuing in the city despite assurances of restraint from the authorities. Speaking in Marathi, the cartmen's jobber stated that 'if they were to terminate the strike they would be cutting their own throats . . . unless promise was given to them that their numerous grievances would be remedied they should continue the strike, or sell their bullocks and carts and go to their native country'.[150]

The strike brought the Municipality, the police and the plague administration to their knees. The reverberations of the urban unrest were felt in the Governor's office, and Sandhurst effected wide-ranging changes in plague administration shortly after the crisis. Soldiers were withdrawn from plague work and arbitrary house inspections were declared illegitimate. The removal of people to hospital without the consent of the head of the family was prohibited – a clear climbdown in the face of the crisis that erupted around the attempt to hospitalize the 'Jhulai' girl. Most dramatically, Campbell, head of the Plague Committee, was asked to go on leave by Sandhurst, and he ended up leaving India for good.[151] A distinguished administrative career, marked by security and power for most of its tenure, was terminated ingloriously as a more or less direct consequence of popular agitation.

The concessions made to popular protest were communicated through a government proclamation issued by Sandhurst, and circulated across the city in English, Hindustani, Gujarati and Marathi, on 15 March:

> His Excellency the Governor in Council desires that all people may understand that the object of all plague measures in Bombay is the benefit of the people. As long as the plague lasts there will be death and sickness, grief and suffering to many. There will also be less trade and less work to do and wages to earn. It is these evils that the Government want to do away with. It is false and absurd to suppose that they wish to oppress the people in any way or cause them suffering or make them discontented. Much suffering there must be as long as the plague lasts, but Government do not wish to make the cure of plague a cause of suffering for the people. The great object of Government is to alleviate suffering. They desire the greatest kindness and sympathy to be shown to all. For the last fourteen days a new plan is being devised, but recent disturbances have delayed its introduction. General searching for plague cases can, it is hoped, be almost wholly given up, provided the people cordially assist to make this new plan effective. To take the place of a general searching, arrangements will be made for ascertaining the house where a death occurs. The headmen must help in this. The people should bring cases of plague to notice that the sick may be cared for in their own caste hospitals, and that those suffering from other sickness than plague may not be taken to hospital. The headmen must help in this also. Where it is necessary to vacate houses, leaders and headmen will be expected to impress on the people the necessity for complete ventilation and temporary removal, as this is the best way of saving life. Careful inquiries will be made to find out whether a death is or is not due to plague, but there will be *no inspection of corpses and no delay of funerals.* If the Plague Authorities are satisfied that a death is not due to plague, the house where it takes place will not be further troubled. Arrangements will be made for the hearing of complaints, and the people should aid Government by exposing attempted extortion.[152]

These provisions amounted to a tacit recognition of the impossibility of sustaining plague control measures in the draconian form they currently existed in. Among substantial sections of the city's elite, this seems to have been interpreted as cowardly capitulation. In a letter to England on 18 March, Hesther Mary Dowson wrote that the Governor's proclamation 'has very greatly appeased the anger of the people, but some of the English are very angry, as it is like giving in to the natives because of the rioting'.[153]

This coincided, as Catanach has pointed out, with a landmark reconsideration of plague policy at the national level. In April 1898 Robert Harvey, the new head of the Indian Medical Service, produced a 'Note on Plague Administration', that urged a retreat from interference with the 'habits and customs' of populations affected by plague and a general easing of restrictions of all kinds. A move towards institutionalization of voluntary inoculation as the basis of plague policy was thus authorized. This had only partly to do with advances in medical knowledge, for it was still not widely understood that plague could not be easily transmitted from person to person.[154] It had more to do with growing apprehension about the disruptive energies that draconian measures of plague control could produce. Plague mortality continued to rise well into the twentieth century: 1899, 1901, and 1903, all claimed more lives than 1897 and 1898 had. However, if we understand the plague crisis as a crisis of authority, then, it reached its terminus in a real sense in mid-1898.[155]

The Plague Crisis and the 'Labour Question'

The form taken by the sequence of events narrated above was significant. A singular, localized event – a riot in a working-class Muslim neighbourhood – produced ramifications that went well beyond its designated frontiers, and released a chain of confrontations which culminated in a city-wide general strike that effectively undermined the existing foundations of plague policy. As demonstrated, the sequence of events in March 1898 gathered within itself tensions and processes that were both long-term and immediate, and articulated them in ways that were impossible to ignore or to refuse.

Viewed in a wider perspective, the consequences of the articulations of public protest by Bombay's working classes in this period were more ambiguous. Spatially speaking, these events represented a revolt of the city's north against its southern elites. The spatial patterns of the Madanpura riot exemplify this, for the crowds on 9 March moved southwards, countering the intrusions of plague authorities with their own forms of intrusion, into alien neighbourhoods and built spaces. The attacks on various symbols of plague authority, the multiple and overlapping refusals of labour, and the eventual articulation of precise demands that more or less were met, all bolster this view. What makes these assertions of 'popular power' all the more arresting is that they were achieved at a point of absolute and often quite literally terminal crisis, marked by death, flight and depopulation, and a demoralization that is hard to imagine. Panic may have defined the situation, but it was a panic that produced its own, fairly coherent patterns of action, and an equally coherent set of immediate consequences.

These events also provide a gloss upon Chandavarkar's suggestion, on the face of it peculiar and even counter-intuitive, that the plague was not only the cause but also the product of the despair that drove the choices and actions of city elites.[156] Here 'despair' is something that should be construed less as a subjective attitude than as an objective, even structural situation. The expansion of Bombay's northern districts, its emergence as a distinctively industrial working-class city, uncontrolled migration from different corners of the country, and the systematic dumping of the social costs of reproduction of labour upon the networks and families of the poor – these were the elements that made up the 'despair' which colonial and municipal officials frequently (and, subjectively, not without sincerity) expressed. Seen in this light, the plague crisis violently arrested this despair, and enforced a relationship between rulers and ruled, elites and urban poor, employers and workers that was much closer – and for that very reason much more openly conflictual –

than earlier. The plague crisis did not, as some of its historians have implicitly suggested, drive an extra wedge between classes in the city, but, paradoxically, forced them closer together through the processes of conflict.

From the side of the state, this took the form of more intrusive behaviour, but also, temporarily, more attention to the social reproduction of labour. The Bombay Improvement Trust, set up in 1898, at least partly as a consequence of the kinds of events described, exemplified this. In its origins, it was a compact between Bombay's colonial rulers and its business elites to shepherd a socio-spatial transformation of the city that responded effectively to the crises that defined its current life. It produced the first attempts to institute a watered-down version of regulated social housing, organized by private capital but overseen by the state. This led to, among other things, the frenetic construction of chawls in the immediate vicinity of the city's mills, which employed, through much of the twentieth century, the major portion of its working poor. This accentuated the social processes described earlier in the essay, extending the colonization of the northern part of the island by private business and the working classes. In time, as the threat of plague receded, the imperatives of social 'improvement' that had defined the Trust faded, and, as Kidambi and Chandavarkar have shown, it became a hyper-efficient mechanism for the transfer of land to mill-owning elites.[157]

Another dimension of the work of the Trust, though, cannot be overstated, which is that from the beginning, it aimed to open up clustered working-class neighbourhoods through the construction of roads that cut across previously opaque spaces, and, in the process, 'improved' and de-fanged them at the same time. The Second Nagpada Scheme, one of the BIT's flagship initiatives, was a striking instance of this. It is no coincidence, perhaps, that it was directed at the very areas that had come most strongly under the control of working-class rioters in 1898. This dovetailed with another very precise consequence of the plague crisis – the development, seen as increasingly necessary by an urban administration that had recognized the pitfalls of an effectively *laissez-faire* attitude to the urban poor – of much more rigorous structures of policing. These structures involved the regulation of festivals like *Muharram*, and also an increasingly intense surveillance of a Girangaon that came to be honeycombed with radical protest in the twentieth century.[158]

The lasting effects of the plague crisis, however, had much to do with the apprehension of the Factory Inspector, who claimed that at the end of the nineteenth century, Bombay was in the throes of a 'Labour Question' comparable to those of Europe.[159] This is a strange assertion to have made about a period when the vulnerabilities of the city's working classes were more pronounced than they had ever been, a time when they were, in a very real sense, *mortally* vulnerable. This very apprehension of mortality, however, made older patterns of political relations between the labouring poor and their rulers untenable, as the threat of death and the intrusions of a fearful state administration coupled to produce various forms of extremely effective popular resistance. In this sense, the plague crisis was a crossroad in

Bombay's history. It expressed and crystallized the existing political regimes and relations that dominated urban life, but also transformed them, both directly and indirectly.

Notes and References

1 For a cross-section of historical analyses of the plague and its impact, see David Arnold, 'Touching the Body: Perspectives on the Indian Plague, 1896–1900', in R. Guha (ed.), *Subaltern Studies V*, New Delhi: Oxford University Press, 1987: 55–90; David Arnold, *Colonizing the Body: State Medicine and Epidemic Disease in Nineteenth-Century India*, Berkeley: University of California Press, 1993; Rajnarayan Chandavarkar, 'Plague Panic and Epidemic Politics in India', in *Imperial Power and Popular Politics: Class, Resistance and the State in India, c. 1850–1950*, Cambridge: Cambridge University Press, 1998; Myron Echenberg, 'Pestis Redux: The Initial Years of the Third Bubonic Plague Pandemic, 1894–1901', *Journal of World History*, 13 (2), 2002: 429–49; Prashant Kidambi, '"An Infection of Locality": Plague, Pythogenesis and the Poor in Bombay, *c.* 1896–1905', *Urban History*, 31 (2), 2004: 249–67; Prashant Kidambi, *The Making of an Indian Metropolis: Colonial Governance and Public Culture in Bombay, 1890–1920*, Aldershot: Ashgate, 2007; Ira Klein, 'Plague, Policy and Popular Unrest in British India', *Modern Asian Studies*, 22 (4), 1988: 72–55; Ian J. Catanach, '"Who Are Your Leaders?" Plague, The Raj and the "Communities" in Bombay, 1896–1901', in P. Robb (ed.), *Society and Ideology: Essays in South Asian History Presented to Prof. K.A. Ballhatchet*, New Delhi: Oxford University Press, 1993: 196–221; Ian J. Catanach, 'The "Globalization" of Disease? India and the Plague', *Journal of World History*, 12 (1), 2001: 131–53.

2 Telegram from Governor, Bombay, to the Secretary of State for India, India Office, London, 21 February 1897: *Papers Relating to the Outbreak of Bubonic Plague in India, House of Commons Parliamentary Papers (PP)*, C.8386, 1897.

3 See Samuel T. Shepard, *Bombay Place-Names and Street Names: An Excursion into the By-Ways of Bombay City*, Bombay: The Times Press, 1917: 126. Ripon Road itself had been built as late as 1885, which indicates the speed with which working-class Bombay was emerging as a distinct spatial unit at the end of the nineteenth century.

4 Shepard, *Bombay Place-Names and Street Names*: 94.

5 I owe this piece of information to Santosh Kumar Rai, personal communication, based on his unpublished Ph.D. research.

6 Jim Masselos, *The City in Action: Bombay Struggles for Power*, New Delhi: Oxford University Press, 2007: 125–53.

7 General Department (Plague Branch), No. 2510, vol. 389, 5 April 1898, Government of Bombay, Maharashtra State Archives (MSA).

8 Ibid.

9 No. 2634/6 R, from R.H. Vincent, Commissioner of Police, to Secretary to Government, Judicial Department, Bombay, 1 April 1898, in Judicial Letter no. 6, 9 April 1898, IOR/L/P & J/3/959, Oriental and India Office Collections (OIOC), British Library (BL).

10 General Department (Plague Branch), No. 2510, vol. 389, 5 April 1898, MSA.

11 Ibid.

12 Ibid.

13 For a more detailed exploration of the relationship between the plague and postulations of community, see Catanach, '"Who are Your Leaders?"'.

14 *Times of India* (*ToI*), 9 March 1898.

15 'Bombay During the Plague, 1897–98: Extracts from the Letters of Hesther Mary Dowson, Plague Hospital Sister Under Government', MSS Eur B. 385, p. 26, fn. 1, OIOC, BL.

16 No. 2634/6 R, from R.H. Vincent, IOR/L/P&J/3/959, OIOC, BL.
17 'Bombay During the Plague, 1897–98: Extracts from the Letters of Hesther Mary Dowson', MSS Eur. B. 385, pp. 18–19, OIOC, BL.
18 General Department (Plague), No. 2510, vol. 389, MSA.
19 'Bombay During the Plague, 1897–98: Extracts from the Letters of Hesther Mary Dowson', MSS Eur. B. 385, p. 31, OIOC, BL.
20 To R.B. Stewart from D.R. Gilder, General Department (Plague), No. 2510, vol. 389, 5 April 1898, MSA.
21 From M.S. Ruknuddin to R.B. Stewart, ibid.
22 From D.S. Gilder to R.B. Stewart, ibid.
23 Ibid.
24 Ibid.
25 From Lt. G. Warneford to R.B. Stewart, General Department (Plague), No. 2510, vol. 389, 5 April 1898, MSA.
26 No. 2634/6 R, from R.H. Vincent, IOR/L/P&J/3/959, OIOC, BL.
27 From Lt. G. Warneford to R.B. Stewart, General Department (Plague), No. 2510, vol. 389, 5 April 1898, MSA.
28 Gilder left the party once it reached the plague office (relatively) safely. 'The Police was informed about this by telephone, and after that as I did not take any active part I know very little', he wrote. From D.S. Gilder to R.B. Stewart, ibid.
29 From Lt. G. Warneford to R.B. Stewart, ibid.
30 No. 2634/6 R, from R.H. Vincent, IOR/L/P&J/3/959, OIOC, BL.
31 Ibid.
32 S.M. Edwardes, *The Bombay City Police: A Historical Sketch*, London [u.a.]: Milford [u.a.], 1923: 99.
33 *ToI: Special Supplement*, 10 March 1898.
34 *ToI*, 10 March 1898.
35 Ibid.
36 Masselos, *The City in Action*: 126.
37 Ibid.
38 *ToI*, 14 March 1898.
39 No. 2634/6 R, from R.H. Vincent, IOR/L/P&J/3/959, OIOC, BL.
40 From R.B. Stewart to E. Ward, Chairman, Plague Committee, Bombay, 15 March 1898.
41 *ToI*, 16 March 1898.
42 *ToI*, 10 March 1898.
43 No. 2634/6 R, from R.H. Vincent, IOR/L/P&J/3/959, OIOC, BL.
44 Ibid.
45 'An Account of the Riots in Bombay on 9 March 1898', unattributed, Judicial Department, Bombay, No. 669, Parts I and II, MSA.
46 Ibid.
47 Ibid.
48 *ToI*, 17 March 1898.
49 *ToI*, 31 March 1898.
50 Ibid.: 3.
51 *ToI*, 15 March 1898.
52 *ToI*, 24 March 1898.
53 *ToI*, 11 March 1898.
54 'An Account of the Riots in Bombay on 9 March 1898', unattributed, Judicial Department, Bombay, No. 669, Parts I and II, MSA.
55 *ToI*, 12 March 1898.
56 Ibid., letter from 'J.P.'
57 Ibid., Letter from 'Observer'.

58 This is an account of urban transformation that is familiar to all historians of Bombay. The clearest expositions of these structural changes can be found in Kidambi, *The Making of an Indian Metropolis*, and Rajnarayan Chandavarkar, 'Bombay's Perennial Modernities', in *History, Culture and the Indian City*, Cambridge: Cambridge University Press, 2009 (posthumously published).

59 Preeti Chopra, 'The City and Its Fragments: Colonial Bombay, 1854–1918', unpublished Ph.D. dissertation, University of California, 2003: 282.

60 S.M. Rutnagar, 'Bombay Industries: The Cotton Mills – A Review of the Progress of the Textile Industry in Bombay from 1850 to 1926 and the Present Constitution, Management and Financial Position of Spinning and Weaving Factories', *Indian Textile Journal*, 1927: 9–24.

61 Ibid.

62 Morris David Morris, *The Emergence of an Industrial Labour Force in India: A Study of the Bombay Cotton Mills, 1854–1947*, Berkeley: University of California Press, 1965: 65.

63 D.E. Wacha, *Shells from the Sands of Bombay: Being My Recollections and Reminiscences – 1860–1875*, Bombay: K. T. Anklesaria, 1920: 50–51.

64 Chopra, 'The City and Its Fragments': 278–95.

65 *ToI*, 25 May 1880.

66 Ibid.

67 No. 686, General Department, 1881, vol. 5, GoB, MSA; Chopra, 'The City and Its Fragments': 292; *Gazetteer of Bombay City and Island*, vol. 2, Bombay, 1909: 188–89.

68 Memorial to Town Council, 15 January 1881, General Department, vol. 5, no. 686, GoB, MSA.

69 Report on the Sanitary Condition of Mills, Factories, and Workshops in the City of Bombay, 1884, V/26/670/86, OIOC, BL.

70 Ibid.

71 Chopra, 'The City and Its Fragments': 278–95.

72 Rajnarayan Chandavarkar, 'Sewers', in *History, Culture and the Indian City*, Cambridge: Cambridge University Press, 2009: 31–59.

73 Ibid.: 35.

74 Chandavarkar, 'Bombay's Perennial Modernities': 18.

75 Chandavarkar, 'Sewers': 36–37.

76 *Abstract of the Report of the Sanitary Commissioner with the Government of India for 1897*: 120.

77 *Abstract of the Report of the Sanitary Commissioner with the Government of India for 1896*: 106.

78 *Abstract of the Report of the Health Officer of Bombay City for 1897*: 228.

79 B.F. Patell, *History of the Plague in Bombay*, Bombay, n.d. (*c*. late 1890s): 32.

80 Indeed it continues to be a contested question today. Where did the oceanically transmitted bubonic plague that hit China, Bombay and various other parts of the world really originate? Was the origin in Hong Kong or did the disease travel in flea-infested bales of Egyptian cotton? Were there perhaps mutations within the genetic structure of *Y. Pestis* (the bacterium that produced the plague, borne on the vector *X. Cheopis*, or the rat flea): did the plague, in other words, arise where it occurred? This would mean that miasmatic theories of the origins of plague, such as those put forward in Bombay in 1896 by Lieutenant Colonel George Waters of the Indian Medical Service, accidentally had a certain purchase upon the realities of the epidemic. See George Waters, *Plague in Bombay. A Lecture Delivered at the Sassoon Mechanics' Institute, Bombay*, Bombay, 1897.

81 From Secretary of State to Governor, Bombay, 23 January 1897, *Papers Relating to Outbreak of Bubonic Plague in India*, *PP*, C.8386 and C.8511, 1897.

82 Kidambi, *The Making of an Indian Metropolis*: 49–71; Kidambi, '"An Infection of Locality"': 249–67.

83 See, for instance, *Abstract of Report of the Health Officer of Bombay for 1874, Report on Sanitary Measures in India in 1874–75, PP*, C.1615, 1876: 124–26).

84 Myron Echenberg, *Plague Ports: The Global Urban Impact of Bubonic Plague, 1894–1901*, New York and London: New York University Press, 2007: 55–56.

85 *PP*, C.8386, 1897, p. 11.

86 *Abstract of Report of the Health Officer of Bombay for 1874, Report on Sanitary Measures in India in 1874–75, PP*, C.1615, 1876: 124–26; M.E. Couchman, 'Chapter 1', *Account of Plague Administration in the Bombay Presidency from September 1896 till May 1897*, Part I, Bombay: Government Central Press, 1897; Catanach, '"Who Are Your Leaders?"'.

87 A prevalent discourse that foregrounded the idea of the instrumentality of bodily contagion in spreading plague and produced strategies of compulsory hospitalization was thus married to a pythogenetic account of plague origins, locating the roots of the disease in the filth of poor neighbourhoods and the insanitary practices of working-class communities. For an important account of the role of pythogenesis in the framing and execution of plague policy, see Kidambi, *The Making of an Indian Metropolis*; Kidambi, '"An Infection of Locality"': 249–67.

88 Couchman, 'Chapter 1', *Account of Plague Administration*, Part I.

89 Couchman, *Account of Plague Administration*, Part I, Chapter 3; Catanach, '"Who Are Your Leaders?"'.

90 Couchman, 'Chapter 1', *Account of Plague Administration*, Part I; Catanach, '"Who Are Your Leaders?"'; *Bombay Gazette*, 8 October 1896.

91 George Lambert, *India: The Horror-Stricken Empire, Containing a Full Account of the Famine, Plague and Earthquake of 1896–97*, Elkhart, Indiana: Mennonite Publishing Corporation, 1898: 400–01.

92 Fascinating descriptions of the way this hospital functioned are contained in letters written by one of the city stalwarts, Dr Thomas Blaney, to the newspapers in early 1897: *ToI*, 6, 8 and 10 February 1897. The most revealing insights, however, come from the letters of Hesther Mary Dowson, who worked for several months in the hospital in 1898: MSS Eur. B. 385, OIOC, BL.

93 Ibid.

94 Arnold, *Colonizing the Body*: 219–20.

95 Lambert, *The Horror-Stricken Empire*: 401.

96 'Bombay During the Plague, 1897–98: Extracts from the Letters of Hesther Mary Dowson', MSS Eur B. 385, OIOC, BL.

97 Ibid.: 9.

98 *Bombay Gazette*, 9 October 1896.

99 *Bombay Gazette*, 30 October 1896; *ToI*, 30 October 1896.

100 *Indian Textile Journal*, 1892 and 1893; *Annual Report of Bombay Millowners' Association*, 1892.

101 For detailed accounts of this riot, see S. Krishnaswamy, 'A Riot in Bombay, August 11, 1893: A Study in Hindu–Muslim Relations in Western India During the Late Nineteenth Century', unpublished Ph.D. dissertation, University of Chicago, 1966; S.B. Upadhyay, 'Chapter 4', in *Existence, Identity and Mobilization: The Cotton Mill-workers of Bombay 1890–1919*, New Delhi: Manohar Publishers, 2004: 111–45.

102 Couchman, 'Chapter 1', *Account of Plague Administration*, Part I: 13.

103 Report from Brigade-Surgeon-Lieutenant-Colonel T.S. Weir, Executive Health Officer, *Report on the Outbreak of Bubonic Plague in Bombay, 1896–9*, IOR V/27/856/7-10, 1897, p. 75, OIOC, BL.

104 Municipal Commissioner's Report, ibid.: 6–7.

105 Ibid.

[106] Ibid.

[107] Couchman, 'Chapter 1', *Account of Plague Administration*, Part I: 9–10.

[108] For an exhaustive and compelling survey of the vicissitudes of untouchable municipal labour in late nineteenth-century Bombay, see Jim Masselos, 'Jobs and Jobbery: The Sweeper in Bombay under the Raj', *Indian Economic and Social History Review*, 19 (2), 1982: 101–39.

[109] Couchman, 'Chapter 1', *Account of Plague Administration*, Part I: 13.

[110] Ibid.

[111] Ibid.: 12.

[112] Ibid.:13.

[113] *Report on the Outbreak of Bubonic Plague in Bombay (1897)*: 9.

[114] *ToI*, 2 April 1897.

[115] *ToI*, 7 April 1897.

[116] Ibid.

[117] *ToI*, 8 April 1897.

[118] Ibid.

[119] *ToI*, 7 and 8 April 1897.

[120] *ToI*, 12 March 1898.

[121] *TOI*, 11 March 1898.

[122] Patell, 'The Plague in Bombay'.

[123] As Ravi Ahuja has pointed out, in nineteenth and twentieth-century European writings, and specifically in administrative discourse, the organic metaphor of the 'artery' that kept the body-politic circulating was frequently deployed to describe the main channels of transport and communication: 'such organicist conceptualizations of social phenomena have the effect of legitimating contradictory social phenomena by naturalizing them'. See Ravi Ahuja, *Pathways of Empire: Circulation, 'Public Works' and Social Space in Colonial Orissa, c. 1780–1914*, Hyderabad: Orient Blackswan, 2009. On the other hand, using precisely this term with all the baggage it connotes, I believe, might indicate more sharply the kinds of tensions and political investments that were at stake in situations like the plague crisis.

[124] S.M. Edwardes, *The Rise of Bombay: A Retrospect*, Bombay: Times of India Press, 1902: 330.

[125] For more detailed examinations of this, see Prashant Kidambi, 'Contestation and Conflict: Workers' Resistance and the "Labour Problem" in the Bombay Cotton Mills, *c*. 1898–1919', in Marcel van der Linden and Prabhu P. Mohapatra (eds), *Labour Matters: Towards Global Histories (Essays in Honour of Sabyasachi Bhattacharya)*, New Delhi: Tulika Books, 2009; Aditya Sarkar, 'Regulated Labour, Unruly Workers: The Making of Industrial Relations in Late Nineteenth-Century Bombay', unpublished Ph.D. dissertation, School of Oriental and African Studies, London, 2010.

[126] *Provincial Report on the Working of the Indian Factories Act in the Bombay Presidency for the Year 1897.*

[127] No. 2161, R.H. Vincent to Private Secretary to Governor, GoB, Judicial Department, No. 669, 10 March 1898, MSA.

[128] *ToI*, 8 March 1898. There may be an interesting clue to the rhetorical strategies of resistance against plague regulations in a petition proposed by Morarjee Nensy, one of the speakers at the *mahajan* meeting, which concluded with the words: 'and if Government, notwithstanding their representations in the matter, were to enact the law, all that they could say was that the Sirkar was the "master" of the situation'. Some of the members objected to the phrasing of the statement, on the grounds that it amounted to a capitulation. Nensy explained that 'the words did not bear the meaning contemplated by some of the speakers'. He was right; the phrasing of the petition is subtle, and a latent threat is conveyed by the deployment of the word "master" (and the quotation marks that encase it) – far from a recognition of mastery, the words

seem to be aimed at compelling the 'Sirkar' to acknowledge its responsibility for the present situation, and therefore of its possible repercussions.

129 *ToI*, 11 March 1898.

130 Ibid.

131 *ToI*, 24 March 1898.

132 *ToI*, 11 March 1898.

133 No. 2634/ 6 R, from R.H. Vincent, IOR/L/P&J/3/959, OIOC, BL.

134 Ibid.

135 *ToI*, 12 March 1898.

136 Ibid.

137 Ibid.

138 Ibid.

139 Ibid.

140 Ibid.

141 Ibid.

142 *ToI*, 14 March 1898.

143 Ibid.

144 Ibid.

145 *ToI*, 12 March 1898.

146 *ToI*, 14 March 1898.

147 *ToI*, 15 March 1898.

148 Ibid.

149 Ibid.

150 *ToI*, 16 March 1898.

151 Catanach, '"Who Are Your Leaders?"': 217.

152 MSS Eur. B. 385, p. 33, OIOC, BL.

153 Ibid.

154 Catanach, '"Who Are Your Leaders?"': 218.

155 Ibid.

156 Chandavarkar, *History, Culture and the Indian City*: 52.

157 See Kidambi, *The Making of an Indian Metropolis*, chapters 1, 2 and *passim*.

158 Ibid.

159 *Provincial Report on the Working of the Indian Factories Act in the Bombay Presidency for the Year 1897*.

Rotting Hides and Runaway Labour

Labour Control and Workers' Resistance in the Indian Leather Industry, *c.* 1860–1960

Shahana Bhattacharya

The production of hides, skins and 'semi-finished' leather in India grew exponentially in the second half of the nineteenth century, responding to the demand in the international market. This growth was achieved by intensification and concentration of work processes, which involved the flaying of carcasses of cattle, sheep and goats, and processing them up to different levels – curing with salt, or unhairing, defleshing and tanning them, to enable transportation. These work processes linked to the production of raw hides and semi-tanned leather were based almost entirely on the labour of 'untouchable' caste groups that were traditionally marked by the stigma of working with carcasses and animal skin. The present essay explores how labour was mobilized, deployed and controlled in this industry to ensure the performance of defiling and hazardous foundational work for leather production at disparate sites where the commodities were produced and processed. The essay also examines the ways in which those who were drawn as workers into the production processes – in rural areas to flay and cure hides, or in the emergent tannery clusters in urban areas – negotiated these forms of control through individual strategies and collective struggles, ranging from evasion and flight to organized resistance.

Three broad themes run through the essay. First, each of the episodes discussed here revolves around struggles on *rights* waged by different sets of workers: from rights over 'raw materials' to rights over their own bodies and movement. These struggles were not linear and their objectives were sometimes opposed to each other, even when the nature of the struggles bore striking resemblance to each other. Second, the essay focuses on how labour control and resistance were crucially mediated by legal and extra-legal regulation. The episodes discussed pertain to the regulation of labour by a redefinition of custom, and a moulding of work patterns and production practices, aimed at securing and 'fixing' labour in different ways. The third running theme is the emergence of various meanings of 'stigmatized labour' and the meanings of the struggles of those engaged in it. What were the particularities of stigma, what was its source and how did it get deployed on the shop-floors of modern tanneries – and in the context of a production chain tied intimately to the international market? In what ways did stigma and labour frame the ways in which workers organized themselves? How did workers drawn into the leather tanning industry negotiate these, and how did these mediate their politics? Divided into six sections, the essay draws upon different historical instances and episodes from various sites and nodes in the production process, to explore these closely intertwined issues.

The Leather Export Boom and the Campaign against Cattle Poisoning

The period between the 1860s and 1880s saw a dramatic escalation in the demand for Indian hides and skins in the international market, and a concomitant growth in their export (see Figure 1, p. 82). The timing of this growth overlapped almost exactly with a period of significant escalation in the number and frequency of allegations of 'cattle poisoning', made by 'dominant caste' cattle owners and by concerned colonial officials across different parts of India. The main targets of these allegations were members of 'outcaste' groups who traditionally flayed and skinned cattle carcasses.[1] The complaints were more insistent and strident in some regions, and somewhat less in others, but they became a source of widespread anxiety that attained the proportions of a 'moral panic' across large areas in northern India. The first section of this essay explores the tensions, ambiguities and contestations that informed this peculiar conjunctural coincidence – of the expansion of hide exports and the growth in allegations of cattle poisoning – and the consequences that spun out of it.

This was a moment that belonged to the early stages of an overall reorganization of the production of Indian hides and skins, as these came to be closely connected to international demand under the colonial economy (see Table 1, p. 83). Further important conditions for this transformation included the growth of domestic military demand entailing import substitution of saddles, harnesses, boots, some machinery parts, etc.; and the availability, in substantial numbers and concentrations, of 'suitable' labour[2] – namely, workers who were willing and able to do the hard and essential work of processing traditionally stigmatized substances like hides and skins before they putrefied.

While there was a prior history of commercialization of hides and skins in India, the order and nature of the demand that emerged during the middle to late nineteenth century, and the political economy within which it was now sought to be met, were new. Both hides (skins of cattle) and skins (of goat and sheep) contributed to the expansion of the export trade (see Figure 1 and Table 1, pp. 82–83), but hides were more significant in terms of value and demand. The demand for goatskins was met directly by the slaughter of greater numbers of goats, largely for food,[3] but the widespread caste-based and ritual taboos against beef consumption and cow-slaughter across India meant that, despite the much higher profitability of *halali* hides (hides from slaughtered cattle), the majority of hides produced for export in India were acquired from cows that had died naturally – 'natural deads' or *murdari*. Thus, the late nineteenth-century reorganization of production of hides for export centred on the collection of cattle carcasses and removal of their hides by rural flayers and workers. However, even as Indian hides and skins got commoditized along new lines, the taboos surrounding cow-hides remained firmly in place. The degree of ritual pollution associated with touching and working with cow-hides was considerable. Procurement of cow-hides was thus a charged issue, in the context of both their immense profitability and the intense stigma associated with them.[4]

It was against the backdrop of a social and economic growth in the demand for and export of hides and skins from India, in the late nineteenth century, that an acute and widespread panic over cattle poisoning gripped cattle owners and colonial state officials alike. They feared that cattle mortality was to a large extent due to cattle poisoning, aimed at recovering increasingly valuable hides. While concerns about cattle poisoning had emerged in earlier decades and continued later, the somewhat obsessive and paranoid quality of these anxieties, and their repercussions and implications, need to be located firmly in the temporal context of the late 1860s to early 1880s.

Cases of cattle poisoning had been increasingly reported from the late 1840s onwards.[5] The report of the Indian Cattle Plague Commission stated that cattle poisoning had occurred in Sholapur in 1846, in Saran district in Bihar in 1851, and Pubna and Jessore in Bengal in 1852–53.[6] There was also a history of executive action against cattle poisoning, especially in the North Western Provinces (NWP), which pre-dated the 1860s. In the 1850s the Magistrate of Azamgarh, George Campbell, claimed to have discovered a 'surprisingly extensive system of cattle poisoning' for the 'sake of their trade in hides'. He believed that there was a clear economic motivation in the crime, stemming from the growing profitability of the trade in hides. Campbell also 'discovered' what he termed as a 'system of cattle poisoning', based on arsenic as the main poisoning agent. He highlighted the close connection between the trade in raw hides and in arsenic,[7] and indicated that the network which had been set up to ensure a steady supply of hides to shippers and exporters at ports was the main factor behind cattle poisoning in the NWP.[8] Campbell proceeded to actively and zealously arrest, prosecute and convict several of those associated with this network, believing that they were guilty of cattle poisoning.[9] Prosecution and conviction were based largely on 'confessions' made in police custody by those arrested, and little actual evidence of involvement in the act.[10]

The 'vast conspiracy' laid bare by Campbell in the 1850s did not, however, lead to the kind of moral panic and executive action that the same issue stirred up a decade or so later, across the hide-supplying regions of India. This difference, to reiterate a point stated earlier, may be attributed in large part to the increased demand for Indian hides and skins, and the concomitant growth in exports from India from the 1860s to 1880s (see Figure 1 and Table 1, pp. 82–83). Dead cattle were now a source of much greater profit.

The panic about 'cattle poisoning' across provinces in northern, western and central India was apparently widespread amongst officials, and led to distinct forms of executive and legislative action to curb it. The anxiety appears to have been most consuming in the NWP, a region which supplied a large number of hides to the international market during this period and where the reported rate of cattle mortality was very high. Several district officials in the province acted on police reports of cattle poisoning by promptly prosecuting the village Chamars, the foremost among them being the Magistrate of Gorakhpur, R.D. Spedding. The most important difference between Campbell's campaign against cattle poisoning in 1855 and that undertaken by Spedding in the 1870s was the scale and number of allegations of cattle poisoning raised against local Chamars, and the subsequent attacks, large-scale arrests and prosecution based entirely on the unproven suspicion that they had poisoned cattle. Following in Campbell's footsteps, albeit two decades later, Spedding claimed to have comprehensively uncovered the close links between cattle poisoning by arsenic and the networks of sourcing hides for the burgeoning hide trade. He held that arsenic acquired from Calcutta by big hide merchants was transported through intermediaries to hide merchants in towns like Dinapore or Patna. It was then distributed to the rural districts through networks involving Iraki Muslim hide dealers and their agents, as well as Chamars from Bengal and local village Chamars, he claimed. In return, hides were collected from them. The network involving Chamars like Boolakee, Toofanee and Lekha, who distributed arsenic to the local village Chamar flayers, became the most consistent target of Spedding's campaign against cattle poisoning.[11]

The fact that possession of arsenic by these and other Chamars, and by Muslim traders involved in the hide trade, could be entirely legitimate was not factored in by Spedding and other officials. By the 1860s, arsenic was being routinely distributed by hide dealers and traders to village Chamars and others involved in the flaying and preliminary processing of hides of animals, including of those that had died of natural causes.[12] This was to ensure that the hides and skins flayed by them, and collected by dealers and merchants for the booming market, did not putrefy in the hot weather during the long journey to Calcutta by boat and train, and thence by ship to destinations like London, Hamburg and other importing ports. Treating flayed skins and hides with arsenic had been found to be the cheapest and speediest way to preserve them. Crucially, it enabled the physical mobilization of hides for export. Yet, even as the procurement network for hides spread to the interiors of northern India, when the hides became profitable possession of arsenic by Chamars in the NWP became the basis of establishing their 'guilt' under the charge of cattle poisoning. Spedding and other officials like Lumsden and Robinson[13] carried out aggressive arrests of Chamars based merely on their being in possession of arsenic or the 'confessions' of others – largely also Chamars – similarly arrested.[14] All those arrested were prosecuted under different sections of the Cattle Poisoning law, and subjected to punishment ranging from 'stripes' to rigorous imprisonment of between six months to ten years.

The most important difference between the earlier official efforts to curb cattle poisoning and that undertaken by Spedding and others in the 1870s was the scale of prosecutions against Chamars. Campbell, in 1855, had been able to rely on 'Mahomedan law'[15] to take action against the Chamar flayers he prosecuted. Recognizing his efforts, the government had passed a law, Act IV of 1856, which declared the crime of cattle poisoning an offence cognizable by the police, and laid down provisions for fines and punishment. Once an offence was declared 'cognizable', a magistrate could act upon it without a court order. However, not much is known about the implementation of this law.[16] In 1873, responding to an apparent epidemic of charges of cattle poisoning, it was deemed necessary to temporarily make this offence 'cognizable', enabling Spedding to carry out his campaign of arresting those he suspected were involved in cattle poisoning[17] and to claim that he had suppressed the offence 'completely within a few months'. Mounting executive pressure amidst widespread fears of cattle poisoning, especially in the NWP, contributed to cattle poisoning once again being declared a cognizable offence by Act XI of 1874. Incorporated as Section 429 of the Penal Code, the law also declared that '[m]ischief by killing or maiming cattle, etc. of any value or any animal of the value of fifty rupees or above' was an offence punishable with imprisonment for a term extendable to five years or fine or both.[18] It was further 'compoundable by the owner of the cattle or animal with the permission of the court'.

Significantly, even though all those involved in the hide trade came under suspicion for cattle poisoning, it was primarily the Chamar flayers, hide traders and contractors who were prosecuted and convicted. Very few of the wealthier and more powerful Iraki Muslim hide dealers were arrested or prosecuted during the campaign against cattle poisoning in the 1870s, even when they were viewed as criminals by colonial officials like Spedding and Lumsden, and their crime of 'instigating' cattle poisoning considered heinous. Moreover, on the rare occasions when they were arrested for possession of arsenic, they were not subjected to the routine treatment meted out to Chamars: namely, capture and torture leading to 'confession' of guilt. Finally, even when identical evidence was available against Chamars like Toofanee or Boolakee on the one hand, and Iraki traders on the other, the latter were not convicted. Colonial officials were aware of the Iraki traders' role in disseminating arsenic, but regarded them as 'parties at the headquarters of the hide trade in Patna and Dinapore' who could not be implicated or arrested. Their status, connections and class distinguished them from the Chamar dealers, and enabled them to circumvent conviction by accessing competent legal help. In a case that Spedding zealously prosecuted in 1873–74 against Chamars and Iraki Muslim hide traders of Bahorwa, Azamgarh, the latter appealed against their conviction in the High Court. Lumsden, the officiating Magistrate, acknowledged that the evidence against them was 'entirely circumstantial, but circumstantial evidence of a very strong and convincing description', and yet the fact that they were 'very wealthy men' and had 'retained an English Barrister to prosecute the appeal'[19] meant that they were able to extricate themselves from penalties. The Chamar flayers could not afford such costly legal defence, and their poverty and lack of access to legal assistance were factors that signified their guilt for colonial magistrates like Spedding. Spedding held that since the convicted Chamars did not appeal against their punishment, this was 'good proof that they admit the justice of their punishments'.[20]

The impact and implementation of the law has to be understood in the context of the widespread and deeprooted popular prejudice across the country against Chamars and other untouchable caste groups, involved in flaying cattle carcasses to remove hides, as 'cattle poisoners'. The members of these social groups stood apart also because of their low social status and vulnerable economic condition in the villages, as well as their exclusive association with the stigmatized work of flaying hides. The law against cattle poisoning, implemented within this matrix, thus rendered large sections of village Chamars considerably more vulnerable and insecure than before. It also enabled the socially and economically dominant sections to retain a degree of control over these 'outcaste' flaying groups and the essential labour they provided – labour that was foundational for both the hide trade and commodity chain in leather, and for the agrarian economy in general.

While the executive crackdown on 'the crime of cattle poisoning' and on rural hide flayers was abetted by the law making cattle poisoning a cognizable offence, it fundamentally contradicted the interests of the expanding trade in hides in Bengal during the period between the 1860s and 1880s. This contradiction got sharpened when some colonial officials began to clamour for another law to legally restrict the possession of arsenic, in view of what they saw as rampant growth of cattle poisoning for hides. In the late 1870s, a proposed all-India law to this effect was debated and discussed at length amongst colonial state representatives of both the Government of India and provincial governments, and a resolution was passed in 1881.[21] During the same period, substantial amounts of arsenic were being officially imported and distributed in Bengal and the NWP, and the procurement network for arsenic was becoming stronger and better knit as the profits from the hide trade soared.

The Bengal government was by this time unequivocally opposed to such a law. Recognizing the 'overlap' between circuits of hide procurement and cattle poisoning, the Secretary to the Government of Bengal observed in a letter to the Secretary to the Government of India:

> The difficulty in the way of restricting or licensing the trade in arsenic is that the people who use the poison for the purpose of destroying cattle belong to the same class and caste as those who require the poison for the legitimate purposes of their trade . . . there is no doubt that arsenic is one of the cheapest and most effective preservatives of leather and skins, any restrictions on its sale would certainly have the effect of materially raising its price and rendering

> it difficult for hide dealers and Chamars to obtain it for the purpose of curing the skins of large numbers of cattle that die of natural causes.

Sir Ashley Eden, Lieutenant Governor of Bengal, argued strongly against restrictions on carrying arsenic, citing the scale and profitability of the trade as important reasons.[22] The only way the trade could be actualized and the demand met, as these colonial officials recognized well, was if the flayers removed hides rapidly and they reached the shipping yard at Calcutta without rotting – a process dependent on the labour of Chamars collecting carcasses and applying arsenic to cure the hides.

The Bengal government was able to scuttle the proposed law restricting possession of arsenic, thereby safeguarding the interests of the big hide traders and the colonial state. And yet those who flayed and cured the hides of cattle remained under the radar of suspicion and could be arrested under the law against cattle poisoning, on the basis of little more than prejudice. Thus, while quashing the proposed law restricting arsenic possession, the Lieutenant Governor of Bengal was quick to advocate that

> something may be done to check the operations of professional cattle-poisoners by more effective police action, by the employment of approvers, and by the deputation of special detectives employed solely for some time in following the movements of the trade in arsenic, and tracing supplies from the centres of the trade, like Patna and Dinapore, to the more remote villages where they are used either legitimately by the village currier for the purposes of his trade or illegitimately for destroying cattle.[23]

While possession of arsenic remained, then, technically legal, it became a source of suspicion, and a justification for arrest, interrogation, torture, imprisonment and prosecution under the law, if the carriers were low-caste flayers who were subject to caste prejudices but who alone could remove and preserve cattle hides for the market. The needs of the market were met through a reification and reinforcement of social hierarchies, and the laws – one that was passed and one that was not – contributed significantly to this process. The operation of the law and the practices of the executive sought to ensure that, even as these groups were accessed as a necessary and exclusive reservoir of labour that made the sourcing of hides possible, they remained insecure and vulnerable, and thus more easily brought under the control of the dominant-caste cattle owners and the state. Hence, while market interests were secured by *not passing* a law banning the sale of arsenic, the second object of securing labour – labour that could be easily controlled and could speedily do the stigmatized work of skinning carcasses and processing hides to ensure that they reached the market – was in turn ensured by *passing* the law against cattle poisoning.

The moral panic over cattle poisoning in the 1860s to 1880s subsided after a while. However, sporadic incidents and allegations of cattle poisoning continued to crop up throughout the period under study. The afterlife of the moral panic extended, at least in a legal sense, to the retention of Section 429 in the Penal Code, and the reincarnation of cattle poisoning in the Poisons Acts of 1904 and 1919.

Contested Rights to Cattle Carcasses

The primary reason for members of 'outcaste' groups involved in flaying becoming 'natural' suspects blamed for cattle poisoning across very distinct regions in India was the widespread and deep ambiguity that surrounded the question of control over cattle carcasses. Once cattle died, 'outcaste' skinners and flayers began to exercise certain customary rights over the carcasses. The developments of the late nineteenth century, the high demand for hides under colonial rule, threw the traditional flayers sharply and directly into conflict with the cattle-owning peasantry. To state an obvious point, cattle owners were also often land owners who belonged to powerful upper or 'dominant' castes, while the flayers, belonging universally to the lowest untouchable castes, were also amongst the poorest agricultural labourers. These structural antagonisms underlay and formed a crucial dimension of the contestation over cattle carcasses, hides and skins, and centrally mediated its outcome.

The traditional systems under which 'outcaste' flayers held customary rights over hides and skins varied across regions and castes. Despite variations in the degree of rights that 'outcaste' skinners and flayers exercised over these materials (ranging from outright ownership to partial control), in all 'traditional' practices, the death of cattle transferred a substantial share of rights of access to and utilization of animal carcasses – meat, hides, horns, etc. – to the workers who laboured to skin them.[24]

Usage rights of 'outcaste' flayers over hides were limited in some places to a few families from among the total population of these castes in the village who customarily performed the labour and were entitled to varying parts of its output. In other areas, these rights were partially dispersed across a larger segment of the village population of these groups. In most regions, after providing the cattle owners or dominant sections of the village community with leather agricultural goods, the flayers could keep a part of the hide for their own 'use' or for sale to makers of leather goods.

Another significant point to be noted is that the work of flaying and skinning, dependent as it was on the occasional death of cattle, was not traditionally the main occupation of any individual member of these castes (Mahars, Dhers, Chamars, or Jatavs, Chakkiliyans, Paraiyans, etc.), but was one of the many labour services they performed for the dominant land and cattle owners.[25] To reiterate, then, when the late nineteenth-century boom in exports occurred, most hide flayers and carcass skinners, whose labour became strategic, were agricultural labourers and farm servants tied in bonds of social and economic subordination and dependence to land and cattle owners.

An inbuilt uncertainty over the degree and extent of cattle owners' control over cattle carcasses and hides connected customary practices across regions. While there were clear rules about the ownership of live cattle, once cows and buffaloes died, the common practice was to cede control over them to the skinners. In most places they would remove the carcasses to designated spots, flay them to remove the hides and eat the meat, which was abhorred by the higher castes. The most important reason for the transfer of control over the dead bodies of animals was the high degree of 'pollution' and strong stigma attached to these – as to corpses, death and dead materials in general. The stigma also extended to all those who touched the hides, skins and leather, and made them singularly untouchable. This, combined with the comparatively limited commoditization of these materials prior to their linkage to the colonial economy, meant that these were, to an extent, traditionally regarded as 'wastes'. In the prior context, therefore, compared to the extent to which contestations over hides occurred in the late nineteenth century, actual ownership of carcasses or hides was not particularly asserted on a regular basis by cattle owners in many regions. Nor were the 'rights' of flayers and skinners over cattle hides clearly demarcated or debated in entirety in the early nineteenth century. The control of the 'outcaste' carcass skinners or traditional 'primary producers' of raw hides over these materials stemmed from their exclusive ability to remove them from the carcasses, and physically 'free' and mobilize them for use and exchange.

The main consequence of the expansion of hide and skin exports in the late nineteenth century was that it converted materials hitherto largely considered 'wastes' into sources of profit. Skinners and flayers thus potentially stood to gain considerably from the death of every cow because of the control they exercised over carcasses and hides by 'prescriptive right'.[26] Returning to the point made at the beginning of the section, it was this factor that crucially underlay the widespread panic and suspicion that cattle mortality was due to poisoning by flayers and skinners, and the latter's arrest and prosecution on a heightened scale in the 1870s and 1880s. As hides became profitable, cattle owners began, in some regions particularly, to clearly assert their ownership rights over the carcasses of their cattle and their hides. This became more common by the 1880s and 1890s, with instances of 'zamindars' in north India demanding cash payment from village flayers for cattle hides, and of Chamars buying hides and skins from them.[27]

However, throughout this period, even as hides became increasingly valuable, contractualization of hide collection did not become the norm across India. The notion that flayers had customary rights over hides persisted and was widely prevalent in official and non-official circles across the largest hide-exporting regions of India for several decades after the 1870s. The issue certainly became a fraught and contentious one, and the subject of everyday negotiations and contestations between cattle owners and flayers over carcasses in distant interior villages and well-connected towns across large parts of India. This was because these groups, even otherwise arrayed in antagonistic hierarchical power relations of caste and class, were now thrown into a potentially constant state of confrontation over access to and control of a 'resource'. The settlement of these conflicts over carcasses and hides depended on a wide variety of local factors, and micro-level political and social dynamics and power balances, as much as on shifts in legal rights and property regimes. This was especially true of most parts of northern India, where the rights of cattle owners over cattle carcasses were not very clearly settled by law.

While cattle owners were able to assert their ownership rights in a few areas, in others the village Chamars were able to contest these efforts through direct confrontation and occasionally in court. A closer look at one such case may indicate how the notion of customary rights of Chamars over carcasses was widely shared and persistent, not just in rural society but also within the judiciary and the state. The case in question, listed as *Manser Chamar and others vs. Gajai Singh*,[28] was adjudicated in the Allahabad High court in 1917. Gajai Singh was 'one of the proprietors of two villages', a powerful land and cattle owner, and Manser and the other defendants were Chamars who lived in one of these villages. An epidemic among the cattle in that village had resulted in the death of sixteen heads of cattle belonging to Gajai Singh. He then offered the Chamars the hides of these animals on a charge of five rupees each. They accepted the offer and removed the hides of the carcasses, but later refused to fulfil their contract of payment. The Small Causes Court, approached by Gajai Singh, ordered that the Chamars pay Gajai Singh some part of what he claimed they owed him. The Chamars then took the case to the High Court where they refuted the existence of any contract with the landlord. They also pleaded that:

> according to village custom, they, as resident Chamars had a right to flay any animal dying a natural death within the boundaries of the village and to remove the hides for their own benefit. The services which they render in return for this privilege they suggest to be (1) the disposal of the carcass of the animal and (2) certain customary services rendered by them [during] weddings and on similar occasions.[29]

Judge Piggott comprehensively overturned the order of the Small Causes Court and ordered a retrial. He recorded that the 'statement of the [Chamar] defendants' regarding this custom (the local custom of disposal of carcasses of cattle) was 'not . . . at all an extraordinary or unusual one'.[30] He also ordered that specific details of the terms of the contract be inquired into, and in case the contract was not found to have been a definite one or if its terms were not clear, he asked the court that would be re-trying the matter to 'consider . . . whether apart from proof of contract the defendants are under any liability to account to the plaintiff [the landlord] for the market price of the hides of any cattle belonging to him which they may have removed'. The judge further instructed the lower court to

> distinctly bear in mind that the question for consideration is not merely

> the benefit which a Chamar may obtain by disposing of the hide, but the remuneration which he would be entitled to charge for disposing of the carcass and for his labour in flaying it. There can be no doubt that the disposal of the carcasses of the animals which had died a natural death is a service to the village community as a whole, and that it is frequently rendered by custom by resident Chamars in return for the right of flaying the carcass and appropriating the hide.[31]

A curious intermingling of frameworks characterizes this judgment. The judge in effect argued that the customary/traditional 'rights' of the Chamars over hides should be maintained, and then, he justified these 'rights' and 'dues' in 'modern' terms by adding up the economic 'worth' of their labour. The labour of flaying carcasses as well as the service to the community at large (by disposing of carcasses of dead animals) were believed to have counterbalanced, substantially, the 'profit' they might have gained out of the hides. The judge thus argued that these should be kept in mind while calculating how much the plaintiff Gajai Singh, the dominant-caste cattle owner, was owed by the Chamar flayers in this case.

The long life and career of these notions of customary rights of Chamars over hides in the NWP are evident from the fact that they were still valid and deeply influential even over six decades after Judge Piggott ruled in Manser Chamar's case. The petition filed by Mohd. Yunus of Meerut in the Supreme Court in 1981 and the appeal made by *Hiralal and Others* of Kanpur district, also adjudicated by the Supreme Court in the same year, were both cases where the petitioners contested the local government's policy of handing over monopoly rights to collect hides to contractors who were 'outsiders'. In both instances the petitioners argued that they were Chamars with customary rights over these materials in their regions, and asked for 'restoration' of their 'age-old' rights to carry on their trade and business in skinning dead animals, and in the hides, bones and horns of dead animals.[32]

Three features stand out starkly in this history of contestation over carcasses and customary rights. The first is the fact that there was, almost invariably, contestation over these materials because the ambiguities surrounding access, utilization and even ownership of carcasses and hides were never completely resolved. Second, as the production of hides and skins got rapidly reorganized in the wake of its linkage to international exports and modern economic structures, the contractual and customary systems of rights over these materials came to coexist and closely intertwine with each other. Thus, by the early twentieth century, in some areas hide collection was contractualized, while in other areas it remained customary in form and content. Third, the 'outcaste' groups who were traditional flayers were rarely altogether denied these rights, and ousted from their association with carcasses and hides. Their rights over carcasses persisted long after colonial rule ended and long after other customary rights were erased. It was only where the political mobilization of this underclass took a different turn, as in the instance discussed later in this essay, when flayers consciously rejected their customary rights as Dalits, that this persistent association was broken.

The trajectory and history of contestation over these customary rights took a somewhat different turn in Bombay, where the colonial state was able to more effectively intervene and regulate the customary rights of 'outcaste' Mahar flayers over cattle hides and carcasses by passing a new law, popularly known as the Watan Act of 1874. It also legally established bourgeois property rights over carcasses and hides in favour of owners of live cattle, and took away from the untouchable caste flayers and tanners the control they exercised. Mahars, who had to do the work of disposing of carcasses of cattle, removing hide, etc., in Bombay villages were appointed as hereditary village servants called '*watandars*'.[33] The Mahar *watan* entitled Mahars, in most instances, to land assessed at a lower rate of revenue and a 'share' of the produce – '*baluta*' – from peasant households, in return for performing caste-based labour services (*maharki*).[34] These services included agricultural labour, acting as watchmen and messengers, and skinning carcasses of dead cattle, among others.

There was stigma attached to the Mahar *watan*, which came from the 'habituated forms of servility'[35] associated with the exercise of these rights. The '*hakk*' or right of Mahars extended normally to a range of 'defiled' things – the *baluta* commonly meant leftovers of food[36] which they customarily had to beg for, as well as defiled substances like carcasses of cattle that had died in the village. The Mahar *watan* thus had a dual characteristic: it was a sign of status and was attached to administrative responsibilities, including the ceremonial honours of being one of the '*bara balutedar*';[37] at the same time, 'it was a form of property that obligated the Mahars to labour in ways that reproduced the very conditions of defilement and degradation that identified them as Mahar'.[38]

The *watandar* Mahar's 'rights' over hides were quite specifically laid down from at least the eighteenth century, prior to colonial rule. The Mahar could take the hides of all disposed cattle except those of plough-bullocks, which they handed over to the former owner of the cattle.[39] While the *ownership* of hides was frequently a source of friction between peasants, cattle owners and Mahars in the eighteenth century as well, the exact nature of these 'traditional' or 'customary' rights in practice was established through negotiation based on local power equations between the Kunbis (peasant caste, land and cattle-owning), Mahars and Mangs.[40] The state was occasionally an arbiter in these confrontations.[41]

Both the Peshwa state and the Bombay Sadr Diwani Adalat that came to be established in the initial period of colonial rule, in 1818, ruled mainly in favour of 'usage of the country' or 'customary practice' in almost all instances of disputes between peasants (largely of the Kunbi caste) and Mahars over the latter's customary services and rights. While other rights of the Mahars were disputed, there seemed to be a widely shared agreement in the practice of the state as well as in the customary claims settlement structures between peasants and Mahars, up till at least the mid-nineteenth century, which was that the 'right' over hides and skins in villages belonged by and large to the Mahars, i.e. the workers who flayed them. In the case of Bombay and other parts of western India, therefore, Mahar workers who skinned carcasses substantially controlled the raw materials for the production of leather.[42]

In Bombay, as elsewhere, the field of contestation over customary rights shifted by the 1860s and 1870s, shaped not just by the linkage of Indian hides with the international market, but also by the increasing adjudication of these rights by a codified law based on the notion of private property. Any lurking ambiguity in the control of cattle owners over carcasses was removed, and the right to cattle carcasses was definitively bestowed upon and confirmed with the cattle owner by colonial law. As a corollary, Mahar workers who flayed the carcasses to remove hides were sought to be dispossessed of their access to and control over these. This was achieved by means of court judgments such as the one passed by the Bombay High Court in 1870, which clearly stated that:

> it has been repeatedly decided in this court, in suits for proceeds of the carcasses of dead cattle between the Mahars and the ryot owners of the cattle, that the person who owned the cattle while alive also has a right to the property in the dead carcasses of such cattle, and may dispose of it to anybody he pleases.[43]

The High Court thus also indicated that similar decisions had been taken previously. Apart from case law, the new property regime that mediated the rights of Mahars to hides was also established through the passing of a new law – the Bombay Act III, or the Bombay Hereditary Offices Act (popularly called the Watan Act) – that was passed, like the amended law on Cattle Poisoning, in 1874. The official reason for passing this Act was to bring the tax-free lands (*inams*) given to *watandars* as part of their perquisites within a general regime of property relations.[44] The Act of 1874 ensured that certain customary rights and duties, and certain hereditary offices, were retained – after they were duly codified, quantified and regulated.

In this process of 'regulating' custom, significant changes were brought into force. Through its crucial Section 18, the Watan Act enhanced the role of dominant peasants in determining disputes over the rights and duties of Mahars.[45] Both Sections 18 and 64 of the Act gave the District Collector powers to register and record *watandars*, and thereby legitimize or de-legitimize their claims. Sections like 64(d), which gave the Collector the power to attach *watans* in case of 'misconduct',[46] pertained particularly to Mahars and were introduced later as a punitive measure, targeting specifically the crime of cattle poisoning which the Mahars were increasingly being accused of. While the Act had a wider ambit, the urgent need to deal with charges of cattle poisoning, and the decision to regulate the relationship between the cattle owners and the actual producers of hides and skins who alone could handle the material, was thus fairly central to the shaping of the Watan Act as far as the 'lower' *watans* were concerned.[47]

The Bombay government stated this in so many words. Responding, in 1881, to an overall enquiry into the effectiveness of the law to curb cattle poisoning (discussed earlier), its representative stated that Bombay had found the law to be effective and, in addition, that they had found it 'useful' to 'suspend the right of the village Mahars to the skins of dead cattle when the deaths of animals in any locality have been so numerous or so suspicious as to suggest the idea of foul play'.[48]

By resorting to the Act, peasants in several villages were able to get the Collectors to attach Mahars' *watans* and to diminish their claims by means of allegations of cattle poisoning, even without any proof. While the district authorities in the NWP, Bengal and elsewhere could (and did) take action against the Chamars who were involved in cattle poisoning by arresting and imprisoning them, in Bombay they had the means, through the Watan Act, to take away what the administrators had identified as the root of the persistent problem of cattle poisoning – namely, the untouchable flayers' access to and control over the newly precious cattle hides. The Bombay law thus effectively shifted the rights of utilization and control over cattle carcasses and hides to dominant-caste cattle owners. A cattle owner could now complain against a Mahar and accuse him of 'misconduct', and the Collector could withdraw the *watan* from him and transfer it to another Mahar, or any other available person or group willing to do this work.

The Mahars, more than other subordinate rural castes in western India, were also traditionally known for their combativeness, especially when they went around in large groups demanding *baluta*, asserting their claims collectively and issuing threats to peasants who refused to give them their 'share'[49] for services performed. Significantly, the threats supposedly issued by Mahars on such occasions often revolved around the death of the higher-caste peasants' cattle, and the so-called 'acts of misconduct' of which Mahars were accused – and for which, after the passing of the Watan Act, their *watans* were taken away – were also frequently allegations of their involvement in cattle poisoning.[50] Colonial officials shared the popular view of the Mahars' aggressiveness. In 1880, for instance, the Ahmednagar Collector, while applying the Watan Act in a similar case where peasants' cattle had died after Mahars had allegedly threatened they would, characterized the Mahars as lawless and was ready to seize their *watans* primarily because of their 'generally menacing attitude'.[51] As in other parts of the country, these allegations of cattle poisoning against the 'outcaste' Mahar flayers were often based on prejudice rather than evidence, but were frequently acted upon by state officials to dispossess them of their customary 'rights', including their control over carcasses and hides.

One of the reasons for peasants' dependence on 'outcaste' flayers across India was the urgent need to secure labour to skin the carcasses of dead cattle, and to extract and process hides rapidly before they could putrefy.[52] In this regard cattle owners in Bombay had an additional advantage due to the presence of the caste of Mangs, also considered untouchables and 'scavengers', who formed another group of village servants though not 'traditional' flayers. Mangs, as well as other, more docile Mahars, were deployed and used under the Act to supplant the assertive Mahar flayers. The law could be resorted to by cattle owners to ensure a more easily controlled, compliant labour force for skinning carcasses, and one that was grateful for the Kunbi patronage and grant of the *watan*. It enabled colonial administrators to legally dismiss the Mahars' claims and access to an economic resource. In practice, the temporary attachment of Mahar *watans* by district authorities frequently resulted in the Mahars permanently losing these. It also brought Mahars into direct contestation with Mangs when they sought restoration of their rights.[53]

Some of the Mahars resisted their removal, and, in the process, also made a bid for their rights in court against the Kunbis and Mangs. In some instances, the courts referred the disputes back to be tried under Section 18 of the Watan Act, to be settled by a 'panchayat' appointed by the Collector or *mamlatdar*. Yet, as in the case of Peth village in Satara district (1911),[54] where the case reached the High Court, the operation of the law could, more definitively and permanently than any other method, deprive the Mahars of their customary rights over carcasses and hides of cattle.

However, it is important to record that the implementation of the Act did not lead to complete disappearance of the Mahar *watan*, and that the Mahars were not wholly ousted from their 'customary rights' and the crucial labour services they performed for a long time after the passing of the Watan Act. The Act, while weakening the customary rights of the Mahars, had inbuilt clauses to ensure the retention of the Mahar *watan* as a form of free or subsidized labour that was important to the locally dominant and to the colonial economy. While Anupama Rao has made this point in her study,[55] I would like to add here that this was particularly true in the case of their strategic labour in skinning carcasses and removing hides. Alternative labouring groups who could do this work were not present everywhere in the region, and ensuring that Mahars were present to perform this labour of flaying and processing carcasses was thus absolutely crucial to prevent them from rotting. The Act sought to ensure that even in cases where *watans* were commuted and *watandars* had given up their 'privileges', the dominant groups in the village could continue to 'exact such service as may be customary from village servants whose *watans* were originally granted or are now held for the performance of such service, but who have been relieved by the Government of liability to perform such service to the State'.[56] This meant that as long as the rural power relations remained weighted against Mahars, and were socially and economically in favour of Kunbis, the state would not intervene if the Kunbis coerced the Mahars to perform customary labour services, including skinning of carcasses, even when the latter ceased to be *watandars* officially.

Formally, the Watan Act ensured that the Mahar *watan* continued long after other, 'higher' village services were commuted.[57] Unlike the higher *watans* where 'village servants' like priests or accountants could, after commutation of their *watan,* get control of the lands they previously held as *watans*, as it was not necessary for the state to resume the lands once the *watan* was commuted in the case of 'inferior village servants', *watan* lands 'given in remuneration for service rendered could be reassigned to other impoverished Mahars or to Mangs',[58] as the case might be. In a situation of land hunger or the absence of other resources of livelihood, this meant that many Mahars remained *watandars*, and, compelled by economic logic and by the inequities of law, they continued to perform customary, often stigmatized and degraded labour services, which also tied them down to their demeaning social status.

The only way in which the Mahars were eventually dissociated from this labour was when they were mobilized by the early Dalit movement led by Ambedkar and others, subsequently abandoning the labour services they performed as well as the *watan*, understanding it as property tied to labour servitude. The degraded and stigmatized labour they had to perform – by the dictates of custom and validated by law – came to be seen by this movement as a source and marker of their low social status. Foremost among such degraded 'traditional' tasks was the skinning of carcasses and removal of hides. Customary practices like collecting *baluta* were also seen as a sign of their inequality as villagers; as Ambedkar wrote, 'instead of treating the *baluta* as payment for services rendered . . . villagers consider it as alms giving and Mahars as beggars'.[59]

The mobilization of Dalits in western India, and the overthrow of *watans* and linked forms of customary labour, was a gradual process. Many Mahars also resisted the move to abolish the *watan*, as it was a sign and source of both 'prestige and of servitude'.[60] The movement for abolition of the *watan* system and abandonment of 'traditional' work that was a source of subordination grew in strength and support over time, gathering pace as those agitating for abolition of *watan* were able to expose its dual nature to a larger number of rural Mahars. The success of the campaign meant that Mahars voluntarily removed themselves from these occupations. The Mahar *watan* was finally abolished in 1959, as a result of these popular campaigns led by the early Dalit movement and with the passage of the Bombay Inferior Village Watan Abolition Act.

Even in western India, however, the work of flaying carcasses continued to be done by members of the lowest, untouchable castes. As many Mahars – the earliest group to be politically mobilized and at the helm of the Dalit movement in the region – abandoned this 'customary' labour because of its association with stigma and subordination, members of other pauperized low-caste groups, who did not share the tradition of Mahar combativeness or a history of rights over hides, came to be employed in the work of skinning carcasses in many areas of the state. The period of contestation by low-caste, untouchable hide flayers in this region for customary rights over cattle hides and carcasses appeared to have largely passed by the 1940s.

Unlike in western India, in other regions of the country, the Ambedkarite movement entailing abandonment of 'traditional' work such as skinning of carcasses did not take root to the same extent, even though there were a few localized, smaller-scale initiatives that sought to mobilize workers along these lines. The peculiar 'rights' over hides and cattle carcasses held by 'outcaste' groups across the country were removed only in those regions, and only at the historical moment when low-caste workers consciously abandoned this work and the 'rights' associated with it as the source of their subjugation and untouchability, in the process of their political self-organization as Dalits. In Bombay, this rejection occurred precisely in areas where earlier Mahar flayers had struggled to secure these rights as cattle owners sought to regulate their control over these profitable materials. The difference lay in the ways in which such 'rights' came to be perceived with the emergence of their own politics, based on an altered understanding of the meanings of labour.[61]

The curious fact remains that the efforts of dominant-caste cattle owners to establish control over cattle carcasses and hides with the help of the colonial state, and to oust low-caste flayers from access to these materials by erasing their customary rights, remained consistently incomplete, even as hides became profitable commodities. Perhaps the most important reason for this was linked to the specificities of the materials.[62] Even where the owners of cattle successfully established their own rights over the carcasses and the 'outcaste' flayers' customary rights were suppressed, workers belonging to the untouchable castes remained continuously, exclusively and universally linked to the work of skinning and flaying hides, i.e. the primary labour processes on which the production of leather was based. For dominant-caste owners of land and cattle, in a situation where even touching raw hides and skins was 'polluting', the need to retain control over these categories of 'outcaste' workers was a pressing one. They alone could give the owners access to the 'raw materials', touch and handle the untouchable hides and skins, and flay, process and mobilize them for export. The owners relied on modes of caste and class domination, as well as the active aid of the colonial state, to do so. The fact that there was a limited labour force which could be deployed for this work contributed to the intensity of the tensions inhering in the social relations of leather production. It created the possibility of labour resistance as much as it triggered intensified efforts towards labour control.

Modes of Protest and Strategies of Control in the Tanning 'Shops'

After the hides were flayed in the rural areas, they were conveyed by flayers, hide contractors or cattle owners to local hide markets, and thence through several rungs of markets and agents to tannery clusters where they were processed and tanned for domestic goods units or for export. This system of organization of production had become finetuned by the end of the nineteenth century as production expanded. Leather tanning clusters, often linked to ports, evolved as dense conglomerations of small, ramshackle units or 'shops' where workers laboured manually to cure and tan perishable hides and skins, to prepare them for the market. Madras province, with a network of several small tanning clusters, remained the most significant region for the production of tanned hides and skins for the international market in the nineteenth and early twentieth century. The small clusters in the province largely produced the famous Madras 'half-tans', lightly tanned leather, which was exported and re-tanned at the importing ports. The United Kingdom was the biggest destination for these 'half-tans'. A web of networks developed, bringing raw hides and skins and tanning bark into these clusters from across the country, and connecting the tannery clusters within the province – such as Ranipet, Pernambut, Ambur in North Arcot; Dindigul and Tiruchirapalli in the south, and Pallavaram in Chingleput adjoining Madras city. Similar networks emerged and connected the smaller tanning clusters in Bombay and Calcutta that emerged later. Kanpur was an early major tanning cluster but had been linked from its inception more to production for the military, and was somewhat distinctly structured and characterized by large-scale production units. When exports began from Kanpur, they passed through Calcutta and even Madras.

A few of the networks through which the commodities were transported from one leather cluster to the other, and then to the Madras port, also became the routes along which workers came into some of the clusters, sometimes from the same areas from where the commodities arrived – as in the case of Chamar workers from Bihar and Uttar Pradesh coming to the Tangra–Dhapa tannery cluster in Calcutta, or Tamil Paraiyan workers from Madras to the Bombay tannery cluster at Dharavi. In other areas, while the raw hides and skins were procured from across the country, workers were locally recruited from the same region and province, again almost exclusively agricultural labourers from the lowest castes. This was true of several tanning towns in Madras province and the Kanpur leather cluster, for instance.[63]

For the owners of the tanneries, recruiting 'suitable' labour and controlling workers once they arrived on the shopfloor, ensuring that they remained at work, became a somewhat desperate problem by the early twentieth century. This section discusses the issue of how owners of tanneries in the clusters sought to ensure that workers stayed to do the hard and brutal work of tanning, and how the workers responded to these efforts. The incident of an escape in 1918 by a group of workers from one tanning cluster to another provides a point of entry to understand some aspects of the regime of labour control, and the forms of labour mobility and resistance, in a modern tannery cluster.

The escape itself was not particularly dramatic. Rather spectacular, however, was the way in which the poorest, most dispossessed workers were able to simply give the slip to the tannery owners and stay out of reach despite the owners' efforts and a powerful colonial law working against them. A crucial condition for this ability consisted in that, by the early twentieth century, tanning and leather working clusters had emerged not just in Madras, but also in the neighbouring, contiguous princely states of Mysore and Hyderabad. These clusters were closely interlinked and these linkages formed a network along which the workers travelled – while running away from one cluster to another, or tramping across to look for work in different tanneries. Moreover, the First World War marked a turning point in the history of the Indian leather industry as the demand for leather reached a peak, far outstripping the supply of labour. It was at this time of chronic labour shortage that this episode of tannery workers' escape occurred.

In December 1917 and January 1918, fifteen workers from the tannery of K.H. Mahomed Yakoob and Sons in Pernambut, near Vellore in North Arcot, Madras province, escaped to Bangalore (administered area) and Nizamabad, the 'industrial town of that name in the Nizamabad district in the Hyderabad state', without paying back the money advances they had taken from the owner or fulfilling the contract they had 'signed'.[64] The terms of the contract show how the tannery owners had tried to secure themselves and 'fix' the workers, by giving money advances and deducting the sum from their wages. The contract stated:

> 1. That the employes [*sic*] have to work in the tannery of the co. since the date of agreement without going to any place.
> 2. That a sum of rupee one has to be deducted monthly from their pay in satisfaction of the advance paid to them.
> 3. That the employe has to work until the advance amount is fully repaid as aforesaid.
> 4. That the employe is liable for criminal prosecution under section 2 Act XIII of 1859, for breach of any of the aforesaid terms.[65]

Act XIII of 1859 was the Workmen's Breach of Contract Act which was widely used to secure labour, and to ensure that workers recruited by means of advances remained in place and that the objective of the advance was realized. The Act criminalized breach of contracts entered into by workers who took money advances from employers, owners of units, and were contracted to work in return, paying back the advance out of their wages. Its specific objective was to prevent workers from absconding with the money taken from owners. In the case of tannery workers, the money advance was in turn a strategic device to ensure the constant presence of 'outcaste' workers on the shopfloors, workers who could be deployed to perform the stigmatized and crucial labour of tanning hides and skins for exports.

There was an old tradition in Madras of using the Breach of Contract Act. In Chingleput district, for instance, an area that became the site of the tannery cluster of Pallavaram–Chromepet, the Act was commonly used in the late nineteenth and early twentieth centuries to ensure the immobility of Paraiyan agricultural labourers. These workers who were tied in different kinds of bonds of agrestic servitude sometimes ran away to seek work elsewhere – without returning their money advances. Some among them were caught, arrested and tried under the Act. Between 1884 and 1891, the number of persons brought to trial under this Act was 1,128.[66] Yet all official reports indicate that despite the efforts to 'secure' them, Paraiyan agricultural workers still found ways of escaping the exploitative bonds of caste and class servitude that tied them to dominant-caste *mirasidar* land holders.[67]

Once tannery clusters emerged in the province and came to employ workers drawn largely from local Paraiyan agricultural labourers, echoing a general practice in the surrounding regions, the Act was sought to be used by tannery owners to ensure that the workers remained in the tanneries. The Pernambut tannery from where the workers escaped in 1918 was one of the tanneries that was supplying War Office orders at the time. It was in dire need of workers and desperate to 'fix' them.

All the workers who ran away from this tannery were Paraiyans (see Table 2, p. 84). Several of their names incorporated place names – possibly their areas of origin or even places they had worked in – which indicated the circuits along which tannery workers had been migrating within the province. The investigations of the Munitions Board revealed that some of the Pernambut workers who escaped to Bangalore had in fact been previously employed there in a tannery belonging to Abdul Razack, almost certainly after having taken advances from him. While employed in Bangalore they had all officially gone on leave 'to their native places' in North Arcot. While in their 'native places', the three workers had evidently taken up work in the nearby, labour-hungry Pernambut tannery, after taking advances and signing the contract cited above. One of the workers had been away from Bangalore for eleven months, and two of them for six months. As it transpired, while 'escaping' from the Pernambut tannery these workers were actually simply returning to Abdul Razack's tannery in Bangalore, bringing with them five other 'escapee' workers from Pernambut.

Despite the desperate efforts of the Pernambut tannery owners, it appears that the runaway workers were never caught. The fact that they had crossed from British territory into that of the states of Mysore and Hyderabad made it considerably more difficult for the tannery owners to pursue them, and to register complaints under the Workmen's Breach of Contract Act. Offences under the Act were not extraditable; Indian states could not thus be compelled to hand over those who absconded. The execution in the 'Native States' of warrants issued under Act XIII of 1859 depended upon 'local custom and the courtesy of the Durbars'.[68] The response of the Mysore Durbar to the Foreign and Political Department's letter – 'no law or rule in force in the State under which such workmen can be prohibited from entering the State and taking up service therein' – showed that they were not particularly eager to intervene to stop the migration of crucial tannery labour. They also categorically declared that it was not possible for them to compel these workers to leave the state. The Durbar agreed, however, to 'caution the tanners against entertaining such men in the future'.[69]

The onus was on the firm to get warrants issued under the Workmen's Breach of Contract Act, while the British authorities pledged to 'support' the tannery owners in any action they tried to take to ensure that their workers returned. The tannery owners were thus free to initiate action under the Act, to use it in a preemptive way as a threat against workers who took advances and to ensure that they stayed. It is unlikely, however, given the elaborate official procedures involved, that many cases were successfully prosecuted across these administrative divisions.[70]

The escape from Pernambut was not unique. The Munitions Board reported that it 'believed' it was 'not an isolated case'.[71] In most instances, tannery workers decamped collectively. The implication is that the illiterate, 'outcaste' workers engaged in the wet, preliminary work of tanning, who provided essential yet stigmatized labour that catalysed the global value chain in leather, were aware, while escaping from the workplaces, of the exact geographical 'boundaries' and limits of the law designed to control their movements. They knew, therefore, how to evade criminal prosecution if they escaped along these networks.[72]

This phenomenon – of workers running away from tanneries after taking advances – was also common in Bombay, the other important centre for tanning in the early twentieth century. Thus a Navsari 'leather merchant, leather factory' owner, R.J. Vimadalal, complained in 1917 of 'Madrasi' workers, among the main skilled workers, frequently running away:[73]

> The Madrasis that we have to deal with have their homes in Madras, and they generally fly from one place to another. Some of these people make it a rule to take advances from here and go away to other places. I mean to say that persons who do like that must be punished in an exemplary fashion so that others may be deterred from doing so. . . . Those that receive advances can be tried and warrants issued.

These warrants, he held, would be under Act XIII of 1859. Vimadalal believed that it would help leather factory owners if 'second class *mamlatdars*' also got jurisdiction under the Act. The reality, as he observed in his deposition, was that 'sometimes' the absconding workmen even came back to the same units and rejoined work, and 'the thing ends there'.[74] He reiterated the need to mete out punishment to absconding workers which would 'set an example to others'.[75] However Sir T.H. Holland, President of the Industrial Commission, did not believe that this was possible. He pointed out that a 'good many practical difficulties' had to be got over before the Act and other government regulations would be effective enough to curb workers from 'flying' and striking work.[76]

The 'success' of legal coercion to fix labour inside the tanneries, through acts such as the Workmen's Breach of Contract Act, or direct economic and physical coercion as was practised by *maistries* in the Dharavi leather cluster in Bombay in the 1920s and 1930s, depended on both market conditions as well as the degree of combination and organization of both workers and tanners, along with the nature of state- and private-controlled coercive and regulatory structures. The *maistries* in the small and informal tanneries in Dharavi in Bombay in the 1920s, for instance, did not resort to the law, but were able to regulate such escape by workers by refusing to employ any worker who had escaped from another tannery.[77] The fact that they were not facing a labour shortage and that the workers in Bombay were more dependent migrant workers from faraway Tirunelveli in Madras, more easily subjected to capital, contributed to Dharavi's success in ensuring labour fixity by coercing workers to remain in the tanneries.

'Escape' of this nature, or 'absconding', remained a common collective strategy that workers in tanneries adopted over time, even during conditions of trade slump. It was therefore not only a way of cheating the tannery owner of the 'advance', but also a way by which workers could escape their context of work – a mode, if not always of protest, of workers trying to cope with their conditions of work, and of informally but collectively resisting the effort by capital and the colonial state to immobilize them through a form of debt bondage.

The reason, perhaps, why the matter of workers absconding from the shopfloor drove tannery owners into a panic was the fear that hides and skins, perishable raw materials of the leather tanning and manufacturing industry, would rot if not processed promptly. Workers took advantage of this peculiarity of tanning from an early stage. The querulous tone in R.J. Vimadalal's deposition on the matter is evident from his testimony before the Indian Industrial Commission in 1917:

> The labour question is very important for tanners. . . . The tannery processes are such that the right things must be done at the right time, delay would be injurious; sometimes whole lots of skins are spoiled beyond repair. Workmen very often strike work at the critical point of a process; this has been a great hindrance experienced. Government regulation should make it as easy as possible for factory owners to take steps against artisans running away or striking work, and getting them punished.[78]

Therefore, apart from losing the money advanced to workers, the fact of workers 'escaping' made tannery owners frantic for another, more pressing reason. They feared that they would not be able to to process hides and skins in time because only workers belonging to certain social groups could do the work. The physical characteristics of hides and skins prone to rotting rapidly in the hot climate created pressure on the owners, and gave the workers important leverage. Once the workers started organizing formal unions, between the 1920s and 1940s, these came to be based on solidarities of both class and caste, as well as on the common experience of brutal labour processes involving routine handling of stigmatized, putrefying materials in which they were universally deployed. Caste, class and work came to be inseparably linked in this context. In the early stages, the most powerful strategy of protest adopted by tannery workers' unions involved stopping work or threatening to stop work at a crucial stage (commonly after soaking the hides in lime). This was also one of the most effective and widely used methods of protest by the unions, and was used across tannery clusters.[79]

It was the main reason for the success of the numerous 'flash strikes' that became a characteristic of the industry. B.V. Narayanaswami Naidu, engaged in labour welfare and counting himself among the 'well-wishers' of labour, recognized this strategic power that workers in tanneries had and, equally, the need to control it. In his influential report, he wrote:[80]

> Due to technical reasons, declaration of strikes in the tanning industry after a short notice or suddenly inevitably inflicts serious losses to tanners. *The workers are in a peculiarly strategic position to bring their employers to their knees when large quantities of hides or skins are in the lime pits or any other stage of tanning.* (Emphasis added)[81]

Naidu was writing after the rise of trade unions in Madras, around 1940–42, when they were militant and very active. He advocated a regulation of the notice period for strikes to curb this power that tannery workers had:

> Too frequent strikes with a view to exploiting the situation will in the long run produce disastrous results to the industry as a whole bringing in its train bankruptcy of tanners and closing down of tanneries. . . . It will be nothing but practical wisdom to qualify the right to strike and at the same time to protect the labourers from exploitation . . . the following scheme for the regulation of strikes is recommended. The workers must give forty-five days' notice of their intention to go on strike.[82]

Following such recommendations by Naidu and others in the Labour Department, changes were brought about in factory regulations in Madras. Till 1 April 1947, workers in tanneries had to give 'only 15 days notice' as in other factories.[83] Subsequently, workers who were engaged in pre-tannage operations and tanning of hides had to give forty-five days notice before striking work; those engaged in tanning skins had to give thirty days notice, the time required for completing the process of tanning.[84] The objective of the regulation was to specifically and directly protect the interests of owners of tanneries, to strengthen their hand so that they were never 'brought to their knees', and to neutralize the advantage the workers had.

While the new strike 'notice' period affected workers in all kinds of tanneries, workers in the more organized tanneries came more easily within its grasp and were perhaps more effectively subjected to such regulations. However, small unregulated units also came under their sway through the implementation of the decisions of the Industrial Tribunal on Tanneries and Leather Factories, set up in 1948 at Madurai.[85] The orders passed by the Tribunal while adjudicating cases pertaining to small and large units were based on Naidu's recommendations.

This did not mean that workers of either regulated or unregulated tanneries immediately stopped flash strikes. The lightning strikes that several owners and owners' representatives accused workers of in the proceedings of the Industrial Tribunal of 1948 testified to the continuation of this mode of protest. The new regulations simply gave the owners and management an additional, common 'legal' basis for dismissing workers easily on this account, and evicting the more vocal or militant workers from the shopfloor.

'Continuous' Work

Reasons similar to those cited by Naidu in arguing for a longer strike notice period by tannery workers had been given by lobbies representing the owners of tanneries much earlier. Their argument was that tanning was essentially 'continuous' work, and therefore distinct from 'normal' work, which was finite and could stop at the end of a working day. Tannery owners became particularly anxious when factory legislation in the early twentieth century began to spell out significant limits to the working day and a weekly holiday for workers, at a time when the demand for leather was escalating. They exerted collective pressure to secure exemption from these regulations so that their workers could work 'continuously', unlike in other factories.

The managements of big factories and tanneries presented petitions to the provincial governments arguing for the distinct nature of the work of tanning. The application presented to the Commerce Department of the Bengal government by the management of the Calcutta-based National Tannery Co. Ltd. is a case in point. Their request that exemption be granted to the industry from the observance of (i) Sunday as a holiday (Section 22), (ii) a working week of 60 hours, and (iii) a working day of 11 hours (Section 28), was accompanied by the following plea:

> The manufacture of leather is a continuous process and the operations involved demand constant attention of the staff. Work cannot be stopped at stated hours for any great length of time, for if it is, the hides under process become damaged.
>
> For the same reason work cannot be entirely discontinued on Sundays . . . some work must proceed, though of course the minimum amount of labour necessary will be employed on such days.[86]

The tannery owners were successful in securing the exemption in Bengal.[87] Workers engaged in the processes of soaking, drying, beating and curing or tanning hides, kips or skins were exempted from Section 22 of the Factory Act of 1911, with the condition that '(1) No person shall be required to work for more than fourteen consecutive days without a holiday for a whole day; and (2) The hours of work of any such person on a Sunday do not exceed six.'[88] The number of workers affected by this exemption and, presumably, engaged in these operations in the five regulated 'factories' in Bengal was 163, out of a total of 489 workers. Most of the workers in the Calcutta tannery cluster, however, worked in informal and unregulated tanneries. These workers numbered about 5,000 in 1946 according to the official count by the Labour Investigation Committee,[89] and the majority of the workers engaged in pre-tanning operations in these units would have worked long hours 'continuously', despite this order.

The notion that tanning was continuous work, and thus exceptional, was raised repeatedly across India by tannery owners. Tannery workers in different areas strongly resisted this exemption. The issue of getting a common weekly off-day became an important plank in the struggles of workers, especially by the 1940s, in the tanning industry in Madras. In the Dindigul sub-cluster particularly, in the years 1951–52, it united workers across regulated and unregulated units. Through the example of the Dindigul workers' fight for their Sunday, this essay explores how the question of whether or not tanning was 'continuous' work became a major site of contestation between capital and labour.

In 1951, an industrial dispute[90] between the two dominant workers' unions in Dindigul – the Tannery Labour Union and Tannery Workers' Union – and the management of eight Dindigul tanneries, large and small (including the well known Jamal Mohideen & Co.), was taken for adjudication before the Industrial Tribunal at Madurai. The dispute involved a range of issues like wages, bonus and provident fund. The demand for a common weekly holiday on Sunday was a part of the list of demands of workers placed before the Tribunal in this dispute. Several tannery owners in Dindigul collectively went to court against the Industrial Tribunal and the workers' unions.[91]

The tannery owners complained to the court that 'at the instance of the communist instigators some labourers in some tanneries have informed the managements on 3 July 1951 that they would completely stop work on Sundays and not adhere to the rotation system of work'. They observed that this was not possible because, '[i]n view of the peculiar condition of this manufacture which requires continuous attention it was decided on several occasions in awards and agreements that rotation system along should be adopted in this manufacture'.[92] Further:

> [t]he tanning industry involving a continuous process spread over 40 days and resulting in heavy loss to the owner if there is a break, the tanning industry has been exempted from the weekly holiday rule under the Shops and Establishments Act. As things now stand workers enjoy weekly holiday in batches by rotation as contemplated in Rule 77 of the Factories Act Rules, and the work in the tannery goes on without a break with the result that the workers themselves stand to gain by having the full quota work on the remaining days.[93]

They then came to the crux of their argument: 'The adoption of one holiday for all would result in lesser production and reduction of work and this would not be beneficial even to the workers.' The tannery owners held that the effort by unions to refer this demand, of leave for all workers on Sunday, to the Tribunal for adjudication was itself illegal.[94] The Labour Officer, asked by the Labour Commissioner to report on the situation, wrote about why, of all the demands made by the workers, the demand for a common 'weekly holiday' had become particularly controversial in Dindigul: '[t]he workers say that the majority being Christians, they have to attend service at Church and observe Sundays as Sabbath days. The real grievance is that the workers are unable to get together for their trade union activities on a common holiday.'[95]

This was perhaps one of the most significant demands for the tannery workers, one that was at once social, cultural and economic. The Labour Officer pointed out in his report that

> [t]he feeling of the workers is very strong on this point and in every tannery which I visited . . . the first question hurled at me was, 'When are we going to have our Sundays to ourselves?' They even hinted at a strike over this issue and I advised them to be patient and not to precipitate matters.[96]

It was no coincidence that the issue was raised so prominently by the Dindigul tannery workers' union. They had a charged history of organization and their union was one of the earliest amongst tannery workers in Madras. The union had been led from around 1942 by communists, and had a core of militant, local caste-based worker-leaders who had initiated the union.[97]

The symbolic power of Christian workers mobilizing for leave from tannery work on Sundays, demanding their right from largely Muslim tannery owners who strongly opposed it, brought an explosive quality to the situation, with class antagonism and religious tensions getting inseparably intertwined. Retired worker and union leader Chinappan, in his account of the history of the union at Dindigul,[98] recalled that the question of a common weekly holiday on Sunday became the context of a confrontation. Matters came to a head on the question of the workers' right to take out a big religious procession at Easter, and on the mobilization of workers against owners on communal grounds.

Under the Factories Act of 1948, workers were entitled to a weekly holiday, though employers were not bound to grant a holiday to all workers on the same day. Interestingly, by 1948, the Dindigul tannery workers, mostly employed in unregulated small tanneries, had been observing Sunday as a holiday for at least one year after successful negotiations with the owners. Their own agitation, it appears, was in advance of factory regulations in this case, and had secured for them greater gains in terms of their weekly holiday. This is why the demand of a common weekly 'day off' had not been an 'issue' in 1948, when the workers and tanners in Dindigul brought their disputes before the Madurai Industrial Tribunal for adjudication, even though they had raised questions of wages, bonus, etc. The workers had already succeeded in getting Sunday as the day off. The Industrial Tribunal, impelled by motives of labour welfare, directed that the regulations under the Factory Act of 1948 be strictly enforced. For the Dindigul tannery workers this meant a setback, though, a curtailment of a right they had won in the course of their own local struggles. The workers were thus 'greatly agitated' over this issue of losing their Sunday holiday.[99]

The fact that the Dindigul workers' union had already won this right meant that the seemingly technical argument that work needed to go on continuously because hides and skins would rot otherwise was less compelling than suggested by employers across India. It was more indicative of an attempt by managements to extend working hours and maximize control over workers. As B.V. Narayanaswami Naidu observed in his report, a few tanneries did actually 'close on Sundays, thereby showing that the process of tanning will not be spoiled, as it is alleged, by the closing of tanneries for one day in a week'.[100] Across the country, tanneries – formal and informal – continued to work on Sundays under even later Factories Acts. The Dindigul tannery workers however won their struggle that year, and got their Sundays to themselves.

The struggles of workers who were drawn into flaying and tanning did not follow a linear trajectory. Given the nature of the work force, the idiom of domination and also resistance were products of negotiations between the customary and the new. Such negotiations were particularly visible in the struggles of workers to get bonuses. At one level the struggle of tannery and leather workers, like that of workers in other sectors, historically, was to get a *regular* bonus (a percentage of the wage) as a right, not as charity given 'at the pleasure' of the owner of the unit. As Justice Horwill, defending the Madurai Industrial Tribunal's decision in a labour dispute involving tannery workers, stated in 1948: 'Bonuses . . . may in one sense be regarded as a recognition of the right of the workers to share in some measure in the profits of the company and encourages workmen to work harder, in the knowledge that by doing so they will secure more gain to themselves.'[101]

The issue of bonus remained a significant one when workers in the Calcutta tannery cluster organized themselves much later. The demand for a regular bonus was the focus of their first major, clusterwide organized struggle in the early 1970s, when the union was particularly dynamic. They wanted a regular bonus as a right and not 'at the pleasure' of the owners. Shamsul Haq, presently a machine operator in the Chinese-run Hobson tannery, and an active union member in Tangra, Calcutta, since 1972, recalled what he had seen when he started out and what older workers used to say then about the past in Dhapa. He said that the Chinese tannery owners in Tangra–Dhapa used to give the workers extra money from time to time, but this was not a fixed amount or percentage. 'They would give you Rs 100 or Rs 200 sometimes *khushi hoye* – if they were happy – they used to call this not bonus but "*bakshish*" or "tip".'[102] The workers demanded that the owners should give all workers a bonus as a right and not as a 'tip' at their pleasure.

In Madras, with its long history of tanneries and of local labour drawn from neighbouring districts, the struggle for bonus carried deeper meanings. The tannery owners in the Madras clusters 'traditionally' gave their workers annual, 'customary' gifts on the occasion of festivals like *Ayudha Puja* and *Pongal*, but no regular 'bonus'. These gifts normally included some length of cloth, mutton and some cash, and were given as per '*mamool*' or custom. These customs, with local variations, closely resembled the customary 'presents' given by powerful land holders and *mirasidars* in the region to Paraiyan labourers employed by them in the late nineteenth century, contemporaneous to and in the immediate vicinity of the tanning clusters. These labourers were tied in bonds described by the Collector of Chingleput in 1891 as ties of agrestic slavery, as *padials* (labourers under debt-bond).[103] Annual cash 'presents' and 'extra presents', apart from 'one cloth a year', for instance, were listed as remuneration, along with minimal wages, daily meals, etc., given to Paraiyan bonded agrarian labourers in 1886 in Chingleput.[104]

These customary gifts carried with them specific histories, and evoked remembered practices of customary dependence and subordination. The rejection of customary 'gifts' given by tannery owners and the demand for a regular bonus for all thus became one of the early demands of the workers in Madras as they began to get mobilized by communists – not least because of the historical associations of these gifts. These demands perhaps also implied a deeper rejection of the exploitative and oppressive structure within which these customs were embedded, a structure of which the workers had been a part for long. Perhaps that is why rejection of these gifts and the demand for their substitution by an annual bonus was a slow and non-linear process, particularly in Madras. There was an additional dimension to the Madras tannery workers' rejection of customary gifts that extended beyond a simpler rejection of dependence upon the 'pleasure' or grace of the tannery owner.

In 1928, in one of the earliest recorded major strikes by tannery workers in Madras province, 600 workers in a tannery at Tiruvottiyur went on strike, and refused the customary gifts of 'a pair of cloths, a seer of mutton, rice and 8 annas in cash'. The owners ceded their demand for a cash bonus only after they went on strike. The workers had to strike work again the following year to ensure that their demands were met.[105] While this early struggle succeeded in ensuring that the workers of this tannery got a bonus, the practice of tannery owners giving customary 'gifts' to workers on festivals instead of a regular cash bonus remained widely prevalent across clusters in the province. Thus, even as late as the 1940s, workers in Dindigul who had been mobilized by the communists had to place their demand for a bonus instead of customary gifts before the Industrial Tribunal at Madurai. In his judgment of 1948, the presiding judge of the Tribunal, T. Subbiah Pillai, clearly ruled in the dispute between the tannery workers and owners in Dindigul that 'hereafter there shall be no gift to workers . . . on occasions of *Deepavali*, *Christmas*, *Easter*, *Pongal* and *Ayudha Pooja*'.[106] A regular bonus based on the number of days of work done by the worker was to be paid instead.

Yet, while bonus remained the long-term goal and was achieved gradually, the workers' rejection of customary gifts on festivals – a part of their customary claims in the agrarian sphere as in the tanneries – was clearly not a move that all workers chose to make. Thus at the same time as the workers in Tiruvottiyur or in Dindigul, strongholds of labour mobilization amongst tannery workers in Madras province, were rejecting customary gifts, workers in other tanneries in the region went on strike because they were not being given customary gifts on festivals. Twenty years after the Tiruvottiyur tannery strikes, on 15 October 1948, workers in the tannery of Abdul Rahman & Co. in the Pallavaram tanning cluster struck work because 'the usual Ayudha Puja present was not given on the Ayudha Puja Celebration Day'.[107] Similarly, workers of Palaniappa Chettiar Tannery in Chingleput staged a token strike the following day demanding 'bonus for the Ayudha Puja'. On 28 January 1948, '[a]bout 500 workers of tanneries in Kurichi and Podanur staged a stay-in-strike . . . as a protest against the refusal of the Proprietors to supply them with cloth for *Pongal*'.[108] This dispute was decided by the intervention of the Labour Officer of Coimbatore. They only resumed work when the 'Company' assured them that it would be given to them.

In the same year, workers of the Chrome Leather Company, organized by a communist-led trade union, raised demands for both bonus (and gratuity and provident fund) and presents for the *Pongal* festival from the Company, along with other demands that it took to the Industrial Tribunal at Madurai. Baktavatsalu Naidu who was presiding over the Tribunal adjudicated the case, ruled in favour of the workers' demand and ordered the Company to give the workers *Pongal* gifts – the workers had asked that 'the learned Tribunal should order the petitioner to give presents of cloth to its workmen at each *Pongal* or to each on that occasion the money equivalent of six yards of handloom cloth'. The Chrome Leather Company appealed against this ruling to the High Court, disputing the powers of the Industrial Tribunal to adjudicate on these matters because bonus, gratuity and *Pongal* gifts were not a part of the Standing Orders of the Company, or of the contract that workers signed with them. The Company's lawyers argued that they were therefore not bound to give these.

These events bear a closer examination. The workers in this case were asking for a customary gift (cloth, etc.) exactly 'as per *mamool*', but appealed to a modern adjudicatory tribunal to secure their 'customary' claim. *Pongal* gifts were part of a set of demands along with 'modern' demands such as bonus, gratuity, provident fund and fair wages, as well as against retrenchment of workers. The Company, on the other hand, was apparently seeking to assert a contractual relationship, and not cede any customary or modern claims not written into the contract. The judgment of the Madras High Court on this matter was significant. Justice J. Horwill ruled in November 1948 that the Tribunal could adjudicate on these matters and upheld the demands of the workers of Chrome Leather Company as valid. He validated the demand for gifts made by workers but established it as their right, rather than as part of a customary regime of claims and obligations. While the appearance of the gifts remained the same, their meaning, significance and location were changed by this judgement, and, in the process, the workers' own politicization. The judge stated that 'presents given at *Pongal* (like gratuities, pensions, provident fund, etc.) may be regarded as deferred wages payable annually at a time when custom and necessity require that new clothing should be purchased'.[109] The High Court's order and the petition of the workers thus showed that the gift was sought to be dislodged from its 'traditional' context and structure. It was not to be considered largesse on the part of the tannery owner but a right of the workers as something they had earned by their labour.

In other tanneries where similar demands were being made, and where matters did not reach the tribunal or the court since tannery owners conceded the demand for gifts, the issue was not perhaps worked out in the same manner. This indicates the non-linear and mediated process of the emergence of a specific workers' consciousness amongst 'outcaste' workers engaged in the wet work of tanning. Even as they came forward to fight for their 'rights' as 'workers', they remained within the ideological ambit of deeprooted, older social relations of production, seeing themselves as 'coolies', 'servants' and 'menials'. This struggle and negotiation can be seen in the contestation over the demand for customary 'gifts'.

It is difficult to posit any teleological shift in workers' demands from gifts to a regular bonus in the case of leather tanneries. Nor is this a narrative of a journey of workers' 'consciousness' from the 'customary' to the 'modern'. The 'rights' that these workers struggled for varied as they were drawn from the different worlds that they inhabited, worlds that met and coalesced and got redefined on the slippery workfloors of tanning clusters.

'In view of their present condition the demands cannot be described as moderate'

When tannery workers began to organize themselves more formally – in Bombay by the 1930s, in Dindigul and elsewhere in Madras province by the late 1930s and early 1940s, and in Calcutta by the late 1940s – the issues they raised were similar, in many ways, to workers' demands in other industries marked by informality and lack of regulation. Yet, in certain contexts, it appears that the earliest struggles of workers in the leather industry to organize themselves, and their attempts to put forward basic demands – including those conceded by law – were met with an extraordinarily high degree of hostility and resistance, especially by state representatives. This included officials who otherwise took a generally sympathetic stance, such as B.V. Narayanaswami Naidu whose influential 1947 report on the conditions of labour in the tanning industry in Madras has been cited before.[110]

In his report, Naidu vividly described the work process, the appalling working conditions and the role of the labour laws in the 'country tanneries', and argued for reform. In the section of the report dealing with 'Trade Unions', he wrote that Madras tannery workers had formed their own union and then went on to list the basic demands of tannery workers submitted by the Madras Provincial Trade Union Congress.[111] These included demands for payment of minimum wages in all leather factories and tanneries, dearness allowance, bonus, and protective equipment – gloves, boots, etc. – for those engaged in hazardous work.[112] The demands were neither very extraordinary nor excessive, but for Naidu these were extreme demands. His disapproval was apparent in his sarcastic comment that 'these demands are mild when compared to those made by the Andhra Provincial Tannery Workers' Union'. The Andhra union apparently had sought to express the 'aspirations of workers' and put forth their own unanimous demands, on 21 February 1947. Naidu recorded these in his report, mainly to draw attention to what he regarded as their excessive nature. That union, again, had asked for minimum wages and, additionally, yearly increments at a regular rate; proper wages for women and children employed in tanneries; leave on Sundays and also some days of casual leave, medical leave; etc. Naidu commented: '[i]t is needless to catalogue the numerous other demands found in their memorandum'. His exasperation with tannery workers making demands based on their own notion of workers' rights comes across clearly in the cold print of his report. This exasperation seemed somewhat puzzling and inexplicable, until he explained it:

> [T]he tannery workers are at present in the lowest rung of society as well as employment; their conditions of service are low as their status in society. *In view of their present condition the demands cannot be described as moderate* [emphasis added]. That is why a series of strikes in the Madras City and its environs did not prove to be a success [here he is referring to a recent spate of strikes led by tannery workers' unions]. Fixing the targets very high may be attractive for some time to the workers; but if they are not attained within a measurable distance by strikes, or by threat of strikes, the members will lose faith in the union activities; such a result will be regretted by every well-wisher of labour.[113]

The implication of what Naidu was writing is clear. The conditions of employment of tannery workers were commensurate with their status in society as members of untouchable castes – both were extremely low. 'Normal' demands and aspirations commonly expressed by workers' unions in other industries, or even struggles to implement rights already granted to labour by law, would be seen as over-ambitious when taken up by tannery workers, and were bound to meet with more opposition and hostility from both capital and the state. This 'well-wisher' of labour was advocating pragmatic acceptance by Dalit tannery workers of the limitations of their entitlement and rights as workers, based on caste and social status.

Naidu's own tacit acceptance of the fundamental inequality of caste on which these differential rights were based was evident. It was also evident that he was not simply representing his individual views but those of the socially dominant classes. After all, he attributed the widespread failure of strikes in the mid-1940s to the prevalence of this attitude. Given how significant Naidu's report was from the point of view of the Labour Department's intervention in the tanning industry in Madras and indirectly at an all-India level, it would not be too far-fetched to estimate that these attitudes also informed the efforts of the government, of the Labour Department, towards workers in this industry.

Caste-based attitudes, which informed the historical development of the leather industry, are notoriously difficult to corroborate in archival and official records, or even in other written records. Naidu's statement with its implicit caste bias is a rare exception as a written document, which exposes that such attitudes were shared by other members of dominant social groups and sections of civil society who were by this time associated with and benefited from the highly profitable leather industry – as owners of tanneries, as traders, or as managerial and technical staff. Oral accounts of the histories of unions, and tannery and leather workers' organizations in different clusters corroborate the constant presence of these attitudes. Demands for dignity and 'proper behaviour' towards workers in tanneries, and rejection of traditional or customary forms of remuneration and behaviour, formed a part of the earliest efforts of workers to organize themselves; and are indicative of the workers' efforts to overthrow caste-based patterns of behaviour, domination and subordination.[114]

The prevalence of caste-based attitudes can also be inferred from largely tangential references in the records – from statements such as the one made in the *Report of the Madras Exhibition* of 1855, which attributed the poor quality of leather production in the province to the 'low rank' of the artisans,[115] to the wide-ranging debates around the syllabus and objectives of industrial training in leather production, and the trajectory of the state-established training institutions that incorporated and recreated the idiom and grammar of caste. Archival sources even suggest that the evolution of industrial training in leather in India fundamentally reinforced a process of congealing caste-based labour. Records pertaining to institutions like the Leather Trades Institute in Madras (established in 1912) and the Calcutta Research Tannery / Bengal Tanning Institute (established in 1919) show how the project of training in leather production was consciously designed to ensure that the actual workers – untouchable Chamars, Paraiyans, etc. – could not access it. 'Outcaste' workers, who formed the bulk of the work force in the tanning clusters and whose foundational labour was crucially responsible for the profitability of the leather industry, were thus excluded from the possibility of moving out of the stigmatized, 'dirty' wet work of tanning into 'cleaner', 'drier' and better paid operations on the shopfloor that now opened up for those with technical training.[116]

Further, as in the case of 'traditional', caste-based skills, these workers who were engaged in unskilled pre-tanning operations, liming, scudding, etc., learnt the work from their relatives and parents on the shopfloors, resulting in hereditary transmission of work skills and reproduction of patterns of caste and stigma. The introduction of industrial training and the reinvention of tanning as a science in the early twentieth century, on the other hand, allowed the entry of educated, upper-caste youth into the profitable leather industry, to perform the better paid, mechanized, 'skilled' and drier work in tanning and leather manufacturing.[117] The shopfloor division of work thus naturalized caste hierarchy and led to a reincarnation of caste in the context of the production of leather, as it got linked to the modern economy and capitalist production in the twentieth century.

Caste attitudes towards the foundational work of tanning were deep-rooted and extended to those who did the work. As C. Sabapathy Mudaliyar, speaking on behalf of tannery owners Messrs C.H. Zain ul Abidin Sahib & Co. (Madras), observed in 1923: 'in a country like India where there is so much of class and caste distinction it is hardly possible to expect a caste man to do the menial work of liming, shaving and drying of skins – practically all dirty work – when a hide or skin is put under tannage'.[118] Dirty work and untouchable-caste workers remained inseparably linked to each other, and this association was even strengthened with the expansion of production, technical training and improvements.

The predominantly Muslim owners of tanneries across Madras also shared several of these cultural notions – or at least the sense of affront that Naidu articulated about these 'outcaste' workers, marked by caste and the 'dirty' work they did, yet daring to articulate even moderate demands. Muslim tannery owners in Dindigul in the 1940s imposed taboos on workers wearing sandals or white *veshti*s (dhotis) when passing through the owners' area of residence, Begumpur, and on visiting tea-shops frequented by higher castes.[119] Muslim as well as non-Muslim owners of tanneries also used derogatory forms of address for untouchable-caste workers.

'Traditional' notions which implied that low-caste groups, because of their inherently subordinate status, were to perform the most hazardous, smelly or tedious work as a service that dominant groups could freely call upon, did not disappear with the rise of the 'market' or the emergence of a commodity chain. In the case of flaying, they got intensified with the increase in the scale of 'production'. They also persisted in the modern leather clusters, stalked the shopfloor, and brought urgency to the efforts of capital and the state to control labour, and to curb workers' self-organization and assertion.

It is not surprising, given this history, that caste became, substantially, the earliest language of class, and also provided the earliest structure for workers' collective organizations and unions. Thus, the Tannery Workers' Union in Dindigul, the first tannery workers' union in Madras formed by Paraiyan tannery workers and educated youth, registered in 1942, metamorphosed from a church-supported, caste-based organization demanding justice, dignity and workers' rights, into a militant communist-led union which continued to centrally raise caste-related issues that affected the workers.[120] In Calcutta's Tangra leather cluster the first union emerged in 1944, and while it was officially called the Tannery Workers Union, it was popularly known simply as the union of Bihari Chamar workers.[121] These workers also organized themselves around the Ravidas Ekta Samiti, formed in the late 1940s, which was based on veneration of the medieval 'saint' Ravidas by Chamars and related castes. The migrant tannery workers in this cluster, coming from different parts of Bihar, eastern Uttar Pradesh and also from Bilaspur–Raipur in central India, could potentially be encompassed in this primarily caste-based organization. In the 1960s, the Samiti members went on to form the core of the earliest communist organization that emerged in the cluster.[122]

While notions of caste – largely shared by state representatives like

Naidu, and tannery owners' agents like C. Sabapathy Mudaliyar or B.M. Das[123] – operated to ensure control and subordination of labour by state and capital, they did not function in a unidirectional or seamless manner. Thus, workers of tanneries in different clusters and regions who built caste and labour-based solidarities (like members of the Andhra Provincial Tannery Workers' Union whose 'excessive' charter of demands had affronted Naidu[124]) were not deterred by official disapproval and opposition by dominant caste–class groups in raising their basic demands as workers. Similarly, the large number of industrial disputes that were taken to the Industrial Tribunal for tanneries and leather factories that sat at Madurai in 1948–49, showed that the workers in these leather tanning and manufacturing units did not particularly heed Naidu's caution about making limited demands given their location on the 'lowest rung of society'.[125] The Chamar tannery workers from Bihar, who had formed a union in Calcutta in 1944, raised demands that were very similar to those raised by the Andhra and Madras unions, i.e. demands which Naidu might have considered excessive and unattainable.[126] Significantly, these workers in Calcutta also simultaneously organized themselves around caste and sect, and there was little distinction between the workings of these different organizations till the late 1960s.[127]

'Caste' was thus neither a 'given' nor a homogenous identity, but was forged anew by workers in these tanning clusters in modern urban conglomerations. Members of the lowest castes, who often belonged to different regions, sub-groups, etc., came together as tannery *workers*, united by the labour process, the hard and essential work they had to do repeatedly and continuously, and the peculiar qualities of the material they had to work with. Caste as a category was to a large extent 'made' along with class. Caste, class and labour process framed and defined each other, and shaped workers' experience centrally and somewhat uniquely in the leather industry as it expanded under colonial rule. Each category, in turn and together, inflected the emergence of the 'identity' of workers in the industry and shaped the nature of their collectivities.

Conclusion

Workers' resistance and labour control in leather tanning in India as it emerged in the late nineteenth to mid-twentieth century, in the context of the international market, was thus continuously haunted by two contradictory sets of relationships. On the one hand, there was constant awareness among the owners of cattle, tannery owners and the colonial administrative authorities, and among workers themselves, of the workers' origins – almost uniformly from the 'lowest rungs' of society – and about the linked template of meanings and associations, hierarchies of ritual pollution and stigma, subservient behaviour patterns and unrecompensated labour services. On the other hand, there was acute dependence of the socially dominant owners of the means of production on the labour of these workers, given the limitations of the labour market. This was due to the stigma of the work itself, which prescribed the creation of a narrowly circumscribed labour market. These conditions, combined with the ever-present threat of rotting hides, gave these low-caste workers the singular capacity to 'bring employers to their knees'.

The stigma of work processes in this line of production, which gave the workers such apparent power, was however double-edged, and also one of the sources of their subordination on grounds of caste. It was vested not just in the work of flaying and tanning, but in the very *materials* – raw hides, skins, leather – that workers had to touch and work with. The 'untouchability' of these materials was in turn transmitted to the *work* of flaying and tanning, and through 'touch' to all those who did this work. These workers were rendered untouchable by their extremely low status in the caste hierarchy and by their work with untouchable materials. The expansion of the modern tanning industry further reproduced and confirmed the stigma of untouchability with regard to these workers. While stigmatized work gave different categories of workers some leverage and created the context for workers' resistance, it carried within it the structural tools of their systematic, caste-based subordination. It is significant, however, that these workers were at the same time subordinated *as workers* to a deeply exploitative labour regime in the new tannery clusters, tied to 'continuous work' by colonial factory regulations created at the behest of capital. Thus the intimate association of these workers with stigma and their subjection to capital as labour occurred simultaneously.

When the workers linked to the industry began to organize themselves, their modes of resistance too had to continuously negotiate both forms of domination, while they themselves had to frame their identity around both – as stigmatized labour. The prevalence of deep-rooted resentment against these workers and their demands, even moderate ones, reveals how stigma and caste mediated the meanings of labour, and shaped the struggles of these workers.

The modes adopted by workers in this industry to negotiate and resist labour regimes that the dominant castes, capital and state converged to create, straddled both 'modern' and 'traditional' strategies, rendering this dichotomy futile. While some workers politicized as Dalits abandoned the 'traditional' work that linked them to defiling substances, others engaged in leather work at different nodes in the production chain, organized themselves as workers and occasionally turned the stigmatized work itself into a tool of resistance. Whatever might have been the method adopted, the workers acted – by selling the hides they flayed, or poisoning cattle in Danapur, Ahmadnagar or elsewhere, by running away from tanneries in Navsari or Pernambut, or striking work after soaking hides at Thangal or Tangra, or going to court to get Sundays off for themselves – and they were thus agents in their own histories. The poor crafted their distinct politics in this industry, precisely under conditions of systematic subordination to both modern and traditional structures of domination.

Figure 1 Escalation of value of exports of hides and skins from India, 1860–1883 (years of maximum anxiety regarding cattle poisoning)[128]

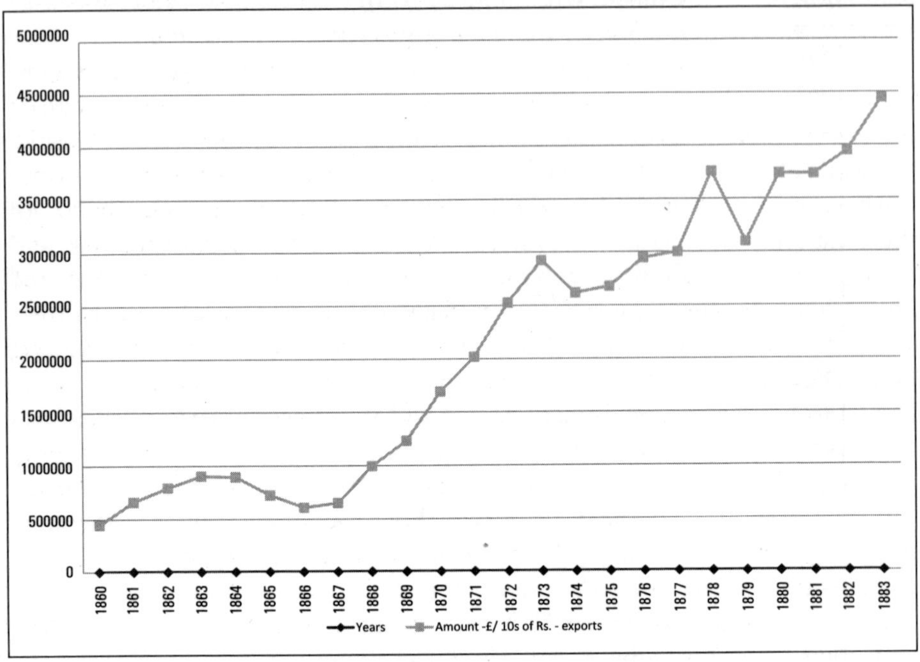

Table 1 Escalation of value of exports of hides and skins from India, 1860–1883[129]

Years	*Amount – £/10s of Rs – exports*
1860	444,537
1861	661,725
1862	794,137
1863	904,280
1864	897,575
1865	725,236
1866	609,803
1867	650,342
1868	994,233
1869	1,230,932
1870	1,691,330
1871	2,020,819
1872	2,525,925
1873	2,921,910
1874	2,618,358
1875	2,677,767
1876	2,944,933
1877	3,000,552
1878	3,757,480
1879	3,097,561
1880	3,738,455
1881	3,735,646
1882	3,950,052
1883	4,444,946

TABLE 2 Names and details of runaway workers from the Pernambut tannery of K.H. Mahomed Yakoob and Sons in Pernambut, Madras in 1918[130]

	Name of Employee	*Father's name*	*Place where employee is believed to be working at present*	*Names of persons under whom employees are now believed to be working*	*What work employees are now doing*
1	Para Mythoti Banga	Para Veeran	Nizamabad	Modi Abdul Gafoor Saib vs. Abdul Hakim Saib and Co.	Tannery
2	Salapettai Peria Abbu	Para Karmatrikara Veeran	Ditto	Ditto	Ditto
3	Mordhana Muthan	Para Govindan	Ditto	Ditto	Ditto
4	Thoppukara Kanayyan	Para Goyyal	Ditto	Ditto	Ditto
5	Sembedu Abhoy	Para Ellan	Kadu Kundlapalli, Hebbalam, Post Bangalore City	S. Abdul Razaq Saib	Ditto
6	Kuthanveetu Pakkalia Gengan	Para Angasala Koothan	Ditto	Ditto	Ditto
7	Mordhana Bheeman	Para Govindan	Ditto	Ditto	Ditto
8	Andi Peri Peruman	Para Kullan	Ditto	Ditto	Ditto
9	Dindigul Ponnan	Ditto	Ditto	Ditto	Ditto
10	Machambut Munyan	Para Peria Munyan	Ditto	Ditto	Ditto
11	Dindigul Rangaswami	Ditto	Ditto	Ditto	Ditto
12	Gummal Perumall	Gummal Gengan	Ditto	Ditto	Ditto
13	Chittoor Mathan	Para Padavettan	Jeevanapalie, Bangalore City	Cholavaram Abdur Rahman Saib	Ditto
14	Poojali Chinnayan	Para Gengan	Ditto	Pallan Lall Batcha Saib	Ditto
15	Cheetamitu Chirma Abbu	Para Chinnan	Kadukundlapalli, Hebbalam, Post Bangalore City	M. Abdul Wahab Saib	Ditto

Notes and References

1 These included castes like Chamar, Mahar, Dher, Paraiyan and Chakkiliyan.

2 The term 'suitable labour' was a euphemism, used to refer to workers who could be recruited into the leather industry. Their 'suitability' effectively lay in their willingness to work with stigmatizing substances like raw hides and skins, and in the hard and degrading labour processes involved in tanning. The term was officially used by informants who deposed before the Indian Industrial Commission 1916–18, like A. Carnegie, a leather manufacturer of Kanpur. See Witness no. 18, A. Carnegie, Leather manufacturer, Cawnpore, in *Indian Industrial Commission (1916–1918), Minutes of Evidence*, Vol. I, Delhi, United Provinces, Bihar and Orissa, Calcutta: Superintendent, Government Printing. The supreme importance of easy availability of labour as a condition for setting up industry was recognized long before the Industrial Commission.

3 The majority of goatskins were a result of slaughter for food, and their production was largely urban. The butchers who slaughtered and skinned goats were more often located in the cities, while the work of tanning, in most instances, would have been done by common groups of tanners who processed both goatskins and cow-hides.

4 The question of who did the work of skinning dead goats and who owned the skins carried as much emotive charge, or was surrounded by as much contestation, as that of cattle carcasses. Skin production was also reorganized, and systematically connected to contractors and markets, but the process was a more direct one as most of the skins exported from India were produced by slaughter and regarded to be of high quality.

5 Some of the implications of this are discussed in Ramnarayan S. Rawat, *Reconsidering Untouchability*, Bloomington: Indiana University Press, 2011. Rawat discusses the emergence of cattle poisoning in the United Provinces in detail, particularly from the point of view of its effect of turning Chamars into criminals. While acknowledging these consequences, I explore some of the same evidence to draw upon the ways in which this late nineteenth-century expansion in cattle poisoning was related to the setting up of a market in hides.

6 Ibid.: 28, citing from *Report of Indian Cattle Plague Commission*, Calcutta: Government of India Press, 1871: 646.

7 Ibid.: 38, fn 38, citing N. Chevers, *A Manual of Medical Jurisprudence for India*, Calcutta: Thacker, Spink & Co., 1870: 128–30.

8 *Papers relating to the Crime of Cattle-Poisoning: Views of Local Governments on the Need or Practicality of a Law Restricting the Sale of Arsenic*, Selections from the Home, Revenue and Agricultural Department, No. CLXXX, Calcutta: Home Department Press, 1881; available at www.archive.org/stream/papersrelatingt00agrigoog#page/n3/mode/2up, accessed on 22 January 2012. Campbell claimed to have unravelled a network of poisoning based on networks of distribution of arsenic – 'a vast conspiracy between leather merchants, buniahs, poison-distributors, and the village Chamars who administered the drug to the cattle'. He linked isolated cases of poisoning by Chamars to 'great parent stems whence the arsenic was disseminated, and from which the whole system flowed'. He hoped to 'commit several hundred criminals' on this charge and felt that he would have to examine 'several thousand witnesses'. He believed this was a 'peculiar crime' which could 'only be fully met by special measures'.

9 Ibid. In October 1854, for instance, Campbell arrested 1,500 Chamars for the crime and convicted 500 of them. These arrests were not based on any evidence except the fact that several of them were carrying arsenic at that time.

10 Ibid.

11 Letter from C.P. Carmichael, Officiating Commissioner, Benares Division, to Secretary to the Government of North Western Provinces, No. 278, 4 December 1873, in *Papers Relating to the Crime of Cattle-Poisoning*, 1881.

12 Report from R.D. Spedding, Magistrate of Goruckpur, to the Commissioner, Benares

Division, No. 77, 11 October 1879, in *Papers Relating to the Crime of Cattle-Poisoning*, 1881. See discussion below.

13 Report by R.D. Spedding, 2 October 1873, in *Papers Relating to the Crime of Cattle-Poisoning*, 1881. J.F. Lumsden was the Officiating Magistrate of Gorakhpur while Spedding was the Joint Magistrate in 1873. A. Robinson was a pro-active Assistant Magistrate in charge of Kussia sub-division of the district.

14 Thus when 'twenty-two and quarter ounces of white arsenic were found in possession of 62 Chamars, and of this 16 ounces were in powder form', Spedding deduced that these were 'doses ready to administer to the cattle'. Report from R.D. Spedding, Joint Magistrate of Gorakhpur, to the Officiating Magistrate of Gorakhpur, No. 410, 2 October 1873, in *Papers Relating to the Crime of Cattle-Poisoning*, 1881. According to the official calculations of dosage by Captain Dodd, 'this arsenic, amounting to 9,600 grains, represents a quantity sufficient to destroy 960 cattle'. But the doses found with the Chamars did not match, and Spedding went on to conclude that 'the number of cattle which would have been destroyed by the arsenic recovered does not probably exceed 500'. He stated that 'the remaining six and quarter ounces were found with Toofanee, the wholesale vendor in Azimgurh', and suspected that these 'would almost certainly have been distributed among the Chamars in a short time'. A large amount was also found in Boolakee's house: 'five seers of white arsenic, or an amount capable of destroying 5,760 cattle, were found in the house of Boolakee Chamar, of Nargaon, near Dinapore. He was the person who supplied arsenic to Toofanee and escaped from the Bengal Police with the five seers in his possession.' This 'evidence' was considered sufficient by Spedding and other North Western Provinces magistrates to arrest and prosecute the Chamars, and establish their guilt.

15 Ibid.

16 Rawat, *Reconsidering Untouchability*: 35.

17 *Papers Relating to the Crime of Cattle-Poisoning*, 1881.

18 Section 429, Indian Penal Code.

19 Letter from Lumsden, Officiating Magistrate, Gorakhpur, to Commissioner, Benares Division, 15 October 1873, in *Papers Relating to the Crime of Cattle-Poisoning*, 1881.

20 Ibid.

21 *Papers Relating to the Crime of Cattle-Poisoning*, 1881.

22 'The total number of hides exported from Calcutta to foreign and Indian ports during the years 1875–76 to 1878–79 and ten months of 1879–80 was 27,373,976 and the total value of the hides was Rs. 7,02,85.71. Any proposal that would interfere with or try to check, an enormous trade of this description should, the Lieutenant Governor thinks, be very carefully considered.' Letter from Secretary, Government of Bengal, Judicial, Political and Appointment Departments, to the Secretary to the Government of India, Home, Revenue and Agricultural Department, No. 3144, 28 June 1880, in *Papers Relating to the Crime of Cattle-Poisoning*, 1881. The Secretary observed: 'Although there are probably substances better adapted for curing leather than any form of arsenic, still there is no doubt that arsenic is one of the cheapest and most effective preservatives of leather and skins, and any restriction on its sale would certainly have the effect of materially raising its price and rendering it difficult for hide dealers and Chamars to obtain it for the purpose of curing the skins of large numbers of cattle that die from natural causes. . . . It must also be borne in mind that the imposition of any restriction upon the trade in which men of the poorer classes in remote villages are engaged places the hands of an uneducated and poorly-paid police an additional power which is at any time liable to be used as a means of extortion and oppression. . . . Having regard to these considerations, and to the orders by the Government of India in 1874, the Lieutenant-Governor is not prepared to make any

further recommendation in favour of bringing the sale of arsenic under administrative supervision.'

23 Ibid.

24 In large parts of north India, Chamars were described as 'recognized village menials' receiving 'as perquisite' the hides of dead cattle which they tanned. 'In return he was bound to supply shoes and other leather articles, such as the skin bag with which water is hauled up from the well to water the fields.' See W. Crooke, *Natives of Northern India*, London: A. Constable & Co., 1907: 122. In the North Western Provinces, Bihar, Bengal, Central Provinces, etc., 'the cultivators of each village' were 'parcelled out among certain families of Chamars'. Chamars performed 'certain services for the cultivators' and received 'the bodies of all the animals belonging to their own particular cultivators which die'. They obtained 'possession of the body [of the dead cow or buffalo] in virtue of a particular right of the nature of a contract'. Communication from Campbell, Officiating Magistrate of Azimgurh, to the Superintendent of Police, the 6th or Benares Division, 21 October 1854, in *Papers Relating to Crime of Cattle-Poisoning*, 1881. In Bombay, however, Mahars in each village did the work of skinning carcasses and flaying hides, as part of their work as designated village servants responsible to the village as a whole and holding hereditary office. In return they received a grant – the '*watan*', which was commonly a piece of land. Hides were considered perquisites of the Mahars for their work. See H.H. Risley, *The People of India*, edited by W. Crooke, second edition, Calcutta and Simla: Thacker, Spink & Co., 1915: 138–39. In Madras, some sections of Paraiyans, referred to as 'village servants' or 'village officials' and called Vettiyans or Toties, did the work of skinning cattle carcasses as part of the labour services they performed for the village. Vettiyans were also responsible for grave-digging and scavenging. As Thurston observed: 'The Vettiyan is said to possess the right of removing dead cattle from villages, and in return to supply leather for agricultural purposes. He is further said to make drum heads and tom-toms from raw hides.' See E. Thurston, *Castes and Tribes of Southern India*, Vol. VII, Madras: Government Press, 1909: 392–94.

25 These castes came to be quite centrally identified in colonial ethnography with leather work despite its limited role in their labouring lives. Studies like R.V. Russell and Hiralal, *The Tribes and Castes of Central Provinces of India* (London: Macmillan and Co., 1916: 16), and the Gazetteers of Bombay confirm this fact. While recording historical evidence, however, the same reports and later writings (see G.W. Briggs, *The Chamars*, Calcutta: Calcutta Association Press, 1920) clearly recognized that the hide flayers were essentially agricultural labourers, and that skinning carcasses constituted a limited and even, at times, negligible component of their aggregate labouring lives.

26 *Papers Relating to the Crime of Cattle-Poisoning*, 1881: 27–28.

27 Writing about tanning in Punjab, Grant noticed as early as 1890 that there was an increasing tendency towards cash payment for work done by village artisans. In Gujranwala, in 1890, *sep* (the system of village service in Punjab) was dying out owing to 'high grain prices', and in Amritsar, 'village leather workers do very little tanning themselves. They either cure the skins roughly or send them into the city to be tanned, and the village mochis for their work buy leather already prepared in the city.' See A.J. Grant, *Monograph on the Leather Industry of the Punjab 1891–92*, Lahore: Civil and Military Gazette Press, 1893: 3. In the United Provinces too, Briggs observed that by 1920 the rights of Chamars 'in respect to hides are . . . being questioned and in some cases being denied altogether', and 'with the marked rise in values, hides and skins, except those of the very poorest quality are becoming more and more difficult for the Chamar to obtain'. See Briggs, *The Chamars*: 53. In Madras, the association of flayers with the work of flaying, and some control over hides and skins, remained alive. See Thurston, *Castes and Tribes of Southern India*, Vol. IV: 309–10; Vol. II: 2.

Guthrie reported in 1929 that cattle owners in Madras branded their cattle to make the hides 'valueless' because the hides of dead animals became 'the property of the members of the sweeper caste'. They told him that a live animal that could work, even though the skin was disfigured with brands, was worth more to them than a dead animal which belongs to 'someone else'. Written Statement of Mr. A. Guthrie, Leather Expert to the Government of Madras and Principal, Leather Trades Institute, *Report of Hides Cess Enquiry Committee,* Vol. II, Evidence, Calcutta: Superintendent of Printing, Government of India, 1930: 269. Evidence in official and academic studies, as well as in literature, shows the simultaneous coexistence in Madras as elsewhere, up till the late 1960s, of the practice of flaying as part of a village service, with the flayers (Vettiyans, Chakkiliyans and Madigas in Madras province) making leather goods for the cattle owners and disposing of the rest of the hides themselves, and, at the same time, cattle owners in other places charging money and paying workers to flay hides. See *Report on the Marketing of Hides*, 1943: 132; Perumal Murugan, *Seasons of the Palm,* translated by V. Geetha, Chennai: Tara Publishing, 2004; Gunnel Cederlof, *Bonds Lost: Subordination, Conflict and Mobilization in Rural South India, c. 1900–1970*, New Delhi: Manohar Publishers, 1997. Murugan and Cederlof record how in western Tamil Nadu these 'rights' over hides remained firmly in place well into the 1960s, but were tied to the persistence of some of the most intense forms of exploitation of the labour of the flayers and tanners.

28 Manser Chamar and Anr. vs Gajai Singh on 7/7/1917, Allahabad High Court; available at http://www.indiankanoon.org/doc/546100/.

29 Ibid.

30 Ibid.

31 Ibid.

32 Evidence from cases like the ones cited below shows that these questions remained relevant for very long. (1) 'In The SC of India Original Jurisdiction – WP No. 1969–70 of 1981 Hiralal and Ors (Petitioners) vs Zilla Parishad, Kanpur & Ors (Respondents). Order dated 1 May 1981 reads: The Court, citing that petitioners were Chamars, appointed Upendra Baxi and Mr Krishna Mahajan as a Commission to undertake a socio-legal investigation with a mandate to ascertain "who flay carcasses and the manner of doing it in Sarsaul district . . . and . . . the impact of the contract system on the lives of those who were originally carrying out the work".' (2) The case of Mohd. Yunus in United Provinces (In the SC of India, Civil Original Jurisdiction, CMP No. 1981, In Civil Writ Petition No. 1862 of 1981) raised the same issues. In Mohd. Yunus S/o Shri Imamuddin, Resident of Mohalla Kabuli Gate, Kasba Mawana, District Meerut UP Petitioner vs Zilla Parishad, Meerut UP, DM Meerut (as Administrator), District Panchayati Raj Adhikari, Meerut, State of UP, Anwar Ahmad, the Respondents asked for their 'age old rights to carry on their trade and business in skinning dead animals and in hides, bones, horns of dead animals by creating monopoly in favour of a contractor. . . . The petitioners cited that they were Chamars and had exercised these rights as such.' Both cases are cited in R.R. Prasad, 'Appendices', *Change and Continuity among the Scheduled Caste Leather Workers*, Hyderabad: National Institute of Rural Development, 1986.

33 *Watandari* was a system of village service prevalent in western India which was confirmed and codified under the Elphinstone Code of 1827. *Watandars* were village servants, ranging from the village priest, headman and accountant, carpenter, potter, etc., down to 'outcaste' village 'servants' like the Mahars. Each *watandar* was supposed to perform certain services and in turn was remunerated with a *watan*. The nature of the *watan* and the conditions of holding it varied, and *watans* were divided into 'superior' and 'inferior'.

34 Anupama Rao, *The Caste Question: Dalits and the Politics of Modern India*, Ranikhet: Permanent Black, 2009: 108. In some areas Mahars did not get land but only their

'share' of the produce (*baluta*) from peasants for the work they did for the village community.

35 Ibid.: 109.

36 'The Mahar's typical baluta (a customary share) was inedible food, used clothing, and the occasional handful of gain.' Ibid.: 108.

37 Ibid.; the twelve 'village servants' characteristic of this system that evolved in western India. Servants included those who performed the work of account-keeping, priests, barbers, watchmen and skinners of carcasses, among others.

38 Ibid.

39 Hiroyuki Kotani, 'Ati Sudra Castes in the Medieval Deccan', in Hiroyuki Kotani (ed.), *Caste System, Untouchability and the Depressed*, Japanese Studies on South Asia No. 1, New Delhi: Manohar Publishers, 1999: 60.

40 Another low-caste labouring group in the village, also considered 'untouchable' and hence having ritual sanction to work with leather.

41 Kotani, 'Ati Sudra Castes': 59–61. In the eighteenth century, socially dominant groups in particular villages occasionally sought to replace the Mahars with Mangs, for performing certain kinds of labour services. For skinning carcasses as well, it appears that there were instances of Mangs being 'recruited' and not Mahars, as evident in Parner village. See, G.C. Vad (ed.), *Selections from the Satara Rajas' and the Peshvas' Diaries*, Vol. VI, Poona and Bombay: 816, cited in Kotani, 'Ati Sudra Castes': fn. 5. Here it is shown that the Mahars appealed to the government when a dispute broke out between the 'peasants' and Mangs on the one hand, and Mahars on the other. The Mahars then appealed to the government asserting their customary and established rights and claims. Two of these demands are revealing: '1. When bulls and buffaloes . . . die in the village it is the custom that we Mahars take their hides except for those of plough bullocks . . . even though peasants have begun to dispute with us over the matter'; '3. When cattle of a Mang's house die, it is the custom that we Mahars take their hides and that mangs should not interfere with this.' It is evident from these demands that disputes over hides would have been germane to this conflict between Mahars on the one hand, and Kunbis and Mangs on the other. The government conducted an enquiry and found that the Mahars' claims in this instance were true.

42 Hiroyuki Kotani, 'Conflict and Controversy over the Mahar Watan in the Nineteenth–Twentieth Century Bombay Presidency', in Kotani (ed.), *Caste System, Untouchability and the Depressed*: 110–11 and fn. 6. Kotani cites evidence from Selected Decisions of the Court of Sudder Dewanee Adawlut of Bombay, Part II: 1848–1850, compiled by James Morris, 1852, pp. 68 ff to make his point. The evidence he presents includes several incidents. For instance, in 1849 a conflict arose in a village over access to hides of bullocks given by Babajee and other peasants to the village Mangs, rather than Suntoo and other Mahar *watandars*. The latter brought a suit for damages against the peasants for not giving them their 'rights'. Through a chequered career, the case was finally admitted to the highest court. There, however, it became clear that neither the Mahars nor the Kunbis in fact opposed customary practice – the Mahars, though they had brought the suit, did not object that the peasants had the right to take back the bullock hides (which they customarily controlled), and the peasants did not object to the Mahars having (customary) access to the hides and skins of other cattle and other animals.

43 Kotani, 'Conflict and Controversy': 112, citing Reports of Cases Decided in the High Court of Bombay, Vol. VIII (Appellate Civil Jurisdiction), 1871, pp. 28ff. The suit had been brought by two *watandar* Mahars of the village Bedzurgi, Bijaour [*sic*] Taluka, against two fellow *watandar* Mahars of the same village, concerning distribution of the perquisites of the Mahar *watan* among them.

44 Rao, *The Caste Question*: 109.

45 Bombay Hereditary Offices Act 1894, Section 18: 'When all or any of the property

of a village watan of lower degree than that of Patel or Kulkarni consists of a right to levy in money or of kind directly from individuals, it shall be lawful for the Collector, on the application of any person interested, to cause the nature and extent of rights and such right and of the duties to be performed, and the persons, families, or classes liable to make payment and to perform the duties, to be defined in writing by a panchayat of five persons, whereof two shall be appointed by the villagers, two by the watandars, and one, who shall be sar-panch by the Collector. The decision shall be in accordance with the opinion of the majority of the panchayat, provided that in case the villagers or the watandars fail to nominate members within seven days, the Collector shall appoint such members as may be required to constitute a panchayat of five:

Provided also that, in case the panchayat do not come to a decision within seven days from the appointment of the sar-panch, the Collector may himself pass a decision. The decision of the panchayat or the Collector, as above provided, shall be final and binding on all persons or classes, or rights, duties or liabilities have been submitted to such decision.'

46 Bombay Act No. III of 1874 (The Bombay Hereditary Offices Act 1874), Part X, Inferior Hereditary Offices Applying to offices lower than Patel or Kulkarni:

'64. 1[(1)] The Collector is empowered, subject to the general control of the Government

(d) to provide for and enforce the joint responsibility of the whole body for the neglect of duty or misconduct of any of their number of their representatives and in cases where the crime of cattle poisoning is prevalent, with the sanction of the Government, to attach during pleasure of the Government, the watans of the persons whom he may have reason to believe to have been guilty of, or to have connived at, the commission of the crime'.

47 Kotani, 'Conflict and Controversy': 116. 'F.S. Chapman summing up the purpose of the bill in the final discussion on 15 October 1874 remarked . . . "this principle of [joint] responsibility has been laid down for the first time in the case of the crime of cattle poisoning of which the mhars of the villages are often believed to be guilty, either from motives of revenge on account of non payment of their dues, or in order to obtain the skins of animals. This is a crime which is most difficult to detect and punish, and which entails the most ruinous consequences on the ryots. I believe the very guarded provision which we have made is most necessary, and I hope it may prove effectual."' Cited by Kotani from *Proceedings of the Council for the Governor of Bombay,* Vol. XIII, 1874: 56.

48 Letter no. 8087, Under Secretary to Bombay Government, Judicial Department, to Officiating Secretary to Government of India, Home, Revenue and Agriculture Department, 6 December 1880, in *Papers Relating to the Crime of Cattle-Poisoning*: 100.

49 Sumit Guha, 'Civilizations, Markets and Services: Village Servants in India from the Seventeenth to the Twentieth Centuries', *Indian Economic and Historical Review*, 41 (1), 2004: 95. Guha cites T.N. Atre, *Ganv Gada* (1915), reprint, Pune: Government of Maharashtra, 1991: 90, 96, 99–102. Atre wrote critically in his pro-Kunbi account, of the Mahars in Maharashtra villages bargaining for the *baluta* long after the villagers in Kaltan, Indapur, in Poona district, had been able to oust them from their 'rights' to these. The Mahars, in Atre's account, went around in a group in the villages, demanding their 'baluta': 'Going in a band means that argument, pressure and threat are deployed. . . . To sum up, claims of entitlement, friendly pleas, begging, flattery and pilferage follow each other like beads on the same thread.' If caught pilfering by an enraged farmer, Atre continued, 'the landless castes appeased him by saying, "Baliraja! We are your footwear! How can we fill our stomachs?" If that does not make him subside, these people say, "Well, well! Is it thus?" and utter words importing

bloodshed and mayhem. The poor farmer [Kunbi] fears that they may fulfill their threats by theft, by arson or by poisoning his cattle. So he perforce allows them to carry away what they have already pilfered.' This was perhaps not entirely true everywhere, given that Atre's work had been 'written exclusively from the landholders' point of view'. Guha cites Atre's description of the Mahars demanding *baluta* and adds: 'Atre presents a vivid but one-sided view of the situation. In reality, here as in North India, the balance of power was tilted in favour of the landowners, and the twentieth century saw a steady decline in the dues received by village servants' (ibid.: 96).

50 Poisoning of Cattle in Poona by the Mahars of Kalthan, Taluka Indapur, No. 149, 1880, Revenue Department, Government of Bombay, Maharashtra State Archives (henceforth MSA); Complaint of Cattle Poisoning by the Mahars of Sangamner, Ahmednagar, No. 1580, 1880, Revenue Department, Government of Bombay, MSA.

51 Letter from J. Ruig, Collector, Ahmednagar, to E.R. Robertson, Commissioner, Ahmednagar, 13 November 1880, Complaint of Cattle Poisoning by the Mahars of Sangamner, Ahmednagar, No. 1580, 1880, Revenue Department, Government of Bombay, MSA.

52 In many other parts of India, the absence of any alternative labouring group that would be able to 'extract' hides meant that the peasants had to be dependent on the Chamars (or other castes whose members could flay carcasses) even if they were able to establish their own claim over the carcasses of their animals.

53 Some of the Mahars went to court against the Kunbis and Mangs over these disputes. In some instances the courts referred the disputes back to be tried under Section 18 of the Watan Act, to be settled by a 'panchayat' appointed by the Collector or *mamlatdar*.

54 Kotani, 'Conflict and Controversy': 118–19. Kotani cites the case of Mahadu vs Krishna, *Indian Law Reports*, Bombay Series, Vol. 47: 95, fn. 12. As the case of Peth village in Satara district (1911) showed, in a dispute of the same type where dominant peasants simply gave the skins of dead animals to Mangs, intruding upon the rights of Mahars, and the Collector (*mamlatdar*) sought to set up a panchayat under Section 18, the conflict between the groups was so acute that they refused to agree on the composition of the panchayat. The *mamlatdar* then nominated the panchayat, which decided in favour of the Mahars. The peasants went to the High Court which found that the provisions of setting up the panchayat had been violated, hence the decision was found to be invalid. The Mahars lost their rights over hides in this village.

55 Rao, *The Caste Question*: Chapter 2.

56 Section 16, The Bombay Hereditary Offices Act, 1874.

57 Rao, *The Caste Question*: 114.

58 Ibid.

59 Ibid.: 111, where Rao cites from B.R. Ambedkar, 'Mahar Ani Tyanche Watan', *Bahishkrit Bharat*, 2 September 1927.

60 Ibid.: 112.

61 There is a contemporary postscript to the historic contest regarding customary rights over stigmatized hides and skins of hide flayers. The move towards abandonment of 'traditional' work like skinning carcasses became part of the Dalit movement especially in certain regions in the decades after independence. One of the consequences of this is a shortage of flayers leading to non-recovery of cattle carcasses, a matter of concern for the Ministry of Commerce and Industry as it directly affects the raw material for the leather industry. A recent report, 'All India Survey of Raw Hides and Skins', prepared by the Central Leather Research Institute (CLRI), Chennai, observes that the value of 'loss due to non-recovery of hides and skins is estimated at Rs 369 crores and loss due to non-recovery of by products as Rs 617 crores in the year 2003'. Further, 'the major cause for non recovery of fallen carcasses is the growing social awareness and stigma attached to the activity. The traditional system is obnoxious.' See *Report on All India Survey of Raw Hides and Skins*, prepared for Ministry of Commerce and

Industry, Chennai: Central Leather Research Institute, 2006: xiv. The report cites the 'lack of traditional flayers' as the most important reason responsible for the non-flaying of carcasses of dead animals, responsible for 42 per cent of the non-recovery. Maharashtra, Andhra Pradesh and Uttaranchal are the three states in India where there are now very few 'traditional flayers' (ibid.: 89).

62 Evidence of the persistence of these customary rights came from different regions. In 1930, the Director of Industries in Bombay, P.B. Advani, observed in his oral evidence before the Hides Cess Enquiry Committee that 'the practice in the rural areas is that dead cattle are thrown out. The owner notifies the local Mahar who drags and skins the animals. After disposing of the flesh the Mahar disposes of the skins or hides. The owner gets nothing. By custom the Mahar gets the hides and the skins'. See Oral Evidence of Mr P.B. Advani, Director of Industries, Bombay, in *Report of Hides Cess Enquiry Committee*, Vol. II, Evidence, 1930: 401. It may be pointed out that Advani was speaking over half a century after the cattle poisoning scare and the first widespread efforts by cattle owners to oust the Mahars from hide collection. This kind of prolonged persistence of these 'rights' despite efforts, administrative and judicial, to circumscribe and control them, could be seen in other parts of the country. In United Provinces, Briggs and others reported in 1920 that the rights of Chamars 'in respect to hides are now being questioned and in some cases being denied altogether' (see Briggs, *The Chamars*: 53). It was not till 1967 that customary rights were overthrown and a contractual system for collecting hides – selling the rights of collection to the highest bidder – introduced (see Prasad, *Change and Continuity:* 95–101).

63 Shahana Bhattacharya, 'Labour in the Leather Industry in India, 1870s–1970s', Chapters 2 and 5, unpublished Ph.D. dissertation, University of Delhi, Delhi, 2012.

64 Measures to prevent absconding workmen from factories, etc., in British India taking service in Native States, in Proceedings of Foreign and Political Department, Government of India, Nos. 191–96, (Internal B), June 1918, National Archives of India (henceforth NAI).

65 Terms of agreement executed by the employees in favour of the Company (Mahomad Yakoob Sahib and Sons, Pernambut), enclosure to Proc. No. 191, ibid.

66 Order, 30 September 1892, by C.A. Galton, Secretary, Revenue Department, Government of Madras, GO No. 1010, 1010 A, 1892, Tamil Nadu State Archives (henceforth TNSA). Out of these 848 were acquitted or discharged, while 246 and 34 respectively were ordered to work out the advance and return the advance. Of the 280 convicted, only 19 appealed. The convictions were quashed in the case of 16 persons and reference was made to the High Court regarding 3 persons with the result that the convictions were set aside. According to the correspondence in the GO, Mr Tremenheere, erstwhile Acting Collector of the district, had alleged that the Act was being widely and wrongfully used.

67 Ibid.

68 Measures to prevent absconding workmen from factories, etc., in British India taking service in Native States, in Proceedings of Foreign and Political Department, Government of India, Nos. 191–96, (Internal B), June 1918, NAI. The Workmen's Breach of Contract Act was one of the British Enactments that could be put in place in Mysore. Hyderabad was not covered by such a notification. The reference is to the Foreign and Political Department's notification No. 111, in British Enactments in Force in Native States, Vol. VI: 156.

69 Proceedings of Foreign and Political Department, Government of India, Nos. 191–96, (Internal B), June 1918, NAI.

70 Letter no. 1634, 2 March 1918, from H.V. Cobb, Resident in Mysore (PRO No. 192), to the Political Secretary to Government of India, in Proceedings of Foreign and Political Department, Government of India, Nos. 191–96, (Internal B), June 1918, NAI.

[71] Ibid.

[72] Ibid.

[73] Written evidence, 20 November 1917, Winess no. 314, R.J. Vimadalal, Leather Merchant, Leather Factory, Navsari, in *Indian Industrial Commission, Minutes of Evidence (1916–1918)*, Vol. IV, Calcutta: Superintendent, Government Printing.

[74] Oral evidence, 20 November 1917, Witness No. 314, R.J. Vimadalal, Leather Merchant, Leather Factory, Navsari, in *Indian Industrial Commission, Minutes of Evidence (1916–1918)*, Vol. IV, Calcutta: Superintendent, Government Printing: 258.

[75] Ibid.

[76] Ibid.

[77] S.V. Parulekar (Member, Servants of India Society, Bombay), *Tannery Labour in India* (booklet), File No. 9134 A, Industry and Labour Department, Government of Bombay, 1932, MSA.

[78] Written evidence, 20 November 1917, Witness no. 314, R.J. Vimadalal, Leather Merchant, Leather Factory, Navsari, *Indian Industrial Commission, Minutes of Evidence (1916–1918)*, Vol. IV, Calcutta: Superintendent, Government Printing: 256.

[79] Ibid. Vimadalal indicated that his workers tended to strike work similarly. Some of the earliest recorded official strikes in Madras, for instance, had adopted the same *modus operandi*. In 1931 Jamal Mahomed, member of the Royal Comission on Labour who had been associated with the tannery owners and leather industry, questioned Sivashanmugam Pillai of the Chingleput Labour Guild about this method used by the workers when they had struck work on 10 November 1928, in the Chingleput tannery cluster. The tone of questioning made it clear that Jamal Mahomed, asking questions on behalf of the Royal Commission of Labour, and member of the Southern India Chamber of Commerce, disapproved strongly of this method of protest in which workers had taken 'advantage of the presence of a large quantity of skins and hides in the factory which needed immediate attention' and struck work, thereby 'spoiling all the skins', which had put 'the proprietors to heavy losses'. The tanneries had subsequently closed down 'on account of heavy losses'. See Oral evidence, Mr. Sivashanmugam Pillai, Patron, The Chingleput District Labour Guild, Kodambakkam, in *Report, Royal Commission on Labour in India, Evidence*, Vol. VII, part 2, Madras Presidency and Coorg, 1931: 162–65.

[80] B.V. Narayanaswami Naidu, *Report of the Court of Enquiry into Labour Conditions in . . . Tanning Industry*, Madras: Government Press, 1947: 141.

[81] Ibid.: 141–43. Naidu further added that during the long notice period, 'the tanners may be allowed to restrict or stop altogether, soaking of hides and skins, but should pay the workers wages which should not fall below their average earnings per month in the three months prior to the issue of the strike notice. The level of wages must be kept up regardless of the availability or otherwise of work. In the meantime the grievances of workers must be referred to the Trade Board of the district.'

[82] Ibid.

[83] Ibid.: 137.

[84] GO No. 2997, Development Department, Government of Madras, 4 June 1948, TNSA. This became the norm in all judgments and decisions of the Industrial Tribunal at Madurai.

[85] The disputes adjudicated by the Industrial Tribunal on Tanneries and Leather Factories set up in Madurai in 1948, in accordance with Narayanaswami Naidu's report, were recorded in a number of Government Orders (GOs) of the Development Department, Madras (TNSA). For instance: GO No. 1349 (Ms), 18 March 1948; No. 587 (Ms), 6 February 1948; No. 2597 (Ms), 20 May 1948; No. 2861 (Ms), 29 May 1948; No. 2425 (Ms), 11 May 1948; No. 2424 (Ms), 11 May 1948; No. 2997 (P), 4 June 1948; No. 2525 (Ms), 17 May 1948; No. 1947 (Ms), 19 April 1948; No. 2591 (Ms), 20 May 1948; No. 3518 (Ms), 30 June 1948; No. 3677 (Ms), 10 July 1948; No. 3868,

(Ms), 22 July 1948; No. 3677 (Ms), 10 July 1948; No. 3868 (Ms), 22 July 1948; No. 3518 (Ms), 30 June 1948.

86 Memoranda on the Royal Commission on Labour in India from R.N. Gilchrist, Deputy Secretary to Government of Bengal, to Joint Secretary to the Royal Commission on Labour in India, File No. 3 C-1, 1929–30, Section IX – Hours, Commerce Branch, Commerce Department, Government of Bengal, West Bengal State Archives (henceforth WBSA): 76.

87 Ibid. The notification regarding the order was registered under 'Ben., Com., Notn. No. 5348 Com., of 27 September 1925'.

88 Ibid.: 9, 79: table, 'Exemptions applicable to individual industries'.

89 As estimated by Ahmad Mukhtar, *Report on Labour Conditions in Tanneries and Leather Goods Factories*, Simla: Government of India Press, 1946: 58. Even accounting for the expansion that took place during the war, the number of workers would have been far greater than the 489 listed here, possibly closer to 3,500 or 4,000. It becomes clear that about one-third of the workers in all these units were engaged in these tasks, and more or less continuously on call.

90 The Industrial Disputes Act, Act No. 14 of 1947, Section 10 (1).

91 Dispute between the workers and the managements of certain tanneries in Dindigul – Reference to the Industrial Tribunal, Madurai for adjudication, G.O. 4605, 9 October 1951, Development Department, Government of Madras, TNSA.

92 Petition from The Dindigul Skin Merchants' Association, Dindigul, to the Minister of Industries, Madras, 5 July 1951, Development Department, Government of Madras, TNSA.

93 Ibid.

94 Ibid.

95 Ibid.

96 Copy of the letter from the Labour Officer, Madurai, to the Commissioner of Labour, Madras, No. C.340/51, 6 August 1951, Development Department, Government of Madras, TNSA.

97 During the period of the ban on communists, local caste-based and militant workers' leaders had taken over. By 1951, when the ban on the communists was lifted, the leaders had returned, and the issue of a holiday on Sunday arose as a major issue then.

98 Interview with Y.S. Cinappan (96-year-old retired tannery worker), member of the Tannery Workers' Union and one of its founder members in 1940–42. Interviews conducted in March–April 2007, Dindigul, Tamil Nadu.

99 Ibid.

100 Naidu, *Report of the Court of Enquiry*: 128–29.

101 Sri Baktavatsalu Naidu, Industrial Tribunal vs The Chrome Leather Co. Ltd. and Anr., Madras High Court, 17 November 1948, available at http://indiankanoon.org/doc/1447636/7.

102 Interview with Shamsul Haq, an active union member and hydraulic press operator (semi-skilled) at Hobson tannery, Dhapa since 1985. The interview was taken at Meeting Ghar, Tangra–Dhapa in March 2006. The '*bakshish*', Shamsul said, also had a sense of a 'gift' given in return for good behaviour and good service.

103 Letter no. 1290, from J.H. Tremenheere, Collector of Chingleput District, to Commissioner of Revenue Settlement and Director of the Department of Land Records and Agriculture, Madras, October 1891, enclosing Tremenheere's 'Note on the Pariahs of Chingleput', pp. 12–16 of the Note: 'The Pariah as an Agricultural Labourer'. These points of the remuneration received were accepted by the Board of Revenue's response to Tremenheere: GO. 1010, 1010 A, Revenue, Government of Madras, 30 September 1892, TNSA.

104 Ibid.: 15.

[105] Strike reports from the Madras Presidency for the year 1929, in File no. L 878 (16), Industries and Labour, Labour Branch, Government of India, 1930, NAI. See: From J. Gray, Commissioner of Labour, Madras, to Secretary, Government of India, Department of Industries and Labour, Simla, 24 October 1929; Letter no. D-1-5070/29, Labour-Strikes-Tiruvottiyur Tannery / submits copy of letter ROC No 11312-29-B-3, 23 October 1929 from Collector of Chingleput to the Commissioner of Labour, Madras; Strike–Labour–Friction between employers and employees; and also Copy of letter no. ROC 11795-29-B-3, 26 November 1929 from the DM, Chingleput, to the Commissioner of Labour, Madras, Labour-Strike-Tiruvottiyur Tannery – Your letter D-1-No. 5070/29, 19 November 1929.

[106] Dispute between the workers and managements of tanneries in Dindigul – Interim recommendation of the Industrial Tribunal, GO No. 2997, Development Department, Government of Madras, 4 June 1948, TNSA.

[107] Extract from fortnightly Confidential report for the second half of October 1948 (Labour Situation Report), Office of the Commissioner of Labour, Chepauk, Madras, Report of Chingleput District, GO 781, Development Department, Government of Madras, 17 February 1949, TNSA.

[108] Ibid., Labour Situation Report for the first fortnight of February 1948, Office of the Commissioner of Labour, Chepauk, Madras, Report of Coimbatore District, Development Department, Government of Madras, 17 February 1949, TNSA.

[109] Sri Baktavatsalu Naidu, Industrial Tribunal vs The Chrome Leather Co. Ltd, Madras High Court, 17 November 1948: 11, available at http://indiankanoon.org/doc/1447636/7.

[110] Naidu, *Report of the Court of Enquiry*: 135–36.

[111] Ibid.: 135.

[112] Ibid.

[113] Ibid.: 136–37.

[114] Workers of Hajee Abdullah and Co. tannery in Kodambakkam, Chingleput district, Madras, struck work in September 1937 because a cooly had been assaulted by a *maistry*. The coolies agreed to end the strike only if the management stopped using abusive language or physical force. See Report of Commissioner of Labour and and Rural Uplift, C.A Henderson, to Government of India, Secretary, Department of Industries and Labour, New Delhi, Strikes for period ending 22 October 1937, Labour strikes and lockouts, Madras Presidency, Weekly Reports 1937, G.O. No 448, Development Department, Government of Madras, 21 February 1938, TNSA. One of the clauses in the resolution of the strike of the first Tannery Workers Union in Tangra–Dhapa, Calcutta, in 1944, was that ill-treatment of workers must be stopped. The management inserted a clause demanding that workers should also behave properly and not 'take undue advantage over their employers'. See Mukhtar, *Report on Labour Conditions in Tanneries*: 81. The Industrial Tribunal on tanneries and leather factories in Madurai in 1948, adjudicating an industrial dispute between tannery owners and workers in Dindigul, upheld the workers' demand for proper behaviour towards workers by proprietors and *maistries*: Interim Award by Industrial Tribunal of Madura, GO 2997, Development Department, Government of Madras, 4 June 1948, TNSA.

[115] A.C. Chatterton, *A Monograph on Tanning and Working on Leather in the Madras Presidency*, Madras: Government Press, 1904, Chapter 1, cited the Report of the Madras Exhibition of 1855.

[116] In the case of Bengal, these processes and their underlying bias against 'outcaste' average workers, Chamars from Bihar, who worked in the tanneries can be seen in a study of reports of the Directors of Industries in Bengal, Agriculture and Industries Department, Industries Branch, Government of Bengal, WBSA. For evidence regarding these courses of study and the ways in which the workmen were left out of the project

of training, see: Imperial Tanning Institute, 3–27, B, April 1921, Agriculture and Industries Department, Industries Branch, Government of Bengal, WBSA; Letter No. 86 D.I. (G), 8 January 1926, from Director of Industries, Bengal, submitting proposal for the introduction of a two-year diploma course in leather manufacture at the Bengal Tanning Institute, Progs. Nos. 1–5, Agriculture and Industries Department, Industries Branch, Government of Bengal, March 1929, WBSA. The concern with ensuring that the *bhadralok* entered the leather industry can be seen most clearly in: File No. I. 5E-3/B April 1923/Nos. 173-175, 1922, Agriculture and Industries Department, Industries Branch, Government of Bengal, WBSA. In the case of Madras, the debates recorded in files of the Development Department, TNSA, map the trajectory of industrial training in leather production and the history of the Leather Trades Institute. The main debates are recorded in Notes to GO No. 148, Development, Government of Madras, 25 January 1923 and in GO No. 137, Development, Government of Madras, 25 January 1924, TNSA.

117 Ibid.

118 Report of the Leather Industry Committee, G.O. No. 137, Development Department, Government of Madras, 25 January 1924, TNSA: 59.

119 Interview, Y.S. Chinappan, Dindigul, March–April 2007.

120 Interviews with Y.S. Chinappan, A. Thangaraj and Munnusami, retired tannery workers and union members (Tannery Workers Union) from the 1940s to 1970s, Dindigul, March–April 2007.

121 Mukhtar, *Report on Labour Conditions in Tanneries*: 81.

122 Interviews with Inderdev Warispuri, Headmaster, Ravidas High School, and Shukul Ram, Tannery Mazdur Union leader, at Meeting Ghar, Tangra, Calcutta, December 2007.

123 Das was the Manager of the National Tannery and also, later, Superintendent of the Bengal Tanning Institute. Cf. Notes on the Tanning Industry in Bengal and the Bengal Tanning Institute for the Hides Cess Committee, B.M. Das, Superintendent, Bengal Tanning Institute, in *Report of the Hides Cess Enquiry Committee, Evidence,* Vol. II, 1930: 112–29.

124 Naidu, *Report of the Court of Enquiry*: 136–37.

125 Ibid.

126 Mukhtar, *Report on Labour Conditions in Tanneries*: 81.

127 Interview, Inderdev Warispuri, Meeting Ghar, Tangra, Calcutta, December 2007.

128 Statistical Abstract relating to British India (from 1840–1865; 1860–1869; 1867/8–76/7; 1876/7–85/6), London: Her Majesty's Stationery Office, 1867, 1870, 1878, 1887, available at http://dsal.uchicago.edu/statistics/, accessed on 6 June 2011.

129 Ibid.

130 Nos. 191–96, (Internal B), Proceedings, Foreign and Political, Government of India, June 1918, NAI.

A Freedom Still Enmeshed in Servitude

The Unruly 'Lascars' of the *SS City of Manila* or, a Micro-History of the 'Free Labour' Problem

Ravi Ahuja

The Problem

'Free labour', it has been convincingly argued for decades, is inadequate *as a descriptive term* for the purpose of providing a clear dividing line between labour relationships germane to industrial capitalism and those of other social formations. A binary model that categorizes historic labour forms as either 'free' or 'unfree' can maintain its sheen only if kept at a remove from the complexity that empirical research into any specific historical labour regime is likely to dig up. While the availability and expansion of a formally 'free' and therefore mobile wage labour force has been a structurally necessary as well as empirically proven underpinning of the development of the capitalist world economy, historical research has brought out with equal clarity that labour regimes under capitalism have consistently combined various labour forms of diverse historical origin in multiple and complex ways. Crucially, the long-term persistence and adaptability of these heterogeneous combinations does not permit to make light of them as marginal phenomena or temporary aberrations from a set linear trajectory towards universal 'free labour', even if the term is understood in its strictly limited formal sense.[1] Instead, the historical evidence available at present appears to resonate with Rosa Luxemburg's claim that the continuation of capitalist accumulation required an ongoing 'metabolism' with precapitalist social formations as an external 'milieu':[2] the continued reproduction and reinvention, in new commodified forms, of labour relations that were, like slavery, unrelated in their origin to capital may be conceived of as one such 'metabolic' process – a process resulting in the continued reproduction of structurally heterogeneous labour regimes.

While historic labour regimes thus show little inclination to abide to easily memorable binary models, it has proved difficult, at the same time, to fully relinquish the free/unfree distinction as a *conceptual tool for analytical purposes*. This difficulty, experienced by many scholars, is arguably due to the fact that the free/unfree distinction is reflective of the tensions and contradictory pulls that inhere every known labour relationship, whether based on contract or not. It is reflective, in other words, of the historically specific *political* conditions that impact in several concrete ways on the constitution of 'labour' (or 'service') as social relationships. Marx hinted at this phenomenon when he famously observed that a 'historical and moral element' inflected the determination of the value of labour power.[3] Hence, as a social relationship, 'labour' is generated in a contradictory field of forces through the exertion of power and counter-power, each force seeking to enhance levels of heteronomy or autonomy, higher degrees of subordination or, indeed, of freedom. This tension is never *fully* resolved, even though the very constitution of 'labour' indicates that an unequal, dependent social relationship, i.e. the subordination of the worker under the employer, has been established successfully for the time being. For this structural reason, I argue, the 'freedom' issue has been and continues to be a major site of conflict between employers/masters and workers/servants across a wide spectrum of historical contexts involving a large variety of labour forms.

In South Asian historiography, however, the unbroken hegemony of a highly adaptable culturalist paradigm and an exaggerated reliance on high- or medium-level official materials have entailed that this site of conflict has rarely been explored. Historians like Gyan Prakash have even discarded the concept of labour 'freedom' as alien and irrelevant to the South Asian context, reducing it to a culturally specific trope of European enlightenment discourses.[4] Much can be learned in this respect from social historians working on former slave societies of the Atlantic rim who have gained new perspectives on the problem by tearing down the sub-disciplinary fence between histories of slavery and labour. Brazilian historians have emphasized, for instance, that no clear-cut division existed between slaves and 'freed' workers with regard to the utilization of extra-economic coercion throughout the nineteenth century. At the same time, however, they have stressed that the ambivalence of the concept of 'freedom' indicated sharp social conflict, resulting in contradictory renderings of the very concept: if employers, slave owners and the state sought to delimit and contain the meaning of 'freedom', slaves and 'freed' ex-slaves had their own take. As importantly, these historians have demonstrated that the 'freedom' slaves sought to achieve and that freed men sought to preserve was an aspiration they held on to doggedly despite the high costs involved and in defiance of the 'structural precariousness' of the 'freedom' achievable through manumission.[5] The precariousness, limitedness, even spuriousness of experienced 'freedom' did not imply, in this context, its ground-level irrelevance as a social category. The Brazilian findings suggest, in my view, that the prevalence, in many parts of the world, of indictments by social or labour movements of '(wage) slavery' or, in the Indian context, of '*gulami*' or '*gulamgiri*', should not be categorized too quickly in purely discursive terms as 'concept metaphors', and much less as minor 'subaltern' discourses exclusively derived from and fully encased within a hegemonic discourse of bourgeois liberalism.[6] Nor should evidence for the everyday vernacular use of concepts of freedom and slavery (for instance, that the recruitment of plantation labour was referred to as 'selling' in some parts of early twentieth-century India [7]) be passed over by historians without exploring the specific social contexts from which such concepts emerged and gained their plausibility.

Other attempts to overcome the inadequacies of binary models have fallen back upon older conceptualizations of the world of labour. Robert Steinfeld has shown that in Anglo-American political discourse, a fundamental distinction between 'free' and 'unfree' labour slowly replaced, from the late eighteenth century onwards, an earlier conception of the world of labour as a '*continuum of unfreedom*'.[8] In recent labour historiography, the now clearly discernible empirical untenability of the 'free/unfree' binary model, and of related assumptions of linear, homogenizing progress from formally unfree to formally free labour under capitalism, appear to have prompted a revitalization of this older notion of a finely graded continuum, if in more sophisticated forms. In what is probably the clearest exposition of this view, Marcel van der Linden thus argues that 'there is an almost endless variety of producers in capitalism, and the intermediate forms between the different categories are fluid rather than sharply defined'.[9] He seeks to capture a 'subtle range of variations' and develop a 'new typology' allowing further differentiation, i.e. a nuanced continuum of many shades.[10] I concede that the notion of the 'continuum' resonates strongly with the variegated material that empirical studies of labour history are likely to unearth, and I readily admit to have extensively relied on the idea of a 'continuum of "free" and "unfree" forms of organizing labour' in my own earlier work.[11] Of late, however, I feel increasingly doubtful of this notion of a fluid 'labour continuum', for typologies based on this notion conceptually arrange forms of socially organized labour along an uninterrupted horizontal line stretching from 'freedom' to 'unfreedom'.

Accordingly, 'freedom' and 'unfreedom' are implicitly reduced to quantifiable units in order to determine the precise location of each labour form on the freedom/unfreedom axis (labour form x = 100 = y 'free'/contractual labour + z 'unfree'/coerced labour). This procedure can be refined but not transcended by presenting the various labour forms on a two-dimensional plane rather than on a one-dimensional axis.[12] It remains taxonomic in its approach and implies the tendency to represent 'labour' as a relatively stable *thing* in (Cartesian) space, as opposed to a *relationship* whose contradictions unfold over time. In historical labour regimes, however, the various labour forms appear to be frequently posited against each other, intercalated or interlocked in contradictory, dynamic and productive ways: workers have frequently combined, at one time and with the assent or against the opposition of their employers, various forms of economic activity individually or as a household. During their working lives, large segments of the workforce have been moving, under diverse historical conditions, in and out of various labour forms, of their own accord and/or in response to economic or political coercion. Crucially, and this is what I am here mainly concerned with, workers and/or their employers have also been known to stretch a labour form to the point of turning it into another, qualitatively distinct form.

According to Steinfeld, the notion of the labour continuum, in its original sixteenth-century form, was developed to depict a hierarchical social order deemed legitimate, not to reflect upon it critically.[13] By arranging social types along a sliding scale, present-day renderings of this idea may inadvertently also suggest a stable parallelism, and conceal tensions, collisions, deflections and transformations within a historic labour regime. More specifically, by emphasizing the 'fluidity' between forms of socially organizing labour, such models may risk underplaying the importance of free/unfree distinctions for the definition of lines of conflict in quotidian, micro-political interactions over the formation of labour relations, and for demarcating boundaries between what appear as acceptable and unacceptable forms of dependency to workers in specific historical contexts.

Hence the notion of 'labour continuum' as well as other spatializing modes of representing historical labour regimes render it more difficult to perceive and come to terms with the 'historical and moral' or essentially *political* element in the constitution of labour relations: the very neatness of the typological sliding scale from freedom to unfreedom comes in the way of understanding the seemingly chaotic struggle that unfolds in assertion of a 'freedom which is still enmeshed in servitude'[14] – the unceasing confrontation from which historical labour relations emerge and are reproduced in the everyday. In much of the relevant literature, on South Asian labour at least, the term 'freedom' has accordingly been reduced to its articulations as an *abstract* analytical or high-level normative concept, while its *concretized* and practical articulations in micro-political conflicts over the constitution of labour relationships have remained unexplored.

This essay attempts to gauge the potential of the concept of 'freedom' as a lens for the analysis *not* of major labour mobilizations for state-level political demands, but of inconspicuous, usually unrecorded conflicts at the shopfloor level over the production and reproduction of 'labour' as a social relationship. In order to provide material for this exercise of conceptual concretization, the following section presents a simple micro-historical narrative which is based, in the main, on a rare account of a series of shipboard struggles on a British merchant steamer during World War I, whose main protagonists were an Indian engine-room crew and their 'white' officers. In the last section, we will return to the theoretical issue of 'free labour' with the objective of developing theoretical devices for the analysis of this account.

The Unruly 'Lascars' of the *SS City of Manila*

In the early spring of 1916, a largely Punjabi engine-room crew reached London on the *SS Newby Hall*, a medium-sized cargo 'tramp' steamer owned by the Ellerman City Line, one of the major British shipping concerns. The engine-room crew had joined the ship in Colombo and was utterly exhausted after a voyage rendered unusually laborious by the need to zigzag in heavy weather all the way from the Suez to Britain in avoidance of German submarines. They hoped for a month's break in London, where the ship was to be inspected and repaired after the discharge of its cargo of Burmese rice.[15] Yet this hope was soon dispelled. Indian crews sailed as so-called 'lascars' on Asiatic Articles, contracts that differed from those of European sailors on many counts. One of these differences consisted in a clause stipulating that the contract could not be terminated outside India. If a vessel carrying a South Asian crew did not return to the subcontinent after its outward voyage, the 'lascars' were to be transferred to another ship, even against their will, to work their way back to Bombay, Calcutta or another Indian port. Indeed, in an official enquiry it had been stated as one of the advantages of employing 'lascars' rather than European seamen, that the former were allegedly 'very convenient and amenable to transfer from one ship to another'.[16] Three days after the arrival of the *SS Newby Hall*, twenty of its Punjabi engine-room men were accordingly informed to get ready for transfer to another vessel.

The group included a sixteen-year-old coal passer from a remote mountain village in the Rawalpindi region. This boy, Amir Haider Khan, would eventually turn into an underground communist militant, hounded for years by the British Central Intelligence Department in India, twice convicted to long prison sentences by the colonial regime – in 1932 and again in 1939 – and later, repeatedly, by its Pakistani successor state. Struggling with the mental strain of imprisonment, Amir Haider Khan embarked on a pursuit that may well have appeared neither feasible nor urgent to a person of his educational and social background under more workaday circumstances. He began to write about – as he put it in the first sentence of his reminiscences of childhood and youth – 'something in which one has never taken any interest', namely the unfolding of his own life's trajectory.[17] The most extensive of his autobiographical manuscripts was written in British–Indian prisons during his second prison term between 1939 and 1942. It was written in a rugged English, acquired in the main during the 'American decade' of his life (1917–26), when he toiled on American merchant ships for five years and then roamed the United States working and attending evening schools in various industrial towns. These 'scribblings', as he called them, emerged in a laborious process. They were first drafted on a slate, then transcribed by himself on to paper and finally turned, after his release from prison and with the help of formally educated admirers, into a typed and edited manuscript of 946 pages.[18] The manuscript avoided, for obvious reasons, a discussion of the political activities he was being prosecuted for. They provided instead, inspired perhaps by Maxim Gorky's famous autobiographical novels, a detailed narrative of his childhood and youth up to the age of twenty-five.

The narrative includes an unusually graphic account of the transfer of Amir Haider Khan and his fellow crewmen from the *SS Newby Hall* and of the ensuing conflict-ridden sea voyage. Many of the tensions and confrontations related in this account were far from exceptional; very similar shipboard conflicts were reported in official sources, though usually as isolated, decontextualized, apparently random incidents and in a format that muted the seafarers' voices. Amir Haider Khan's narrative is unique only in that it allows insights into the quotidian world of maritime labour *as sequentially experienced and interpreted* by an Indian seafarer in the early part of the twentieth century, thus providing specific contexts and references for otherwise opaque or even unintelligible incidents. While all general limitations of memory-based ego documents apply, Amir Haider Khan's radical candour and politico-ethical sense of full accountability induced him to attempt an explicit separation of a scrupulous rendition of his experiences from occasional reflections emerging from his later intellectual and political development. Accordingly, he did not spare ugly details, and confessed to partaking in dispositions and practices even if they appeared undiscerning, fallacious or – like the consumption of commodified sex or racist attitudes against African-Americans – deeply repulsive to the author at the time of writing.[19]

The following account is mainly based on the pages of these memoirs dedicated to the author's voyage on the *SS City of Manila* but draws on additional materials where necessary. I have divided the account into five episodes, which will be contextualized and discussed in the concluding section of the essay.

The Ship 'meant every thing'

> Hence twenty of us were ordered to get ready immediately. Indeed there was nothing for us to get ready except to wash off some black and dirt of the flues and boilers with which our whole bodies were covered from top to toe. However we were ready within two hours after bathing and changing into some clean cotton overall or ordinary linen clothes which are used by poor Punjabis in streets of Bombay. Unfortunately it was not Bombay, but it was London; that too, in the earlier spring when still there was cold. But it could not be helped since we had nothing else to put on. In the meantime, there came near the ship down in the dock an open horse waggon in which we had to load all our dirty beddings, mats, the ugly looking wooden boxes and all other paraphernalia. Shortly we were ordered off from the ship down in to the dock [*sic*]. From there we had to follow behind the horsewaggon, which was loaded with our belongings, through some of the London streets without knowing as to where we were going. But in the olden days the galley slaves were never told about their destination. In the eyes of our civilized British masters we were not any better.
>
> With our troubled, starved and clumsy appearance, with our heterogeneous cotton clothes, and with the dissimilar footwear and head

> gears, with our bed-bug-ridden beddings, mats, boxes and other things on the waggon (and behind it our procession!) we were an awful scene.
>
> But we appeared very amusing to the civilized Londoners, who grinned and some even openly laughed at us, as if we were an object of ridicule and fun-making and some street urchins even followed us some distance as if we were a circus or a carnival.[20]

The inability of Indian seafarers to terminate their labour contracts in a foreign port not merely contributed to conferring on them the structural status of a coerced, bound workforce. It also implied, in this case, the humiliation of being paraded through the streets in a condition that rendered exclusion and subordination highly visible. In Amir Haider Khan's narrative, the metaphor of the 'galley slave' or 'chattel slave', the notion of experienced unfreedom, seems central and recurs frequently. It is employed to highlight the colonial dimensions of the 'lascar's' labour relationship,[21] as well as employer practices that kept the 'lascar' in the dark by denying him even the most basic information, for instance the ship's destination.

The group found themselves transferred by train to West Hartlepool, a port town in northeast England, where they were to supplement the Indian engine-room crew of a considerably larger, newly built cargo steamer, the *SS City of Manila* (7,452 GRT), that was likewise owned by the Ellerman City Line.[22] The crew was comprised of almost one hundred men in total, the majority of which were Indians, while deck crew and officers were European. The first stage of its maiden voyage was to cross the Atlantic in order to load a new cargo mainly comprising of kerosene in New York, then traverse the Panama Canal to reach India on a circuitous route via Vladivostok, Yokohama, Shanghai, Manila and Singapore. The twenty men from the *SS Newby Hall* had no inkling of all this when they reached West Hartlepool after a day without food.[23] Amir Haider Khan remembered their mood as follows:

> Due to sudden transfer to unknown destination while on the way in the train, our feelings, our doubts, our fears, and our mental reactions and speculations were similar to those of a group of Indian prisoners who often are in the same way transferred from one jail to some other jail in the country without informing them where they are being taken to.
>
> Hence, just as we entered the quarters our first question to the men (who had already woken up due to the noise) was 'How is the ship'. *It meant every thing* [emphasis added]: the working and living conditions and the official treatment to the men. In the same way, the first question a newly transferred prisoner would ask to another one when he gets a chance would be, 'How is the jail'.[24]

'*It meant every thing*' – the ship was, in other words, more than a site of the real subsumption of labour under capital. It was, as Markus

Rediker put it, a 'totalitarian work environment'.[25] The ship was a space where the real fiction of a separation of labour power from the process of human life was more transpicuous than elsewhere: the extraction of labour power implied, in more radical, immediate and unconcealed forms than at other worksites, an effort at controlling the worker's existence *in toto*. Amir Haider Khan's comparison of ship and prison should not be discounted as mere rhetoric. A sense of intense existential confinement had been tangible on his preceding voyage on the *SS Newby Hall* when a desperate fireman had attempted to drown himself in the Red Sea after being punished for seeking temporary relief at deck from the oppressive heat of the engine room. 'Such incidents are not rare among Indian seafaring men', commented Amir Haider Khan.[26] Suicides among South Asian engine-room men on board ship were in fact frequent enough to be recognized as a larger phenomenon in British and even German shipping records.[27] The British consul at Suez noted, for instance, in 1904 that fifteen such suicides had been reported to him within two years. He reasoned that the 'lascar' was 'practically . . . a prisoner on board', thereby using the same analogy as Amir Haider Khan for pointing out the strong sense of spatial and social confinement among steamship crews.[28]

The 'Serang' Incident

'*How the ship was*', the twenty men found out the same evening. Their new shipmates informed them of acute conflicts with the *serang*, the Indian boatswain, and his followers who attempted to extract payments from the other members of the crew.[29] *Serangs* were the maritime version of the Indian jobber or *sardar*: they doubled as recruiters and boatswains, as labour subcontractors and supervisory staff. In order to be given the job of recruiting a crew, a *serang* had to bribe port officials and European ship's officers – expenses they needed to recover from the seafarers in addition to a share they appropriated themselves. Balachandran and the present writer have written extensively on the contradictory position of the *serang* and on the structure of informal payments in the Indian maritime labour market,[30] while the role of 'jobbers' in other industries has been a core concern of Indian labour historiography.[31] Suffice it for our present argument to refer to Amir Haider Khan's memoirs, where he calculated that more than half of the annual earnings of a seafarer employed from Bombay had to be 'invested' as follows: two months' wages went to the *serang* at the beginning of the voyage, another two to the *derawala* or boarding house keeper, yet another two were spent on the loan that had enabled the sailor to reach Bombay for employment and on the expenditures incurred for returning to the village. In addition, a full monthly wage was needed for work clothes, soap and other items required for work but not provided for by the employer.[32]

If this structure of payments had assumed a status of contested normalcy, as reflected in the use of the term '*dasturi*' (customary payment),[33] the engine-room *serang* of the *SS City of Manila* raised demands that were deemed excessive and unacceptable by the engine-room crew. For, after the transfer to the new cargo steamer, he and his ring of supporters had apparently pressed for an additional 'collection' of dues from the rest of the crew. The latter now hoped to change the equations of power in the engine room by winning over the newcomers from the *SS Newby Hall*. According to Amir Haider Khan's account, a consensus was soon reached that the *serang* was a hopeless case and needed to be removed from his position of power by collective action.[34]

How difficult and risky this decision seemed to the crew is indicated by their unlikely choice of a spokesman: the youngest member of the crew was apparently chosen – a boy whose physical development, as Amir Haider Khan observed of himself in hindsight, had been slowed down by malnutrition and early toil.[35] In his memoirs, he remembered to have had a reputation of hot-headedness (wielding an iron rod, he had forced a *serang* on a previous voyage to return coerced 'bribes'[36]) and of being fluent in English (though he had merely picked up a few words during his deployment among British troops in Basra in 1915).[37] Both reasons are instructive – the distinction of being 'hot-headed' or '*sar-garam*' qualified for shopfloor leadership under conditions of coercive labour regimes, as Zafar Shaheed has argued perceptively for a later Pakistani context.[38] Using a reckless youngster as a frontman may thus have appeared to be a device of risk mitigation to more experienced workers who felt that they were forced to turn, despite their fears, against a *serang* who could rely on backing from the employer as well as from the state authorities in a British port. The ability of making oneself understood even in the most rudimentary English was, furthermore, clearly of paramount importance under circumstances where English was the language of contract and negotiation with the authorities, while only two of the Indian crew members, including young Amir, appear to have been literate even in their own language.[39]

The following day saw a scuffle between the *serang* and one of the more 'hot-headed' Indian seafarers, resulting in a slight facial injury of the latter. The 'anti-*serang*' group had waited for such an occasion; they immediately downed their tools and forced their way off the ship despite futile attempts on the part of officers, quarter masters and other European crew to block the gangway. In effect, the protesters apparently carried along most of the Indian engine-room men. In a short meeting they agreed to demand the removal of the *serang* from the ship and elected Amir Haider Khan as their sole spokesman, deciding at the same time that no one else was to respond to any question directed at them.[40] The effortlessness and flexibility with which an elementary device of self-organization for conflict was thus recurred to by the crew should not be lost – an effortlessness that is difficult to reconcile with the once influential hypothesis that Indian workers could articulate themselves politically solely in a primordial language of '*ma–bap*' paternalism.[41]

The crew then proceeded, under the indifferent eyes of onlooking

English dockers,[42] to the Shipping Master's Office, where they 'spontaneously stood at attention in two straight rows, with silent but grim faces, as if we were ready for a military drill'[43] – again a canny, 'untraditional' form of expressing their protest through an ambivalent display that provided cover against the accusation of breach of regular discipline, while at the same time applying pressure on the authorities by turning this discipline against them. In response to the Shipping Master's paternalistically phrased question – 'What is the matter, boys'[44] – Amir somehow managed to convey that a crewman had been injured by the *serang*. Ordered to return to the ship, he recounted to have made his point with admirable precision and economy of words: 'Serang shore – me ship. Serang ship – me shore.'[45] The Shipping Master's attempts to break up the group by addressing other crewmen and to browbeat them by calling in a bulky policeman failed. Eventually, the elderly shipmaster of the *SS City of Manila* entered the scene and tried to communicate with various crew members in the simplified 'sailor's Hindustani' or '*lascari bat*' that served as a language of command on British merchant ships.[46] When all efforts to cajole the crew back on to the ship remained fruitless, the following exchange occurred, according to Amir's memoirs:

> . . . the captain while facing us asked 'Bager Sarang hum jahaz kaisa chalayega' (without a Serang how can I run the ship?). I immediately replied to the captain in Hindustani that 'we will give you another sarang'. Again he asked 'Kahan hai dusra sarang?' (where is the other sarang?) I at once pointed with my finger towards the senior water-tender by name Rehma[n] who was standing in the front row. The captain moved just before him and asked him in Hindustrani 'kya tum sarang?' (What! You a sarang). The senior water-tender who was close to six feet in height and [a] well-built stalwart wrestler from the rural area of the Gujrat district of Punjab replied by nodding his head. Since the captain had no alternative thereupon half-heartedly he accepted our candidate for the sarang's post and ordered us back to the ship.[47]

On reaching the quay, the captain sought to renege on his promise, but the crew refused to re-enter the ship until the deposed *serang* had physically left the vessel with his baggage.[48] Amir Haider Khan commented himself that 'the peculiar situation at that time was responsible for our success'.[49] Indeed, British ship authorities agreeing to the election of a *serang* by an Indian crew and removal of their own man would have been an unlikely outcome under conditions other than those of an extreme wartime scarcity of maritime labour. Even under war conditions, the shipmaster's handling of the situation may well have seemed unfortunate in hindsight from the perspective of the ship's bridge and the shipping company's office: we shall see that the crew never returned to the level of 'docility' that British shipowners expected from the Indian 'lascar', and the Ellerman City Line saw itself ultimately saddled with higher labour costs. When the same company was confronted in Salford five years later with a very similar conflict on the *SS City of Shanghai*, the owners decided not only to transfer the *serang* and four of his relatives to the *SS City of Lahore*, but also to break up the recalcitrant crew and transfer part of it to yet another vessel.[50]

Working Hours and the Question of Obedience

To resume our story, the maiden voyage of the *SS City of Manila* was interspersed with a series of covert tensions and overt conflicts between its Indian engine-room crew and the ship's officers. While crossing the Atlantic, the new machinery needed to be worked in and had to be stopped repeatedly requiring the repair work of the British engineers and the Indian oilers. Amir Haider Khan noted that the firemen and coal passers who tended to the boilers were of little use during these repairs, but would have been compelled to remain in attendance in the engine room under normal circumstances 'because the Sarangs force them to do so.' Yet as the *serang* had been removed, the crew actually worked according to a shift rhythm of four hours work followed by eight hours rest.[51] This was a significant difference. No labour law regulated the working hours of Indian seafarers;[52] informal mechanisms of control did, with the labour intermediary as the key institution. 'In a British ship which carries an Indian crew,' wrote Amir Haider Khan, 'it is a sarang through whom the authorities make man [*sic*] work for unlimited hours.'[53] Even though the extremely strenuous work in the engine room could only be physically endured for *limited* (in the best case, four) hours without rest,[54] the practice of arbitrarily demanding unpaid services outside the usual working hours and in the absence of situations of emergency was an assertion of claims to subservience: it underlined that 'lascars' were *always* compelled to obedience.[55] The removal of the company-chosen *serang* had thus deprived the ship's officers of a potentially powerful disciplinary tool. Consequently, the engine-room crew, during the remainder of the voyage, 'flatly refused to do any extra work outside our shift, which was not connected with the running on sea'[56] – an important qualification to which we shall return.

The Quarantine Incident

While the crew's refusal to work extra hours without pay does not seem to have escalated to open conflict despite some shouting between the elected *serang* and the officers,[57] another critical incident occurred when the *SS City of Manila* reached the port of Vladivostok, forty-five days after entering the Pacific from the Panama Canal. The engine-room crew was keenly expecting to be granted land leave in accordance with their 'articles', but the Russian authorities decided not to take down the yellow quarantine flag after the usual medical inspection. Nevertheless, dock workers immediately began to unload the ship's cargo, while various Russian soldiers and officers came on board, too, some trying to buy shoes and other items from the Indian seafarers. Moreover, the Indian engine-room men observed, the steamer's European crew did visit the shore despite the quarantine restriction imposed on the *SS City of Manila*.[58] It appeared, wrote Amir Haider Khan, 'as if the quarantine was meant for us Indians only'.[59] The engine-room men thus remained on duty, but on the following Sunday three of them, including young Amir, decided to visit the town in defiance of the humiliating quarantine order.

> At the gangway of the ship we were physically obstructed by the European quartermaster who was on guard duty. We actually after pushing him aside went on our way. Some other European officers of the ship were watching the scene but they did not dare to come near us. . . . Just when we reached the outer gates of the docks, we met the captain by chance. He was returning from outside to the ship. At the sight of us he shouted at us in the sailor's Hindustani as to where we were going. He ordered us that we must immediately return to the ship, otherwise we would be arrested. We did not reply nor did we pay him any attention.[60]

Both employers and state authorities of various countries sought to reduce the ability of Indian seafarers to make use of their contractual right to land leave, though for divergent reasons. Owners and shipmasters dreaded costly delays in foreign ports due to the disappearance of crewmen – a risk that could be avoided more easily when employing 'lascars' and other non-European seafarers who had fewer means to enforce their rights. State authorities in Australia, the United States and further countries wished to prevent the illegal immigration of 'coloured' people for openly racist reasons. They registered all incoming Indian seafarers and imposed considerable fines on shipping companies for each 'lascar' who went missing in one of their ports.[61]

Since the *SS City of Manila*'s logbook cannot be traced in the Ellerman City Line archives, we do not know the exact circumstances of the curious quarantine order in Vladivostok. Yet it is clear that the quoted act of defiance was directed against one of the main grievances of Indian seafarers: practices that extended their spatial confinement beyond the periods at sea and deprived them of their freedom of movement even when in port. The collective character and legitimacy (in a plebeian common sense) of what could otherwise be interpreted as a mere act of individual recklessness is born out by the further escalation of the conflict.

> The next morning just as we put on our working clothes and footwear . . . and were ready to go down for the day's work, the captain demanded that the three who had gone to the shore must be produced before him, to punish [*sic*] for defying the quarantine's prohibitory order and also his personal order.
>
> . . . Just as soon as we three were called to the bridge, instead of three of us, the whole crew, 50 strong, rushed towards the captain's cabin, which was on the top deck under the bridge. The officers who had come to take

> us three, when they saw the crew rushing towards the bridge, they tried their best to stop the men from going ahead. But no one paid any attention to their shouting. Then the officers ran ahead of us and tried to stop us on the stairs. There too their attempt failed. All of us forced our way upstairs, by brushing the officers aside. Thus by rubbing, the officers' faces, clothes, and hands were all blackened. When the captain saw that the crew was threateningly rushing towards him, he too tried to explain by some sign and broken Hindustani that he only wanted three and all other[s] must go. No one bothered to hear him; on the other hand we all surrounded him. He was panic-stricken and was making all sorts of gesticulations with both of his hands that 'we must go, go'. And he did not want any one. Then we left.[62]

According to Amir Haider Khan's account, the ship's officers were thrown off their guard (or 'terror-stricken', as he puts it) when they discovered that what had seemed to be a case of individual breach of discipline enjoyed the backing of the crew and bore the potential of seriously unsettling the ship's structure of authority. The incident could have been legally interpreted in various ways, but neither do the memoirs reflect on this possibility nor did the captain apparently decide to take any further steps at this point. This may well have been out of practical considerations since Vladivostok was far away from the usual recruitment areas of the British merchant marine, implying that the ship's officers may have felt they had to bear with their unruly engine-room crew for the time being.

The Water Incident

As the *SS City of Manila* continued her voyage, the engine-room men's quotidian experience was mainly shaped by the characteristic monotony of ship work,[63] only briefly interrupted by more remarkable incidents like those in West Hartlepool and Vladivostok, or by bouts of sensual escapism in the gin mills and brothels of port cities like Shanghai.[64] After Vladivostok, the engine-room crew of the *SS City of Manila* was surely regarded and perhaps dreaded by their officers as recalcitrant, but none of the 'lascars', including young Amir himself, had any consistent political motivation prompting them to keep up the heat on their 'white' superiors. However, the chain of confrontations extended well into the summer of 1916. As the steamer steered a southern course from Shanghai to Manila, outside temperatures soared, further increasing the heat in the boiler room. Yet the officers had rationed the fresh water supply each seafarer received for cooking and drinking. On a hot day, the afternoon shift, after cleaning the scorching furnaces, sent their fireman to the engineer in-charge to ask for more drinking water but met with an outright refusal. As the crew believed that fresh water was available in sufficient quantities, the engine men persisted and their water tender (or *tindal*, foreman) went up to the first executive officer of the deck department, only to receive the same negative response.[65] This resulted in a spontaneous, apparently unplanned reaction:

> . . . the men from twelve to four shift stopped attending their furnaces. Some even left the boiler room, which was too hot and came up to deck to have some fresh air. Thus immediately the steam pressure went down. When the engineer went to the boiler room to shout at the men some of them had already left their places; one or two were there, they too were lying under the ventilators breathless. Hence he had to stop the engine at once to preserve some steam for the auxiliary machine.[66]

Such incidents were not unheard of in steam shipping: European seamen had been reported to be prone to leave the furnaces when temperatures soared in the 'tropics' in order to cool themselves – a practice condemned by shipmasters and owners since it implied fluctuation of boiler pressure and greater consumption of coal. Employment of 'lascars' had been justified as a remedy for this problem since the 'Asiatic' allegedly did 'not care so much for the heat'.[67] Yet, in this case, the 'Asiatics' did react, as a group, much in the way their European counterparts did, which created a situation of extreme tension.

> When the ship stopped there was paniclike excitement as stopping a ship in high sea is an extraordinary incident, specially when it is due to refusal on the part of the crew to work. *It is considered to be mutiny* [emphasis added]. Hence at first the officers of the ship took up very firm and threatening attitude towards us, though it was not a premeditated action on our part at all. In fact the men of [the] two other shifts who were sleeping or resting did not know anything about it.[68]

The fear of German sea raiders aggravated the situation, and the captain decided once again to avoid an open confrontation with the crew. The shipmaster, according to Amir Haider Khan, addressed the engine-room men in a conciliatory tone, ordered his officers to give them 'some water' and warned them of the dangers of stopping the ship when enemy raiders might be near. The ship workers appear to have insisted, however, on getting unlimited access to freshwater supplies. In Amir Haider Khan's later formulation: 'We are not going to attend the boiler till the water pump is completely unlocked, so that we can have water whenever we need it, instead of being required to beg it from you.' The captain finally gave in.[69]

Two aspects seem significant with regard to this last incident. First, it was *similar* to the two earlier incidents in that it concerned issues of personal autonomy rather than the labour process itself; it concerned what was apparently perceived as an elementary and existential right one should not have to beg for.

Second, this last incident *differed* from the former two in that it did not buoy up the crew's self-confidence even though the workers reportedly succeeded in getting free access to drinking water. Stopping the ship on the high seas could be interpreted, as Amir Haider Khan pointed out, as 'mutiny', a serious criminal offence, though the earlier incidents could also be construed as cases of 'disobedience' which were equally punishable by imprisonment. Yet Amir Haider Khan emphasized that so far they had always carried out their 'sea duty' out of an 'instinctive sense of discipline' despite the various disputes they had had, and pointed out severally that stopping the ship had not been a premeditated act.[70] He also narrated that on reaching Manila, 'instead of merry-making our minds were preoccupied over the recent incident',[71] and that during the remainder of the voyage 'we were extremely cautious to avoid any more conflicts with the ship's officers'.[72] They feared prosecution on their return to India in a summary, i.e. unrecorded, trial before a colonial court since shipping companies avoided more public and transparent court proceedings against 'lascars' in European and other countries.[73] This gloomy mood appears to have reached its climax when the *SS City of Manila* reached Singapore, the first port under direct British control. The shipmaster now acted swiftly: he discharged all the Indian engine-room men, replaced them with a newly hired Malayan crew and sent the former back to India on a different vessel as deck passengers, as was his obligation according to Indian maritime law in cases when 'lascar' contracts were terminated outside the subcontinent. Amir Haider Khan recalled that the sudden removal from the ship was 'somewhat embarrassing to us all', but a sense of relief 'to be free from the horrible toils at least for a short while' and for not having been punished more severely is also discernible in his narrative.[74]

The crew clearly benefited from the war in various ways – the severe scarcity of maritime labour forced a more conciliatory approach towards Indian seafarers upon British shipmasters and shipping companies than in other periods, and strengthened their bargaining power. And even the one potentially dangerous disciplinary measure the shipmaster eventually decided to apply, namely an entry in red ink in their '*nullies*' or discharge certificates, remained inconsequential under war conditions: several of the 'redlisted' former engine-room crew of the *SS City of Manila*, including Amir Haider Khan, were soon engaged by shipmasters in desperate search of men who were willing to take the increased risk of wartime employment.[75]

The Limits of 'Labour': Concretizing the 'Free Labour' Problem

'Precarious Freedom' and Micro-Politics of Labour

The simmering tensions and open conflicts on board the *SS City of Manila* revolved around various, seemingly unrelated issues: resisting the oppressive dominance of a middleman and his clique; refusing to be available at all times, i.e. outside the usual if formally unregulated working hours; insisting on the right to land leave and thus on freedom of movement; asserting free access to the most existential resource of life. Was any pattern discernible in this series of conflicts? Clearly, it was *not* the labour process, *not* the transformation of the employer's right to make use of the worker's labour power into actual work or 'output' that was at the heart of these conflicts.

Matters of performance were not at stake in any of the engine-room men's encounters with their superiors and Amir Haider Khan, even when looking back on the events as a militant labour organizer and jailed revolutionary, did not question the need for doing one's 'sea duty'. Instead, he insisted that a 'sense of the instinctive discipline is innate in the men while the ship is on sea'.[76] This naturalization of discipline as '*instinctive*' and '*innate*' could be interpreted as being reflective of the hegemonic understanding of ship hierarchies as 'natural'.[77] However, when comparing the workplace of the engine room with his later experiences in Detroit car factories, Khan moved beyond naturalizing images by hinting at the disciplinary mechanisms that were built into the labour process itself. While the crew could (and, as we have seen, did) refuse 'to do any extra work outside our shift, which was not directly connected with the running on sea', they

> never could refuse the engine which without even a single word was compelling us all to do our task at all cost without grumbling.
>
> It was just like the conveyor system in the big motor car plants in the USA which extract the task from the men without the bosses even opening their mouths. In the same way it is [in] the engine room department in sea-going steam ships. It, by the very process of its running, forces the men to do their respective task instinctively without any bossing . . . every one of us was obliged by the impersonal and mechanical process of running the ship to go on with our work despite the hardships and even semi-starvation so that the ship could keep running.[78]

Accordingly, no general breakdown of discipline is observable even for the unusually unruly maiden voyage of the *SS City of Manila*. The dangers of confronting nature that are implicit in seafaring, aggravated still by additional war-time perils, may well have generated a certain level of acquiescence to the disciplinarian structure of the ship. Nor does our evidence suggest that ship workers resisted the imposition of industrial work discipline as such. They accepted tacitly (or 'instinctively', as Amir Haider Khan chose to put it) their transformation into appendices of the ship's quadruple expansion engine, their real subsumption under capital. Hence, if Indian engine-room men repeatedly went against the *SS City of Manila*'s 'white' officers, this cannot be interpreted as indicative of a refusal to submit to capitalist wage labour as such.

Rather, I suggest, the series of conflicts points to a more limited and specific micro-politics of labour. It highlights micro-political activities suggesting an attitude Hegel described as '*Eigensinn, eine Freiheit, die noch innerhalb der Knechtschaft stehen bleibt*' ('self-will, a freedom which is still enmeshed in servitude'). This, according to Hegel, was an attitude rooted in the social practice of work itself – 'it is precisely in his work wherein he [the bondsman] seemed to have only an alienated existence that he acquires a mind of his own' (in the original: 'eigener Sinn') – an attitude thus reflecting the *fact* of subordination and, at the same time, the inextinguishable *limitedness* of subordination.[79] While Alf Lüdtke, who introduced the concept of 'Eigensinn' ('self-will') to German social history, found it useful for bringing into view a 'waywardness' informing non-collective, individual behaviour of workers that ran counter to homogenizing and teleological conceptualizations of class consciousness,[80] I am using it here for understanding the micro-politics of groups of workers – groups that are formed through shared (work or other life) experiences. 'Self-will', in this usage, refers to individual dispositions (such as the 'hot-headedness' directed at superiors, mentioned above) *and* collective modes of behaviour (such as those of a 'recalcitrant' engine-room crew). For individual and collective articulations of 'self-will', I argue, combine to generate a group's micro-politics, both relying on shared notions of appropriateness or acceptable 'normalcy' with regard to labour relations. Further, I proceed from the assumption that such shared notions are not mechanical reflexes of the workers' position in the social division of labour, but products of an ideological process, under specific conditions of hegemony, of making sense of this division. Whether (and to what extent) the potential for dissidence from dominant structures that is inherent in 'self-will' *or* its simultaneous potential for conformism is released in a particular situation hence requires an empirical reconstruction of how social forces related to each other concretely in a specific historical constellation.

How are these observations applicable to the analysis of the series of shipboard conflicts presented in the previous section of this essay? In this case, conflicts arose at points where the specific wage labour relationship of an early twentieth-century Indian seafarer blended into forms of personal subordination that seemed unacceptable to the engine-room men. Rather than struggles over levels of extraction, these were struggles of definition – conflicts over the determination of the *specific limits* of the labour relationship itself. What was the nature of 'legitimate' or socially acceptable authority derivable from a wage labour contract (in this case, from 'lascar articles')? Where lay the bounds beyond which this authority could not be exercised legitimately? In other words, the constitution of 'labour' as a social relationship *began* only with the conclusion of a labour contract; 'labour', in its concrete articulation, was produced and reproduced in a drawn-out process of social interactions, including conflicts of the kind under discussion.

It is in this context that the free/unfree distinction (or, more precisely, a multilingual semantic field of related terms) obtained utility as a quotidian conceptual device for purposes of articulating the micro-politics of labour. First, these terms could be used in everyday discourse for marking out contradictory tendencies within a labour relationship (see below); and second, for distinguishing forms of subordination considered acceptable by workers in a specific historical context from those deemed unacceptable. But how does the evident usability of the free/unfree distinction as a workaday or 'vernacular' concept relate to its utility as an analytical category?[81] At this point, we need to return to the theoretical debate on the 'free labour' problem that is mentioned in the introductory section of this essay.

As distinct from the enlightenment notion of a natural right to freedom including control over one's own labour, the definition of 'free wage labour' *as an analytical concept*, introduced by Karl Marx, and taken over by Max Weber and many scholars up to the present, is of course that of a double freedom of the wage worker under capitalism: first, the *formal* freedom to sell one's own labour power (or freedom to conclude and terminate a work contract); second, freedom (or an often involuntary separation) from all means of production and subsistence.[82] The first half of this definition has been frequently, though not without problematic consequences, expanded to imply the worker's freedom from exposure to (extra-economic or 'non-pecuniary') coercion.[83]

If the 'freedom' of selling one's labour power is qualified as being *formal*, this should not be understood as indicating the total absence of any actuality in social relations of this 'freedom', or of its *complete* incoherence with material reality. Even Jairus Banaji's sophisticated essay on the 'free labour' problem veers, in its early part, towards depicting labour's 'freedom' as *no more* than a liberal ideological artefact when refuting the assumption 'that it had anything to do with the "ultimate development of human freedom"', and asserting, in effect, an indistinguishability in terms of coercion (and hence unfreedom) of non-wage and wage labour forms.[84] Later in the same essay, Banaji turns to a richer Marxian understanding of the 'formal' freedom of labour as '"one of the essential mediating forms of capitalist relations of production" which is nonetheless a mystification of the "essential nature" of wage labour',[85] i.e. a mystification of its inescapable subordination not under a single capitalist but under capital as a whole: workers can leave an individual employer but most of them cannot avoid a dependent relationship to capital in one or the other labour form.[86] In this reading, 'formal freedom' is thus no simple fiction in the sense of a fanciful construct but a mystified, blurred projection of very real social relations. Yet even here the 'fiction' of 'formal freedom' (or freedom as a legal construct) is perceived as *nothing more* than a structural precondition for alienation, a *mere mechanism* of turning workers into accomplices in their own exploitation. The wage worker's formal freedom, Banaji argues by quoting Sartre's powerful phrase, is a freedom that takes 'upon itself everything which crushes it'.[87] This is not a 'freedom which is still enmeshed in servitude',[88] but a hopeless, lifeless, static freedom that has been reduced to a mere function of servitude.

The disadvantage of this conceptualization is its one-sidedness: by precluding the possibility of inner tensions (or conflicting interpretations of 'free labour' by different social forces), it prevents us from tracing the *history* of the legal construct or 'fiction' of formally free labour. As an alternative, I suggest to examine 'formally free labour' as a normative concept that acquired plausibility (or hegemonic potential) only when capital accumulation required the availability of a mobile labour force and bore of course the marks of prevailing structures of social domination, *but* assumed, at the same time, concrete shapes only in specific political processes, articulated at many levels in a conflictual field of forces.

Yet how is a concretization of the free labour problem, the stated objective of this essay, to be achieved in a historical case study? As pointed out before, the definition of formally free labour possesses value as an analytical concept only if it is clearly understood to be an abstraction from the much richer and more complex reality of concrete historical situations, with the purpose of marking out larger historical *tendencies*. 'Concretization' thus cannot imply to treat 'free labour' as a conceptual container to be filled up with corroborating lumps of evidence. For as soon as we try to 'apply' this definition to concrete labour forms in this way, we run, more often than not, into endless difficulties. The labour relations of the Indian seafarers under discussion here are as much a case in point as those of South Asian factory workers of that period. Hence, much of the evidence on the so-called 'lascars' toiling on British steamers at the time suggests that most of the *SS City of Manila*'s engine-room crew would have been petty landowners themselves, or contributed to a household economy based on a combination of wage labour, rural smallholding and other resources – this was certainly the case with the narrator, Amir Haider Khan.[89] A total separation between means of subsistence and production was, in other words, rather unusual.

As for the Indian seafarers' ownership of their labour power, we shall see below in greater detail that their freedom to terminate a contract and freedom from extra-economic coercion were severely restricted and, to borrow Sidney Chaloub's felicitous phrase, '*structurally precarious*'.[90] Their labour relationships, with regard to the limits imposed on the worker's right to terminate the contract, resembled those of indentured labourers. The captain's official denomination was 'shipmaster', which was fully appropriate in that it clearly reflected his position of not being merely the agent of one of the parties to the labour contract; the shipmaster represented both the employer and state-sanctioned authority as he held the right to punish 'disobedient' seafarers physically, by incarceration or by fine.[91] Moreover, 'extra-economic coercion' in the most unconcealed form of physical violence appears to have been frequent on board ships, especially on vessels manned by legally inferior seafarers from colonies like India, with middlemen (like the *serang* in Amir Haider Khan's account) or British officers being the main perpetrators, and with shipboard labour leaders establishing themselves through 'hot-headed' counter-violence.[92]

If freedom from extra-economic coercion thus appears to have been either absent or unenforceable in the concrete form that Indian maritime labour relations assumed in the early twentieth century, this does not imply, however, that it was irrelevant as a normative concept or as a key feature of an appropriate labour relationship as understood by the workers themselves. This is implicitly but impressively indicated by Amir Haider Khan's report on the conflict in West Hartlepool with the engine-room *serang*: while the root cause of the conflict was the *serang's* demand for additional payments from the engine-room men (which was both legally unwarranted and considered illegitimate by the 'lascars'), the reason foregrounded in negotiations with the British authorities for removal of the *serang* was not his raising of illegal fees but his resort to violence, which, according to the account, was the welcome result of a provocation on the part of one of the engine-room men. Hence, a complaint against physical violence of a foreman appeared to the engine-room men more compelling than a complaint against what would quite possibly have been conceived of, by British officials, as a corrupt, legally unwarranted but 'customary' practice. The notion of formal 'freedom' thus had some lingering presence even under conditions of a racially segmented labour market where the 'structural precariousness' of 'free labour' was particularly pronounced.

Similarly, Amir Haider Khan's repeated comparisons of the ship with prison may be reflective of more than the individual perspective of one of the twentieth century's numerous 'political jail-birds'. As has been pointed out by Rana Behal, for instance, in his study on Assam, even senior colonial officials were convinced, in the early years of the twentieth century, that 'amongst the coolies the whole plantation system was commonly regarded as a *phatak* [prison]'.[93]

The Temporal Limits of 'Free Labour'

That tensions within wage labour relationships could be articulated concretely in terms of the 'free labour problem', which thus assumed immediate relevance for the micro-politics of labour (like those examined in the case study undertaken in this essay), is even more clearly observable if we take account of an aspect of Marx's discussion of a crucial precondition for the continued availability of wage labour as a commodity that is only seemingly banal and has received less attention in the 'free labour' debate:

> For this relation [of legally equal sellers and buyers of labour power] to continue, the proprietor of labour-power must always sell it for a limited period only, for if he were to sell it in a lump, once and for all, he would be selling himself, converting himself from a free man into a slave, from an owner of a commodity into a commodity. He must constantly treat his labour-power as his own property, his own commodity, and he can do this only by placing it at the disposal of the buyer, i.e. handing it over to the buyer for him to consume, for a definite period of time, temporarily.[94]

In stating this precondition for the continued availability of 'free' wage labour, Marx reformulated, expanded upon and explicitly referred to the distinction 'between a slave and present-day servants [*Gesinde*] or a day-labourer'[95] in Hegel's 'Philosophy of Right':

> Single products of my particular physical and mental skill and of my power to act I can alienate to someone else and I can give him the use of my abilities *for a restricted period, because, on the strength of this restriction,*

> *my abilities acquire an external relation to the totality and universality of my being* [emphasis added]. By alienating the whole of my time, as crystallized in my work, and everything I produced, I would be making into another's property the substance of my being, my universal activity and actuality, my personality.[96]

Wage labour, according to this conceptualization, was distinguishable from other labour forms by having a temporal limit. 'Free' wage labour thus had a *measure* in the Hegelian sense: within this measure (or scope of temporal properties) wage labour remained intact with regard to its defining quality (formal freedom); beyond this measure it turned into something else. This conceptualization differs significantly from that of the 'sliding scale' of labour relations referred to earlier in this essay: the latter postulates 'fluid boundaries' between 'free' and 'unfree' labour relations, and thus questions the relevance of this distinction except for purely taxonomic purposes; the former, too, allows for a wide range of gradual differentiations within wage labour, while defining at the same time a *threshold* of qualitative change or a *zone of transformation*. This threshold, the zone where formal 'freedom' was lost or gained, is not to be understood as a timeless given but as a product of human action. Crucially, it cannot be conceived of as a consequence of abstract, unconscious and mute economic force ('the market'), but as the outcome of confrontations between concrete social forces and hence as an essentially *political* product. This understanding of the boundary zone between 'free' and 'unfree' labour as a politically constituted and embattled frontier is implicit already in the explanatory footnote Marx attaches to the statement quoted above.[97] More importantly, it underlies his subsequent discussion of the 'limits of the working day', where it is developed further in ways relevant to our more specific discussion:

> . . . *the nature of commodity exchange itself imposes no limit to the working day*, no limit to surplus labour. The capitalist maintains his rights as a purchaser when he tries to make the working day as long as possible, and, where possible, to make two working days out of one. On the other hand, the peculiar nature of the commodity sold implies a limit to its consumption by the purchaser, and *the worker maintains his right as a seller when he wishes to reduce the working day to a particular normal length*. There is here therefore an antinomy, of right against right, both equally bearing the seal of the law of exchange. *Between equal rights, force decides*. [Emphases added.][98]

From Hegel's and Marx's elementary observations on the temporal limitedness of wage labour, it is possible to proceed further and develop two hypotheses that allow for a concretization of the 'free labour' problem in significant ways.

First of all, the worker 'treat[ing] his labour-power as his own property' or 'maintain[ing] his right as a seller' is not, in Marx's rendering, conceived of as a singular act separating capitalism from earlier social formations, or setting apart 'contemporary' and 'natural' labour forms from 'earlier' and 'unnatural' ones (as is implicit in Hegel's earlier definition). Rather, the determination of temporal limits on wage labour is reconstructed as a long-drawn and contentious historical process (in Marx's words, a 'protracted and more or less concealed civil war'[99]) not only within one social formation (in the case he studied, capitalism), but even within the process of producing and reproducing the 'free' wage labour relationship itself. Marx reconstructed the history of wage labour in Britain, to some extent, *through* the history of struggles over the working day. By implication, maintaining the worker's formal 'freedom' (or the proprietorship in and ability to sell one's own labour power) is recognized as a crucial 'moral' or political 'element' of the prolonged conflictual process of actualizing the wage labour relationship in concrete, historically contingent forms.[100] In other words, this conceptualization allows us to understand *conflicts over the temporal limits of labour* not as mere negotiations over secondary modalities of the wage labour relationship but *as being constitutive of the wage labour relationship itself*.[101] Further, the relevance of this conceptualization is arguably not restricted to the form of *wage* labour alone: the threshold separating formally 'free' and 'unfree' labour relations can be shown to have remained embattled from both sides. Just as workers have sought to preserve proprietorship of their own labour power by defending the temporal limitedness of wage labour, slaves on sugar plantations of the Caribbean strained against the bounds of slavery, as Dale Tomich has pointed out, by securing the right to be unavailable to the slave owner during specific periods of time – the conflicts revealing the tensions and limits of the master–slave relation and prompting its evolution, potentially even its transformation, into new labour forms.[102] The persistence of conflicts over the temporal restriction of labour relations can thus be understood as an issue connecting what have too often been regarded as separate histories of slavery, wage labour and other labour forms.

The second hypothesis is based on the first and permits further concretization. We begin with the observation that the temporal limits of the wage labour relationship are not exclusively determined by formally and effectively separating the 'working day' from a section of the day dedicated to 'non-work' (i.e. practices that may or may not generate use value but do so, in either case, outside an employment relationship). Rather, conflicts over the temporal limits of the wage labour relationship have taken various forms. They have included confrontations over the duration of the labour contract, restrictions on the worker's right to terminate it, and entitlement to temporary leave or work breaks. In nineteenth-century England, as Robert Steinfeld observes, the 'length of the contracted-for service appears to have been the crucial factor separating free from unfree, rather than whether a worker could be compelled to perform a contract through criminal punishment'.[103]

To appreciate the importance of taking into account the whole range of possible temporal restrictions in the wage labour relationship, it is instructive to turn to a distinction within the category of 'wage labour' that Marcel van der Linden has highlighted recently: 'in the Antique period, the wage labourer was regarded as a "hireling" who did not so much "hire out" (or, if one prefers, temporarily sell) his labour power, but who placed himself temporarily with his whole person in a dependent position'.[104] In explaining and developing this distinction, van der Linden continues as follows:

> Wage labour was . . . conceptualized differently than we do today: not as the hire of labour power, but as self-hire of a worker plus his or her labour performance. The person and labour performance were, to be sure, distinguished but the hire was simultaneously applied to both aspects . . . the most important conclusion is that wage labour existed *before* it was conceptualized in the 'modern' way.[105]

These two conceptualizations (that of the 'hireling' and that of the 'free' wage labourer) are clearly discernible in historical debates on wage labour, but I argue that the gap separating them can be overdrawn. What is it that renders them recognizable, after all, as two varieties of the *same* labour form? According to van der Linden's definition, they *share* the property of being temporally limited labour relationships and *diverge* in that this temporary subordination to an employer is stated in different terms: temporary renunciation of the right of self-determination as a 'person' or temporary renunciation of the right to dispose over one's personal capacity to work. Yet this separation of the person from the 'mental and physical capabilities existing in the physical form, the living personality, of a human being'[106] is both a potent expression of the real commodification of social relations *and* a piece of fiction concealing the loss of personal independence implicit in wage labour relationships.[107] Hence I argue that the 'hireling' and the 'free' wage labourer do not inhabit two clearly demarcated spheres, and question the assumption, *pace* van der Linden, that 'free' wage labour has fully displaced the 'hireling' under capitalism or 'modernity' even at the conceptual level. Rather, they should be understood as divergent tendencies emerging from a contradictory field of forces – divergent tendencies that could find concrete expression even *within a single*, seemingly incoherent labour form straddling the gap between the 'free labourer' and the 'hireling'. Such labour relations were, for instance, those based on the master and servant law that was slowly phased out in Britain in the latter half of the nineteenth century, but bolstered up or newly introduced in colonies of the British empire even much later.[108] Arguably, in many labour arrangements of the nineteenth to the twenty-first century, ranging from indenture via domestic service to soldiering and other militarized forms of labour such as seafaring,[109] it has been a matter of social conflict, often over the form of the temporal restriction of wage labour, whether the 'free labourer' or the 'hireling' prevailed.

To sum up the argument thus far, conflicts over the temporal limits of wage labour were constitutive, at a general level, of the wage labour relationship itself, and these decided, in particular, whether historically evolving varieties of wage labour bore a greater resemblance to the notion of 'free wage labour' or with that of the 'hireling'. These observations seem particularly relevant with regard to maritime labour relations. They can help to explain why, even beyond the specificity of colonial labour regimes, 'seamen occupied the boundary waters of free labour status', as Leon Fink put it so graphically.[110]

Wage Worker or Hireling? 'Lascars' and 'Freedom'

In the Anglo-American maritime world, the ship emerged in the eighteenth century, according to Marcus Rediker, as 'one of the earliest totalitarian work environments' where the captain was invested with 'near-dictatorial powers'.[111] The merchant ship thus was a space where labour's 'freedom', even in its most fleshless, formal embodiment, found few crannies to survive. Penal sanctions, i.e. legally endorsed means of coercion like corporal punishment or imprisonment, for vaguely defined misdemeanours such as 'mutiny', 'desertion' or 'wilful disobedience' were, for instance, crucial devices for defining the British seaman's wage labour status as one that closely resembled the status of the 'hireling'. These sanctions did not disappear with the rise of capitalism. On the contrary, they were drastically reinforced in the eighteenth and early nineteenth centuries, as Conrad Dixon has shown. Yet, while prison sentences for 'desertion' persisted as a legal option in British maritime law until 1975,[112] the actual ability of employers to use these disciplinary devices against British seamen declined in the last quarter of the nineteenth century. Around the *fin de siècle*, employer spokesmen complained that the jurisdictional powers of shipmasters and the device of 'summary', i.e. unrecorded, court proceedings had been diminished, that seamen were using courts against their employers with increasing success, that so-called 'sea lawyers' or half-educated troublemakers exerted a mischievous influence on many ships, and that the naïve British Jack Tar of olden times had been replaced by the cunning trade unionist.[113]

It is significant that this was also the period when the employment of 'lascars', i.e. South Asian seafarers, skyrocketed numerically, bringing their share in total employment in the British merchant marine up to one quarter by the interwar years.[114] Colonial conditions helped to give the 'hireling' (or 'servant') a new lease of life within the structure of maritime wage labour relations. While the relinquishment of many, though not all, attributes of the 'hireling' had to be conceded to the British seaman, a separate colonial maritime labour law for British India allowed for the preservation of various grey zones, such as the persistence of summary trials and significant gaps in the legal regulation of labour relationships. These grey zones served as a habitat for the 'hireling'. If British maritime law insisted that Indian seafarers were 'lascars' and not 'seamen' in a strictly legal sense, this was more than idle nitpicking.[115] The terminological distinction between 'seaman' and 'lascar' marked diverging tendencies within the development of maritime wage labour relations: one towards formally 'free labour' and the other, backed by colonial modes of power, towards preservation of the 'hireling' in the racialized form of the 'coolie'.

How were these diverging tendencies articulated concretely? In the early years of the twentieth century, when the growing presence of South Asian seafarers in the international maritime labour market elicited controversial responses within British society, the advantages and disadvantages of 'lascar' employment were examined in great detail by an official commission of enquiry appointed by the House of Commons.[116] The arguments of the supporters of 'lascar' employment, closely associated with commercial shipping interests in various capacities, were summed up conveniently in a rambling treatise by one Captain W.H. Hood. That the following quote from this treatise is rather lengthy may be excused on the grounds that it specifies in detail where, in addition to much lower wages and other labour costs, the key advantages of 'lascar' employment lay for ship owners and their agents.

> If the vessel should go to Europe and return to Bombay, the [South Asian] crew are, of course, discharged in the usual way as the voyage is ended; but if the vessel does not return to Bombay but goes trading anywhere within the scope of the articles [i.e. labour contract], and the scope is very wide, the crew remain until the time – twelve months – is expired, and it is specially provided for that in the event of a steamer being under charter, or bound for India or Burma when that occurs, they bind themselves if required to complete the voyage to such destination. Thus with these crews there is no change of men at the end of each passage. They make, except in the case of a direct return to Bombay, two, three or four complete voyages; they are on board in port in India, in the United Kingdom or the Continent, and stick steadily to their work, and are always there when wanted at times out of the ordinary hours of working, such as shifting about the quays, dry-docking or changing docks. They do it willingly, too, well understanding that ship-work cannot always be regulated in the same manner as the hours of labour in a shop on shore. They are quite ready when required to shift into another steamer, going over as a whole crew, and are thus more completely the servants of the shipowner while under engagement than any other group of men doing similar work that shipowners have ever had to do the work for them. At sea, the ordinary watch and watch system does not obtain among Lascars, but that which is known to Europeans as the Calassie watch, i.e., 'all hands at all times.' They work all day, and sleep o'nights like other men, except those, of course, who are told off for the 'lookout'. Taken altogether, a much more efficient state of discipline prevails on the Lascar-manned steamer than can ever be hoped for on similar vessels manned by the ordinary type of European crews.[117]

In brief, the major advantages of 'lascar' employment for British shipping industrialists were, according to this account:[118]

(i) South Asian seafarers were engaged not for single voyages but for periods of twelve months at least, and their contracts could not be terminated outside India. In effect, they were bound to one employer much longer than their European counterparts, namely for three to four voyages at a stretch, which reduced the rate of attrition, recruitment costs and, crucially, expensive lay days in port. 'Lascar' contracts also stipulated the employer's right to transfer 'lascars' from one ship to another without their consent.

(ii) 'Lascars' remained, if required by their officers, on board ship when in port, since their contracts did not expire with the end of the voyage. This implied uninterrupted availability and controllability as well as reduced risk of desertion – the latter being one of the main complaints ship owners and officers raised against European seafarers.

(iii) South Asian seafarers were allegedly 'more willing' to accept unregulated working hours and acquiesced to a system of 'all hands at all times', as opposed to the regular watch system that applied to their European counterparts.[119]

Extending the period of employment by restricting the worker's right to terminate the work contract; denying leaves of absence when in port during the period of employment; avoiding any formal restriction or 'normalization' of the working day – these were the key elements of the shipping interests' politics of the labour contract with regard to Indian seafarers, a politics ensuring a 'more efficient state of discipline' to such an extent that 'lascars' were 'more completely the servants of the shipowner while under engagement than any other group of men doing similar work'.[120]

If the temporal limitedness of the 'free' wage labour relationship thus appeared as a disciplinary problem to shipping industrialists, officers and officials, the urgency of this problem was aggravated as shipping schedules became more inflexible with the rise of capital-intensive steam shipping in the late nineteenth century. As a senior shipping official put it in 1902:

> [s]teamships have to sail at a fixed hour, whilst olden days sailing ships went to sea just when they were ready, without any special reference to the hour. If the men were not aboard in time, and she was detained a tide, it did not matter very much, but if a steamer is delayed half an hour now it means a great deal of inconvenience and loss, and therefore the trouble caused by the seaman is more marked.[121]

Sir Thomas Sutherland, chairman of the Peninsular and Oriental Steam Navigation Company (P&O), similarly explained why his concern had turned into one of the largest employers of 'lascars': 'a liner, and by that I mean a mail steamer, has to be at each point at a given date, and we found our European crews would not bring us to those given points at those given dates'.[122] In other words, the transformation of shipping into a highly centralized, capital-intensive industry, whose tall, steel-hulled liners were among the most visible beacons of the 'modern age', generated pressing needs at the level of individual capital that were diametrically opposed to the general tendency, in late nineteenth-century Britain, towards an abolition of legal provisions restricting the formal freedom of labour.

The employment of colonial labour, of 'coolies' or 'lascars', permitted to sidestep this tendency – manifest in the abolition of the ancient Master and Servant Law in Britain in 1870 – and to avoid the temporal limitedness of what was now being established as the regular labour contract in the metropolis. Employment of 'lascars' allowed shipping industrialists and their agents to fortify their status as 'masters', while the place of the worker as a 'servant' was marked out clearly. As British sailors asserted, with considerable success, the formal freedom of temporally restricted wage labour in the metropolis, the maritime 'hireling' was reinvented in the colonial empire along the lines of the old master and servant legislation, and the 'indenture' contract. Though the Workmen's Breach of Contract Act (1859) and certain sections of the Indian Penal Code that provided for the imposition of criminal penalties on 'disobedient' workers, including seafarers, were repealed as being 'anachronistic' in 1925,[123] the Indian Merchant Shipping Act of 1923 *confirmed* imprisonment as a penalty for desertion and 'other misconduct'. Even the postcolonial Merchant Shipping Act of 1958 retained imprisonment of up to three months as a penalty for 'disobedience'.[124] At least as importantly in terms of everyday work experience, the legal grey zone with regard to the temporal limits of labour was studiously maintained: though the issue of regulating the working hours of Indian seafarers became a subject of official deliberations time and again since 1920, under the influence of ILO (International Labour Organization) debates, neither legislative measures nor collective agreements had materialized even a quarter of a century later.[125] The distinction between 'free' and 'unfree' labour was thus, in this context, not just a matter of ideological concealment; it was articulated *politically*, through legislation, social conflict and political action at various levels as a tendency towards a differentiation within the wage labour form.

If late nineteenth-century imperialist societies tended to systematically racialize social phenomena, the rise of the South Asian maritime hireling was publicly justified in exactly this way. The superintendent of Liverpool's Mercantile Marine Office thus echoed the prevailing common sense among British ship owners, shipmasters and port officials when he stated, in 1902, that 'lascars' were 'more amenable to discipline, of sober habits, and not given to going on shore at every port', while 'their physical inferiority was practically an advantage in the stokehold', allegedly enabling them to cope with excessive heat more easily.[126] The 'lascar's' 'docility' was thus 'discovered' as a racial trait rendering him particularly adaptable to a disciplinary regime that British sailors were increasingly unlikely to accept.[127] However, even though the attribute of 'docility' was predominantly ascribed to the 'oriental' maritime worker, there are interesting instances of it being applied to non-British Europeans too. Hence the German and Scandinavian seafarers were stated to be more '*docile*' than the English Jack Tar,[128] while the sailor from Greece or Italy was reportedly preferred because, unlike his British counterpart, he did not have the 'idea he has to work only a certain length of time a day'[129], i.e. he did not insist on a clear separation of the '*ship's time*' from his '*own time*'.[130]

This hints at *political structures* underlying what was pronounced, in British discourses, as 'racial' behavioural patterns. Political reforms in Britain had strengthened the citizens' rights and bargaining power of the British working classes in the closing decades of the nineteenth century, which were expressed, in the case of the seamen, through the rise of a new resolute though jingoistic trade union.[131] 'Alien' seafarers, whether 'white' or not, were however excluded from the political resources newly available to British workers. Those subjected to a more authoritarian colonial legislation, resulting in contractual forms like the 'lascar articles' that continued to be based on master and servant law, were even '*more amenable*' to the disciplinarian requirements of British shipping capital.

Unfortunately for employers, the 'lascar's' presumably primordial 'docility' rubbed off rather soon, especially under the conditions of massive maritime labour scarcity during the two world wars. A wave of labour militancy among South Asian steamship crews has been observed especially for the early years of the Second World War,[132] but the drive towards trade union formation set in among 'lascars', even more than among other industrial workers of the subcontinent, in the wake of the First World War.[133] This is the specific historical setting of the story of the *SS City of Manila*'s unruly maiden voyage – simmering, unresolved tensions within the wage labour relationship were more likely to be brought out in the open in this context. The significance of Amir Haider Khan's account lies in the fact that the issues raised by the series of confrontations on board the *SS City of Manila* are a precise mirror image of the list of advantages of 'lascar' employment presented to the public by the advocates of British shipping interests in the early years of the century: acquiescence to a wage labour relationship that was temporally less restricted, vaguely restricted or unrestricted (longer duration and reduced right to termination of contract, transferability to another ship, unregulated working hours and right to leave of absence), and to informal structures that enforced such acquiescence (namely the appointment of *serangs* by the ship's officers) – these were, apart from their 'cheapness', the main items on the employers' list of 'lascar virtues'. The breakdown of the 'lascar's' proverbial 'docility' that Amir Haider Khan remembered, at least for one voyage of a British merchant steamer, revolved around exactly the same issues regarding the temporal restriction of the wage labour relationship. That the virtues listed in one account mirrored the grievances detailed in the other was no mere coincidence. It reflects, I argue, the defining power of temporal properties with regard to the quality of labour forms, or, in other words, the indispensability of temporal specifications for determining a historically concrete location of the threshold between formally 'free' (or 'self-willed') and 'unfree' (or 'docile') labour at the level of everyday social and political conflict.

Temporal restriction of the labour contract was thus an issue where labour was experienced and made sense of in terms of 'unfreedom', and where, accordingly, 'freedom' acquired workaday relevance, though in the severely limited form of a '*freedom which is still enmeshed in servitude*'. For in all the episodes on the *SS City of Manila*, issues of relative autonomy *within* the absolute limits of the wage labour relationship were being pursued by the Punjabi engine-room crew: not the refusal to submit to labour intermediaries in general, but the right to refuse a specific *serang*; not a questioning of the wage labour relationship as such, but insistence on its temporal limitedness. Accordingly, when their contracts were terminated before the stipulated time by the shipmaster, they were, according to Amir Haider Khan, in some ways relieved but also somewhat embarrassed. Writing in hindsight from his cell in Nasik Road Central Prison, he still characterized the *SS City of Manila*'s engine-room crew as '*rebellious*', and within his narrative this voyage assumed the status of an initial step of his metamorphosis into a '*confirmed "Red"*'.[134] A close reading of the episodes discloses a somewhat more ambivalent wilfulness or, in the sense discussed above, 'self-will' – a disposition expressed in various forms that oscillated between instances of individual, spontaneous and reckless 'waywardness' (e.g., absence without leave in Vladivostok), and cases of collective, considered and carefully calibrated behaviour (e.g., lodging a complaint with the Shipping Master of West Hartlepool).

Yet Amir Haider Khan's memoirs also suggest that these limited efforts towards individual or shopfloor autonomy provided a bridge to more expansive conceptualizations of 'freedom' and 'unfreedom' – a bridge that remained precarious and was more easily discernible in times of crisis like the two world wars. They created, in other words, new possibilities for making sense of the larger world. The humiliating experience of being paraded through the streets of London while being transferred by an employer to an unknown destination could be enriched with meaning by conscious acts of thought – for instance, by comparing it to galley slavery, or by connecting it to issues of colonial subordination and national liberation. Conversely, the experience of the irresolvable quotidian tension of a 'freedom which is still enmeshed in servitude' may have rendered it *possible* (but by no means inevitable) for workers to appropriate contemporary political discourses of freedom from colonial rule, caste oppression or class domination, and to endow them with historically specific meanings. The 'formality' of the achievable 'freedom' within wage labour thus did not imply its total absorption within an assumed prestabilized economic cunning of capital. Even this ragged and haggard freedom persistently provoked social conflict and political contention; the temporal limits of the labour relationship remained an embattled threshold of transformation within the differentiated landscape of labour forms. Conflicting tendencies never subsided even within the wage labour form itself: while capital *at large* required and promoted the availability of mobile, 'free' labour forces (for instance, by consenting to labour demands in Britain for the abolition of the master and servant law), capital *in particular*, such as the British shipping industrialists of the early 1900s, defended the ancient figure of the 'hireling' tooth and nail.[135] This conflict over the constitution of the wage labour relationship, i.e. over the concrete articulation of 'formal freedom', spelled itself out in the everyday. Here it became a site of the micro-politics of labour, a politics that brought out the 'hot-headedness' of individual members of a seemingly apolitical engine-room crew of the *SS City of Manila* and spurred it into collective 'self-will' for one eventful voyage at least. While such micro-politics did not challenge the unfree content of formally free wage labour, it threw into sharp relief, for a moment, the political within the economic, and hence the historical limits of the labour relationship.

Notes and References

1 Important contributions to this debate include: Marcel van der Linden, *Workers of the World: Essays toward a Global Labour History*, Leiden/Boston: Brill, 2008, Chapters 2, 3 and 4; Jairus Banaji, *Theory as History: Essays on Modes of Production and Exploitation*, Leiden/Boston: Brill, 2010, Chapter 5; Robert Steinfeld, *Coercion, Contract and Free Labor in the Nineteenth Century*, Cambridge: Cambridge University Press, 2001; Tom Brass and Marcel van der Linden (eds), *Free and Unfree Labour: The Debate Continues*, Bern: Peter Lang, 1997; Tom Brass, *Labour Regime Change in the Twenty-First Century: Unfreedom, Capitalism and Primitive Accumulation*, Leiden: Brill, 2011.

2 Cf. Rosa Luxemburg, *Gesammelte Werke*, Vol. 5 (*Ökonomische Schriften*), Berlin: Dietz Verlag, 1990: 315 (Chapter 26 of *Die Akkumulation des Kapitals*).

3 Karl Marx, *Das Kapital* (1983), Vol. I (*Marx Engels Werke*, Vol. 23), Berlin: Dietz Verlag, 1983: 185; Karl Marx, *Capital: A Critique of Political Economy*, translated by Ben Fowkes, London: Penguin, 1982: 275.

4 Cf. Gyan Prakash, *Bonded Histories: Genealogies of Labour Servitude in Colonial India*, Cambridge South Asian Studies, Vol. XLIV, Cambridge: Cambridge University Press, 1990: 1–12, 218–25.

5 The *International Review of Social History* (*IRSH*) has contributed substantially in recent years to make the results of this exciting debate available to a wider international audience of labour historians. See Henrique Espada Lima, 'Freedom, Precariousness, and the Law: Freed Persons Contracting Out Their Labour in Nineteenth-Century Brazil', *IRSH*, 54 (3), 2009: 391–416; Marcelo Badaró Mattos, 'Experiences in Common: Slavery and "Freedom" in the Process of Rio de Janeiro's Working-Class Formation (1850–1910)', *IRSH*, 55 (2), 2010: 193–213; Sidney Chaloub, 'The Precariousness of Freedom in a Slave Society (Brazil in the Nineteenth Century)', *IRSH*, 56 (3), 2011: 405–39. Personal communication with Henrique Espada Lima in particular has made me aware of the relevance of these findings for other labour regimes.

6 For the former, more sympathetic view, see Anupama Rao's discussion of Jotirao Phule's famous 1873 treatise, *Gulamgiri*/Slavery, where she points out rightly that Phule used the reference to Atlantic world slavery to reframe the discourse on caste relations in India. The book was in fact dedicated to the '*good people in the USA*' who had fought slavery. However, what remains unexplained is why this

pamphlet gained such immense popularity and, more specifically, how the concept of '*gulamgiri*' resonated with everyday discourses or 'common sense'. Cf. Anupama Rao, *The Caste Question: Dalits and the Politics of Modern India*, Berkeley: University of California Press, 2009: 12 f, 272 f; G.P. Deshpande (ed.), *Selected Writings of Jotirao Phule*, New Delhi: Leftword Books, 2002: 23–99. For the latter, more dismissive view, see Prakash, *Bonded Histories*.

7 See, for instance, Nitin Varma, 'Producing Tea Coolies? Work, Life and Protest in the Colonial Tea Plantations of Assam, 1830s–1920', unpublished Ph.D. dissertation, Humboldt University, Berlin, 2011: 132.

8 Robert J. Steinfeld, *The Invention of Free Labour: The Employment Relation in English and American Law and Culture, 1350–1870*, Chapel Hill: University of North Carolina Press, 1991: 104.

9 van der Linden, *Workers of the World*: 22.

10 Ibid.: 35 f.

11 The quote is from Ravi Ahuja, 'Labour Relations in an Early Colonial Context: Madras, 1750–1800', *Modern Asian Studies*, 36 (4), 2002: 806.

12 For a two-dimensional representation of a 'labour continuum', see, for instance, the diagram in van der Linden, *Workers of the World*: 22.

13 Steinfeld, *Invention of Free Labour*: 104.

14 G.W.F. Hegel, *Phenomenology of Spirit*, translated by A.V. Miller, Oxford: Oxford University Press, 1977: 119. The German original of this quote from Hegel's reflections on 'lordship and bondage' carries more dynamic connotations as it describes the phenomenon as one of an interrupted *movement*, not of a *state* of detention: 'eine Freiheit, welche noch innerhalb der Knechtschaft stehenbleibt' (a more appropriate translation might be: 'a freedom, which yet pauses in servitude'). G.W.F. Hegel, *Phänomenologie des Geistes*, Frankfurt: Suhrkamp, 1986: 155. The relevance of this formulation for the problem under consideration is discussed more fully in the final section of this essay.

15 Amir Haider Khan, 'I Break with the Old World', typescript, Pakistan Study Centre, University of Karachi: 203–12. Numerous corrections and deletions were made by the author and/or his editorial aides to this typescript, which have been disregarded in this essay in order to preserve as much as possible of the earliest, most unfiltered version of the memoirs.

16 Examination of Duncan Mackenzie, Superintendent of Mercantile Marine Office at Glasgow, in *Report of the Committee Appointed by the Board of Trade to Inquire into Certain Questions Affecting the Mercantile Marine* (hereafter *Report of the Mercantile Marine Committee*), Vol. II: Evidence, London: Wyman & Sons, 1903: 43, 48.

17 The preservation and publication of the autobiographical writings of 'Dada' Amir Haider Khan (1901–1989) is to the sole credit of Professor Hasan N. Gardezi. Gardezi had edited the autobiographical manuscripts in consultation with the author by the mid-1980s, and a first volume was published in 1989 by Patriot Publishers, New Delhi. However, the second half of the edited manuscript remained unpublished at that time and was lost subsequently. Gardezi later edited, once again, this latter part of the autobiographical writings, and a complete two-volume set was published under the same title: Hasan N. Gardezi (ed.), *Chains to Lose: Life and Struggles of a Revolutionary. Memoirs of Dada Amir Haider Khan*, Karachi: Pakistan Study Centre, 2007. The editor's objective was clearly to attract a wide readership to this, in many ways, unique historical document, which is why sections of the manuscript he considered 'overly exhaustive and repetitious' were omitted in the published version (cf. ibid.: xvi). The original manuscripts were deposited at the Pakistan Study Centre, University of Karachi, however, and I was able to consult them thanks to the generous support of the Centre's director, Professor Syed Jaffar

Ahmed. All quotes in this article are from the original manuscript entitled 'I Break with the Old World'. For the quoted phrase, see ibid.: 1.

18 Cf. ibid., 'Preface'.

19 In the Preface, the author made explicit the limitations as well as the ethico-political impetus of his memoirs. He thus clarified that at the time of writing no notes or documents had been available to him to prop up his 'hazy memory'. He also stated that, in his view, the 'role of the progressive writer is to expose everything bad in society, no matter how ugly it may be; those who do not like it, let them work for ending the same.' For accounts of visits to brothels and of being 'infected' with the racism prevalent in the US, see ibid.: 181, 321 f, 341, 366 f, 400 f.

20 Ibid.: 212 f.

21 See also ibid.: 230, 494, 550.

22 Available at http://www.wrecksite.eu/wreck.aspx?17009 and http://uboat.net/allies/merchants/2075.html; accessed on 31 January 2012.

23 Khan, 'I Break with the Old World': 214 f.

24 Ibid.: 215.

25 Marcus Rediker, *Between the Devil and the Deep Blue Sea: Merchant Seamen, Pirates and the Anglo-American Maritime World, 1700–1750*, Cambridge: Cambridge University Press, 1987: 212.

26 Khan, 'I Break with the Old World': 208.

27 See, for instance, F. No. 54-M. II/31, S. Nos. 1–42, part B, Department of Commerce, Merchant Marine II, January 1932, National Archives of India (hereafter NAI). Various other files regarding 'death on board ship' can be found in the 1932 and 1933 indices of this series of records, though several were apparently 'not transferred' to the NAI. See also Oral Testimony by H.F. Darvell, Shipping Master Calcutta, in *Royal Commission on Labour in India, Evidence*, Bengal, Oral Evidence, Vol. V, part 2, London: His Majesty's Stationery Office, 1931: 279. The shipping authority of Bremen, home base of the Hansa DFG (the largest German employer of Indian seamen), put on record that 61 per cent of the 106 trimmers and stokers who committed suicide between 1901 and 1912 were 'coloured'. See Hartmut Rübner, 'Lebens-, Arbeits- und gewerkschaftliche Organisationsbedingungen chinesischer Seeleute in der deutschen Handelsflotte. Der maritime Aspekt der Ausländersbeschäftigung vom Kaiserreich bis in den NS-Staat', *Internationale wissenschaftliche Korrespondenz zur Geschichte der deutschen Arbeiterbewegung*, 4 (1), 1997: 1–41, 19.

28 W.H. Howell, Board of Trade, Marine Department, to Under Secretary of State for India, 12 December 1904, Bombay Marine Proceedings, IOR/P/7191, A228, Oriental and India Office Collections (hereafter OIOC), British Library (hereafter BL); D.A. Cameron, British Consul in Port Said, to Board of Trade, Marine Department, 3 November 1904, ibid., A229.

29 Khan, 'I Break with the Old World': 215 f.

30 G. Balachandran, 'Searching for the Sardar: The State, Pre-capitalist Institutions and Human Agency in the Maritime Labour Market, Calcutta, 1880–1935', in B. Stein and S. Subrahmanyam (eds), *Institutions and Economic Change in South Asia*, Delhi: Oxford University Press, 1996: 206–36; G. Balachandran, 'Recruitment and Control of Indian Seamen: Calcutta, 1880–1935', *International Journal of Maritime History*, 9 (1), 1997: 1–18; Ravi Ahuja, 'Die "Lenksamkeit" des "Lascars": Regulierungsszenarien eines transterritorialen Arbeitsmarktes in der ersten Hälfte des 20. Jahrhunderts', *Geschichte und Gesellschaft*, 31 (3), 2005: 323–53; Ravi Ahuja, 'Networks of Subordination – Networks of the Subordinated: The Case of South Asian Maritime Labour under British Imperialism (*c.* 1890–1947)', in H. Fischer-Tiné and A. Tambe (eds), *Spaces of Disorder: The Limits of British Colonial Control in South Asia and the Indian Ocean*, London: Routledge, 2008: 13–48.

31 The most advanced discussion of this subject, in my view, is in Rajnarayan

Chandavarkar, 'The Decline and Fall of the Jobber System in the Bombay Cotton Textile Industry, 1870–1955', *Modern Asian Studies*, 42 (1), 2008: 117–210.

32 Khan, 'I Break with the Old World': 167.

33 In colonial documents, the term '*dasturi*' was used to legitimize informal payments ('bribes') as unavoidable in the specific cultural context of India. See, for example, *Report of the Seamen's Recruitment Committee*, strictly confidential, Delhi: Superintendent of Government Printing, 1922: 17 f (S. Nos. 1–7, A, Department of Commerce, Lascar Seamen, August 1922, NAI). This has been reviewed critically elsewhere, but Amir Haider Khan's account demonstrates graphically that the seafarers' consent to various informal payments was given grudgingly, and in recognition of the fact that access to the maritime labour market could only be gained by contributing to a complex system of payments to various levels of labour market intermediaries, including European ship officers. Cf. Khan, 'I Break with the Old World': 161 f.

34 Khan, 'I Break with the Old World': 215–17.

35 Ibid.: 494.

36 Ibid.: 197 f.

37 Ibid.: 220.

38 Zafar Shaheed, *The Labour Movement in Pakistan: Organization and Leadership in Karachi in the 1970s*, Oxford: Oxford University Press, 2007: 169, 187 fn 7.

39 Khan, 'I Break with the Old World': 219.

40 Ibid.: 217–20.

41 The most influential exposition of this hypothesis is to be found in Dipesh Chakrabarty, *Rethinking Working-Class History: Bengal 1890–1940*, Princeton: Princeton University Press, 1989.

42 Khan, 'I Break with the Old World': 218 f.

43 Ibid.: 220.

44 Ibid.

45 Ibid.: 221 f.

46 Ibid.: 221–23.

47 Ibid.: 224.

48 Ibid.

49 Ibid.: 225.

50 S. Nos. 156–157, Filed, May 1921, Department of Commerce, Lascar Seamen, NAI. For similar *lascar–serang* conflicts over payments, see also F.S. Purnett, Chief Collector of Customs in Sind and Shipping Master Karachi, to Commissioner of Sind, 21 February 1913, Bombay Marine Proceedings, IOR/P/9342, A212, OIOC, BL; R.H.H. Hopkins, Shipping Master Bombay, to Secretary to Government of Bombay, Marine Department, 29 March 1913, ibid., A213–214; Indian Seamen's Union, Resolution on the Pending Grievances of the Indian Seamen, 31 August 1943, M.A. Master Papers, I. Subject Files, A. Scindia Steam Navigation Company, File 150, Nehru Memorial Museum and Library (hereafter NMML), New Delhi.

51 Khan, 'I Break with the Old World': 228.

52 See section under the sub-heading 'Wage Worker or Hireling? "Lascars" and "Freedom"' below, in this essay.

53 Khan, 'I Break with the Old World': 225.

54 Ibid.: 168.

55 For an account of a *serang* who purportedly used his power to demand unrecompensed overtime work as a lever for extracting informal payments (or 'bribes') from a unionized crew, see Report by Calcutta Censorship Authorities, 31 July 1944, translation of a petition by eleven Muslim deckhands and union members to the President of the Indian Seamen's Union, IOR/L/PJ/12/630 (Indian Seamen: Unrest and Welfare), f. 175f, OIOC, BL.

[56] Khan, 'I Break with the Old World': 238.

[57] Ibid.: 237.

[58] Ibid.: 239–40.

[59] Ibid.: 240.

[60] Ibid.: 240 f.

[61] This is discussed in greater detail in Ravi Ahuja, 'Mobility and Containment: The Voyages of Indian Seamen, *c.* 1900–1960', *IRSH*, 51 (supplement S14), 2006: 120–25.

[62] Khan, 'I Break with the Old World': 242 f.

[63] Interestingly, Amir Haider Khan's memoirs reconcile a strong sense of 'worker's pride' in one's own technical knowledge and skill with an equally strong emphasis on the monotony and boredom inherent in the labour process in a steamer's engine room. For the latter, see Khan, 'I Break with the Old World': 227 f.

[64] See, for example, ibid.: 245–50.

[65] Ibid.: 251 f.

[66] Ibid.: 252 f.

[67] Examination of Captain H. Henderson, *Report of the Mercantile Marine Committee* (1903), Vol. II: Evidence: 21.

[68] Khan, 'I Break with the Old World': 253.

[69] Ibid.: 253 f.

[70] Ibid.: 252 f, 258.

[71] Ibid.: 255.

[72] Ibid.: 258.

[73] Ibid.: 257.

[74] Ibid.: 259.

[75] Ibid.: 260 f.

[76] Ibid.: 252.

[77] Such an understanding of a special necessity for a rigid disciplinarian regime in seafaring has been acceptable, in fact, even among prominent representatives of seamen's trade unions. Cf. Leo Barnes, *Evolution and Scope of the Mercantile Marine Laws Relating to the Seamen of India*, New Delhi: Maritime Laws Association of India, 1983: p. 61.

[78] Khan, 'I Break with the Old World': 238.

[79] Hegel, *Phenomenology of Spirit:* 119. Cf. Hegel, *Phänomenologie des Geistes*: 155.

[80] Alf Lüdtke, *Eigen-Sinn: Fabrikalltag, Arbeitererfahrungen und Politik vom Kaiserreich bis in den Faschismus*, Hamburg: Ergebnisse Verlag, 1993: 9–13. Even though 'self-will' appears to be the closest rendering, any translation of the term '*Eigensinn*' into English will miss out on some of its connotations. For an explanatory note, see Alf Lüdtke (ed.), *The History of Everyday Life*, Princeton: Princeton University Press, 1995: 313 f.

[81] I borrow this distinction between 'vernacular' and 'analytical' concepts from Frederick Cooper, though for different purposes. See Frederick Cooper, *Colonialism in Question: Theory, Knowledge, History* (Berkeley: University of California Press, 2005: 60.

[82] Marx, *Das Kapital*, Vol. I, p. 181–83; Marx, *Capital*: 270–73. See also Max Weber, *Wirtschaft und Gesellschaft: Grundriss der verstehenden Soziologie*, reprint of fifth revised edition, Tübingen: J.C.B Mohr, 1990: 70–71, 86–87, 123, 439–40.

[83] Cf. Steinfeld, *Coercion, Contract and Free Labour*: 4.

[84] Banaji, *Theory as History*: 132–34.

[85] Ibid.: 138.

[86] Ibid.: 142.

[87] Ibid.: 152.

[88] See above.

89 Khan, 'I Break with the Old World': 1–22; see also ibid.: 167. For a more systematic discussion, see Ahuja, 'Networks of Subordination'.

90 Chaloub, 'Precariousness of Freedom', *IRSH*: 406.

91 See below for details.

92 Cf. Ahuja, 'Die "Lenksamkeit" des "Lascars"': 329.

93 Rana P. Behal, 'Coolie Drivers or Benevolent Paternalists? British Tea Planters in Assam and the Indenture Labour System', *Modern Asian Studies*, 44, Special Issue 1, 2010: 39. For similar evidence, see also Prabhu P. Mohapatra, 'Assam and the West Indies, 1860–1920: Immobilizing Plantation Labour', in D. Hay and P. Craven (eds), *Masters, Servants, and Magistrates in Britain and the Empire, 1562–1955*, Chapel Hill/London: University of North Carolina Press, 2004: 477.

94 Marx, *Capital*, Vol. I: 271. Cf. Marx, *Das Kapital*, Vol. I: 182.

95 My translation of: 'Unterschied zwischen einem Sklaven und dem heutigen Gesinde oder einem Tagelöhner.' G.W.F. Hegel, *Grundlinien der Philosophie des Rechts*, Frankfurt: Suhrkamp, 1986, §67: 145. This additional explanatory remark by Hegel is not contained in the English translation quoted below.

96 G.W.F. Hegel, *Philosophy of Right*, translated and with notes by T.M. Know, London: Oxford University Press, 1978: 54. The German original reads: 'Von *meinen besonderen, körperlichen und geistigen Geschicklichkeiten* und Möglichkeiten der Tätigkeit kann ich *einzelne* Produktionen und einen *in der Zeit beschränkten* Gebrauch von einem anderen *veräußern*, weil sie nach dieser Beschränkung ein äußerliches Verhältnis zu meiner *Totalitat* und *Allgemeinheit* erhalten. Durch die Veräußerung meiner *ganzen* durch die Arbeit konkreten Zeit und der Totalität meiner Produktion würde ich das Substantielle derselben, meine *allgemeine* Tätigkeit und Wirklichkeit, meine Persönlichkeit zum Eigentum eines anderen machen.' Hegel, *Grundlinien*, §67: 144 f.

97 Marx, *Capital*, Vol. I: 271. Cf. Marx, *Das Kapital*, Vol. I: 182.

98 Marx, *Capital*, Vol. I: 344. Cf. Marx, *Das Kapital*, Vol. I: 249.

99 Marx, *Capital*, Vol. I: 412. Cf. Marx, *Das Kapital*, Vol. I: 316.

100 Marx stated, however, that the 'civil war' over the working day was to end, at one point, with the victory of capital, but from the structure of the theoretical argument it is difficult to see how the tension with regard to the temporal limitedness of wage labour can be resolved without dissolving the wage labour relationship itself. Marx, *Capital*, Vol. I: 412. Cf. Marx, *Das Kapital*, Vol. I: 316.

101 Dale Tomich has made the following similar argument: 'In this conception, struggles of labour and capital over the working day develop capitalist production while the freedom of labour from the domination of capital depends on the shortening of the working day.' Dale W. Tomich, *Through the Prism of Slavery: Labour, Capital, and the World Economy*, Lanham: Rowman and Littlefield, 2004: 27. I disagree in what I think are more than nuances: rather than 'depending' on the shortening of the working day, I would argue that the issue of 'freedom of labour' is articulated in a concrete yet limited form in conflicts over the temporal restriction of wage labour.

102 Ibid.: 149 f, 167 f.

103 Steinfeld, *Coercion, Contract and Free Labour*: 13.

104 van der Linden, *Workers of the World*: 40.

105 Ibid.: 41.

106 Marx, *Capital*, Vol. I: 270. Cf. Marx, *Das Kapital*, Vol. I: 181.

107 I agree with Jairus Banaji's observation that 'since labour-power is never disembodied, what employers buy when they "buy" "labour-power" is command over the use of the workers' bodies and their persons.' Banaji, *Theory as History*: 132. However, I disagree with his conclusion that the differentiation between 'wage-labour' and 'hired labour' is fully irrelevant (ibid.: 135), which seems overdrawn and linked to a conceptualization of 'formal freedom' that has been criticized earlier in this essay.

108 For a brilliant survey of the manifold articulations of 'master and servant' law, see Hay and Craven (eds), *Masters, Servants and Magistrates*. For a brief comment on the theoretical implications of Hay and Craven's path-breaking research initiative, see Ravi Ahuja, 'Making the Empire a Thinkable Whole: Master and Servant Law in Transterritorial Perspective', *IRSH*, 52 (2), 2007: 287–94.

109 Even Leo Barnes, long-term chairman of the National Union of Seafarers in postcolonial India, observed approvingly that the '*discipline at sea is analogous to the discipline needed in the Army or Navy*'. Barnes, *Evolution and Scope*: 61. The role of military forms of employment in shaping labour relations, it seems to me, needs to be explored more systematically, however.

110 Leon Fink, *Sweatshops at Sea: Merchant Seamen in the World's First Globalized Industry, from 1812 to the Present*, Chapel Hill: University of North Carolina Press, 2011: 60.

111 Rediker, *Between the Devil*: 212, 209–11.

112 Conrad Dixon, 'Seamen and the Law: An Examination of the Impact of Legislation on the British Merchant Seaman's Lot, 1588–1918', unpublished Ph.D. thesis, University College, London, 1981: 204, 219–23, 268, 297, 300.

113 Examination of Captain H. Henderson, *Report of the Mercantile Marine Committee*, Vol. II: Evidence, 1903: 27, 41. For a publication summing up these complaints, see (Captain) W.H. Hood, *The Blight of Insubordination: The Lascar Question and Rights and Wrongs of the British Shipmaster*, London: Spottiswoode & Co., 1903.

114 Cf. Ahuja, 'Networks of Subordination': 11 f.

115 Cf. ibid.: 12 f.

116 See *Report of the Mercantile Marine Committee*, Vol. I.

117 Hood, *The Blight of Insubordination*: 48 f.

118 For another graphic account stating the reasons of the City Line to replace British sailors with 'lascars', see Examination of Duncan Mackenzie, Superintendent of Mercantile Marine Office, Glasgow, in *Report of the Mercantile Marine Committee*, vol. II: Evidence, 1903: 48. See also Examination of Frederick Shaw, Superintendent of Mercantile Marine Office, Cardiff, ibid.: 61.

119 This was confirmed by Joseph Havelock Wilson, chairman of the National Sailor's and Firemen Union, whose objective of reducing 'lascar' employment was contrary to that of the shipping concerns, as represented, for instance, by Hood: 'They [the owners] can get Lascars to work hours that Britishers would not work.' Ibid.: 199.

120 Hood, *The Blight of Insubordination*: 48 f.

121 Examination of W.H.D. Deacon, Superintendent of the Mercantile Marine Office, Victoria and Albert Docks, London, in *Report of the Mercantile Marine Committee*, Vol. II: Evidence: 98.

122 Quoted in *Report of the Mercantile Marine Committee*, Vol. II: Evidence: 77.

123 *Labour Legislation in India*, International Labour Office (ILO), India Branch, New Delhi, 1957: 11.

124 Barnes, *Evolution and Scope*: 176–80.

125 Memorandum on Regulation of Hours of Work of Indian Seamen, 1 August 1945, M.A. Master Papers, I. Subject Files, F. International Committees and Commissions, file 896, NMML. For detailed evidence, see Ahuja, 'Mobility and Containment': 116 f (fn 22 f). See also 'Indian Labour Problems: Mr. Joshi's Work at Geneva', *The Servant of India*, XIX (3), 16 January 1936: 35.

126 Examination of Captain H. Henderson, in *Report of the Mercantile Marine Committee*, Vol. II: Evidence: 21.

127 I have explored this in greater depth in Ahuja, 'Die "Lenksamkeit" des "Lascars"': 323–53.

128 The superintending mercantile marine officer of London's Victoria and Albert Docks described the advantages of German and Scandinavian sailors using exactly the same

expressions as was usual with regard to 'lascars': 'they are preferred for their greater sobriety, and shall I say, docility. They do not answer back as readily as the Britisher, they do not give ships' officers so much trouble.' Examination of W.H.D. Deacon, in *Report of the Mercantile Marine Committee*, Vol. II: Evidence: 98.

[129] Examination of James Henson, Secretary of the South Shields branch of the National Sailors', Firemen and Fisher Men's Union, ibid.: 268.

[130] Examination of Joseph A. Bellamy, JP and former Mayor of Plymouth, ibid.: 516.

[131] Jonathan Hyslop, 'Steamship Empire: Asian, African and British Sailors in the Merchant Marine *c.* 1880–1945', *Journal of Asian and African Studies*, 44 (1), 2009: 58 f.

[132] OR/L/PJ/12/630 (Indian Seamen. Unrest and Welfare), OIOC, BL; G. Balachandran, *Globalizing Labour? Indian Seafarers and World Shipping*, New Delhi: Oxford University Press, 2012: 258–62.

[133] Cf. N.M. Joshi, 'Trade Unions in India. II. A Historical Survey', *The Servant of India*, IX (48), 13 January 1927: 610; Theodore G. Mazarello, *Maritime Labour in India,* book supplement to the Special Maritime Labour Issue of *Oceanite: Maritime Magazine of India*, August 1961, Bombay: Maritime Union of India; Frank Broeze, 'The Muscles of Empire: Indian Seamen and the Raj, 1919–1939', *Indian Economic and Social History Review*, 18 (1), 1986: 43–67; see also Balachandran, *Globalizing Labour*: 230–32.

[134] Khan, 'I Break with the Old World': 260 f.

[135] Jairus Banaji has forcefully argued that the needs of 'social capital' (capital as a whole) and of 'individual capital' must not be conflated: 'the real issue of theory here is whether we can sensibly visualize the accumulation of capital being founded on unfree labour (in the strict sense just noted) at the level of the expansion of the total social capital. And the obvious response is, no, since the mobility of labour is essential to the mechanism of capital at this level.' At the same time, he writes, 'individual capitals are indifferent to the nature of the labour force'. Banaji, *Theory as History*: 142 f. The case discussed in this essay suggests, similarly, that the needs of 'social' and sections of 'individual' capital can be opposed to each other under certain circumstances.

The Rowlatt Satyagraha and the Railway Strike of 1920

Radical Developments in the Language of Plebeian Protest in Colonial Punjab

Ahmad Azhar

This essay identifies the immediate years post the First World War (roughly 1919 to 1922) as a period signifying radical departures in the plebeian political culture of Lahore. Diverse ideological currents were reflected in the efflorescence of local political movements under the rubric of the pan-Islamic Khilafat and national Non-Cooperation campaigns.[1] Coalescing in unusual proximity and frequently overlapping around the urban centres of Lahore and Amritsar, these diverse yet interconnected political currents need to be carefully unpacked in order to unearth their distinct ideological underpinnings. The analytical distinction between domains of elite and plebeian politics emerges from a desire to delineate divergent ideological repertoires that nevertheless shared certain elements of a common language, and, therefore, appear as inseparable elements of a single political discourse. Through exploring tensions and complementarities between elite representations and plebeian political praxis, the essay aims to grasp the extent to which elite ideologies of the time either became hegemonic or were forced to accommodate popular pressure, and to ask whether there were fundamental breaks with the languages of class, religion and politics of the pre-war period.

Through revisiting this rich historical conjuncture, the essay attempts to tease out some of the anxieties and aspirations of certain plebeian elements, emerging from their peculiar experiences, as they fed into broader popular movements. The pan-Islamic Khilafat movement, the Congress/Gandhian Non-Cooperation campaign and the labour movement on the North Western Railway form the explicit focus. I argue that these umbrella movements could be less than the sum of their more radical parts by focusing on particular moments during these political movements when plebeian aspirations can clearly be seen as straining against the conservatism of their elite stewardship. The reverse could be true as well, as we shall see in the case of the railway strike, where the anti-colonial dimension of the struggle seems to be clearly exaggerated both by contemporary political observers and historians.[2]

The methodology involves retaining a sustained focus on the politics of railway workshop labour of Lahore as representative of a distinctly delineable, yet sufficiently embedded component of the contemporary spectrum of plebeian political culture. The North Western Railway strike of 1920 is looked at in detail in order to generate empirically grounded insights into the world of plebeian politics. The choice of the term 'plebeian', as opposed to 'working class', is born of an acknowledgment of the shifting terrain of the politics of the poor during this conjuncture; the working class, empirically as well as heuristically, cannot be abstracted from its broader social milieu, and even more so in a context that is defined primarily in terms of extreme proximity and consistent overlap of diverse political currents.

Of particular interest will be the specific forms of articulation adopted by popular movements, which, because of their ambivalent situation at the confluence of 'traditional'[3] and novel modes of expression, can help in identifying emerging ideological shifts. The difficulty involved in such a task becomes clear as attention is diverted from the national stage to consider the variations in localized expressions of these broad movements. Consider, for instance, the programme of a local, village chapter of the Khilafat Committee, which principally included forming roving bands of children who would go around at the break of dawn, exhorting Muslims to come out and say their *fajr* prayers (the early morning prayer) or else face the wrath of God. The lengthy ballads they had composed would predict the terrible fate of Muslims heedless of their religious duties, which included supporting Khilafat.[4] Warnings to the rich, and especially the hoarders, were thrown in for good measure as well.[5] To top it off, these early morning processions were referred to as *prabhat pheris*. So what we end up with is a form with origins in Sikh religious practice being used to awaken Muslims for morning prayers, as part of the political programme of a local chapter of the anti-imperialist Khilafat movement. Besides illustrating the complexity of these forms the account is relevant since it comes from Mirza Muhammad Ibrahim, who would in the 1940s emerge as the leader of the communist trade union movement on the North Western Railway. The anti-colonial and nationalist content of the Khilafat movement sat comfortably within ostensibly communal/religious forms. As we shall see, around the concrete space of the neighbourhood alleys and the community mosques, varied forms of popular protest targeting colonial rule were struggling to find expression. This discontent was linked to but qualitatively different from that which found expression through elite representations in newspaper columns and the legislative councils, and that is why such micro-level, bottom–up perspectives are essential for unpacking broader political movements.

The strike movement of 1920 is here considered a pivotal point through which radical ideological departures in plebeian consciousness achieved a concrete, albeit precarious existence. Their presence, however, can be traced to the period preceding and following the strike, first as premonitory glimmerings during the Rowlatt Satyagraha and later as extended after-glows illuminating the enduring struggle of the railway workers.[6]

The following section surveys the relevant historiographical literature in order to situate this research in the broader theoretical and methodological debates. In the subsequent section the Rowlatt agitation is looked at in its immediate context, and it is argued that it represents a moment when a 'plebeian' alliance begins to emerge. However, this ostensibly unified coalition breaks down under closer scrutiny to reveal tensions within the domain of plebeian politics. How these tensions result in a fracturing of the plebeian, especially in so far as the working-class politics of Lahore begins to acquire a relatively autonomous domain, forms the subject of the last section dealing with the railway strike of 1920.

Popular Politics in the Interwar Period: A Historiographical Note

The immediate post-war years (roughly 1919–22), when the Khilafat and Congress Non-Cooperation movements came together, are generally accepted to be exceptional years of Hindu–Muslim unity. The conjuncture marked a watershed moment which ushered in an era of unprecedented involvement of urban plebeian classes in political movements across colonial India.[7] Along with the observation that this conjuncture provided a glimpse of an unrealized secular nationalism as foreshadowed by popular politics of the time, academic scholarship has frequently discerned premonitions of the subsequent development of Muslim separatist tendencies back to this period of Hindu–Muslim rapprochement. These movements embodied a range of aspirations which, for urban Punjab, have not been systematically explored by the otherwise fairly substantial and rich historiography of the region. Subordinated to the needs of broader narratives of nationalism and religious communalism, these complex, multifaceted movements have traditionally not been analysed on their own terms. Lahore's large organized body of industrial railway workers provides a window on to studying such diverse plebeian socio-political movements of late colonial Punjab.[8] However, an overwhelmingly disproportionate historiographical focus on partition of the province in 1947 has resulted in a blinkered view of pre-partition socio-political movements, where they all in some way or the other form part of an inexorable drive towards a foregone conclusion.

Partition occurred amidst the most brutal forms of religious communal violence, with even the more conservative estimates of casualties fixing the death toll at several hundred thousand; forced migration along religious communal lines meant that millions had to cross over into the newly created states of India and Pakistan. It is not difficult to understand why most historical reconstructions of the interwar period have at some level been 'attempts at incorporating partition in broader narratives'.[9] However, in direct opposition to this approach, a recent trend in academic output within the flourishing field of partition historiography addresses itself to capturing the experiences and memories of participants. Six decades later, the intense trauma of partition still clearly comes out through these studies.[10] Unfortunately, there have not been attempts to reconcile the two approaches. The workshops make a compelling case for the necessity of such reconciliation. If in 1947, at the eve of partition, the workshops are a site of communal violence, it is worth reminding ourselves that only a year earlier they had been at the forefront of a nationwide agitation, as part of a movement where communal antagonisms appear to have been subsumed, at least momentarily, to class solidarity. Teleological narratives, therefore, either of increasing communalization or of growing class solidarity, are in and of themselves as inadequate as fragmentary studies of such moments.

Official versions, sanctioned by the postcolonial states of Pakistan and India, had for long dominated the historiography of this period. The 'two nation theory', originally as the rationale and later on as justification for the creation of a separate nation-state for the Muslims of colonial India, argues that Muslims and Hindus had always comprised two separate, irreconcilable nations.[11] Not much unlike nationalist historiography anywhere else, it is essentially a dramatized rendering of constitutional battles fought on the lofty plains of high politics. For historians concerned with contextualizing political and ideological developments within the broader context of the eventful interwar years, the essentialist and ahistorical conception of religious community advanced by proponents of this theory is not very useful.

Nationalist historiography across the border has been similarly marred by a dogmatic approach towards the causes of partition, even though it offers the much more empirically compelling argument for viewing Muslim religious nationalism in the subcontinent as a product of particular historical forces. In this view secular nationalism, seen as the exclusive preserve of Congress, ultimately lost out to the forces of religious communalism represented by the politics of the Muslim League and nurtured by the policies of the colonial state.[12] Although diametrically opposed to each other in their conclusions, these nationalist histories have much in common as far as methodology is concerned. In all these accounts the focus is exclusively on political machinations at the all-India level between the Congress, the Muslim League and the colonial state, and therefore, sources that can give insight into these political developments are privileged. The underlying assumption that partition was the end result of a drawn out battle between forces of religiously informed nationalism (referred to pejoratively as communalism) and rational secularism buttresses them both.

Increasingly, however, historical practice is reflecting an appreciation of the severely limited explanatory potential of imposing these overarching frameworks of religious communalism and secular nationalism on a highly differentiated and complex political terrain. The ground for such critical re-evaluation was laid by historians who traced the roots of Muslim separatism not to any putative differences, but rather to the conscious manipulation of powerful symbols of group identity, primarily language and religion, by a political elite in a bid to forge a communal sense of identity for their own interests.[13] Others, while adopting a regional perspective focusing on Punjab, located the impetus for the articulation and privileging of communal identities in the political and legal structures introduced by the colonial state.[14] Such scholarship has contributed significantly to understanding the institutional bases of political developments leading to the partition of Punjab by providing detailed analyses of the organizational structures of the Muslim League and the Unionist Party.[15]

Similarly, the role of religious organizations and ideologies in enabling and perpetuating the culture of popular politics of interwar Punjab comes out clearly in several extremely detailed studies of the Khilafat movement.[16] With varying emphases, these studies explore the ideological, institutional and political dimensions of this pan-Islamic movement and its overlaps with other political movements of the time, especially the Congress-led Non-Cooperation campaign. Similar studies exist for the role of the Hindu revivalist organization Arya Samaj in fostering communal antagonism in Punjab.[17] These studies, however, fail to explain the role that popular participation at the level of the plebeian classes played in the emergence and growth of communalism. Like political histories in the tradition of the Cambridge School, they admittedly 'concern [themselves] with organized politics at the top', while acknowledging 'the existence and importance of tensions at the base'.[18] Criticized for their elitist bias in exploring the underpinnings of communalism/nationalism through intellectual and cultural production within the elite strata of society, these writings downplay the extent to which both evolve through constant interplay. They also tell us virtually nothing about ideological reception and construction at the grassroots level.

Sandria Freitag shifted attention to the public arena to take in changing forms of collective activities – including religious festivals, processions and neighbourhood organizations – from which she reads off the development of a communal consciousness.[19] One major shortcoming of this otherwise welcome shift to questions of plebeian agency in crafting communal identities lies in the uncritical privileging of the ostensibly religious content of forms of cultural expression. Suranjan Das's study of communal riots in Bengal during the early twentieth century shows how, on several occasions, class antagonisms were expressed in the language of communal rivalry.[20] The work of George Rudé, Eric Hobsbawm and other social historians of Europe provided the template, which Das then applied to the study of crowds involved in communal riots in Bengal.[21] This contributed to, and was indeed part of, a broader re-evaluation initiated by the subaltern studies group to restore plebeian consciousness as an agent in political movements that had traditionally been looked at from an elite perspective. Perhaps it is Subho Basu's nuanced study of popular politics in interwar Calcutta which comes closest to capturing how plebeian politics in a localized context could converge with the pan-Islamic Khilafat movement and the nationalist Non-Cooperation campaign without being completely absorbed by them.[22]

Recent research in the field of South Asian labour history has begun to show a much greater sensitivity to developments in plebeian discourse, as well as changes in form of popular cultural practices.[23] Joshi takes a step towards reconstructing workers' particular renderings of universal and abstract concepts associated with religion, nationalism and socialism, while Gooptu's work is a detailed exposition of how this process unfolds in a particular urban context through changing forms of popular culture over the long-term. This emerging corpus highlights how elite ideological constructs, themselves not immune from subaltern influences, were negotiated and subsequently recast by the plebeian classes in a bid to express their social aspirations. These are just a few of the more prominent examples of a continuing stream of output by labour historians that traces the interconnectedness of caste, religious, ethnic, gender and class concerns, and the complex and historically dynamic mentalities of the urban working classes.[24]

It is with the purpose of tracing important shifts in these mentalities that the next section looks at a particular agitation, emanating from the Council Hall debates over the passing of the Rowlatt Bill and culminating in what can arguably be construed a popular, albeit short-lived, revolt in the streets of urban Punjab. However, it should be stated at the outset that this essay does not attempt an in-depth study of the Rowlatt Satyagraha; certain events that occurred in Lahore and Amritsar during April 1919 are revisited to extract insights into, and help concretize radical departures from, existing forms of plebeian politics. While the most frequently commented upon aspect of this movement is the brief consensus reached between the communities and across classes, there were other interesting processes at work, signifying more horizontal solidarities. Forms of popular protest emerging during this movement – like the mock funeral, the use of military forms of expression in popular political movements, and an active reworking of ideas on kingship and government – comprise some of the elements that would be carried over into the vocabulary of protest of the railway workers' strike of 1920.

Rowlatt Satyagraha in Lahore: The Making (and Unmaking) of the 'Plebeian Moment'

Official sources, while locating the impetus for the disturbances in the machinations of the 'political' classes, defined loosely as a grouping of lawyers, students and professional agitators, are quick to point to tough economic conditions as the underlying cause of discontent.[25] Inflationary pressures, in other words, rendered the working classes susceptible to being exploited in the interests of the aforementioned political classes, whose irresponsible meddling with this combustible material resulted in anarchy.[26] That there was steep inflation and that the initial thrust came from the educated classes are reasonably uncontroversial observations.[27] Railway employees affected by this general inflation had been petitioning for a raise and intelligence agencies were predicting a strike in case their demands were not met.[28] Whereas the official report places economic hardship at the root of the disturbances, the Congress report reverses this order: inflation being one factor behind 'intensifying' existing political 'discontentment'.[29] Purely economistic frameworks prove insufficient as they elide questions of the local government's important role in precipitating and determining the course of events leading up to the declaration of Martial Law on 15 April.[30] More importantly, designed as this narrative is with the primary consideration of apportioning blame, it does not directly address questions of subaltern initiative, which, it will be shown, was asserting itself with unprecedented force and in unexpected ways.

The Indian Association, led by and representative of the Hindu middle classes of Lahore, had been holding protest meetings in the Braudlaugh Hall at Lahore since February. The Rowlatt Bill was passed on 18 March, after which Gandhi gave sanction for his *satyagraha* campaign.[31] Popular leaders, in their efforts at mobilizing public opinion, exercised considerable creativity in interpretation and representation of the Bill. This '*Nadar Shahi*' (roughly translatable as tyrannical) order, which allowed '*na daleel, na vakeel, na appeal*' (no defence, no counsel, no appeal), was like 'a black serpent which could only travel in the dark'.[32] A particularly sore point of contention that came up repeatedly during the Rowlatt agitation was that the present King was *inaccessible* and did not *hear* his subjects' grievances. Precolonial monarchs, especially the Mughals, had set a precedent for spectacular (albeit arbitrary) public dispensation of rough-and-ready justice for the common folk. Institutions like the *Diwan-e-Aam* ensured that at least in theory, everybody had a claim to the King's audience – a principle that the colonial state consciously tried to retain through regular '*darbars*' at the Commissioner's office. The Rowlatt Act, then, could be perceived as the final blow to this already crumbling façade of kingly benevolence. Distinct from the formal, structured ideological debates in the legislative council, the content of such public speeches helps to grasp the emerging irregular contours of popular ideology. The following discussion will further explore the forms the Rowlatt Act was acquiring in popular imagination.

On 30 March, when unarmed protestors were shot down in Delhi, the movement picked up and a *hartal* was declared for 6 April in Lahore.[33] Even official accounts admit that the *hartal* was an unqualified success, with businesses in the city shutting down voluntarily. During the day processions marched through the city, usually preceded by a black flag with Gandhi's picture on it. In the afternoon a meeting was convened at Bradlaugh Hall and the charged-up crowd spilled over into the streets once the proceedings came to an end. The crowd headed towards the city chanting cries of lamentation like '*Hai Hai Rowlatt Bill!*' and, more interestingly, '*Hai Hai George Mar Gaya!*' (George has died).[34] The authorities, in characteristic fashion, did not attempt a deeper reading of this slogan than as a straightforward declaration of seditious intent, even though the report notes the novelty of such a direct assault on the figure of the King.[35]

The figure of the king as well as popular nationalist leaders, foremost among whom would be Gandhi, surface frequently and ambivalently in popular discourse of the period, but unless properly contextualized, such pronouncements obscure more than they reveal.[36] In the Congress report on the Punjab disturbances, Gandhi began by clarifying in great detail the true meaning and purpose of *satyagraha* as conceived by him, particularly its emphasis on eschewing violence, and thereby categorically dissociating it from the actions of the 'mob' that chanted '*Gandhi ki jai!*' while burning down government buildings and murdering Europeans.[37] The doctrine of *satyagraha*, as well as recourse to what Gandhi referred to as the 'age old institution of *hartal*', for him, could not lead to such 'mob' excesses. He cited the peaceful *hartal* on 6 April to exemplify what an agitation based on the principles of *satyagraha* and in line with the *ancient* custom of *hartal* would look like. Moreover, in order for *satyagrahic* principles to translate to political praxis, what was required was a simple 'extension' of the virtues of patience and self-sacrifice practised in everyday life by individuals, as part of a family, to the public/political sphere. The only room for 'misinterpretation', Gandhi went on to concede, lay in the civil disobedience or passive resistance component of the campaign, for which the people had not been sufficiently primed;[38] the doctrine of *satyagraha* here was clearly distinguished from the politically strategic use of civil disobedience. It is doubtful whether this understanding of the precepts of *satyagraha*, particularly the centrality of *ahimsa* (non-violence), was shared, let alone practised, on a mass scale anywhere in political agitations of the time; but it is not discernible in the actions of the people who, quite literally, rallied under his banner to challenge the Rowlatt Bill.

Throughout this broadbased popular movement, as with the more specific labour movement of the railway workers, which will be discussed later, public discourse repeatedly drew a distinction between the King and Government. In popular imagination the bureaucracy or, in other words, the colonial state, had grown into a leviathan, crushing the very rights it was supposed to safeguard. Consider, for instance, the following extract from a speech delivered by Dr Kitchlew (along with Dr Satyapal, the most popular leader of Amritsar in the build up to the disturbances and till much after), which is representative of this changed attitude:

> He [Dr Kitchlew] assured government that they were more loyal to His Majesty the King-Emperor than the Bureaucracy. The only difference was that Indians wanted full freedom like other colonies . . . as these rights would deprive the bureaucracy of their present high salaries and other privileges enjoyed by them, it therefore always stood in their way and created disunion.[39]

The anarchist–libertarian thread in Gandhi's political–moral philosophy is reflected in denunciations of government, but not always taken to its logical conclusion; categorically listing the government's flaws carried within it the negation of the principle that government by its very nature is antithetical to liberty. During the charged political scene immediately preceding the disturbances this cleavage appeared even more pronounced; the sense of betrayal and disenchantment was conveyed with passion through the language employed, not infrequently with recourse to sarcasm. The following excerpt from one of the last big public meetings at Jallianwala Bagh in Amritsar, before Martial Law brought an end to them, highlights these sentiments.

> . . . the bureaucracy had often passed laws to snatch liberty from the Indians,

> but this law, which had brought about calamity from one end of India to the other was unprecedented . . . women could not feed themselves fully at night. For want of clothes they passed time warming themselves by the fire. *Parda Nashin* women, whom the sun blushes to see, wandered about with their hands out begging for a handful of corn. In face of these things some people called the government the mother of kindness. Instead of a mother what was it becoming . . .[40]

This passage is interesting for several reasons. For instance, it is interesting to note how the Rowlatt Bill was being linked to the prevailing economic discontent and through that to the question of *izzat* (honour). The ideal held up for the conduct of the state towards its citizens was a 'motherly' disposition. The statement also appears to admonish those who clung to the idea of the government as '*sarkar*', i.e. as essentially benevolent, making appeals to its paternalistic duties. The central trope was the familiar one of women, but of course only the 'respectable', *parda nashin* ones at that, being the repository of national honor. Not only was their honour at stake but the honour of the entire nation had been compromised. Within this patriarchal discourse it appeared a seamless move from holding up women as exemplars to trivializing their contributions to the nationalist cause, their bold actions serving as a wake-up call for men to reclaim their honour, as seen in the following excerpt: 'the daughter-in-law of M. Munshi Ram has signed the Satyagraha vow and it is a shame for us men if we decline to do so while females are doing it'.[41]

In the course of the same meeting, the speaker then went on to emphasize the humiliating injustice of the bureaucracy in dismissing the loyal sacrifices made by men in the Great War.

> To protect the King-Emperor India helped with men and wealth in different forms and ways. Indians then said that they would not sell their blood, which they were prepared to shed for the King-Emperor without condition or consideration. Just compare that time with this time. Even the rain had not been able to wash away the blood that had been shed by the lakhs who sacrificed themselves for the King. Thousands of cripples and wounded were present in India on account of the war. This compensation of the bureaucracy would be ever remembered. Bureaucracy was compelled [to do this] by its habits.[42]

In so far as such rhetoric of these popular leaders began to identify the bureaucratic form of government as being antithetical to the exercise of liberty, the radical, anti-authoritarian strain of Gandhi's political philosophy was briefly discernible. Later on we shall see how, when carried through in the actions of the urban poor in refusing even this bourgeois leadership, there was a retreat from this position and a tacit acceptance of government as a necessary check on the anarchist tendencies of plebeians. The *logic* of the bureaucratic machine – the trajectory of this 'giant wheel'[43] – constantly brought it in the path of British justice. In other words, the problem was clearly being identified as systemic; the bureaucracy was not 'really executing the commands of His Majesty the King-Emperor'[44] because it could not do so without compromising its own interests. This message was loud and clear.

In referring to the monarchy, however, the tone changed to that of a jilted lover, hurt by an indifferent attitude but not yet committed to a final break-up. The following excerpt, from another such public meeting, captures this beautifully:

> ... we are not treated as Her Majesty the Queen Victoria and other Kings proclaimed, that there would be no difference between Indians and Europeans in any respect.
> Will the CID please take careful note:
> *Agar teri tarah ham se koi jhute wade karta*
> *Tumhi munsafi se kehdo kon itibar karta*
> [If anyone else had made such false promises with us, could you honestly say who was to believe him?][45]

Cries of '*Hai Hai Rowlatt Bill!*' and '*Hai Hai George Mar Gaya!*' can then be interpreted as serving the dual purpose of lamenting the *passing* of the Rowlatt Bill and mourning the symbolic *passing away* of a beneficent, and very much alive, sovereign who was supposed to be the guarantor of his subjects' liberty. For it would naturally have been inconceivable for him to have allowed this – a clever bit of satire really, but sadly, not picked up by the more literal-minded intelligence apparatus of the state.[46] In other words, the moral stance adopted against the Rowlatt Bill invoked the idea of British government as one based on the rule of law and the image of the King as the embodiment of this principle. This symbolic burial of a living King who could not, or deliberately would not, intervene on behalf of the *legitimate* political rights of his subjects appears to signify a sharp escalation in the tenor of political protest invoking the King, and the introduction of forms like that of the mock funeral to the repertoire of plebeian political forms of protest. Destroying effigies or pictures of the King signified another aspect of this. However, while violence (verbal or through actions) towards the figure of the King reflected rage, mock funerals pointed to his impotence, and in that sense denote a radical departure from appeals couched in the language of paternalism.

Questions concerning how far this was a deviation from traditionally held expectations and ideas on kingship require further research; we have already considered the right to audience by the King as an established principle. Anything in the way of a coherent social contract, however, cannot be reconstructed here. As far as the form of the mock funeral is concerned, it appears unlikely that the *Muharram* procession did not serve as a template. A report on events that occurred in Kasur on 12 April contains the following observation:

> . . . the crowd rapidly grew to several thousands; excitement was enhanced by bringing out at its head a bed covered with a black flag, as an emblem of the death of *liberty* [emphasis added], and at about ten o'clock it took its way, under the direction of Nadir Ali Shah,[47] to the railway station. It now resembled a *Muharram* procession; there were general cries of lamentation, and beating of breasts; it was deliberately working itself up into the state of frenzy which *Muharram* processions frequently exhibit.[48]

Consider it alongside this excerpt from a report on a railway employees' procession during the same period:

> A crowd of about 150 Railway Shop labourers passed through Railway Road to city shouting '*Hai Hai*' saying that the Railway Shops were closed and not one is to go there and another crowd was noticed carrying a bed covered with cloth representing the same as the *cuffen* [burial shroud] of His Honour [most probably referring to the Governor].[49]

British representations of *Muharram* (both official and literary), going back to the eighteenth century, are revealing of a deep sense of anxiety at the opacity of this complex and ambiguous social phenomenon.[50] For observers like Kipling, the social composition of the mass of 'rioters', predominant amongst whom were faceless 'fellows of the baser sort', held dangerous portents for law and order; mutiny lurked just beneath the surface of *Muharram*. It is entirely plausible that confronted suddenly by the biggest threat to British sovereignty since 1857, the official mind was quick to conflate the two. Still, barring the possibility of fabrication on the part of colonial authorities, we could grant that the similarity between the conduct of this political procession and the *matam* (beating of the chests, or *sine-zani* in Persian) witnessed during *Muharram* was not purely imagined. *Matam*, as just one element of Muharram processions, is a solemn form of expression of grief that traditionally only the fringe orthodox elements of the Shiite community employ, and to be engaging in it reflects how deeply the agitation had struck roots with these participants.[51]

Mock funerals in the ostensible form of a *Muharram* procession, like the one mourning the loss of *liberty*, were directed more towards conveying a feeling of helplessness and grief on the part of the participants. The element of critique implicit in the mock funeral both of abstract rights and of particular individuals appears blunted in the case of the former, subordinated as it is to the principal task of expressing a deeply felt sense of injustice and loss. During this period, bareheaded (baring the head being a sign of grief, even shame) congregations chanting cries of '*hai hai*' were not uncommon in Lahore city, and in fact it was exactly such a procession which tried to make its way over to the Mall on 10 April, triggering the chain of events that led to the imposition of Martial Law.[52] Whether in the explicit form of *Muharram* processions or through other means, an acute feeling of hurt was being expressed until the state's heavy-handed response pushed it towards confrontation.

When a 'mob' assembled during the evening of 10 April marched to the city, ostensibly to protest in front of the Government House, it was not without precedent. Spontaneous processions had on occasion been allowed to register their grievances directly to the Governor in a ritual that helped reinforce the image of the government as '*maibaap*', an image that had been carefully nurtured by the 'paternalist' Punjab government.[53] As long as they pandered to such ritualistic reinforcement of this image of colonial rule, processions were considered legitimate and even encouraged, or at the least, not shot at. Consider the following newspaper report on a spontaneous procession of railway workshop employees to the Government House:

> . . . on the 13th instant thousands of employees of the NWR workshops went to the Government House, Lahore, and began to cry out 'hunger'. When His Honour was apprised of the arrival of the crowd, he at once summoned the Commissioner, the Deputy Commissioner, and the Superintendent of Police, who went to the Government House and conversed with the crowd. The latter complained about the high prices of foodstuffs and starvation. His Honour asked whether they would be satisfied if their salaries were increased by one anna per day. The latter said that this would not be sufficient to fill their stomachs and that if flour was not sold at the rate of at least 10 seers per rupee they would die of starvation. Thereupon they were told that grain merchants would be consulted and orders on their representation communicated to them by Monday. The men then came back.[54]

The fact that the procession was chanting 'hunger' removed any ambiguity and with it reason for alarm that such a massive procession could otherwise create. On this occasion, the workers categorically refused the Governor's spontaneous offer to raise their wages and instead demanded that the state intervene in checking the spiralling prices of foodstuffs.[55] The Governor had misinterpreted their plea as an industrial grievance that could be resolved through a wage increase, which the workers immediately rejected. His willingness to consider their petition clearly validated the demand as legitimate and falling within the purview of the state's obligations. Interestingly, during the period of Martial Law following the Rowlatt *Satyagraha*, while the state imposed a slew of restrictions that trampled on basic civil rights, it simultaneously enforced strict price control.[56] Intervention in the operations of the free market, both of a permanent nature and in exceptional periods like this one, had the dual purpose of identifying certain interests as legitimate and then safeguarding these against encroachments from other groups. The Land Alienation Act illustrates how this paternalism was translated into legislation that clearly pitted landowning peasantry against urban capital; in this instance and during the period of Martial Law, the state's intervention was presented as being on the side of the urban poor and against rapacious 'hoarders'. More research is required to ascertain precisely how and to what extent this practice drew upon established understandings of moral economy, and particularly, the state's role in its regulation. The purpose of tracing the pre-history of these practices is not to categorize them as 'pre-industrial' or 'reactive'.[57] Customary – although not primordial as Gandhi would claim – forms of protest like this were proving inadequate vehicles for the expression of popular will; where these forms could not be bent to serve this purpose they could be replaced.

The agitation against the Rowlatt Bill in Lahore assumed the form of a mass movement beginning with the *hartal* on 6 April, and petered out with the imposition of Martial Law on 15 April. Behind every act of the 'mobs' that formed in Lahore between 6 April and 15 April, authorities were quick to identify strong anti-government feeling. Even fraternization between Hindus and Muslims during the *Ram Navami* festival on 9 April 'connoted a union that had only one purpose, a combined attack on government'.[58] That the form of a religious procession had been usurped for the purposes of articulating political sentiments is another accurate observation of a practice that became general during this period. In passing it is also noted that the band accompanying the procession played 'God save the King' when it passed by the Deputy Commissioner.[59] Arguably, in pre-empting a revolution the local government inadvertently forced the hand of social forces that had been ambivalent, if not sufficiently wary, of raising the pitch of their protests. The predicament of prominent 'leaders' leading up to and in fact even during the events of 10 April reveals the strain they were already feeling in mediating between a paranoid government and an impatient populace. The Deputy Commissioner had summoned prominent political leaders on the eve of the scheduled *hartal* on 6 April to deliver a thinly veiled ultimatum aimed at getting them to call off the strike. Their reluctance to offer any assurances betrayed the same helplessness they professed during their depositions to the commission of inquiry later. Events during the next couple of weeks would corroborate this.

The government-appointed commission of inquiry conceded that the 'mob's' 'collection was more or less spontaneous', and during its march from the *Lahori* Gate to the Mall it 'did no damage to shops, nor had it, up to the point at which it encountered the police, assaulted any Europeans'. According to officials' testimonies, the way events unfolded at Amritsar earlier in the day had alerted them to the danger involved in not checking the 'mob's' progress into the civil station. In fact, if anything, events at Amritsar had shown the risk of doing precisely that, since in that instance the 'mob' had only turned violent when confronted by the police. Unable to force the 'mob' to retrace its steps, the police opened fire; official figures put the resulting casualties at one dead and seven wounded. Assisted by a party of cavalry called up from the cantonment, the authorities were able to drive the 'mob' back up to *Anarkali* but could not make it disperse. At this point Pandit Rambhaj Datt tried to buy time to reason with the crowd and, according to newspaper accounts and the findings of the Congress report, he was able to get the aggravated 'mob' to listen, but the brief period of time allowed him was not sufficient, at the expiry of which the police opened fire again. This time the official figure placed the number of casualties at three dead and twelve wounded, but the 'mob' was finally dispersed and made to retreat to the city where, in the words of the commission, it was given free rein to 'wage war against the king' over the next few days.[60]

It is interesting to quote excerpts from the official narrative verbatim, to capture its breathless sense of awe at reporting on what it perceived as clearly a series of truly extraordinary events, of observing a world turned upside down. The spectre of revolution haunted the official mind.[61]

> On the morning of the 11th all shops were closed and an enormous crowd of Hindus and Muhammadans (said to number 25,000 people) collected in the Badshahi Mosque, inside the gate of which a banner was hung bearing the inscription: 'The king who practises tyranny cuts his own roots underneath' . . . the crowd was addressed from the pulpit by Rambhaj Datt and others, and was told to stand and face death if necessary. He referred to an expected decision of the Satyagraha committee that the orders of the police and other laws should be disobeyed even if death were involved. After the speech of *Rambhaj Datt* a railway *khalasi* named Balwant Singh, an ex-sepoy, was brought in. . . . He shouted a false story that Indian regiments had mutinied in Lahore Cantonment and were marching on Amritsar and Lahore. He also stated that they had killed about 200–250 British soldiers and that he himself had killed six. He claimed to be a soldier and was dressed as one. He was garlanded and carried in triumph to the pulpit of the mosque. . . . More speeches were made and a committee of management of the hartal was elected. As a result of this orgy of oratory the rabble left the mosque headed by hooligans carrying sticks and marched through the city, shouting seditious cries and destroying pictures of Their Majesties.

Commenting on 'the unusual nature of a mass meeting in such a place', the commission claims to concur with *orthodox* Muslim opinion, determined in this instance by the pronouncement of the secretary of the Muslim League, which termed such appropriation of the mosque as 'sacrilegious'. A written apology and guarantee that the premises of the Badshahi Mosque would not be made available for the purpose of political meetings was teased from the *Anjuman-i-Islam*, a committee comprised of influential Muslims of Lahore and appointed for managing the mosque.[62] In fact the custodians of the mosque were quite incapable of offering any such guarantees, just as the conservative and moribund Muslim League was powerless to check the grassroots-level political rapprochement between the communities.[63] To the authorities, however, such 'union' could only have been 'temporary', motivated by immediate political considerations, as opposed to the natural/primordial friction between the communities; of course that begs the question as to why the state then actively involved itself in forming oversight committees for the mosque. The report is brutally honest, however, in its reason for condemning such use of the mosque, connoting as it did a 'union that had only one purpose, a combined attack on government'. Such sustained micro-management of public spaces reveals the concrete modalities and implications of the divide and rule policy of the colonial sate. It reveals the state's active role in ensuring that such periods of rapprochement proved artificial, inherently contradictory and hence readily collapsing conjunctures in an overarching narrative of growing communalization of popular politics. If anything, this marks the beginning of a process that resulted in a clear politicization of the pulpit through grassroots initiative of popular firebrand *maulvis* like Maulvi Ata Ullah of Amritsar, estimated to have given upwards of 10,000 speeches during his lifetime. Not only were demagogues like Maulvi Ata Ullah wresting influence away from the politically conservative elements that had previously represented Muslim opinion, from the elite leadership of the Muslim League to politically apathetic *mullahs*, but also creatively reworking Islamic doctrine and history to find religious sanction for merging the Khilafat and Non-Cooperation cause. The following excerpt, one of countless such, from the abstract of an Intelligence report illustrates this, while showing how the concept of *satyagraha* allowed an immense range of appropriations: 'Referring to the Satyagraha movement, started by Gandhi, he [Ata Ullah] remarked that it was not a new movement as it was started by the Holy Prophet of Mecca'.[64]

However, coming back to the account of the meeting in *Badshahi* mosque, the reference to the banner, far from positively establishing a conspiracy against the King, reveals the extent of the state's desperation to prove a popular uprising in so far as it had to rely upon such evidence. By prosecuting on these grounds, the government only helped to reinforce the feeling, already more acute in Punjab because of particularly repressive press laws,[65] that legitimate political rights of expression granted to citizens in the metropolis, as well as other colonies, were being denied. The government's reactive approach arguably served only to push political forces to employ more radical and spectacular means to convey newer horizons of expectations, which were acquiring coherence in contradiction to the state's determined reaction. Rumours like the one circulated by the railway *khalasi* in the mosque straddle these frontiers, and that is where their usefulness lies; in special circumstances they can simultaneously stretch the boundaries of plausibility and inspire actions otherwise unthinkable. In this case, the rumour galvanized people to form a committee for management of the *hartal*, which Kumar rightly describes as the *popular party* and the authorities referred to as the 'revolutionary party'.[66] Interestingly Rambhaj Datt – a close confidant of Gandhi and an avowed *satyagrahi* who had emerged through participation in this movement as a popular leader – too had got in on the act, and was wrongly pre-empting the Satyagraha Committee's programme by predicting a course of action that was more in tune with people's heightened expectations but quite detached from Gandhi's principle of non-violence.

Besides challenging established structures of authority, exceptional periods like this can embolden popular will to articulate itself with unusual assertiveness, imposing strain on existing forms of popular protest, infusing them with new meanings, and where these forms are unable to bend sufficiently to accommodate popular will or if their target remains too diffuse, they are discarded. *Satyagraha*, the way it was envisaged by Gandhi as a form of contesting injustice, while useful for providing cover to divergent political and ideological currents, was still insufficiently elastic to accommodate the range of popular energies unleashed during the Rowlatt agitation, which sought expression through other, more uninhibited forms like the '*Danda Fauj*' (lit. 'baton army').

The official report reflects the tension between acknowledging that the '*fauj*' (army), 'recruited exclusively from Muslim artisans and workers',[67] was not much more than a 'band of hooligans' and the need to prove the hidden hand of 'organized' forces behind it. The *fauj* was certainly exhorting people to obey Gandhi, but simultaneously it was commanding obedience to the Prophet Muhammad, while swearing allegiance to the Kaiser, the Caliph and the Amir of Kabul; in a way, by professing loyalty to all these it was claiming allegiance to none. The commission described the nefarious activities of the *fauj* thus:

> They marched two deep carrying their sticks as if they were rifles at the slope or trail. At constant halts they knelt, by numbers, as if in a firing position. On numerous occasions Chanan Din made inflammatory speeches proclaiming that he and his band were rebels and looked, not to His Majesty the King, but to Germany, Turkey and Kabul as their suzerains. He invoked the assistance of God and of those powers to overthrow the British Government. He also made reference to the Rowlatt Bill. Chanan Din's speeches were applauded by the mob and the fauj as it passed along was joined by recruits who were supplied with sticks.[68]

The following is an excerpt from a poster attributed to the *Danda Fauj*: 'O Hindu, Muhammadan and Sikh brethren, enlist at once in the Danda Army, and fight with bravery against the English monkeys. God will grant you victory.'[69] It seems the *fauj* was caricaturing the white 'monkeys' that formed the target of its assault, and doing so in a manner sufficiently ludicrous to voice the most deeply felt grievances under the cover of satire. If the *Danda Fauj* wanted to make serious threats of violence, it would *not* have brandished the sticks as rifles; had they just waved those sticks around angrily it would have been more intimidating, but by pretending that they were rifles it gave the impression that they were mocking through mimicry.[70] The *Danda Fauj* is also significant in so far as it appears to be a precursor, foreshadow as it is, of more enduring and better defined formations, like the '*Ghareeb Fauj*' of the railway workers which emerged a year later. The metaphor of the *danda* figured prominently in the discourse of the *Ghareeb Fauj* as well; at that point too the *danda* appears to serve purposes other than a declaration of violent intent. As far as the *Danda Fauj* was concerned, ambiguities regarding its composition notwithstanding, its purpose appears clearly one of mocking the very foundations of colonial rule; of spectacularly dispensing with the artifice that normally serves to render unspeakable the truth of naked force, of the proverbial sword, as the ultimate guarantor of colonial rule.

Another indicator of the shrivelling away of inhibitions that normally regulated a superficial harmony of relations between the rulers and the ruled was the changed public attitude towards those perceived as collaborators, from the *khan bahadurs* right down to subsistence-wage CID reporters.[71] There are, however, clear and consistent distinctions drawn between the paid staff of the Intelligence department and the honorary workers reporting to the authorities. While the former were seen as fulfilling their duty and serving as a means of conveying public sentiment to the government, the latter were nothing short of 'devils in the garb of men'.[72] In this way the moral stance against CID-*wallahs* got the force of religious disapprobation behind it.

An incident that occurred on 12 April during the course of a public meeting at the Badshahi Mosque (again attended by Hindus) can be seen as a moment when the social pretence, which had thus far helped maintain the veneer of civility defining relations between CID informants and the public, broke down. When a 'mob' attacked CID informant Ali Gauhar, it was not so much to cause physical harm as to humiliate and ostracize him. In the words of the commission, 'they had him at their mercy, but did not kill him'.[73] There is no indication in the relevant records that they intended to do so. However they did chase him back to his house and later on burnt his *pagri* (turban) in the mosque, as part of a communal ritual meant to disgrace individuals. The customary burning of the *pagri* displaced the rage of the 'mob' on to a symbolic gesture, conveying clearly the community's disapprobation without resorting to 'extremes'. This event can be seen as a critical conjuncture in an increasingly ambivalent relationship with the CID. Earlier on the same day that Ali Gauhar's *pagri* was being burnt in the mosque, there were groups appealing vociferously to the police to fight alongside their Indian 'brothers' and court '*shahadat*' (martyrdom).[74] They were regarded as sell-outs, but at the same time there was an appreciation that they performed the necessary function of serving as a channel for conveying the popular mood to an otherwise disconnected government.[75] Maulvi Ata Ullah, commenting on the relationship between CID and political malcontents, drew this interesting analogy: 'The sepoy's duty was to be vigilant; the thief's to be on the alert.'[76]

At this particular moment, however, the ubiquitous intelligence apparatus of the state was not essential for conveying popular sentiment.[77] It was saying to the government that it had to intervene, which it did in customary fashion by bringing in the cavalry. On the morning of 12 April a police force with military escort converged on the mosque and ordered that its premises be vacated immediately. The dispersing crowds were fired upon, supposedly upon provocation, and there were further casualties. Ironically, the funeral procession of the Hindu youth during the ensuing commotion again became a spectacle of the newfound communal camaraderie that was behind the government's move to purge the mosque. Influential loyalists were employed to mediate with the 'popular party' on the government's behalf, but the negotiations failed and the *hartal* continued despite the proclamation of emergency. The turbulent proceedings of this meeting showed that popular discontent was at such a pitch that even the aforementioned 'revolutionary party' could not, despite its willingness, broker a deal at this point. The massacre at Jallianwala Bagh occurred on 13 April, and the province came under Martial Law from 15 April. The *hartal* was crushed soon afterwards, as much a result of the state's coercion as due to the withdrawal of support from elements within its leadership, which were suddenly confronted with a situation that made them wary of losing all control over the movement.

In retrospect, this brief period can be seen as an exceptional conjuncture when anti-establishment forces achieved an unusual degree of proximity, despite underlying contradictions of class and community, to mount a concerted assault against colonial rule. The open-endedness of the movement and the prevailing political climate enabled it to absorb divergent ideologies in a manner that showed, albeit in the form of a fleeting shadow, the possibility of actualizing the ideal of a nationalist front cutting across boundaries of religious identification. It also clearly marked a critical, though temporary rapprochement between the domains of elite and plebeian politics. The railway workers of Lahore represented one particularly well-documented strand of plebeian politics, and it is instructive to trace the trajectory of their political movement inasmuch as it allows for isolating from the broader political milieu, developments that emerged from within the realm of plebeian politics.

During the disturbances, attendance at the railway workshops remained extremely low, reduced to less than one-third of the total number employed on 16 April. The clerical staff of the railways in particular, representing the '*babu*' class, had to sneak their way to work at the risk of social stigma, and the meagre attendance at the workshops was made possible only by providing armed escorts to the workmen's train coming in from the city.[78] In dealing with the absenteeism at the workshops, the railway management believed it was not altogether linked to the wider unrest and had roots in economic grievances preceding the Rowlatt agitation. It appears reasonable to assume that this class would have felt the financial pinch with particular intensity, but from that it cannot be inferred that their participation in the anti-colonial agitation was devoid of conscious ideological commitment or even empathy. For their concrete, everyday experience of social relationships at the workplace did lend itself to nurturing the kind of general resentment against the inherent injustice and unabashed hypocrisy of colonial rule that provided coherence to the Rowlatt agitation.[79] Let us reconsider the mock funeral procession of the railway workers:

> A crowd of about 150 Railway Shop labourers passed through Railway Road to city shouting '*Hai Hai*' saying that the Railway Shops were closed and not one is to go there and another crowd was noticed carrying a bed covered with cloth representing the same as the *cuffen* [burial shroud] of His Honour.[80]

The similarities to the mock funeral of King George are immediately visible. Also clear is the deviation from the form of that procession of railway workers which called on 'His Honour' to ask for a reduction in the price of grain. This example appears to mark a clear break with established modes of protest that invoked the state's paternalistic duties. Arguably, this connotes a radical departure for this organized workforce which, though no stranger to periods of concerted agitation, was nevertheless marked by its disciplined and constrained forms of protest. Such radical departures incubated within, and developed in relation to, various elements of the plebeian culture of protest that was emerging through this broadbased nationalist agitation. Anti-colonialism was here fused with the question of social equality in working-class politics. However, the only reported instance of the workers resorting to violence refers to their attacking the Time Office at the workshops; a very precise target that seems to convey industrial grievances more than anything else.[81]

The point is that certain features of popular forms of protest were emerging through the course of this agitation, and were subsequently carried over into and refigured through the politics of the railway workers. In other words, a language of plebeian protest was coming into being and part of the vocabulary for that developed in this period. The railway labourers of Moghalpura, however, in adopting these forms for their specific needs, established them as a legitimate and legible repertoire for the articulation of plebeian politics. Already during the Rowlatt agitation plebeian initiative appears to be straining against the rather limiting horizons imposed on the movement by its less radical, middle-class leadership.[82] The subsequent growth of organized labour politics can then be seen as constituting attempts at demarcating a separate domain for adequate representation of plebeian aspirations. Over time, the sphere of plebeian politics itself would fracture and working-class politics would begin acquiring a relatively autonomous domain.

The Strike of 1920: General Miller and the 'Army of the Poor'

The early months of the year 1920 witnessed some localized rumblings of discontent among the railway staff of the NWR, including a strike at Saharanpur where one of the 'ringleaders' was a railway guard by the name of J.B. Miller.[83] This event proved to be a symptom of much more general discontent, which finally boiled over and took the shape of a system-wide strike that began in the workshops and at its peak included tens of thousands of railway employees of the North Western Railway. However, as the official government publication, the *Civil and Military Gazette*, was forced to acknowledge, this strike was novel in that it was not restricted only to formally employed railway workers; even 'the "number" coolies who [were] not railway servants but [plied] for hire for the public were also induced to leave work and thus put the public to great inconvenience'.[84] In fact, the *Civil and Military Gazette* was particularly well placed to appreciate the inclusiveness of the railway strike movement as its own staff went on strike to protest against the printing of a veiled threat to the railway strikers.[85]

By 27 February 1920, a newly formed association of railwaymen, drawing the bulk of its support from the Moghalpura workshops at Lahore, could openly boast 4,000 members.[86] There were repeated warnings by the intelligence agents to check the activities of Miller who was becoming extremely popular with the railway workshop employees, creating a nuisance by attracting huge crowds composed of 'the riff-raff of Lahore Bazaar' to daily meetings of the strikers outside Mochi Gate.[87] When the strike collapsed and the meetings stopped, intelligence agents noted with relief that 'meetings of strikers are not held daily and the Mochi Gate is no longer the rendezvous of a *resentful idle crowd* [emphasis added]'.[88] Terms like 'riff-raff' and 'idle crowd' are reflective of a general tendency on the part of the colonial state to be wary of agglomerations of the urban poor.[89] The cult of Miller was fast expanding and might not have been limited to the railways strikers; the myth of Miller would continue to spread through the streets of Lahore through 'poetasters' singing 'popular poems' in his praise.[90]

The warnings came true on 22 April when the dismissal of seven fitters from the Carriage and Wagon workshops resulted in a complete strike in these units within two days. By 29 April, employees from the locomotive workshops had also joined the strike, bringing the total number of strikers in Lahore to 15,000.[91] Intelligence reports observed that the railway strike was feeding into the 'prevailing discontent especially in Lahore itself where 15,000 or more of the strikers [had] for many weeks been wandering about without work and attending almost daily meetings at which their grievances were set forth'.[92] The relationship between the strike movement and the prevailing field of nationalist politics, however, cannot be reduced to a simple absorption of the former into the latter in a manner where both remain unchanged. Focusing on points of overlap between the politics of this self-proclaimed 'army of the poor' and contemporary nationalist political movements, particularly the Khilafat movement, help in bringing their peculiarities to sharper relief.[93] In other words, contextualizing the strike within its political and social milieu helps identify certain distinct and enduring characteristics of working-class political culture and ideology that developed during the course of the strike.

Unravelling, for instance, the idiom of militarism, which enveloped and suffused so much of the discourse around the movement, can lead to an appreciation of the underlying ideological battle lines that were being drawn. From the very beginning of the strike, Miller's commitment, and the workers' ready acceptance, to adopting ostensibly militaristic representational forms become clear. Miller and his 'lieutenants' riding into 'Moghalpura on horseback with a band and the "Union Jack" . . . ordering the men to fall in, four abreast, and march[ing] them to the city',[94] marked the beginning of a movement that helped establish such processions as an enduring form of working-class politics in Lahore, especially as far as the railway workers were concerned.[95] The inherent contradictions and difficulties involved in grasping the ideological underpinnings of such popular political forms come out when overtly anti-colonial declarations are followed by processions led by trade union spokesmen on horseback, accompanied by a brass band and Union Jack. Interestingly enough, at the conclusion of the strike, the railway authorities had to succumb to the demand that Miller be allowed to march his proverbial troops back, just as he had led them out. The metaphor of *fauj* was a carefully crafted rhetorical device. 'General' Miller after all carried a bugle, frequently employed the services of a brass band and demanded military precision in public processions. Such fragments give insight into how 'General' Miller's persona was created and sustained through these practices. There is an interesting anecdote about how 'he kept a bugle with him, and was, therefore, nicknamed as the "bugler". A blow upon it was a signal for workers in Moghalpura railway workshops to abandon work and gather around him.'[96] A magical charm was attributed to this whistle, considering how it seemed to impose itself on the rhythms of the workplace in so far as under normal circumstances these were regulated through the sound of buzzers.[97] The following represents a highly dramatized account of a particular confrontation between the union and the railway authorities, where the whistle was instrumental in tilting the precarious balance in favour of Miller.

> When the men assembled at 8 am on the 19th for their roll call, Mr Miller gave his whistle. It was a sight worth seeing. We hope the men who saw it would never forget it. The Station Master had posted his Anglo-Indian subordinates at every gate to stop the men. Mr Miller was standing on a high place just in front of the railwaymen but out of the Railway limits. The whole army of strikers and a large number of spectators stood on either side of him. There was excitement among the staff. They wanted to obey. They dared not step out. The two generals, Mr Miller and Mr Norris, stood firm and resolute – the one summoning, the other restraining. For a minute the whistle seems to have lost its magic.[98]

Unusual as this excerpt – drawn from what was essentially a strike bulletin – might appear, it was by no means unusual in the context of the inspired representational styles adopted by the union. The enchantment of symbols drawn from the quotidian world of union politics could not occur without a concomitant disenchantment of everyday markers of authority; conditioned to be in thrall of booming engines, these workers were increasingly marching to the beat of Miller's drum. Authority divested thus was invested in the figure of 'General' Miller and enacted publicly through displays of unconditional surrender.[99] Miller, in turn, adopted techniques of mobilization which reflected his absolute ability to control and discipline his troops.

Before discussing the explicit impact and underlying motivations of these techniques of exercising control over the movement, and crucially, in demonstrating it in the form of public spectacle, it would be expedient to briefly consider the possible reasons for naming his army the '*ghareeb*' (poor) *fauj* instead of, say, the '*mazdoor*' (workers) *fauj* or any other such variant. The most straightforward explanation would be that although the bulk of the union membership and its more militant core came from the railway workshops, it was not exclusively a workers' (*mazdoor*) union. Strategically, it was imperative that the 'native' subordinate, white-collar staff in the Traffic and other departments struck as well. By claiming to speak in the name of the poor, as opposed to the working class, the union left the door open to different cadres within the railway hierarchy, including casual – or what would be called today 'informal' – employees linked to the railways. Strategically, it made sense to not use the term *mazdoor* in order to include the various grades of clerical and supervisory staff; the following analysis of the leaders' rhetoric leads one to believe that at this moment there was a real possibility of forging a broad plebeian front. The nomenclature made allowance for bringing in various strands of class-based politics of the poor working classes, cutting across the formal–informal sector divide, and involving blue and white-collar workers. Not simply a matter of semantics, the use of the term '*ghareeb*' needs to be seen in the context of a dominant discourse that tried to marginalize the poor; it can then be seen as a countermeasure aimed at asserting pride in poverty. *Ghareeb* and *bhooki* (hungry) army were the terms interchangeably used to refer to this movement, and the question of bread was constantly foregrounded as the central issue in the campaign in order to emphasize its class-based tenor. Such a clear demarcation was necessary if the movement wished to participate in the contemporary political sphere on its own terms.

Miller continued efforts to organize employees of other government departments, including the *patwaris* and police subordinates, though with limited success.[100] His control over the 'army' that he did manage to amass, however, was under no doubt, and he wasted no opportunity for a demonstration. One such opportunity presented itself when Zafar Ali Khan finished lecturing a public meeting of the strikers outside Mochi Gate.

> On the evening of 5th May there was a spectacular congregation of railway workers outside the Mochi Gate. Such meetings take place regularly in Lahore. The audience numbered 15,000. Maulvi Zafar Ali Khan got there around the time of *Maghreb* prayers and delivered a rousing speech. Referring to the confrontation between capital and labour, he prophesized that the workers would prevail and the capitalists, representing an avatar of *Yamnoon Al-Maun*, will be crushed. Then he said that 'you create this ruckus over food but be careful lest your carnal desires distract you from your duty to God. I have noticed that a handful of Muslims have offered the *Maghreb* prayers. *You should consider your religious duties paramount* [emphasis added]. It is also incumbent upon our Hindu brothers to pray in their own way. *If you get your bread at the cost of forsaking God it will only be a source of shame and ill-fortune. Remember God in all your political movements and bow only in front of him* [emphasis added].' Mr Miller and M.A. Khan of the labour union then spoke in support of Zafar Ali Khan, saying that they too believed that the labourers should practise their respective religions, as that would ensure their welfare.
>
> The audience clapped enthusiastically three times. The way they went

about it was that *Mr Miller would 'whistle' and the applause would begin. He would then gesture with his hand and the clapping would stop* [emphasis added].[101]

Perhaps the faintest hint of a covert tussle can be sensed here; one that would repeat itself whenever political 'outsiders' were to address these meetings.[102] Maintaining the integrity/identity of the *Ghareeb Fauj* as a distinct social movement around specific demands of plebeian groups required negotiating the centripetal forces of political currents that its communally diverse composition and the prevailing political scene rendered it susceptible to. Arguably, Zafar Ali Khan was not simply illuminating a pre-existing esoteric dimension of the workers' movement; he was in fact, by dismissing its profane demands as secondary, assigning a radically different meaning to the struggle, from outside (and above). This intervention may have been interpreted as an attempt at cooption that compromised, at least potentially, Miller's efforts to foster class-based solidarity among the workers. It is not being suggested that class-based mobilization necessitated the annihilation of communal identifications, or that identitifications in categories of 'class' could ever completely avoid religious symbolism. In this instance, Zafar Ali Khan used an analogy from the Quran to identify the capitalists in language that would have resonated with the Muslims in the audience. Yamnoon Al'Maun probably refers to Surah Al'Maun, which discusses

> the character of those who claim to be Muslims but are oblivious of the hereafter. These people deprive the orphans of their rights, are heedless to the dues of the destitute, and pray without holding God in remembrance, forgetting the objective behind prayer. *Their charitable acts are a display of their false piety, since they do not give for the love of God* [emphasis added].[103]

While analysing the discourse around this strike movement we find other instances where religious vocabularies provided useful metaphors for pushing a secular agenda; this intervention by Zafar Ali Khan, however, cannot so easily be categorized as such. His moralistic speech reflected ideological differences with this non-communal, class-based movement. Just as workers had intervened in the Rowlatt agitation, which essentially was a quarrel between representatives of elite interests and the colonial state, the elite were now showing reluctance to give this sphere of politics free rein.

Compare Zafar Ali Khan's speech with the following excerpt from an intelligence report of a speech by Miller, and the contrast becomes clear:

> . . . he [Miller] was not an agitator and did not mean to fight government . . . the Afghans and the Bolshevists . . . are coming shortly and *the empty stomached persons* would be *obliged* to join hands with them . . . *they were hungry and demanded food*. They were naked and demanded clothes, and were *not in need of anything else* [emphases added].[104]

The question of bread here comes across as the primary need rather than a secondary concern, as argued by Zafar Ali Khan. By seconding Zafar Ali Khan's stance, Miller responded in the only way available that would not preclude the support of popular political leaders, and ensure against hurting the religious sensibilities of his troops. However authority, both moral and temporal, could not that easily be conceded; while his followers were free to pray behind Zafar Ali Khan for the attainment of their spiritual needs, for getting their worldly grievances addressed they were asked to surrender absolutely to Miller's leadership. That little demonstration at the end where Miller, not much unlike the conductor of an orchestra, coordinates the applause, was a gentle reminder that although indulgent towards outside influences, this army ultimately marched to the beat of its own drum. Invariably the nationalist press commented admiringly on the discipline shown by the *Ghareeb Fauj* and the novelty of the elaborate forms it manifested itself through. But the possibility that these forms could have represented overt displays of a closing of the ranks against interference from outside political currents is not rendered explicit in these contemporary reports. Various ideological tendencies emerging under the umbrella of the pan-Islamist Khilafat movement and the Congress Non-Cooperation campaign were articulated through grassroots initiatives at the local level; from campaigns aimed at banishing prostitutes from the neighbourhood, enforcing prohibition and banning cow slaughter to communist mobilizations, the entire ideological spectrum from right to left was represented. Thus the *Ghareeb Fauj* was not, for instance, free from the influence of patriarchal social values. In fact it could be argued that the hyper-masculine culture of the workshops contributed to a hardening of patriarchal social structures, and of course would also have linked up with the military language of protest we have been considering. Reporting on Miller's tactics of mobilization an intelligence report quotes him as saying: 'The strikers were behaving like women; they should remain true to their cause and obey the orders of their general.'[105] And:

> Mr Miller's activities are the talk of the town of Lahore. His interesting methods of persuading the people to join him are described by the people with delight. 'Are you a man or a woman?' asked he of a booking clerk. 'I am a man' replied the latter. 'Come and sign this paper and join the railway labourer's union' and the man joined. This is his method and he is said to have enlisted five thousand men up to now.[106]

It was the intertwinement and overlap of diverse ideological repertoires and political currents that necessitated a clear demarcation of the *Ghareeb Fauj* without isolating it from other popular political movements.[107] Going back to Miller's preferred practice of marching his army under the Union Jack, it can be seen as a way of distancing his movement, with its concrete and well-defined economic motivations, from the anti-colonial sentiment-animating offshoots of the Khilafat and Non-Cooperation campaigns. Displacing it to the formal, and hence more ambivalent, discursive level provided an alternative to unequivocally rejecting anti-imperialism, which, however dispersed, was a powerful sentiment informing his followers' sympathy with the Khilafat and Non-Cooperation campaigns.

The accoutrements, like the bugle and the standard, served as props, but not in the way they are used in theatre to render artifice more believable. On the contrary, here they served to present a dramatized narrative of real events. The most important audience to this drama of course was the state, split in its response at the local, provincial and all-India levels. With the embarrassing experience of the Martial Law of 1919 behind it, Government of India, under increasing pressure from the Office of the Secretary of State, was extremely wary of imposing the Seditious Meetings Act to counter the strike. While local government, and especially the Intelligence branch, was shocked by the violence of the language employed by the leaders of the strike movement, the requests to apply the Seditious Meetings Act were promptly snubbed by the higher authorities. At a meeting held by the Lieutenant Governor of the Punjab at Lahore, and attended by the top bureaucrats, to discuss the Hijrat movement and the proposed extension and application of the Seditious Meetings Act to the Lahore division, it was mentioned by the Home Secretary that 'he had been informed that 290 of the railwaymen now on strike and several clerks from the Audit Office had given in their names as volunteers for hijrat'.[108] According to a newspaper report submitted by Miller, at a public meeting it had been 'resolved that the strikers having cried hoarse over their grievances from the 23rd April to the 8th July and all their representations to the authorities for better conditions having failed the only thing advisable [was] to leave a country which [could not] procure sufficient food for them and where none [heard] their grievances'.[109] He claimed that nearly 100 men had given names for *hijrat* and more names were expected to follow, and that local chapters of the association should furnish names to the relevant *hijrat* offices.[110] A police abstract of intelligence concerning a meeting held a few days later at Badami Bagh Station, Lahore, to welcome a train carrying '*muhajirs*' (migrants) from Sindh en route to Afghanistan, also points out how Miller was present as a member of the reception committee comprised of notable Muslim political figures of Lahore such as Zafar Ali Khan. Speeches were made, and during his speech Miller announced 'his intention of proceeding to Kabul as soon as he had collected 1000 volunteers from among the railway strikers'.[111] It is important to note that this desperate bluff was made when the strike had all but collapsed.

In order to further explore the question of how far this strike movement was linked to anti-imperialist political currents like the Khilafat movement, the complex public persona of J.B. Miller, the avowed general of the *Gharib Fauj*, deserves closer inspection. A brief biographical sketch gives insight into his past:

> J.B. Miller was born in 1880 in Ceylon. He started his career on the EIR but was dismissed from service during the EIR European locomen's strike

> of 1907. Then he served for a while in the canal factory at Rurki and also served in the army before he rejoined the ORR as a guard in Saharanpur. He was again dismissed from service during the ORR loco strike in 1920. He was fond of athletics and was *popular with the Indian staff at Saharanpur* [emphasis added] because he organized sports and games. He had a sister who kept a shop in Rawalpindi in 1920.[112]

J.B. Miller, a working-class Irishman born in India but to European parents, by virtue of Indian domicile status and class background, was part of a community situated, both in terms of legal categories and lived experience,[113] ambivalently between the British colonial oligarchy and the Eurasians; the former were unwilling to integrate them and the latter they did not want to identify and assimilate with. However, conflicts over self-identification within this embattled community, important though they might be, are peripheral to this particular research. What is important for our purposes is to ask how, if at all, race and social background figured in the popular myth of Miller. The following excerpt from a popular vernacular newspaper of Lahore, reporting on a large public meeting of the strikers, addresses this question.

> Yesterday, 6th May, during the evening there was the usual meeting of railway strikers at Mochi Gate. Maulvi Zafar Ali Khan delivered a speech in which he said that what separated this meeting from earlier meetings was not the fact of Hindu–Muslim unity, since that had been in evidence before. The fact that more than 20,000 people had gathered there too did not distinguish it, since Lahore had witnessed even bigger public meetings. *What made this particular meeting stand out was the presence of Anglo-Indians, foremost amongst whom was their benefactor Mr Miller*, along with guards of the railways etc.
>
> It is generally presumed that the Anglo-Indian community stays aloof from nationalist movements, but *this question of bread is such that it dissolves all differences of race or community*, and in their stead a feeling of mutual love and cooperation takes root . . . *Miller is British. His skin is the same colour as yours.* If you won't listen to him whom will you listen to? [all emphases added][114]

Initially, the term 'Anglo-Indian' denoted all British in India, the oligarchy as well as working-class people like Miller, while descendants of a 'white' father and an Indian mother were called 'Eurasians'. Later the term 'Eurasians' was officially discarded because of its discriminatory connotations and, by the time we are concerned with here, the same community had inherited the denomination 'Anglo-Indian'. However, for conceptual clarity, we shall draw on the distinction between European and Eurasian where it is necessary. For the use of the term Anglo-Indian in the discourse we are analysing frequently conflates these categories, as Zafar Ali Khan did in this instance. When referring to Miller along with the railway guards, who by this time would have been mostly 'Eurasian', he used the term Anglo-Indian. However, he also followed that up by calling him 'British' on the basis of the colour of his skin.[115]

Despite such ambiguity, there was never any confusion about whom Miller was actually representing; for an outsider like Zafar Ali Khan at least, Miller's militant stance did not seem to express the aspirations of the Anglo-Indian ('Eurasian' or working-class white) community whose interests, particularly in railway employment, were usually articulated through adopting a loyalist stance and appealing for continued preferential treatment based on considerations of racial background. As pointed out by Zafar Ali Khan, the participation of a limited segment of the Anglo-Indian ('Eurasian') railway employees highlights the radical expansion of the sphere of plebeian politics where even the exceedingly loyal 'Eurasians' were brought in. It was, after all, through racially discriminatory policies that the Anglo-Indian community had come to occupy privileged positions in the railways. Upper subordinate positions such as those of drivers, guards and workshop supervisors were reserved almost exclusively for this community.[116] Zafar Ali Khan, tongue firmly in cheek, was in fact saying that this rapprochement represented a volte-face driven purely by immediate material considerations; after all in that earlier speech his attitude towards movements centered purely on questions of bread was made clear when he admonished the Muslim audience that 'bread at the cost of forsaking God could only be a source of shame and ill-fortune'.[117]

However much sense it made for Zafar Ali Khan, a *khilafat*ist and a nationalist, to use this opportunity to pass yet another barbed critique of the Anglo-Indian community's 'anti-nationalist politics', Miller's public posturing never dwells on this Anglo-Indian connection. In the popular imagination the colour of his skin contributed to the aura of 'General' Miller by presenting him as *a rebel against his own people*, and thereby imbuing his defiance with greater import. Intelligence agents certainly argued that '*Miller is a popular hero for opposing his own countrymen* [emphasis added] and championing the cause of the railwaymen.'[118]

For the workers of Moghalpura white skin was an immediate marker identifying their concrete, flesh-and-bone masters at the workplace. How exciting it must have been, and how unlikely not to draw parallels between them and the person of Miller. However it is important to appreciate that the 'Anglo-Indians' (both 'Eurasians' and working-class whites) occupied vastly different roles in the colonial social hierarchy in general, and the railway organization in particular. Especially tasks of supervision involving direct interaction with the Indian workers usually fell to the 'Anglo-Indians'. Their importance as a buffer, and what that could have meant in terms of mediating everyday relations at the workplace between European officers and Indian workers, comes across in an anecdote from the memoirs of Norman Charles Watney who had a long career with the Moghalpura workshops – beginning with his recruitment in a mid-level supervisory position and terminating with his appointment as Divisional Superintendent of the workshops.[119]

> I found that the role of the Anglo-Indian in the railways was absolutely paramount. They occupied almost every possible supervisory position in the sheds, in the workshops and even on the locomotives themselves. Without this fraternity I feel sure that the railway would have come unstuck. It must be remembered that . . . even the bulk of the drivers was entirely illiterate. . . . And the result was that they occupied quite a strong position, for without them no views could come from the illiterate to management. *The management in any case were never able to speak and act as could the Eurasian. He knew the fads, the foibles and what is more he knew exactly how to speak which we never did* [emphasis added]. I shall never forget that when I was in one shed one of the Anglo-Indian foremen started to what I thought tear off an immense strip to one of them. But the staff around him started to laugh and I asked him why he was laughing. Oh, he said, I have been abusing him and his grandparents from A to Z, but don't you ever try it. . . . I realized that there was a method of speaking to the Indian and these people could do it.

The unenviable position of the 'Anglo-Indian' (both 'Eurasian' and poor white), not to yet speak of the plight of workers who had to suffer verbal abuse from them, ambivalently situated as it was at the fringes of both European society and native 'culture', has been reasonably well explored.[120] While European 'blood' entitled them to certain privileges vis-à-vis the Indians, the refusal on the part of the European community to fully assimilate them left the 'Anglo-Indians' in the awkward position of being stuck in a state of limbo; part European and part Indian, they ended up being neither. Housed in relatively enclosed European-style railway colonies, educated in missionary schools and automatically enlisted into the Indian Defence Force,[121] the Anglo-Indians (Eurasians) were socially and spatially kept at a remove from both the Europeans and Indians. The workplace, however, be it the engine room of locomotives or the shop floor at the workshops, helped bridge these distances. At the workshops Indian workers enjoyed camaraderie with their 'Anglo-Indian' ('Eurasian' and white blue-collar) supervisors, which, while nothing extraordinary perhaps, would still have been unthinkable with their caste superiors or the *chaudharis* of the village. A common refrain against hiring educated, high-caste Indians for supervisory posts requiring a more hands-on approach was that they refused to do any form of manual labour, which legitimized the hiring of Europeans and Anglo-Indians in these positions since they had no such qualms, given of course that the price was right.[122] For the railway workers, rubbing shoulders with whites at the workplace or on the sports field, while ostensibly not much more than a gesture, could have helped put in perspective the experience of racial inequities through comparison with their everyday experience of more rigid caste, *biraderi* and class distinctions. These distinctions were not left behind at the gates of the workshop. Yashpal, in his novel *Dada Comrade*, dedicates a chapter to a conversation with a railway workshop employee of Moghalpura. The worker in this semi-autobiographical work of fiction insists that the true exploiters were the jobbers and the *mistris* who, he points out, were not white but brown-skinned like him. He talks about bribes and other forms of extortion, along with the preference of higher-caste brahmins to recruit from their own community, representative of the most intimately felt forms of exploitation – again also because these were not restricted to the workplace. He ends the monologue with the question as to why he should participate in anti-colonial struggles if that meant promoting these people to the positions occupied by the whites. Arguably, in determining the form of any anti-colonial resentment these workers could have harboured, quotidian experiences at the workplace are no less important than the sensationalist anti-colonial rhetoric they were increasingly being exposed to, be it through the urban elite or local neighbourhood *moulvis*.

Every morning thousands of labourers from as far out as Sialkot would board a special train to bring them to the workshops; this train, interestingly, was popularly referred to as the *babu* train. Although meant partly in jest – and no less revealing as a consequence – this observation helps shift attention to what government service (or *sarkar ki naukri*) could have meant to these workers drawn from the lower castes and traditionally engaged in agricultural labour or as village artisans. The introduction of wage labour through *sarkari naukri* helped erode traditional ties of deference. In the process, opportunities for limited social and spatial mobility presented themselves in the form of workshop employment. Becoming a *naukar* of the colonial government (the North Western Railway was a state enterprise) allowed some leeway in negotiating the bonds of servitude experienced within a caste and class-bound social hierarchy. Being labelled as *babus* represented the prestige society attached to government service and how this form of employment contributed to developing the self-esteem of an otherwise disenfranchised labouring poor. For these subalterns this represented the obverse of the dark side of colonialism.[123] Far too often, engagement of plebeian movements with broader social movements is taken as hegemony of the latter over the former.[124] Such frameworks, in so far as they refuse to probe deeper than ostensible overlaps to the nuances of an essentially dialogic process, are inadequate tools for approaching questions of plebeian consciousness. By imagining the colonial state as a leviathan such frameworks fail to account for the complexity and contradictions within and between its institutions.

Any exploration into the anti-imperialist credentials of the movement, or the lack thereof, would be inadequate to the task as long as it glosses over the apparent contradiction of a white person leading it.[125] The following excerpt can offer insight into how such contradictions were reconcilable, perhaps more so at this juncture than any other.

> The Afghans and the Bolshevists, he [Miller] said are coming shortly and the empty stomached persons would be obliged to join hands with them. *He belonged to the Indian Defence Force and knew how to use arms* [emphasis

> added], and would teach the same to his force . . . if India was internally united no force, he asserted could invade or govern it.[126]

Membership of the Indian Defence Force, a marker of his identity as a European and symbolic of his community's identification with the imperatives of colonial rule, with a flourish and with complete nonchalance, was disconnected from its symbolic baggage and presented as a potentially enabling agent against fighting the injustices of colonial rule. Miller could make such uninhibited references to his racial lineage because he was simultaneously making ostentatious displays of solidarity with the starving workers, such as when he promised to 'live on parched grain' until he got them their demands.[127] The fact that Miller was able to establish himself as the undisputed spokesman of the *Ghareeb Fauj* (or army of the empty stomached, as he referred to them in the excerpt above) sits uncomfortably with efforts aimed at subsuming it within the field of contemporary political movements, which were more unequivocal in the expression of anti-colonial sentiments.[128] Having a white person at the helm of the movement very clearly separated it from the aggressively nationalist political currents that had a tendency to assume racial overtones. It conveyed the secular and class-based tenor of the movement and enabled it to comfortably engage with various strands of communally organized politics.

Nothing in the way of memoirs exists for Miller, making it much more difficult to explore questions of self-identification. On one occasion though, during the course of a public meeting held in connection with the strike, Miller declared with much aplomb that he was an Irishman and would follow the example of his brave countrymen in fighting oppression.[129] Obviously there is no reason to presume that this was the only, or even the strongest, sense of belonging he had. This, after all, is the same person who a few months earlier had felt no compunction in leading his army of strikers under the Union Jack. Therefore, instead of parroting out clichéd disclaimers about how identities are fractured, in flux, multiple, layered, etc., we could perhaps, more usefully, direct our gaze outward to the ways in which Miller chose to project himself and the movement he spearheaded. Arguably, it is through these verbal and non-verbal forms of expression, which have been considered in the preceding section, that the ideological content of the movement can be reached.

By all accounts the Hijrat movement, as a corollary of the Khilafat agitation, failed to actually mobilize the railway strikers, who sought employment elsewhere in the city or chose to go back to their villages instead of migrating to Afghanistan. In an immediate sense, therefore, the movement did not have an impact on this labour movement. However, it was through their travels on this ostensibly religious pilgrimage that individuals like Fazal Elahi Qurban turned communist. Having received a lukewarm reception from the Afghan government, which had neither explicitly supported nor rejected the Hijrat movement during its build-up, these *jihad*ists eventually ended up at communist training institutes in Tashkent and Moscow.[130] Fazal Elahi Qurban represented a small coterie that had turned from political Islam to communism and which, beginning with the late 1920s and continuing beyond partition, would provide leadership to the various working-class movements in Punjab including the increasingly sympathetic one on the railways. Defections from political Islam to left-wing politics as in the 1920s, or from communism to Islamism in Pakistan during the 1970s and 1980s, are bewildering only if considered at the level of pure theory. It is arguably at the much fuzzier level of praxis at the grassroots level that these appear as gradual transitions and not sudden reversals. Sustained focus on the railway workers' world of politics can help illuminate the processes through which these ideologies were negotiated at the grassroots level and reworked as a consequence.

As we have seen, plebeian aspirations that came within the ambit of a large and organized social formation like that of the railway strikers were able to find expression through a somewhat distinct and distinguishable repertoire of forms of political articulation; the development of this language of labour, however, neither occurred in a vacuum, nor remained confined to the domain of organized labour politics. The organized activities of the *Ghareeb Fauj* represented attempts to assert social identification in terms of class – attempts that were struggling to find adequate vehicles for their articulation; coming up, inevitably, against metaphors ostensibly reflecting community consciousness. However, as a consequence of the dialogue necessitated by this encounter between political ideologies and existing vocabularies for their articulation, such metaphors could be extracted from one context and transplanted into a different chain of meanings. The following excerpt from a strike meeting by a prominent Muslim lieutenant of Miller's 'army' helps illustrate this.

> They say we are poor and small in number, but those who are so, are always successful. The Arabs were haughty and idolators. God sent Muhammad to infuse in them the Unity of God. At first *a few men, who were very poor* [emphasis added] became his followers. He, by means of those few converted all the Arabs to Islam and was at last successful. So we, comparing our Miller's case with him, deduce the inference that he too will be successful. We are now not fighting for the removal of our poverty, but we are fighting for the honour of our country and forefathers.[131]

Muhammad's followers could quite easily, and more in tune with the dominant interpretation, be singled out for their piety, but the speaker here chooses to focus on their poverty. The original followers of Muhammad are distinguished by their poverty and humility, in stark opposition to the haughtiness of those who refused to heed his message; here is an attempt at devising a moral category of the 'poor', in direct opposition to 'riff-raff'.

Miller, Mahatma, Muhammad – between these varied appropriations and the murky world of constantly shifting alliances of union politics, the one constant was the undeniable 'appeal of Miller's bugle'[132] to the railway workers. It is arguably to Miller, therefore, that we need to direct our gaze if anything in the way of a general comment on the essential characteristics of the movement is to be extracted from the historical context of its relationship with the broader field of force of political movements, as well as divergent tendencies within the movement. Enduring *forms* of plebeian protest, although emerging from specific conjunctures, in so far as they transcend their immediate context, have been investigated for the same purpose and their possible functions explored.

Conclusion

The immediate post-war period, particularly the Rowlatt Satyagraha agitation, brought together various strands of elite and plebeian politics under the broader rubric of the nationalist and pan-Islamist movements. This analysis of political upsurge of the early 1920s shows that there was an unusual degree of overlap between elite and plebeian politics. The broad-based Rowlatt agitation, for instance, was a moment when elite hegemony appeared established in so far as the nationalist movement, hitherto restricted mostly to the sphere of elite politics, brought on board virtually all segments of society. The analytical distinction between domains of elite and plebeian politics, however, is borne out by evidence of tensions within the broader field of force of popular politics as it was being formed at this moment. This essay has tried to show that within a field of shared forms of political expression, elite and plebeian culture challenged each other and began to assume separate shapes in the process.

Already discernible during the Rowlatt agitation, the contradictory thrusts of plebeian and elite politics, by the time of the railway strike of 1920, had resulted in a further hardening of these respective spheres. The discussion of the strike has tried to demonstrate that the language of protest around the strike movement clearly borrowed certain elements from the vocabulary of popular protest that had come together through the interaction of elite and plebeian politics during the Rowlatt Satyagraha. However, these shared forms of political expression, by their appropriation and articulation through the strike movement, were becoming associated with a particular brand of class-based and non-communal plebeian mode of politics. This is borne out by tracing the recurrence of such forms in the politics of the Moghalpura Railway workshops in particular, and the broader field of plebeian politics of interwar urban Punjab in general, over the next decades. In Amritsar, Bashir Ahmed Bakhtiar, the driving force behind the formation of the hugely popular Amritsar Labour Federation, borrowed heavily from Miller's tactics to forge a broad plebeian alliance.[133]

If the 1920s are compared with the 1940s, another transformation of the political culture of Moghalpura railway workshop workers becomes discernible. The sphere of plebeian politics, never fully formed or completely under elite hegemony, witnesses a significant break in the 1930s. By the 1940s, the field of urban politics in Lahore had been further differentiated to an extent that 'plebeian politics' no longer was a viable category for subsuming the politics of railway labour in Lahore. Moghalpura's politics of labour had acquired a greater measure of (relative) autonomy from both elite and broader plebeian politics in regard to both form and content: while the city was increasingly immersed in conflicts along the hardening line of religious affiliation, a parallel space emerged simultaneously where joint action based on shared experiences at the workplace served as a conceivable option for large bodies of workers at least at some, however transient junctures. The (no doubt dominant) process of 'communalization' of both elite and plebeian politics that has been the exclusive focus of much of the existing historiography, was shot through with as yet unappreciated counter-tendencies in Lahore's now more easily distinguishable domain of labour politics.

Notes and References

1 For detailed academic studies on the Khilafat movement, see Gail Minault, *The Khilafat Movement: Religious Symbolism and Political Mobilization in India*, New York: Columbia University Press, 1982; and M. Naeem Qureshi, *Pan-Islam in British Indian Politics: A Study of the Khilafat Movement, 1918–1924*, Leiden: Brill, 1999. For a contemporary account from the perspective of the intelligence agencies that were closely following these developments, see P.C. Bamford, *Histories of the Non Co-operation and Khilafat Movements*, New Delhi: Deep Publications, 1974.

2 See Lajpat Rai Jagga, 'Formation of an Industrial Labour Force and Forms of Labour Protest in India: A Study of the Railways, 1919–1937', unpublished Ph.D. dissertation, Jawaharlal Nehru University, New Delhi, 1983: 121–31. The title of his dissertation notwithstanding, it is precisely Jagga's lack of serious engagement with the discourse and forms of labour protest which leads him to uncritically bunch together the railway workers' movement with other anti-colonial movements. Also see Ravinder Kumar, 'The Rowlatt Satyagraha in Lahore', in Ravinder Kumar (ed.), *Essays on Gandhian Politics: The Rowlatt Satyagraha of 1919*, Oxford: Clarendon Press, 1971. Kumar makes a compelling case to view the events of this period as signifying a radical break from the existing political culture of Lahore.

3 Not to be understood as primordial. Eric Hobsbawm and Terence Ranger (eds), *The Invention of Tradition*, Cambridge: Cambridge University Press, 2009. The book presents several excellent empirical studies which, taken together, form a compelling argument for being circumspect about the implied historical continuity of rituals. Nandini Gooptu, *The Politics of the Urban Poor in Early Twentieth Century India*, Cambridge: Cambridge University Press, 2001 and Chitra Joshi, *Lost Worlds: Indian Labour and Its Forgotten Histories*, New Delhi: Permanent Black, 2003 grapple with the question of how pre-existing cultural forms with roots in rural society are imbued with new meanings in the process of being transposed to an urban context.

4 Mirza Muhammad Ibrahim's video interview, recorded in 1999, translated by me from the Punjabi original. The village in question is Qila Gujaran, near Rawalpindi, Punjab.

5 Ibid.

6 This formulation is borrowed from Ernst Bloch, *Principle of Hope*, Vol. I, reprint, Cambridge, Massachusetts: MIT Press, 1995: 48. 'New and unexpired ideas appear as premonitory glimmerings and extended after-glowings, shining ahead or continuing to bathe history in their unextinguished light.'

7 See, for instance, Gooptu, *The Politics of the Urban Poor*.

8 See Ian J. Kerr, 'The Railway Workshops and Their Labour: Entering the Black Hole', in Ian J. Kerr (ed.), *27 Down: New Departures in Indian Railway Studies*, Hyderabad: Orient Longman, 2007. These workshops comprised of two separate facilities located

adjacently, classified according to their function as either the carriage and wagon shops or the locomotive shops. Entirely new locomotive workshops were built opposite the main carriage and wagon shops at Lahore in 1912. These locomotive shops employed about 5,000 men by 1926. The carriage and wagon shops employed about 5,600 men, bringing the total number of employees of the Moghalpura workshop complex to over 10,000 men in 1926. To put this in perspective, in the year 1928, out of 51,613 people employed in factories in the province of Punjab, 13,624 or roughly one in four were engaged by the railway workshops.

9 David Gilmartin, 'Partition, Pakistan and South Asian History: In Search of a Narrative', *The Journal of Asian Studies*, 57 (4), 1998: 1068–95. Shabnum Tejani, 'Reconsidering Chronologies of Nationalism and Communalism: The Khilafat Movement in Sind and Its Aftermath, 1919–1927', *South Asia Research*, 27 (3), 2007: 248–69 attempts to point out how this 'teleological' pull distorts reconstructions of the Khilafat Movement.

10 Urvashi Butalia, *The Other Side of Silence: Voices from the Partition of India*, London: C. Hurst, 2000; Gyanendra Pandey, *Remembering Partition: Violence, Nationalism and History in India*, Cambridge: Cambridge University Press, 2001; Ian Talbot, *Divided Cities: Partition and its Aftermath in Lahore and Amritsar 1947–1957*, Oxford: Oxford University Press, 2006; V. Z. Yacoobali Zamindar, *The Long Partition and the Making of Modern South Asia*, NewYork: Columbia University Press, 2007.

11 I.H. Qureshi, *The Struggle for Pakistan*, Karachi: Karachi University Press, 1969; K.K. Aziz, *The Making of Pakistan: A Study in Nationalism*, Lahore: Sang-e-Meel Publications, 1988.

12 Bipan Chandra, *India's Struggle for Independence 1857–1947*, Harmondsworth: Penguin, 1989; Mushirul Hasan, *Nationalism and Communal Politics in India 1885–1930*, New Delhi: Manohar Publishers, 1991.

13 Paul Brass, *Language, Religion and Politics in North India*, Cambridge: Cambridge University Press, 1974; Francis Robinson, *Separatism among Indian Muslims: The Politics of the United Provinces' Muslims, 1860–1923*, London: Cambridge University Press, 1974.

14 Imran Ali, *The Punjab under Imperialism 1885–1947*, Princeton: Princeton University Press, 1988; Gilmartin, 'Partition, Pakistan and South Asian History': 1068–95; David Page, *Prelude to Partition: The Indian Muslims and the Imperial System of Control, 1920–1932*, New Delhi: Oxford University Press, 1982.

15 Ian Talbot, *Provincial Politics and the Pakistan Movement: The Growth of Muslim League in North-West and North-East India, 1937–47*, Karachi: Oxford University Press, 1988.

16 Minault, *The Khilafat Movement*; Ayesha Jalal, *Self and Sovereignty: Individual and Community in South Asian Islam since 1850*, London/New York: Routledge, 2000; Qureshi, *Pan-Islam in British India*.

17 Kenneth W. Jones, 'Communalism in the Punjab: The Arya Samaj Contribution', *The Journal of Asian Studies*, 28 (1), 1968: 39–54; John Zavos, 'The Arya Samaj and the Antecedents of Hindu Nationalism', *International Journal of Hindu Studies*, 3 (1), 1999: 57–81.

18 Ayesha Jalal and Anil Seal, 'Alternative to Partition: Muslim Politics between the Wars', *Modern Asian Studies*, 15 (3), 1981: 415–54.

19 Sandra Freitag, *Collective Action and Community: Public Arenas and the Emergence of Communalism in North India*, Berkeley/Oxford: University of California Press, 1989.

20 Suranjan Das, *Communal Riots in Bengal 1905–1947*, New Delhi/New York: Oxford University Press, 1991.

21 George Rudé, *The Crowd in History: A Study of Popular Disturbances in France and England, 1730–1848*, New York: Wiley, 1964; and E.J. Hobsbawm and George Rude, *Captain Swing*, London: Lawrence and Wishart, 1969.

22 Subho Basu, *Does Class Matter? Colonial Capital and Workers' Resistance in Bengal 1830–1937*, New Delhi/Oxford: Oxford University Press, 2004.

23 Joshi, *Lost Worlds*; Gooptu, *The Politics of the Urban Poor*.

24 For monographs that engage seriously with questions of gender, see Janaki Nair, *Miners and Millhands: Work, Culture and Politics in Princely Mysore*, New Delhi: Sage, 1998; Samita Sen, *Women and Labour in Late Colonial India: The Bengal Jute Industry*, Cambridge/New York: Cambridge University Press, 1999.

25 See the note by A.J.W. Kitchin, Esq. CIE, ICS, Offg. Commissioner, Lahore Division, in District and Miscellaneous Reports on the Punjab Disturbances, 5 July 1919, IOR/L/PS/20/F206, Oriental and India Office Collection [henceforth OIOC], British Library [henceforth BL]. Particularly p. 108: 'Legal practitioners, newspaper editors mainly culpable for inciting the students and the schoolboys, and their instruments . . . the riff-raff of the towns, i.e., artisans and menials, who make up 40 per cent of the convictions by the Special Tribunals.'

26 See *Memorandum on the Disturbances in the Punjab, April 1919*, Lahore: Sang-e-Meel Publishers, 1997. The subsequent account of the Rowlatt Satyagraha draws extensively on this report for establishing the sequence of events. See also House of Commons Parliamentary Papers East India (disturbances in the Punjab, etc.), Report of the committee appointed by the government of India to investigate the disturbances in the Punjab, etc., (Cmd. 681), which contains the Minority Report as well.

27 See Kumar, 'The Rowlatt Satyagraha of 1919': 272–74 for a discussion of prevailing inflationary trends, and ibid.: 276 for profiles of individual 'middle class' leaders of the movement.

28 Secret Punjab Police Abstracts of Intelligence [henceforth SPPAI], 1920, National Documentation Centre, Islamabad [henceforth NDC]); and District and Miscellaneous Reports on the Punjab Disturbances, IOR/L/PS/20/F206, OIOC, BL.

29 See Memorandum on the Disturbances in the Punjab for the former, and the Congress Report on the Punjab Disorders for exposition of the latter perspective.

30 Of course there was rampant inflation and it would have been an underlying cause, perhaps the most important one. However, the form this resentment adopted for its public expression was to a degree determined by the state's reaction.

31 The 'Anarchical and Revolutionary Crimes Act, 1919' was commonly referred to as the Rowlatt Act. Interestingly, it was also referred to as the 'Black Act', which links it to Gandhi's campaign against the Black Act in South Africa.

32 'It is a way of the bureaucracy to form commissions for satisfying the people. More than Rs. 3,00,000 had been spent on the Industrial Commission, but when the time to pass the bill came they said they had no time. It was just to the contrary in connection with the Rowlatt Bill when His Excellency the Viceroy kept awake the members of the Council up to 1-30 A.M. (cries of shame). This the Viceroy did, perhaps, because he thought that the black serpent could only travel in the dark.' And: 'This act nullified the right of an appeal by an offender. If once one offence was committed under this law, all the doors would be shut against the accused. Was it not a Nadar Shahi order?' See SPPAI, 1919, para 494, NDC.

33 See Memorandum on the Disturbances in the Punjab for a chronology of events.

34 Ibid.: 41.

35 Ibid.: 'the slogan "hai hai George margiya" in evidence here for the first time'.

36 See Shahid Amin, 'Gandhi as Mahatma: Gorakhpur district, Eastern UP 1921', in *Subaltern Studies: Writings on South Asian History and Society*, edited by Ranajit Guha, Vol. 3, New Delhi: Oxford University Press, 1984, for a nuanced study showing how the image of Gandhi was being reworked in ways that did not necessarily converge with that being promoted by Congress and Khilafat committees.

37 Memorandum on the Disturbances in the Punjab: 6.

38 A tactic resorted to by Gandhi in calling off the Non-Cooperation movement after

the events of Chauri Chaura, effectively displacing the blame for the outrage from the infallible principles of *satyagraha* on to the people who were as yet incapable of practising them.

39 Public speeches from the period are replete with clear and precise identification of the 'bureaucracy' (*daftari hakumat* was one variant of the vernacular terms used) as the target of polemic. SPPAI, 1920, para 284, NDC.

40 SPPAI, 1919, para 494, NDC.

41 SPPAI, 1919, para 531, NDC.

42 SPPAI, 1919, para 532, NDC.

43 Speech by S. Annubhava Nand, an Arya Samaj preacher and a resident of the United Provinces: 'are there not such regular processions (Muharram and Dusserahs) in these native states as well? We do not say that the source of all these troubles is our Government, but we can say that the real source is the giant wheel of bureaucracy, which is going on since 50 years. Really, it has spread a poison.' SPPAI, 1919, para 532, NDC.

44 Ibid.

45 SPPAI, 1919, para 531, NDC.

46 King George, after all, had not really passed away just yet.

47 It cannot be claimed with absolute certainty but the name sounds distinctly Shia.

48 Memorandum on the Disturbances in the Punjab: 56–57. Kasur, a town with a population of roughly 30,000 inhabitants at the time, was overwhelmingly Muslim. It had a large community of leather workers.

49 Report on Punjab Disturbances, 1920, Evidence, Vol. IV: Lahore and Kasur, L/PJ/6/1669, IOR NEG 14658: 581, OIOC, BL.

50 David Pinault, *The Shiites: Ritual and Popular Piety in a Muslim Community*, London: I.B. Taurus and Co. 1992: 63–76.

51 Prabhu P. Mohapatra, 'The Hosay Massacre of 1884: Class and Community among Indian Immigrant Labourers in Trinidad', in Arvind N. Das and Marcel van der Linden (eds), *Work and Social Change in Asia: Essays in Honour of Jan Breman*, New Delhi: Manohar Publishers, 2003: 187–230. Mohapatra unravels some of these layers of meanings of the *Muharram* procession, albeit in the much distant regional and social context of indentured plantation labour in late nineteenth-century Caribbean plantations.

52 *Paisa Akhbar*, 10 April 1919 (consulted at Punjab Public Library, Lahore). The article makes the observation that such a huge gathering of Hindus and Muslims had never been witnessed in Lahore. According to the article this procession was unique in that the participants were required to take off all headgear and were beating their chests, not unlike a *Muharram* procession.

53 Much has been written about the 'paternalism' of the Punjab government. For instance, see Tan Tai Yong, *The Garrison State: Military, Government and Society in Colonial Punjab, 1849–1947*, Sage Series in Modern Indian History, New Delhi: Sage, 2005, for a detailed study on how this self-identification with 'paternalism' translated into concrete policy measures towards the army recruitment districts.

54 Indian Newspaper Reports, January–December 1914, IOR/L/R/5/195: 101, OIOC, BL. Extract from *Zamindar*, Lahore, 15 February 1915.

55 Ibid.

56 Memorandum on the Disturbances in the Punjab: 53.

57 David Arnold, 'Industrial Violence in Colonial India', *Comparative Studies in Society and History*, Vol. 22 (2), 1980: 234–55, traces the tradition of rural violence to its origins in a peculiarly rural political and moral economic framework. While integral to the process of determining moments of rupture, such a line of inquiry ignores interesting processes of how older forms were being reworked and infused with new meanings.

58 Memorandum on the Disturbances in the Punjab: 46 and *Paisa Akhbar*, 10 April 1919.

59 Ibid.

60 Memorandum on the Disturbances in the Punjab: 45.

61 The following excerpts are drawn from reports of commissions that were appointed during the period of Martial Law to prosecute individuals on charges of sedition, and as such foreground the more radical rhetoric and actions of the crowds, possibly indulge in exaggeration, and might even contain fabrications.

62 Memorandum on the Disturbances in the Punjab: 52.

63 'The Muslim League has become a mere appendage of the Congress and is content to play second fiddle to the latter, so fully has it, in recent times, fallen under the influence of the older, better organized and more ably worked institution. Judging by its proceedings at Amritsar, one looks in vain for anything to justify its existence as a separate body from the Congress. Indeed so complete is the metamorphosis that the League, a Muhammadan body selected, of all places, the Bande Matram Hall of Amritsar for its annual meeting'; SPPAI, 1920, para 169, NDC.

64 SPPAI, 1920, para 419, NDC.

65 Several newspapers were proscribed, like Zafar Ali Khan's hugely popular *Zamindar*, restarted on 21 April 1920; SPPAI, 1920, para 971, NDC.

66 Kumar, 'The Rowlatt Satyagraha in Lahore'.

67 Kumar does not explain how he determined the composition of the *danda fauj* but appears confident in this assertion; ibid.: 293.

68 Memorandum on the Disturbances in the Punjab: 45–46.

69 Ibid.

70 One contemporary interpretation offered for referring to the British as monkeys was that they believed in Darwin's evolutionary theory. 'he [Dr Kitchlew] addressed the audience and said that the Maulvi [Ata Ullah] referred to the English as white monkeys because they believed in Darwin's theory!'; SPPAI, 1920, para 1060, NDC.

71 Kumar, 'The Rowlatt Satyagraha in Lahore', shows how the *khan bahadurs* and *raises* were losing influence; SPPAI reports confirm his account.

72 SPPAI, 1920, para 1060, NDC.

73 Memorandum on the Disturbances in the Punjab: 47.

74 Ibid.: 46.

75 Numerous excerpts from the secret abstracts; SPPAI, 1920, paras 747, 931 and 995, NDC.

76 SPPAI, 1920, para 995, NDC.

77 Punjab Police Report's annual review mentioning that the special branch was under unprecedented stress and its resources stretched thin due to the vastly increased number of political meetings during the year. 'The NWR Railway strike, the Hijrat movement and the adoption of non-cooperation . . . threw a heavy burden on the department. Criminal Investigation Department records were taken of over 1400 public political meetings and 375 of those were attended by officers of the CID to report on the speeches made.' 'Report on the Police Administration of the Punjab during the year 1920', Punjab Home Proceedings, Part A, October 1921: 49, OIOC, BL.

78 Report on Punjab Disturbances (1920), Testimony of Mr C. C. Ryan, Station and Assistant Traffic Superintendent, NWR, Lahore Junction, L/PJ/6/1669, IOR NEG 14658: 567, OIOC, BL.

79 Lajpat Jagga, 'Colonial Railwaymen and British Rule: A Probe into Railway Agitation in India, 1919–1922', *Studies in History*, 3 (1) and (2), 1981: 120.

80 Report on Punjab Disturbances (1920), Evidence Volumes, IOR L/PJ/6/1669, IOR NEG 14657 and 8: 581, OIOC, BL.

81 Ibid.: 44.

82 Kumar, 'The Rowlatt Satyagraha in Lahore', tries to establish this primarily through looking at testimonies of the 'leaders' to the inquiry committee.

83 For an account of this strike, leading up to the dismissal of Miller, see Jagga, 'Colonial Railwaymen and British Rule', and *Tribune*, 18 January 1920.

84 *Civil and Military Gazette*, 2 May 1920, Colindale Newspaper Archive, London.

85 *Zamindar*, 3 May 1920, National Archives of Pakistan, Islamabad.

86 'An association of NWR employees has been formed in Lahore, for which thanks are due to Mr. Miller, and his other colleagues. So far nearly 4,000 members have joined the association. Others who are desirous of becoming members, should apply to the Secretary NWR Association, Brandreth Road, Lahore'; *Tribune*, 27 February 1920, Centre for South Asian Studies, Cambridge.

87 Weekly Report of the Director Central Intelligence, 1 March 1920, Home Political (Deposit), Proceedings, March 1920, OIOC, BL: 'The dismissed railway guard Miller has, for some time past, been haranguing large crowds in Lahore and inducing men to join the railway labour union which he has brought into being . . . the meetings that he arranges and the speeches that are delivered thereat by himself and his intimate co-workers are looked upon as a sort of amusement and relaxation by the riff-raff of Lahore bazaar who muster strong at these gatherings.'

88 SPPAI, 1920, para 1433, NDC.

89 Gooptu, *The Politics of the Urban Poor*. George Rudé's writings remain the best guide to demystifying categories like crowds, mobs, etc., and understanding them as historical agents. See Rudé, *The Crowd in History*.

90 'The praises of Mr. Miller, the leader of the railway strikers, have been sung by some street "poetasters" in their popular poems having little poetic merit but plenty of fun'; Report on publications registered in the Punjab during the year 1920, Punjab Home Proceedings, July 1921, Part A: 10, OIOC, BL.

91 The following account of the strike is based primarily on the newspaper *Tribune* and Jagga, 'Colonial Railwaymen and British Rule'.

92 SPPAI, 1920, para 493, NDC.

93 Intelligence reports from as early as February 1920 note that Miller was popularly referred to as the Railway Mahatma Gandhi and also the Railway General; SPPAI, 1920, para 530, NDC. Miller himself actively promoted this image when, for instance, he proclaimed during a meeting, again outside Mochi Gate, on 15 February that 'he was a general and a leader no doubt and was collecting his forces'; SPPAI, 1920, para 493, NDC. Newspapers like the *Zamindar* had taken this up and were using the term *Ghareeb Fauj* for General Miller's proverbial troops; *Zamindar*, 3 May 1920. Also see, 'Theory and Practice', *Civil and Military Gazette*, 12 May 1920, where it is stated: 'Here is a fair sample of the argument of the strike organizers who are seeking a dubious notoriety as the champions of the "hungry army".'

94 'NWR Workshop Strike', *Civil and Military Gazette*, 27 April 1920: 'On Saturday afternoon as the men were about to enter their special [train] to return to the city, they were stopped from doing so by the leaders of the railway union who came in to Moghalpura on horseback with a band and the "Union Jack". They ordered the men to fall in, four abreast, and marched them to the city.'

95 Consider this excerpt from an Intelligence report more than a decade later: 'On 16 September, 1932, Dr Shuja Ullah addressed some 700 workmen, whom he marched round the workshops in formation and ordered them to salute their officers with closed fists, instead of in the usual manner . . . and said he proposed to teach drill to the workmen, as they were to lay down their lives. . . . He ended his pernicious speech . . . the audience was then marched in military formation to the workshops'; SPPAI, 1932: 543, NDC.

96 Jaspal Singh, *India's Trade Union Leaders*, New Delhi: National Publishing House, 1981: 166.

97 A speaker addressing a meeting of the strikers when the strike had almost collapsed 'complained that Miller's whistle had lost its *whilom charm*; and this he ascribed to a lack of unity'; SPPAI, 1920, para 1523, NDC. Kipling's description of Jamalpur workshops in Rudyard Kipling, *Among the Railway Folk*, ebooks@adelaide, html

version: http://ebooks.adelaide.edu.au/k/kipling/rudyard/railway/chapter2.html, Chapter 2, originally published 4 August 1888 in the *Pioneer*. 'The "buzzer" howls, for it is nearly tiffin time. There is a rush from every quarter of the shops, a cloud of flying natives, and a procession of more sedately pacing Englishmen, and in three short minutes you are left absolutely alone among arrested wheels and belts, pulleys, cranks, and cranes.'

98 'Wazirabad strike', *Tribune*, 20 May 1920.

99 In fact the railway management refused to even negotiate with the Association founded by Miller, since doing so would mean officially recognizing it. The workers, on the other hand, made it clear that they would not have anybody else representing them.

100 See SPPAI, 1920, para 2133. The geographical sphere of his activities spread further in the next few years as he made extensive efforts to organize the workers of the Dhariwal Mills.

101 *Zamindar*, 3 May 1920; my translation from Urdu.

102 Zafar Ali Khan was the editor of the hugely popular, Muslim nationalist and pro-Khilafat newspaper called the *Zamindar*, which exercised influence on the plebeian Muslim classes of Lahore. However, the fact that the workers would have accepted his leadership on political matters does not mean they would have followed his lead in this instance.

103 Maulana Muhammad Ali, *The Holy Quran: Arabic Text, Translation and Commentary*, Lahore: Ahmadiyya Anjuman-i-Ishaat-Islam, 1951.

104 SPPAI, 1920, para 493, NDC.

105 'OM's All-India Letter, 15 March 1920 – with Letters from the Provinces', Prog. no. 57, Home Political, Deposit, March 1920, OIOC, BL.

106 Ibid. Of course such patriarchy was not the exclusive preserve of male working-class culture. Refer back to Dr Kitchlew's reference to *parda nashin* women.

107 India Home (Political) Proceedings, Part A with notes, IOR NEG 8622, September 1919 to February 1920, OIOC, BL. 'The latest report I have seen indicated that the railway strike was losing rather than gaining ground, that in fact Guard Miller had not met with much success outside Lahore, that funds were short and the position getting rather desperate for the strikers. . . . So far as I understand the strike has been run on purely industrial lines and political complications and more particularly the Khilafat agitation have been kept out of it. Action under the Defence of India Rules might have the result of importing non-industrial considerations into the struggle.'

108 Ibid.

109 Police Abstract of Intelligence Punjab, Simla, 24 July 1920, IOR NEG 8956, September 1920 to December 1920, OIOC, BL; 'NWR Strikers Decide on Hijrat', extract from *Leader*, Allahabad, 12 July 1920.

110 Ibid.

111 India Home (Political) Proceedings, Part A with notes, IOR NEG 8956, September 1920 to December 1920, OIOC, BL. Police Abstract of Intelligence Punjab, Simla, 24 July 1920. 'Paragraph 1515 Railway, 11-7-20 – The special train conveying the Sindhi Muhajirin from Larkana to Peshawar reached Lahore Junction at 1-31 am, some 5 hours behind the schedule time. . . . After a 20 minutes halt the train proceeded to Badami Bagh. . . . At Badami Bagh an hour's halt had been arranged for refreshments and by 5 pm a large crowd, numbering anything from 25,000 to 30,000 spectators, had assembled. The crowd included many students from the various local schools and colleges and some 2000 railway strikers. The long interval between 5 pm and 2 am, the time at which the special train arrived, was mainly occupied in listening to speeches from Maulvi Ata Ullah, Zafar Ali, M.A. Khan and Miller. The latter announced his intention of proceeding to Kabul as soon as he had collected 1,000 volunteers from among the railway strikers. . . . The principal representatives of the Reception Committee were Zafar Ali, Ata Ullah and Miller. Miller shook hands with

Jan Muhammad, the leader of the emigrants, and asked him to convey his respects to the Amir and inform him that he hoped to visit his country shortly.'

112 Jagga, 'Colonial Railwaymen and British Rule': 120.

113 Laura Bear, *Lines of the Nation: Indian Railway Workers, Bureaucracy and the Intimate Historical Self*, New York: Columbia University Press, 2007.

114 *Zamindar*, 5 June 1920; translated from Urdu.

115 Bear, *Lines of the Nation*, argues that class and race were constitutive of each other, through looking closely at the 'Anglo-Indian' community.

116 Report of the Royal Commission on Labour in India, Evidence, Vol. VIII, part I (Railways). See especially, the Memorandum submitted by the North Western Railway Union: 359–75. Muslims, in particular, were severely under-represented in these higher posts.

117 *Zamindar*, 5 June 1920; translated from Urdu.

118 SPPAI, 1920, para 1196, NDC.

119 Private Papers of Norman Charles Watney, Institute of Civil Engineers, London.

120 Bear, *Lines of the Nation*.

121 This, however, included Europeans as well.

122 Anglo-Indians got higher wages than Indians on the same pay grade. Report of the Royal Commission on Labour in India, Evidence, Vol. VIII, part I (Railways). See especially, the Memorandum submitted by the North Western Railway Union: 359–75.

123 Army, canal colonies, and railway workshops and sheds provided a source of employment to these groups.

124 Jagga, 'Colonial Railwaymen and British Rule', and Kumar, 'Rowlatt Satyagraha', take overlaps between the strike movement and nationalist political agitations as a sign of the latter coopting the former. The terms of engagement are not scrutinized.

125 Jagga, 'Formation of an Industrial Labour Force'.

126 Weekly Report of Director Central Intelligence, 8 March 1920, Home Political, Deposit), Proceedings, OIOC, BL.

127 OM's All-India Letter, 15 March 1920 – with Letters from the Provinces states, 'Mr. Miller's activities are the talk of the town of Lahore. His interesting methods of persuading the people to join him are described by the people with delight . . . "This is the grain I live upon and shall continue to live upon it till I get you promotions." He shows the parched grain and eats it up before the audience and thus he wins the applause of the people'; Prog. no. 57, Home Political, Deposit, March 1920 , OIOC, BL.

128 Again, Secret Police Abstracts capture the escalation of such rhetoric during the period.

129 Extract from letter no. 4623-5-36-20, 8 July 1920, from the Assistant Inspector-General, Government Railway Police, Punjab, to the Deputy Inspector-General of Police, CID, Punjab, India Home (Political) Proceedings, Part A with notes, IOR NEG 8955, August 1920, nos. 71–72, OIOC, BL.

130 For a detailed account of the Hijrat movement, see Naeem Qureshi, 'The Ulama of British India and the Hijrat of 1920', *Modern Asian Studies*, Vol.13, 1979: 41–59.

131 'Extract from a report made by Sub-Inspector of Police, Multan City, on a meeting of the NWR Association, Multan section, held on the 1st July 1920, at about 6 pm in the Langah Khan gardens'; India Home (Political) Proceedings, Part A with notes, IOR NEG 8955, OIOC, BL.

132 *MCCP*, Letter by Philip Spratt, 1929, P. 1975, Exhibits 1501–2000, ZMO, Berlin: 'Miller has just started a new campaign to form a red NWR Union. The "recognized" Union had [as] such almost nothing, and obstructed progress. It is interesting to see the enthusiasm with which the men assemble when he blows his bugle.'

133 Bashir Ahmed Bakhtiar, *The Labour Movement and Me*, English translation of the Urdu original, first published in this volume.

'Dirty Work, Filthy Caste'

Calcutta Scavengers in the 1920s

Tanika Sarkar

A long time back, when I was working on popular politics in late colonial Bengal, I came across some interesting references to strikes among Calcutta municipal scavengers in 1928.[1] They seemed important for several reasons. First, municipal politics had long been fiercely contested by nationalists. From the 1870s, Congress councillors in the Corporation had been trying to wrest control over civic space from European residents and state officials, and by the 1920s, they were largely successful. The brightest stars of the Bengal Congress – C.R. Das, J.M. Sengupta, Subhas Chandra Bose and many others – often filled mayoral posts and other positions of authority. J.M. Sengupta, a leader of the Swarajist Party – the electoral wing of the Congress – was the mayor during the scavengers' strike in March 1928, and Bose was elected to the post in 1930–31.[2] The Corporation, therefore, provides an important site for evaluating incipient nationalist governance, especially its class perspectives and labour policies.

Congress leaders used the Calcutta Corporation, above all, to create employment for the educated nationalist gentlefolk. Persecuted families of revolutionary terrorists were the prime beneficiaries of such employment expansion, and the clerical staff of the Corporation easily outnumbered the manual workers. Subhash Mukhopadhyay recalled how, around the 1930s, Corporation councillors would get a fresh increment to their salaries if they had the good fortune to be arrested from nationalist processions and demonstrations.[3] European councillors looked after the needs of European urban residents alone, and tried to form factions with non-Swarajists of various stripes. The municipality in the age of nationalism was thus predominantly a political and factional arena. Bengal nationalists – as well as their rivals – tried to compete with rousing rhetoric and insinuations, rather than with administrative excellence or public welfare.

All groups largely ignored the urban poor, and scavengers fell out of the loop of municipal improvement projects or of benefit schemes for Corporation employees. Neglect was unavoidable. The early Indian councillors came from highly privileged aristocratic backgrounds and from three dominant caste clusters: *Dakshin Rarhi Kayastha*, *Rarhi Brahman* and *Saptagram Subarnabanik*. Even though their ranks slowly opened up to somewhat lesser elements from district towns and from the professional middle classes, their caste composition did not change to any noticeable extent.[4] *Subarnabaniks* did belong to the unclean Shudra category. But the caste-based lowliness was overcompensated by their great wealth and urban influence. The social gulf between nationalist councillors and 'untouchable' scavengers – the meanest of Corporation employees – was no less oceanic then, than was the distance between Europeans and 'natives'. In fact, racial boundaries were considerably more porous than the caste barrier. The fate of scavengers was no concern of Corporation factions till independent labour activists and communist leaders began to unionize them from 1927.

A study of scavengers thus takes us to yet another political realm: that of early communist bases among the urban poor under the Workers' and Peasants' Party (WPP), a mass front of Bengal communists. This was a small group of extremely dynamic young men – all of them men, at this stage – active in working-class belts in and around Calcutta. They provided a pool of highly organized and motivated personnel of labour activists. Entirely committed to the politics and strategies dictated by the Communist International, they had recently been instructed to follow a sectarian line of separation from the nationalist bourgeois leadership of the Congress and to conduct an independent project of working-class-based anti-imperialist action.[5] They were equally abhorred by the Congress and by the colonial state, and, in 1929, most of their leaders would be arrested under the Meerut Conspiracy Case.

There were independent labour leaders too. Surprisingly, some of them were upper-class women, Hindu as well as Muslim.[6] One of them, Prabhabati Dasgupta, founded the first All Bengal Scavengers' Union in 1927; and another, Begum Sakina, would lead a scavengers' strike in 1940. In the mid-1930s Maitreyee Bose, a doctor, led a scavengers' union at Metiaburz in Calcutta.[7] Women activists deliberately cultivated social closeness with scavengers and harvested a kinship-based intimacy from their warm personal overtures. Both Prabhabati and Sakina were called *dhangar ma* or mother of scavengers.[8] They opened up an alternative route to labour activism which communists, in contrast, undertook with a more straitlaced and impersonal approach that typified professional organization men. Prabhabati Dasgupta was the daughter of a well-established business family in Calcutta. Freshly returned from studies abroad with a Ph.D. degree, and from a decisive meeting with M.N. Roy in Germany which made her turn to working-class areas on her return to India, she began to visit their slums day after day from late 1927. She aimed at cultivating familiarity and friendship with workers before she plunged into union work. To break through the yawning social gap, she regularly ate at their meagre teashops, and proved that she was immune to ritual taboos about forbidden food and water. Her gesture at first 'amused' scavengers but when she returned their banter with rough humour of her own, they were impressed. Only thus was she able to break down their innate suspicions about her class and caste situation, and develop an ascriptive kinship.[10] The work of these women unionists overturned primal gender and caste taboos, and radically redefined their social selves in terms of a most extreme form of defiance. It can be linked – at least partially – to an interwar phase in middle-class gender history in Calcutta when youthful, avant-garde women from privileged backgrounds experimented with bold and transgressive lifestyle changes. It was, perhaps, as much a personal revolt against inherited social prescriptions, a defiant journey into a prohibited world, as their commitment to a leftist political ideology – which, of course, was also strong and vibrant.

Prabhabati was arrested in June 1928 for apparently using abusive language against municipal carters who tried to break up a strike. It was unthinkable in those times that a young woman, alone amidst low-caste working men, should engage in a scuffle with another set of 'lowborn' workers in a public space. Instead of being openly castigated and expelled from her own social group, however, she enjoyed a sympathy wave. Protests were organized citywide as she was a young woman, an educated one, and also because she came from a highly respected and wealthy family that had close nationalist connections. Latika Basu, Secretary of the Mahila Rashtriya Sangha, issued a protest letter from 'ladies of Calcutta' and called for a protest meeting which would be addressed by Basanti Debi, widow of the Congress leader C.R. Das, and a renowned nationalist herself. The wife of Sarat Bose visited Prabhabati's mother to convey public sympathy for her plight. *Forward*, the Swarajist newspaper and a major mouthpiece of Bengal nationalists, expressed great indignation at the arrest.[11] But public sympathy had its limits. Ordinary scavengers faced brutal flogging and humiliation in police hands, and Muzaffar Ahmad, a young communist unionist, too was arrested on the same day. These did not lead to civic protests or create any noticeable sympathy for the strike as such. Prabhabati's defiance against her class, caste and gender prescriptions was thus softened by the very privileges she wanted to abjure. It was received, revised and reframed within the familiar nationalist critique of police tyranny against Bengali political celebrities.

The All Bengal Scavengers' Union was founded in 1927. Prabhabati was its president; Muzaffar Ahmad[12] of the WPP – an indefatigable organizer, traversing several strike areas at once with superb skills in 1928 – was the vice president; and Dharani Goswami was the secretary.[13] During the two strikes in 1928, Prabhabati and the WPP worked closely and harmoniously, even though she was no communist and her mentor, M.N. Roy, had already lost the trust of the Comintern.[14] She was the first leader to organize scavengers, and the WPP – a latecomer in the arena – could not do without her influence and cooperation. She, on the other hand, needed an organization to work with as her initiative was an entirely individual one. Jute mill strikes in 1928 and 1929, however, saw a major rift between Prabhabati and the WPP, and she more or less disappeared from the political horizon after the late 1920s. The strikes of 1928 reveal the importance of the highly personalized approach of the individual activist, as well as of the collective organization animated by a systematic political ideology. Together, and symbiotically, the two strategies of mobilization worked extremely well.

Reform was another mode of organizing scavengers. Aghore Sen, a homeopathic doctor at Dacca, gained considerable influence among local municipal sweepers and scavengers. He used to hold classes for their children and disburse medicine among them. The Dacca Congress Committee, however, removed him from his base in early 1928. Interestingly, just before his removal, WPP activists had been trying to unionize the Dacca scavengers. After the entry of the Congress on the scene, however, scavengers and sweepers succumbed to the pressure of municipal authorities. Meetings called at the Coronation Park by Philip Spratt and Muzaffar Ahmad failed to achieve a significant turnout as workers were warned of grim retaliation by the authorities. The Dacca experience is important for several reasons. It shows that scavengers valued education and responded warmly to a leader who offered it. It reveals the reach of constructive reform. Union organizers avoided this mode altogether, probably because their resources were small and badly stretched across several working-class movements. It also shows that even philanthropic work alarmed the Congress nationalists who had Sen replaced with one of their own men, even though he was not trying to unionize workers.[15]

There was another possible model of collective action that Calcutta scavengers avoided. This was self-organization as an occupation-based *jati* rather than as a working-class union. In December 1928, washermen or *dhobis* of Calcutta and Howrah held caste *panchayats* at Puddopukur Road, and decided not to work under the Dyeing and Cleaning companies but only under the direction of prosperous members of their own caste. They resolved to outcast anyone who flouted the decision.[16] This was a caste association whose powerful leaders reinforced their economic authority with the traditional disciplinary mechanism of outcasting. As a slight but significant deviation from this, Mymensingh scavengers set up a union in March 1928 under a *jamadar* which called itself the Mehtar and Dom Union of Mymensingh. It organized a brief strike in July under WPP leadership.[17] The naming reveals a double-barrelled sense of identity where union and caste-based occupation intermingle.

It is possible that municipal scavengers did not have strong caste-based *panchayats* to regulate their social life. Their absolute poverty would have flattened out internal hierarchies and prevented the formation of a leadership from within the profession. But caste, occupation and class-based identities were sometimes fluid and porous for them, even for union leaders. On 4 March, the first day of the first strike of 1928, Muzaffar Ahmad addressed a public meeting of scavengers as 'Dear Mehtar, Dom and Dhangar brothers'.[18] He used designations where caste and occupation overlapped. Both were then reconfigured within their new unionized identity. The striking difference between the two urban forms of subaltern organization – one that gave priority to *jati*-based occupation and the other which preferred non-caste unionization – complicates and largely contradicts Dipesh Chakravarty's argument: that working-class identities and union–worker relations were merely a replication of traditional rural cultural hierarchies, where union leaders stood in for caste superiors among urban workers.[19] Scavengers definitely spurned the caste-based organizational model, and chose to ally with a non-traditional and non-status-based political group.

At the same time, a study of Calcutta sweepers and scavengers has to be a conjoint exploration of caste and labour, as there was a tight interlock between the nature of their work and their social status/stigma. A relatively small proportion was Muslim but most were Hindus from the most absolutely polluted untouchable castes: Doms and Hadis (or Haris), or equivalent castes from eastern United Provinces and Bihar. In the 1891 Census, out of a total of 15,375 Corporation sweepers and scavengers in Calcutta, only 1,232 were Muslims. No other categories were mentioned.[20] In 1911, the last Census where we get a break-up of the population in 'Industries Concerned with Refuse Matters – Sweepers, Scavengers, Dust and Sweeping Contractors', out of a total of 15,381, Hindus constituted 13,823 and Muslims were 1,539. We find mention of sixteen Christians and three unspecified 'others'.[21]

In the 1931 Census, Doms of Calcutta were described as 'basket and mat makers, scavengers and drummers', while Haris were described as 'scavengers and menials'.[22] Risley described the Mehtar both as 'a sub caste of Haris who remove night soil', and also as 'a section of Maghaya Kumhars: a title of Nunias, of the Dhusia and Dohar subcastes of Chamars: a section of the Kulsunri subcaste of Sunris and of the Dharkar subcaste of Doms'.[23] Of his two different entries, the first seems to indicate that this was an occupation exclusively reserved for a specific caste. The second suggests that the occupation was also widely scattered among a spectrum of other low and untouchable castes. One may guess that Haris were generally identified with night soil removal. But the occupation also occasionally recruited from fractions of other castes that had been traditionally endowed with different labour forms: potters or brewers. One can also guess at processes of downward mobility that drove this second group into the ranks of night soil removers. Doms – the other group associated with scavenging – seem to be a very large and heterogeneous caste, spread across Bengal, Bihar and the North Western Provinces, and subdivided among many diverse occupations and status positions. In 1891, when Risley published his ethnographic glossary on tribes and castes of Bengal, he argued that they came from aboriginal origins and much later acquired an untouchable *chandala* nomenclature. An upwardly mobile segment moved into landless agricultural labour and small-scale tenancy, another took to 'habitual thieving', and yet another engaged in scavenging. Wives of agricultural Doms were employed as midwives in rural households.[24]

Night soil removers were the lowest of the low, even among untouchables, and in popular Bengali parlance their occupational and caste names signify the most absolute state of degradation.[25] Not just the prospect of touching but the very sight of them polluted and produced acute physical revulsion. Bishnunath Motilal, a Bengali gentleman, wrote to the municipal authorities in 1837 in great horror, that these days scavengers are actually *seen* on the streets 'at all hours of the day'. This literally turns the stomach of the well-born Bengali, he complained, especially if he has just had a full meal. Houses where they worked had backyard entrances which led just to the lavatory, so that they did not have to set foot anywhere else.[26] We do find mention of a Bala Chamar who accused union leaders of assaulting him for strike-breaking in June.[27] His presence among scavengers shows that the occupation was not entirely caste-related as Chamars, or leather workers in terms of their designated caste occupation, were untouchables who would still be ritually a notch above Doms and Haris. We do not know if he was a sweeper or a night soil remover. Most other names mentioned in the strike reports do not carry surnames. As a result, their caste is difficult to ascertain.

Even though leftist, middle-class literature in Bengali frequently made various categories of subaltern classes their subjects, and despite the fact that jute workers quite often featured in fiction written by prominent novelists like Manik Bandyopadhyay, Tarashankar Bandyopadhyay and Samaresh Basu, scavengers hardly ever make an appearance here. Practically the sole exception is a brief passage in Samaresh Basu's semi-autobiographical novel, *Yug Yug Jiye*. Its young, middle-class, leftist hero loses his way in wartime blackout one night on the outskirts of Calcutta. He stumbles into what appears then as a black hole in the middle of nowhere, and which, the next morning, is found to be a slum harbouring scavengers who clean latrines in jute mills. The hero, otherwise quite familiar with working-class habitations, is nonetheless stupefied by their grime-encrusted hovel, their stinking food and the reek of cheap liquor, as well as their strange guttural speech that was almost incomprehensible. But the lowest depths signify – in true leftist literary mode – their inner richness in the same proportion. The scavenger couple who brings this lost hero home shares their scanty food and decrepit bed with him, and the wife is told to serve the guest with her body as they have nothing else to offer. The sheer sexuality of the encounter is however transcended by her overflowing maternalism and nurture, which embrace him, the husband and the baby in equal measure. Even though their simple, non-possessive goodness raises them above the surrounding stench and filth, the point that emerges with great force is the overpowering animality of these lives, their absolute otherness.[28] What gets established is the sheer non-representability of their lives in middle-class language, however sympathetic or even admiring, except as a string of negatives – darkness, filth and stench.

There is another very interesting entry of scavengers in *Char Adhyay*, a late novel by Rabindranath Tagore. The revolutionary terrorist hero, Atin, is called by his friends to visit a scavengers' slum at night and to preach temperance to them. Atin refuses: 'So, you will take away their drinking. But what will you offer them in its place?'[29] An angry sense of the nothingness that frames these lives and of the irrelevance of middle-class good intentions is presented.

But a very different kind of middle-class intervention did find rich resonance among scavengers of unions and strikes. There was good reason why the 1928 strikes – the first where workers were unionized – breached their non-visibility. Their caste status ensured that they were the only people who cleared homes and streets of human and animal waste, the latter being profuse up to the 1920s as much of urban transport was still animal-driven. They therefore had a virtual monopoly over this indispensable yet devalued work. And a very useful monopoly it proved to be during strikes when substitutes from other castes were hard to find. In some wards, a group of middle-class heroes and near-martyrs did emerge. They demonstratively cleaned streets under the direction of the Corporation Health Associations, albeit not very efficiently. They were directed to either burn their domestic refuse or to sweep it into main collection depots and leave it there. Winds blew the filth around and added to sanitary risks.[30] But public and domestic latrines were not cleared even by these intrepid social workers. In 1941, during yet another scavengers' strike, 'civil guards' drawn from upper-caste, *bhadralok* sections were made to take their place. That reduced their recruitment into this rather coveted occupation as their parents objected to the terrible loss of caste.[31]

Strikes also brought home an important lesson to scavengers and to the city they cleaned: that urban health, indeed urban survival, was crucially dependent on their despised labour. Nandini Gooptu refers to the access to self-esteem that accrues when migrant untouchables lose the face-to-face humiliation of their rural existence in the social anonymity of big cities and learn to regard themselves as government employees, not as servants of high-caste individuals.[32] In the case of scavengers, however, their work and caste combined to ensure a ghettoized urban existence that preserved and continued the rites of distance pollution characteristic of the lives of rural untouchables. Strikes alone translated degradation into strength.

Revisiting the material, I obviously wanted to reach out beyond strikes into the larger world of scavengers. Predictably, I encountered severe problems of sources. Scavengers were casual workers and they were not recorded on the rolls of municipal conservancy departments of these times. Corporation council proceedings have not been available, and most Bengali and nationalist newspaper holdings have large gaps in them. Sanitation records have fascinating material about urban waste disposal, but relatively little about men and women who disposed of it.

Pre-1911 censuses provide figures of Corporation workers, ward by ward. They also have elaborate tables for urban castes. But the two are not correlated. That is, we know how many Haris and Doms there were in the city, and how many scavengers, but we do not know how many came from which caste or what other castes they came from. We cannot distinguish among sweepers, coolies, night soil removers and other menial workers as they are lumped together as a single, undifferentiated category of scavengers. Censuses mapped urban migration patterns but did not specify the occupational profiles of different categories of migrants. Home Political files, Intelligence Branch,

Special Branch and the Meerut Conspiracy Case proceedings chiefly tracked the strike activities of communists. Scavengers, almost entirely illiterate, left no written records. Because they were a mobile labour force without a spatially fixed workspace, their actual mode of work was never observed or described.

We need, then, to ponder on the paradoxical nature of this work: work that was mobile, peripatetic, yet centralized under a single employer – the Corporation. Work done by government employees who were nonetheless casual workers on a life-long basis; who performed labour that was hidden, polluted and polluting, utterly filthy yet absolutely essential. For, unlike all other labour strikes, theirs alone had the capacity to make an instant difference to the entire urban population and not just to their immediate employers. Essential work, therefore, but nonetheless work that was 'non-productive', as it is difficult to conceptualize work without invoking its indissoluble link with the production of tangible commodities. Since scavengers produced nothing but subtracted filth, the analogy that readily comes to mind is with female domestic labour, usually also classified as non-productive. But scavengers, in contrast to housewives, did paid work under impersonal employers. Even though their labour produced no obvious exchange value, a rather strange kind of use value did emerge out of 'non-production', which 'disappeared' waste. Ordinarily, however, the subtractive effort, conducted behind public gaze, did not register itself on public consciousness as work that creates use value – until they went on strike. So, once again, the nature of their work produced the same sense of blankness or absence that marked their lives as well.

It bears little resemblance, too, to other kinds of urban services performed by low-caste manual labour, like that of washermen or *dhobis*. The level of caste degradation and work-related filth that marked scavengers is nowhere comparable with the *dhobi* profession. Clothes washed by low-caste *dhobis* would be allowed to touch upper-caste skins; what scavengers took away would not return to defile upper-caste bodies as they worked with human and animal waste which rendered their touch totally intolerable, as much as did their most degraded untouchable caste. Work and ritual status produced each other in an unbreakable cycle.

There is yet another paradox. Even though they were strictly segregated, at the same time, unlike other categories of workers, their work constantly intersected with upper-caste, European and rich urban homes and streets which they cleaned on a daily basis. Their living areas – however hidden from view – abutted on all these wards where the rich and the privileged lived. They probably saw more of the lives of others than any other group of workers, except for domestic servants.

There is uncertainty about the very designation. Their name – scavenger or *dhangar* – has a curious definition. It refers to tribal people originally migrating from Central India and described by polite society as barbarians, 'non Aryans' – *asabhya*. Probably, the word had once signified tribal migrant labourers but in Bengali usage it came to be exclusively associated with scavenging.[33] Used as a singular noun, it actually refers to several deeply stratified subdivisions. It includes sweepers or *jharudars*, waste contractors or *jamadars*, Mehtars or night soil removers, coolies or porters, and *muddafarsh* or cremation site workers who burnt corpses. A Bengali-language encyclopaedia, published first in 1909, describes Mehtars as 'shit cleaners of untouchable caste'. It thus uses the word as both a caste and an occupational name.[34] In our case, the 1928 strikes involved sweepers and night soil removers.

There is, therefore, silence as well as confusion about their identity. We need to look at lateral sources and highly diffused evidence, and think in terms of a decentred narrative where workers are scattered and embedded among several disparate fields: municipalization of urban life; technologies of waste disposal; communal, nationalist, left and gender politics; and caste.

II

Let me first situate the scavengers within a very brief sketch of municipalization of urban services and labour practices.[35] As in Britain, the process started in Calcutta from the late eighteenth century. At first, a rudimentary municipal administration was set up under a royal charter and was entrusted to a civil servant of the Company. In 1753, a new royal charter rather ineffectually tried to establish a municipal fund with taxes which were to be utilized for clearing jungles and draining marshes in the city. But apart from constructing the Marhatta Ditch, little else was done. In 1794, the Governor General appointed Justices of Peace who would make regular assessments and levy taxes. Municipal work was now divided into three departments: assessment, executive and judicial. The second handled conservancy concerns. It acquired an Engineer to look after roads and conservancy.

Lord Wellesley's Minute of 1803 was the first official document to draw serious attention to conservancy needs.[36] 'The health of the Town', he wrote, 'would be certainly considerably improved by an improvement of the mode of draining and cleansing the Streets, Roads and Esplanade.'[37] In contrast with debates in Britain about the ethics of using money generated by gambling,[38] lottery funds were quickly institutionalized in Calcutta with the establishment of the Lottery Commission in 1814. It was assisted by various other committees like the Fever Hospital Committee and the Municipal Improvement Committee which disbursed funds for urban improvement schemes. Predominantly official bodies with European residents as members, they would, at times, nominate a few prominent natives of Calcutta: Prasanna Kumar Tagore and Dwarkanath Tagore, for instance.[39]

In 1833, an abortive experiment was made with representative government, and suggestions were made that ratepayers should elect municipal committees to look after conservancy needs. Act XVI of 1847 transferred conservancy work from the Justices to a Board of Commissioners, most of whom would be elected. Calcutta Corporation was formally instituted in 1856 to raise funds for public utilities from ratepayers, and the same year, 'a very complete conservancy Act' was also passed. Notwithstanding this, sanitation remained horribly deficient and urban health was precarious, vulnerable to regular and deadly bouts of epidemics and fevers. As late as 1878, an official report described mortality rates in the city as 'excessively great' and attributed it to the neglect of proper drainage.[40] In the 1880s, prodded by furious civic body complaints, a Commission was set up; and another Act was passed in 1888 increasing the number of Commissioners, most of whom would be elected. A third Act, however, reduced the number in 1899.[41]

From 1876 to 1877, a limited electoral principle was put in place, bringing important nationalist figures like Surendranath Banerjee into Corporation administration. As the election of Indian councillors became an established fact, the Corporation emerged as a critical site where nationalist criticism of governmental despotism and racial discrimination was sharpened and articulated. There were frequent complaints in the nationalist press about misgovernance and neglect, especially of the concerns of rich Indian ratepayers. But nothing was said about the living and labour conditions of menial employees.[42] In 1923, a new Act extended franchise to lesser middle-class ratepayers, and this ensured the long reign of nationalists. The Mayor would be henceforth annually elected and assisted by five aldermen and ninety councillors. Executive powers were vested in the Chief Executive Officer, appointed by the Corporation.

Around 1923, government controls were reduced and funds were enlarged. Swarajist councillors came to dominate the Corporation at this propitious phase. They made fine welfarist promises: of free schools, milk supply, medical relief and housing for the poor.[43] Though sadly forgotten soon, these still did create a horizon of expectations, even for menial workers. Strike demands could now be articulated as a betrayed trust. Nationalism, therefore, was aporetically pressed between twin incompatible compulsions. It had to appear inclusive, in order to distinguish itself from the racialized elitism of the European authorities. At the same time, its own social privileges made it, for much of the time, blind to the needs of the urban poor and untouchables. As it came to rule over the Corporation, it increasingly appeared as the obvious tyrant figure at times of strikes, exposing the limits, or even the hollowness, of its representational claims on behalf of the people as a whole. This was a burden that its European rivals did not have to share. Strikes were therefore enormously inconvenient and embarrassing to nationalists in particular.

In March 1928, at the time of the first round of strikes in this year, Swarajists were the ruling party in the Corporation. In April they were defeated by a coalition of Muslim and non-Swarajist councillors, and they faced the June–July strikes as leaders of the opposition. Their stances towards the two strikes, therefore, differed significantly. In the earlier round, they called in the police, turned a blind eye to the floggings, intimidation and arrests of workers, and negotiated with the union only when uncleared waste seemed to threaten epidemics. At the same time, they did open negotiations sooner than non-nationalists wanted that to happen. The non-Swarajist Chief Executive Officer sharply criticized Mayor Sengupta for losing his nerve and opening a dialogue with the union. But we cannot push the difference too far. When accused of compromising prematurely, Sengupta did not refer to the problems and needs of scavengers, nor did he justify their demands. He merely pleaded that he was not told in time that the strike was already failing; had he known, he would not have agreed to a settlement. In June–July, in contrast, the Swarajist press reported on scavengers' demands with far greater sympathy, and they were more vocal in Corporation debates on behalf of scavengers.

As Corporation funds and functions expanded, it became a major source of power and patronage. Elections were therefore exceptionally hard-fought. Posters and leaflets carried scurrillous charges and counter-charges: about financial corruption, hooliganism and, above all, the anti-patriotic tendencies of non-Swarajist candidates.[44] Little was raised about the quality of urban services in election campaigns. Nothing at all was said about workers' lives. As urban residents who did not pay rates, they did not form an electoral constituency and could therefore be easily forgotten.

Factions were volatile and council debates could be dangerous occasions. In July 1928, when a very important Council meeting was scheduled to discuss the scavengers' strike, Shams ul Huq, a Muslim councillor and secretary of the Hackney Carriage Drivers' Association, was apparently abducted from the streets at gunpoint as he went to vote. He had, until recently, been a member of the Swarajist Party and his abductors accused him of basely defecting from it. He was kept a prisoner until the time of debate was safely over.[45]

III

Municipalization had already entered an ambitious phase in the late nineteenth century when Calcutta finally began to look like a great modern city with access to many new urban facilities. From the 1860s, the Corporation began to draw up plans to supply a reasonable bundle of facilities to the ratepayers: to bring piped water at least to the richer residential areas; to construct drains and sewage dumps that would cover much of the city. By the 1880s, urban facilities in the metropolitan capital were no longer remarkably different from those in the imperial capital. For much of the nineteenth century, London too suffered atrociously from sewage problems, stench, garbage deposits and epidemics. Calcutta's water, supplied by Corporation pipes, was better in all respects except one than the water in London.[46] In 1889, Florence Nightingale congratulated Viceroy Lansdowne for his advanced notion that a school of sanitary engineers should be set up for improving waste disposal methods.[47] Gradually, the white town–black town gap was considerably replaced with a class divide, as prosperous Indian houses and streets began to enjoy the fruits of urban improvement. The Tagore residence in Jorasanko had piped water supply as early as the late 1860s.[48]

A lot of the improvement was, no doubt, uneven and irregularly enforced; a matter of planning rather than of actual implementation. Even in 1932, a Bengal Municipal Act was still urging municipal residents to abide by basic rules of sewage removal.[49] Nonetheless, by the 1920s, improved sanitation technologies had been made available to most well-off residents, Indian and European. They stimulated the development of small industrial units, all capitalized in India and many owned by Calcutta-based Indian entrepreneurs. The *Calcutta Municipal Gazette* of 1935 carried many illustrated advertisements of new sanitary gadgets: covered pans, pull-flush commodes and covered municipal rubbish carts. There were also pictures of new drainage and sewer building material which called themselves 'revolutionary'. Municipal conservancy, then, provided a field for Indian private capital investment and profits, a local labour market, minor capital goods production, as well as a new civic and patriotic pride. A Bengal Iron Company advertisement proudly proclaimed that it used 'Indian material, Indian labour' alone for its sewer pipe production. No doubt, nationalists dominating the Corporation were careful to invite tenders largely from patriotic businessmen who were likely to liberally fund Swarajist coffers.[50]

Waste removers – sweepers and scavengers – of Calcutta presented a stark contrast to this happy narrative of improvement. Municipalization of urban facilities had severely curtailed their freedom to bargain with employers.[51] Till the early nineteenth century, some scavengers were employed by private households. Otherwise, garbage and night soil were simply dumped into adjacent ponds, wasteland or open drains that lined the streets. Conservancy began to acquire a more organized shape only from the 1830s. Rubbish was now transported by municipal carts – later by light railways – to new sewage depots, which disposed of it in the Hooghly river until 1866. Afterwards, it was pumped into the eastern wetlands or the 'salt lakes' towards which the city naturally tilted and whose saline marsh water had deodorizing properties: yet another idea that was first mooted by Wellesley in his Minute of 1803.[52] From the 1870s, Bhabanath Sen, a very enterprising Bengali, leased a part of this land and innovated the profitable cultivation of fish and vegetables on waste-enriched marshes. Even though there were occasional pleas to fill up the lakes for fear of the miasma that supposedly emanated from garbage deposits, other environmental and sanitary views prevailed and the lakes were preserved to receive urban waste.[53]

Special sanitation commissions were set up from the 1880s. They set afoot various slum 'reforms' whose major task was to demolish shacks that could not afford to instal latrines or pay for night soil removal. A number of these were demolished to make room for expensive and sanitary residences, for the Presidency and Medical Colleges, and for commercial establishments. So, those who ensured sanitary health were often evicted from their living spaces for offending sanitary norms.[54] As they crowded into the remaining slums, European officers wondered why they 'chose' insanitary areas rather than better parts of the city. Sanitation officers deplored the persistence of the rural habit among them of defecating on open ground. They ignored the fact that public latrines were almost non-existent.[55]

We find a typical motif of urban development planning at work. The living spaces of the urban poor are first left out of the network of sanitation facilities altogether. As slum dwellers are paid too little to provide these for themselves, the absence of basic sanitation is ascribed to their peculiar lifestyle choices. Dangers to urban health from such filthy living patterns are then underlined, and finally, they are displaced from their homes or are continually threatened with eviction as punishment for endangering urban health. City fathers then rebuild the urban form and add to the profits of real estate developers by making the demolished slums sites of sanitary and expensive living areas. The rhetorics of public health and urban reform are therefore very dangerous matters for the urban poor.

By the late nineteenth century, a growing number of rich homes had private privies while poorer ones shared a toilet among four to five huts, each of which might house scores of people. Many used the few available public toilets and most were forced to use the open ground. In earlier times, privately hired night soil removers used to collect waste. This had allowed them some bargaining power. They were supposed to bring the waste to specified Tolla Mehtars' depots, from where municipal boats would carry it to the river and dump it there. An Act of 1863 began to centralize cleaning operations under the Corporation. It fixed wages, and put scavengers under *sirdars* licensed by the municipality and provided with buckets and carts for hire. At first, there was a division of labour between Tolla Mehtars and Corporation *sirdars*. Soon, however, conflicts started over the payment of Corporation fees for leasing the depots to which Tolla Mehtars brought their garbage. With rapid municipalization of night soil services in the 1870s, the Mehtars lost their earlier leeway; in 1877, they struck work in protest. They were remarkably well-organized and tenacious, even though unions did not yet exist. They spread rumours among municipal sweepers who turned up for work that the Corporation would eventually pack them off to the West Indies. They also sent emissaries into district municipalities to extend the strike. The strike failed to stop the process and in 1877, the Coporation notified that Tolla Mehtars would be replaced with municipal ones.

At this point, their pay ranged between 8 annas per month for cleaning houses which were valued at Rs 50 per year, and Rs 8 for cleaning houses whose owners paid rates at Rs 5,000 and above per year. A spatial hierarchy structured highly uneven terms of work and put cleaners of richer households at considerable monetary advantage over those who cleaned poorer areas.[56]

In the same year, rice was priced at Rs 3.10 per maund and the high price of most vegetables made them unaffordable for the poor.[57] 1878 was also a year of very high urban mortality, and municipal authorities debated if this was due to starvation or insanitary living conditions of the poor. Whatever the cause, scavengers would be the primary natural victims of both. Every day they manually removed huge deposits of solid waste and rubbish from streets and public latrines without any protection against infections. The Corporation was congratulated by the Army Sanitary Commission for the accelerated progress of street cleaning. But out of a total of 39,756 listed houses in Calcutta that year, only 5,400 were directly connected with sewers. From 11,496 *pucca* or concrete houses of the better-off, night soil was still removed by private arrangement; the rest was cleaned by the municipal Mehtar establishment which employed 'about 1,100 Mehtars' who also cleaned the 68 public latrines or *mehtartattis*.[58] Not only was the pressure of work on each individual scavenger extraordinarily arduous, they worked with filth which made them particularly vulnerable to diseases and infections. Censuses do not break down mortality figures according to occupation, but it stands to reason that scavengers would provide a very large category of the dead. They cleaned stagnant ponds from time to time, and they regularly cleaned the growing miles of underground brick-lined sewers of which the city fathers were so proud. Many of those who went down to clean them would never come up as they succumbed to the noxious fumes or were suffocated to death.[59]

In 1900, the Corporation congratulated itself on its conservancy performance: 'It is in the matter of disposal of night soil that great improvements have been effected.' Reverend Moule's invention of dry earth latrines where waste was buried under earthen trenches was now supplemented by a further technological innovation: construction of large central sewage depots at Hazra Road and Budge Budge where garbage was carried and emptied, and then pumped into the large central Circular Road sewer.[60] But methods of manual and unprotected cleaning persisted. There was, furthermore, no municipal investment in the sanitary health of *bustees* or slums where the scavengers lived and which crowded around each ward that they cleaned. As municipalization of urban facilities accelerated, it was admitted that the 'worst parts of the town – bustees and their huts and tanks – have gained nothing . . . it is thus with sewers, as with the water supply, the more substantial householders who have benefitted . . . the new night soil service . . . makes no provision against daily and hourly deposits on bustee lands'.[61]

Conditions worsened for the urban poor as sanitary consciousness expanded among the privileged, and as ever-growing land prices threw up a class of real estate speculators. Between 1905 and 1911, a major spate of land acquisition occurred in various parts of the city, all at the expense of the insanitary *bustees*. In three predominantly European quarters – Baman Basti, Hastings and Collinga – Bustee Regulations either thinned out the slums or demolished them altogether. Landlords, inspired by rising rents and development of trade, destroyed the small, *kutcha* or non-concretized dwellings of the poor and built large masonary ones, converting slums into shops. The line of social demarcation was not really racial but class.[62] The Corporation vacillated between suggestions of filling up open drains and ponds where poor people defecated, and projects of *bustee* removal or demolitions to make way for more expensive, sanitary residences, which would immediately put them beyond the reach of the poor tenants who rented the huts.[63]

In the late 1920s, most labourers in 'public works' – and this would have included Corporation scavengers – were migrants, recruited by labour contractors who were sent into the 'highways and byways' of distant rural catchment areas to gather workers, in exchange for fixed rates of commission. *Sirdars* combined many operations: of supervision, of finding workers their living quarters, of granting leave, of renewing recruitment after leave was over, and of conveying information from Corporation authorities to the workers. Women workers were sometimes provided with women supervisors who rose from their ranks. Actually, strikes were the only point of a direct contact between the Corporation leaders and the menial labourers. All other contact was mediated by the *sirdars*. The Corporation knew that they fleeced the workers when they gave them jobs and when they returned the jobs to them after their leaves of absence.

The Report of the Royal Commission on Labour observed with some sympathy the profound alienation that migrant workers experienced when they came to the city for work. Totally deprived of the open spaces that the most impoverished of them still had access to in their villages, they lived their days and nights in the city in horribly cramped huts. They lost their access to fresh food, their dietary habits changed and nutritional levels declined, and their health declined drastically. The language they encountered in the city was often strange to the point of incomprehension, and city ways defeated them. For a minimum of human interchange, they huddled together with their countrymen in accommodation that was inhumanly overcrowded.[64]

They often went back to their villages for very long periods, paying the *sirdars* an entire month's salary to get back the job when they returned as they had no leave facilities at all. Villages were essential to their survival: in cases of illness, accidents, old age, for family life and festivities, and for extra income during harvest seasons. So villages, whose extreme poverty had pushed them out into the ranks of the migrant workforce in the first place, had to bear the real burden of producing and reproducing the labour force as urban employers entirely denied all responsibility for workers.

In 1924, when the nationalist leader C.R. Das was the Mayor of Calcutta, scavengers briefly struck work and presented a list of their grievances. Das met them – it was considered a big gesture – soothed them and promised them much. It is significant, though, that he would not promise to give them the wage increment they wanted without consulting the Congress. The Congress withheld its approval. Das set up a committee of largely Swarajist councillors to look into their grievances. The grievances were: high prices of daily necessities, extremely high rents for houses, exorbitant interest rates that Kabuli or migrant Afghan moneylenders charged, the *bharti* or admission charges paid to Block *sirdars* when they returned from home, great delay in receiving monthly wages, no regular water supply at slums, problems of raising money for funerary expenses or compensation to family even when they died during work.[65]

There are some interesting aspects to the list. All their problems flowed from the fact that the Corporation would not provide the basic necessities for mere survival: accident and health care, death benefits, housing, living wages. Second, what *sirdars* charged from them was described as a routine part of their expenses; it was not yet described as bribe. The committee did admit that problems existed but did nothing to alleviate them.

In 1928, the scavengers had been unionized by a small but extremely efficient communist group. The WPP studied their conditions and reported on their problems, elaborating on and clarifying what the scavengers themselves had brought to the Corporation's notice in 1924. These were: dangerously insanitary slums, usually without any water supply and always without electricity or proper ventilation; exorbitantly high rents, as being untouchables they found few slum owners who would defile their property by renting it out to them unless they made a neat profit out of it. The Corporation did not arrange for housing. They had no rights to leave of any sort and dismissal was always round the corner, depending on the whim of the supervisor. There were no medical benefits whatsoever, though they were sorely needed 'due to the nature of the work'. There was no 'death benefit' for the family, though death frequently occurred due to the Corporation's negligence 'through suffocation or poisoning of drains' which they cleaned without protective gear. The burden of bribes – to get a job, to get it back after absence – to various categories of *babus*, *chaprasis* and supervisors was often equal to a month's pay. Almost all of them were indebted to highly oppressive and violent 'Kabuli' moneylenders, to an extent the debtor himself may not know. The interest rate was about Rs 2 a month. They received a monthly salary between Rs 10 and Rs 12 a month, plus a grain allowance of Re 1. Even if they had worked for fourteen consecutive years, they got no increments. Though Corporation authorities alleged that their actual earning was double of what they alleged, as most worked double shifts, the union insisted that out of a total workforce of 13,000 sweepers and Mehtars, only 1,000 did double shifts and they had to pay a considerable bribe for the privilege. Double shift brought them a salary of Rs 14 per month. The union insisted that most of them could not afford to drink. It prepared a monthly budget of the average scavenger living on a maximum salary of Rs 10 to Rs 14: rice, at 20 seers per family – Rs 4 and 8 annas; lentils – 4 seers – Re 1; mustard oil – 4 annas; vegetables – 15 annas; drinks – Re 1 and 9 annas; soap (an absolute necessity, given what they had to handle) – 4 annas; rent – 12 annas per head; interest on loans – Re 1 and 4 annas; kerosene – 4 annas; fuel – 10 annas; bribes – Re 1 and 8 annas. The total came to Rs 12 and 14 annas, which left nothing whatsoever for medicine, schooling for children or entertainment of any sort. As it exceeded the monthly salary for many, the debt burden was permanent and insuperable.[66]

The union alleged that the Bombay municipality paid a higher salary to its scavengers.[67] It is interesting that payments to *sirdars* were now definitely classified as bribes. But bribes were looked at somewhat differently by union leaders and by Swarajist corporators. The Swarajists insisted that bribery was the main problem that plagued scavengers. In the union's analysis, in contrast, this was mentioned as a part of the larger picture but not the chief cause of distress. In their understanding, Corporation negligence and non-provision of basic necessities were the real culprits. Faced with a highly dangerous civic situation that the strike brought about and with an irate body of ratepayers that constituted their electoral constituency, Swarajists chose to pick out the middle rung of employees as culpable, rather than admit to their own gross callousness towards their employees. At a critical Corporation councillors' meeting to discuss the March strike that had just ended, only Alderman Daud – a non-Swarajist – asked about their demands and problems. He got no reply. Eventually, the Corporation admitted that there was a lack of medical and housing benefits. But it would not provide them. The strike was already over and they were under no pressure to be accommodating. They refused to consider a pay increase. Once again, they identified bribery as the sole problem and promised to check it.[68] That, however, was an empty promise unless major changes were made in structures of recruitment and supervision; such changes were never made.

According to the very detailed 1911 Census, in 'Industries Concerned with Refuse Matters (Sweepers and Scavengers, Dust and Sweeping Contractors) in Calcutta', men counted for 7,210 and women numbered 1,889.[69] A minuscule proportion of Hindus had stable, land-based subsidiary occupations. This implies that most came from families of landless labourers. Not a single Muslim scavenger had links with land. This shows that they joined the ranks of scavengers only when they were totally destitute. Both supported a large number of dependants.[70] In the 1931 Census, we find that the number of those employed in 'public works' was rising steadily, in comparison with the city's industrial workforce whose numbers had declined. City boundaries expanded and more cleaners had to be found. The Census, however, does not provide occupational tables for different categories of workers in the public works.[71]

IV

Quite certainly, scavengers were familiar with certain forms of non-class political and cultural activity. Prabhu Jagatbandhu and Atulchandra Champati, Vaisnav proselytizers in the 1910s, preached an ardent devotionalism to Calcutta's slums. While Jagatbandhu offered the urban poor mystical–philosophical messages as a route to salvation, Atulchandra, working among labourers and poor prostitutes, combined preaching with moral reformism, cautioning them against drunkenness and immorality. Another such figure was Swami Haribolananda, the founder of *hari sabhas* or open congregations which collectively chanted sacred words to ward off disease and distress. These were a solace to the fearful urban poor in the plague years of the 1890s. Surprisingly, anti-caste reform organizations seem to have been entirely absent among them. [72]

Muslim migrants from Bihar and the United Provinces imbibed some of the ideology of religious segregation that north Indian reformist sects propagated at the end of the nineteenth century. Both Vaishnavs and reformist Muslim sectarian leaders were active in the 1926 communal riots in Calcutta, where music before mosques became a potent instrument for fomenting violence when Vaishnav processions insisted on passing by at prayer time. Muslim *jamadars* from upcountry origins organized paramilitary bands.[73] Tablighi organizations had brought their communal messages to Calcutta Muslim labourers from the early 1920s, providing a tangible focus for their everyday grievances against a Corporation that was so obviously dominated by Hindu nationalists, often in alliance with highly communal Hindu Sabha councillors. Subhas Bose had tried to recruit Muslims into the upper ranks of Corporation employees but he was fiercely resisted by other Hindu councillors. After the riots, municipal elections were viciously communalized and nationalists made little attempt to distinguish themselves firmly enough from Hindu Sabha electoral propaganda.[74]

We also find several Arya Samaji *sadhus* who organized scavengers for strike action in 1928: Swami Kumarananda, along with Swami Biswananda who was also active on other labour fronts. In a speech at an early public meeting called by the union in February 1928, Swami Kumarananda asked scavengers to combine and assert their rights like the workers of Russia, China and Germany. He told them that Russian workers had overthrown the Czar and were 'now practically ruling the country themselves'.[75] They, however, were not independent unionists but worked under WPP guidance.

V

As scavengers' strikes began in Calcutta, *The Statesman* made a very perceptive observation. In 1924, when scavengers downed tools, they presented 'grievances'. In 1928, they had 'demands'.[76] The shift in vocabulary suggests a cognitive leap.

In 1924, the scavengers had no union which would consolidate and direct their discontents and their energies. Totally illiterate, quite innocent of legal technicalities and bereft of help from outside, they could only draw upon their own resources. In 1928, they possessed a union led by middle-class, highly educated and experienced labour activists. The union taught them to raise regular subscriptions, to put together a fund for a possible strike and to articulate their everyday grievances as a written charter of strike demands. It solicited help and money from the Bengal Federation of Trade Unions and the All India Federation of Trade Unions; it introduced scavengers to foreign labour activists like Philip Spratt, and to news of strikes in other parts of Bengal, in India and abroad. It taught them basic dos and don'ts in strikes, especially about what constitutes legal action and what is defined as criminality.[77] Above all, by working very closely with untouchable scavengers without a shred of purity–pollution taboos, union leaders taught them a new measure of self-respect and a surge in confidence, without which a strike would have been impossible to sustain among such a desperately impoverished and vulnerable people.

We tend to think of unions in somewhat fixed terms: as signs of the political consciousness of workers or of the maturity of a political organization, as facilitators of collective bargaining for higher wages and for a better standard of living. All that is true. But the real significance of unions for untouchable scavengers lay in touch, in the very fact of a contact between impossibly distant worlds and in a new intimate, collective identity that was, significantly, cross-class and cross-caste. The empowering contact with different worlds helped them to transcend the demeaning boundaries that had locked them into a class and caste apartheid. It helped them to translate grievances as demands through the new language of organization and strikes. Recognition of their union was one of the first demands scavengers raised in the strike. We have already noted the absence of caste reform among scavengers. The union, by exemplary action if not through caste-focused discourses, played the role of a caste reformer.

Strikes were indeed much in the air at this time. The Congress began to harness large crowds for protest action against the all-white Simon Commission that had come to India to ponder on constitutional changes. A general strike was called in Calcutta on 3 February 1928. In a preparatory demonstration just before that, about 4,000 scavengers showed up along with dock and tramway men at the Maidan to pledge their support to the general strike. A common, though transient platform was forged in this joint action as scavengers stood with transport workers and with middle-class Congress activists. They were moreover applauded by leading nationalists of Bengal like Bose who presided over a large meeting of workers. He said that politics and labour were causes that were 'indissolubly bound together'.[78] The solicitation of support from the lowest category of workers – essential to ensure that public protests could become a spectacular event – put scavengers on a footing of brief but real equality with leaders of national stature, with middle-class youth and the large urban public.

Nationalism, therefore, was simultaneously a release and a constraint. It broke down lines of division and segregation, but it did so for a single day. It avoided, moreover, any engagement with the specific problems of the scavengers which were, at this point, largely a creation of nationalists in the Corporation. Significantly, even though they were called to participate in the demonstration, scavengers were exempted from the *hartal* itself. Their participation would have put urban ratepayers – the chief Congress constituency – into a situation of acute discomfort.

The WPP itself would not have liked such solidarity with nationalists. It was a distraction from union activities, vital at this stage for the impending strike. The WPP was now at a point of transition in its relationship with nationalism. If the Executive Committee Report of 1927–28 still adhered to a broad framework of unity and struggle with Congress movements, the breakdown of the Communist–Nationalist alliance in China heralded a far more sectarian line for the Comintern.[79] In 1928, Indian communists were cautiously probing an independent form of anti-imperialist politics, opposed to the Congress and based on working-class activism. The target was to immobilize the government through a general strike of several categories of workers at once. Scavengers and sweepers were crucial elements as their strike would truly paralyse the city. The WPP was quite confident of bringing this about. It had undoubtedly emerged as the leader of trade union activities in Bengal and Governor Jackson testified to the success of the alternative line of anti-imperialism: 'It is common knowledge', he would soon write, 'that the encouragement of the anti-British propaganda is the main work of the Communists.'[80] The Corporation, ruled by nationalists, provided them with an obvious arena of conflict with the Congress where nationalists doubled up as direct employers of many thousands of workers. In the Preliminary Report of the WPP in April 1928, Swarajist repression of scavengers in the March strike was described as a form of 'Fascist activity'. At the same time, the Report warned that communist distrust of the Congress should be expressed cautiously, as the Congress was whipping up popular sentiments against communists as 'anti-national': again, in a typically facsist manner.[81] At this critical juncture, scavengers' participaton in the nationalist rally was troublesome. It showed that however important their union was to them, scavengers still made independent political decisions.

The union was a surprising phenomenon. It was directed by the WPP which itself had been formed only in 1926. A very tiny group of full-time activists, twelve when it was first formed, it contended with surprising success against the massive popular support of the Congress in general and the influence of Muslim organizations among the Muslim urban poor. It was run by very young middle-class activists who had just begun to converse with working men. With extremely meagre resources – the extent of Moscow money was vastly exaggerated – it launched into an ambitious strategy of bringing about a general strike wave in the city and in all industrial areas simultaneously. Its manpower and time were constantly overstretched. Its activities were both protracted – continuing for the entire year and beyond, intermittently – and compressed; often, on the same few days, it would look after several strike actions at once.

Sometimes the WPP leaders were too preoccupied elsewhere to fully control developments in a particular area. This is precisely what happened with the first strike of scavengers on 4 March 1928. As Muzaffar Ahmad later recalled: 'As we sat in our European Asylum Lane office in the morning of 4 March, two to three *jharudars* came and said: "we are on strike." We rushed out everywhere to spread the news and to extend the strike where it had not occurred yet.' A very important strike was about to occur at the Lillooah railway workshop which involved about 14,000 workers. The WPP leaders were no doubt busy with its planning and knew nothing, consequently, of the scavengers' strike decision.[82] During the second strike in June, the union was so short of men that they called Philip Spratt, the English communist, from another strike situation to move among the scavengers' slums and help them organize.[83] There was an additional difficulty about organizing scavengers. Unlike mill workers, they were not distributed at specific points: at factory gates or workshops. Nor were their living areas spatially concentrated. They were scattered all over the city, living in slums that were attached to each ward. They worked on an individual basis. Union leaders had to be constantly on the move in order to communicate with them. Mobilization was extraordinarily difficult and so was the organization of strikes.

Though most of the workers were illiterate, we do find instances of WPP leaflets circulating among them: instructing them about their conduct during the strike, bringing them information about the strike situation from day to day, and also giving them news about strikes elsewhere in Bengal and in India. One of them was an Urdu leaflet titled *Tariq ki Talab* or 'Call of the Times'.[84] Intelligence Bureau informers reported on the circulation of red and yellow leaflets in May which were signed by Dharani Goswami. They urged scavengers to go on a second strike as their demands had not been met, in order to 'realize their rights'.[85]

Informers summarized other WPP pamphlets at greater length. One may speculate that the language of appeal and the content of discourse would have been very similar in all cases, cutting across sectoral differences among workers. All emanated from a tiny circle of activists who shared the same concerns and values. Since the strikes were very tenacious, we may infer that they had considerable mobilizational potential, that their language of appeal created or confirmed ideas that resonated powerfully among the workers. These may constitute something like 'controlling narratives' that were enthusiastically received by workers but which were born outside their circles. We find in them, as Patrick Joyce does in a different context, not quite a working-class discourse but a populist one.[86] Their popularity – especially of *Lal Paltan,* a small magazine for railway workshop labourers – makes them something like a consensual discourse, producing a shared imaginary.

Though written by communists, they were nonetheless quite different from the usual run of communist writings in India. They did not use the Marxist historical logic of class formation, transformation, struggles and revolution. Nor did they define or explain capitalism. Unlike the WPP reports, written for and by Party activists, these did not use categories like communism, socialism or fascism. Poverty rather than class relations was the dominant motif. They had a thin, simple, present-oriented narrative, contrasting the distress and poverty of manual workers with the profits of employers: sometimes using visual illustration, like a fat capitalist being thrashed by a skeletal worker. The language was highly charged: workers abroad have 'girded up their loins' for a fight; 'the lolling tongues of fire of the revolution from hundreds and thousands of mouths' will devour enemies; those 'who daily suck the blood of workers' are to be punished.[87] As counterpoint, they evoked a utopic vision of the Soviet Union – not so much as a classless society under proletarian dictatorship, but as a state where workers were fully and permanently employed and lacked for nothing. The present of the Soviet Union was taken to be the future of Indian workers, and strikes opened up a passage between the two.

They spoke much about workers' strikes in other parts of the world, especially in England and in China, and always in terms of success. The British General Strike of 1926 was described as something happening in the immediate present and as something poised to win: not as a failed strike that had happened two years back. Nor did they mention the communist debacle in China, already a year old. We may guess, from their tone of passionate certainty, that the authors themselves believed in the chronicle of victories even when they were fully aware of the debacles. This was the law of history, moving inexorably towards its revolutionary telos: defeats could only be temporary. This particular logic rendered their writings an act of genuine faith, rather than a manipulative strategy.

Scavengers must have been amazed to find a genuine *sahib* who came to them on behalf of the WPP: the English communist Philip Spratt who visited their slums, worked hard to keep the strikes going and talked about identical struggles among British workers. His presence was living irrefutable proof of the pervasiveness of global strikes. The globality of militancy was a very important resource.

There were, in this discourse, four concentric thematic rings circling one another. The innermost ring would describe themselves and their strike. Next, supplementary evidence would come from strikes among related categories of workers; for Calcutta scavengers, these would include scavengers' strikes in Howrah, Mymensingh and Darjeeling, as well as similar strikes in Delhi and Simla. These would be surrounded by references to contiguous categories, close to them in spatial and temporal terms. In our case, this would include strikes in Bengal among jute, paper, oil and railway workshops, and strikes in Bombay's cotton mills. Indian events would be framed within news of strikes elsewhere in the world: in Britain, in China, in Europe. The final, or outermost ring, was composed of the Soviet Union, which had 'workers' *raj*' as contrasted with the mere political *swaraj* of Indian nationalists.

Workers were offered a large world of solidarities and identifications. Scavengers sent a pledge of solidarity to the Lillooah railway workshop labourers on strike, just as the All India Trade Union Congress sent them messages of support. Some of the Calcutta jute, oil and paper mill workers who were also on strike would be their neighbours or men from the same districts, castes, communities, even villages. They now came to share something more: the common time of strikes. This time was also a global temporality.

What ensured this seamlessness, what conferred authenticity to the narrative and finally proved its moral, was the existence of the Soviet Union. Since no Soviet leader had yet emerged as an undisputed messiah, an entire conditon – its problems and struggles for survival unmentioned – rather than a personality cult propelled the hope and justified it. The Soviet Union was not so much a classless society as one without dearth, a country of full employment where all basic needs of all workers were met. It was the apex of the political imaginary whose actuality confirmed the possibilities that strikes envisaged. It had happened and it still existed. It was the goal, the way and the dream. Above all, it was a call for action, for strikes.[88]

We have another set of controlling narratives in the speeches of labour leaders. Since it was difficult to address highly dispersed scavengers collectively at any given time, these public meetings were crucial for mutual communication. They became especially urgent and intense during strikes. Interestingly, we find several different inflections and modes of address among WPP leaders. On the first day of the first strike, for instance, there were two speeches, one by Dharani Goswami and one by Muzaffar Ahmad. Goswami spoke in broken Urdu and apologized for it. It seems clear, then, that there were few or no Bengali-speaking scavengers in the audience. First, he assured them about the legality of their strike acion. On 29 January, after a union meeting, their demands had been written down and sent to the Corporation 'in a registered cover'. The union had received an acknowledgement from the Corporation and the letter was published in all newspapers. The legal conditions for serving the strike notice had thereby been fulfilled. He advised workers not to speak to any outsider who might ask them about the strike. They were merely to say: 'You may address our *anjuman* (union). We know nothing.'[89] Ahmad reiterated this: 'You should remain firm as long as you do not get your rights. You have done nothing against the law.'

Legal points were important. The Chief Executive Officer staunchly maintained that their letter did not amount to a proper strike notice, even though a Corporation committee had already held a meeting to discuss it. In the absence of a proper notice, according to Section 57B of the Corporation Act, the strike was an illegal stoppage of work.[90] Since this was a ticklish issue, the union placed a mandate of silence on the workers with special emphasis: not as a mode of control but as a necessary precaution against inadvertant confession of criminal action.

The notion of problems and demands – something that scavengers were familiar with – was now translated into a new language of militant politics: as a matter of rights. Ahmad formalized them as a union charter. He cited ten demands: union recognition, monthly pay of Rs 10, well-ventilated houses with latrines, rent fixed according to income, free medicine and treatment, end to the corruption of Block *sirdar babus* who extracted a month's salary to provide jobs and also deducted Rs 2 a month, fifteen days of annual casual leave, and paid leave for a month every year. He included provisions for leave for accidents and injuries incurred during work, a month's notice before dismissal and, in case a worker died in harness, transfer of his pending salary to his heir. Women workers should get three months' fully paid maternity leave and some child care provisions. There should also be old age provisions for workers with a long-term service record and free schools in their slums. The Corporation should open banks for workers and give them loans at affordable interest rates.

Ahmad blamed the 'inhabitants of the city' for their indifference to scavengers: 'It appears that they do not care for you a bit.' A strike would force them to put pressure on the Corporation. This proclaimed an ideal of mutual care: a notion of the city's public, and not just employers, taking responsibility for workers who looked after the city's health. He warned that the strike would cause pain to workers but, at the end of it, they would get 'good food'.

Radharaman Mitra's speeches on 8 March presented the theme of exploitation. Labourers get less than a rupee for food while *babus* ride cars, drink freely and 'dine in big hotels'. While scavengers are wrongly accused of blowing their earnings on drink, *babus* drink themselves silly. The set of contrasts denaturalized privilege and deprivation. He asked them to stand firm against threats as well as against pity when educated men would come and plead with them to save the city from cholera. The power of upper-class appeals was greatly feared. In May, Ahmad urged scavengers to prepare for another strike as all Corporation promises after the first strike went unheeded. He appealed to their masculinity: 'Do you want to live like men or not?' Living like men involved a desire for just revenge: 'Do you want to take revenge or not?' He built on the experience of the first strike. Then they had been beaten up, but they could also negotiate on equal terms with Corporation bigwigs who were afraid of their action. It was the strike that gave them power over the mighty of the land. After all, the Chairman of the Corporation was but an employee, 'just as you are'. Do not heed appeals to older notions of loyalties, he told the workers; loyalty to the union was important, not loyalty to 'munibs'. If the union was to replace older ties, Mitra tried to inculcate a stronger sense of equality by referring to it as a body of 'clerks' gathered to assist workers. Masculinity sometimes involved a competitive militancy. Referring to the strike by Howrah scavengers in April, Ahmad asked Calcutta workers at a public rally: at Howrah, sweepers did battle for eleven days and they won; '[w]e have 12,000 brethren who could not do as much work as did the 3,000 men of Howrah!'[91]

During the early days of the first strike, Goswami described the Swarajya Party as oppressors.[92] In her letter to the Bengal Trade Union Federation, Prabhabati made the same point.[93] The fact that Swarajists had called in the much abused colonial police to beat up and arrest their own compatriots was shocking to even their critics. This was quite natural as the nationalists berated foreign rule primarily because of police oppression. The Intelligence Bureau observed that a 'noteworthy feature . . . of the various meetings held during the strike had been the outspoken condemnation of the Swarajist Corporation who were severely criticized for taking police help to break the strike'. It also observed that even Bose's faction in the Bengal Congress occasionally sympathized with the workers; Bose wanted to oust the Chief Executive Officer and take his place, even if that meant adding to the embarrassment of his own party.[94] The Bengal Congress was sharply divided between Bose and Sengupta who was the Mayor during the first strike.[95] His discomfiture would not have been entirely unwelcome to his rival.

Given the constraints within which the WPP operated, they had little time for constructive welfare work or for labour reform. They formed unions to bring about strikes in the immediate future. After the strikes were over the union practically disappeared, and it had to be rebuilt at the time of the next strike. The contact between the workers and the union was profoundly transformative, but it was also tantalizingly transient. Strikes were therefore the only school the union provided for the workers. What workers heard at meetings and what they read in the leaflets taught them a new language and a new ability – to translate grievances into demands and demands into rights.

VI

There were two rounds of strikes in 1928: one between 4 and 9 March, involving 9–10,000 scavengers and sweepers: another between 25 June and 5 July, involving about 3,000. The first strike was handled by the nationalists. They had to answer to an increasngly outraged public as the city reeled under a total sanitary breakdown. Garbage piled up dangerously and the stench became unbearable with the onset of hot weather in March. Epidemics were predicted and even middle-class newspapers blamed them for not attending to the workers' demands.[96] Eventually, the Mayor agreed to negotiate with the workers' representatives as he felt the strike could not be broken. They agreed on a Re 1 monthly wage increase, release of all arrested workers and restoration of pay during the strike period. A committee was formed to look at work conditions in general.

When the strike was on, Swarajists cracked down very hard on strikers. Hundreds of picketers were beaten up mercilessly; 70 workers were arrested on a single day. Workers were threatened, blacklegs were freely imported, and scavengers were excluded from cheap-price shops and water supply. Worst of all, their access to public latrines was cut off. The Corporation claimed that even a Re 1 wage increase was excessive and undeserved.[97]

The police reported that intimidation proved useless and that the pickets remained disciplined and well-organized even under great pressure. Even the better-off scavengers, who cleaned European homes, ignored blandishments of preferred treatment and joined the pickets. When *sirdars* were approached to provide an alternative labour supply, they confessed that they could not find an adequate number of men.[98] This could have been the result of quite a few things. Despite their notorious corruption, the strike was more about wage, housing and compensation issues, and about the exorbitant interest rates that workers paid to Kabuli moneylenders. The latter, being both oppressive and foreign, drew most of their wrath. Workers shared a more complex relationship with them, that was made up of dependence, greater everyday interaction as well as resentment. Equally, the strength of the pickets and the public shaming devices to humiliate blacklegs worked so well that few dared to break the strike. Quite often, truckloads of scavengers imported from distant parts were blocked and turned back by the picketers.[99] What helped scavengers most of all was their caste-based monopoly over this work. No other caste would demean itself with night soil removal in public, and recruitment possibilities were therefore severely restricted. Their degraded caste became a source of great power in the strike situation.

From April, the union began to prepare for a second strike, taking great care this time to fulfil all legal technicalities about proper notice. On 2 April, it sent a letter to the Corporation, asking for the promised withdrawal of cases against workers and demanding a response within three days. A second letter was posted on 14 April, citing instances where the mayoral agreement was violated and threatening a strike the following month. There seems to have been a lull after this, and it is possible that the WPP was fully preoccupied with a short but ferocious bout of strike by Howrah's municipal scavengers in April. This became a reference point for the subsequent strike in Calcutta in June–July.

The Mayor called a meeting only on 2 July, after the second strike was well under way. The Corporation played a waiting game, hoping that the threat would come to nothing. Significantly, the visitors' galleries were full when, after a week's stoppage of work, the Corporation at last decided to pay attention to the issue. Swarajists fully supported workers' demands this time and poured scorn on the new Corporation leaders for ignoring the settlement that their Mayor had promised. Apart from that, however, they did nothing to help the strike. The coincidence of the strike with the monsoon rains created an awful situation as garbage floated around and the stink of rotting waste became unbearable.[100] Scavengers had finally managed to force their presence on the entire urban public – ironically, by their non-work. This is exactly what the union had predicted in late May. Ahmad then exhorted the workers to be patient as soon there would be public pressure on the Corporation. 'Inhabitants must see whose mischief it is' and step in. They must realize who clean their city for them, even at the cost of their lives at times.[101] By the time of the second strike, then, the urban 'public' had entered the scene as an interested third party in the dispute – a very rare occurrence in strikes. After another meeting in the Mayor's room, the second strike was finally settled with a unanimous agreement on a Re 1 monthly pay hike and with the Chief Executive Officer's promise to persuade the police to withdraw cases against workers. He was 'requested' by the union to sanction strike pay and prevent victimization.[102] There was a minimum of gain as more effort went into ensuring non-victimization and release of arrested workers than in enforcing the original demands: a problem that plagues all strikes where the collateral damage during a strike situation often becomes more important than the original problems.

During the seventeen days of the two strikes, the new visibility of scavengers was signified in two different ways. First, their fundamental importance to Calcutta life became manifest as garbage choked the city and the entire urban public appealed to the Corporation to negotiate with them. Second, as the strike persisted, their meetings occupied more and more important civic centres: Hazra Park, Deshbandhu Park, the Ochterlony Monument and the Maidan – the largest, most beautiful and well-kept green in the entire city; a pleasure ground of the rich and the *sahibs*. Meetings were held in the late afternoons and early evenings; when shops, offices and workshops closed down, workers of various kinds poured though these central spots. This was also when the privileged leisured classes strolled through the parks and grounds. They would hear all about the workers' conditions and problems. The city thus became the theatre of strike action with large and immensely varied slices of the urban public drawn in as concerned audiences.

For the scavengers, this temporary inhabitation of the city centre would have been a sign of the world turned upside down, albeit in the immediate present and not in any long-term or permanent sense. They could not have been naive enough to believe all was going to change; at the most, they bargained for a bit of wage increase and non-victimization. Yet strikes were a moment out of time. They were a liminal intercession, interrupting the structures of everyday and creating a sense of festive *communitas* which, in the strange year of 1928, seemed to encompass the workers of the world. The experience of becoming unhidden, public, of swelling into the heart of the city, of occupying what was previously non-touchable, was something that stood apart from their quotidian lives of work and degradation, and from the prosaic and limited demands they set to the authorities as bargaining points.

The world changed in other ways, too. Often, workers shared the platform with labour leaders and, once or twice, they too made public speeches. Their leaders had advised them to tell the authorities: 'Ask our *anjuman* [union], we know nothing.' Nonetheless, belying this passive image entirely, they spoke in public and they spoke in accents of their own. An Intelligence Bureau report on a meeting observed that a 'stout *methrani*' sat next to the main speaker and it was because of her vigorous interventions from the podium that workers finally decided to continue the strike. Ram Nagina, a very vocal worker, advised scavengers to use violence without hesitation if they were attacked. He suggested that they should pour night soil on picket breakers as this would be an irresistible mode of attack. Often, workers suggested violent retaliation against police flogging. Crowds of workers, as they listened to the leaders' speeches, would interject from time to time bringing new information of their own: about Corporation attempts to bribe recalcitrant workers, for instance.[103] The March strike began when workers first declared it and then came to the WPP office to tell them they had gone on strike. So union leaders did not make up their minds for them; they relied on their own counsel.

Women *methranis* were energetic on strike days. During the Howrah scavengers' strike, they drove away Anglo-Indian sergeants by upending pots of excreta on their heads, thus turning the signs of their degraded caste and work into a weapon of offence. The sergeants fled, tearing off their uniforms and vowing never to return. The middle-class woman leader Prabhabati would not handle excreta. Still, she too defied norms of class and gender as she used unwomanly, abusive language against strike breakers.

We have talked of cross-class solidarities. But the working class itself was a matter of divided interests. From day to day, scavengers of different wards vacillated, nearly came out of the strike, and joined back again when the strike seemed almost lost. Their decisions were local, contingent, fluctuating: another sign of their autonomy as the union had a clear and firm policy. Strike breakers and imported blacklegs were threatened and beaten up, and mutual clashes were frequent. Scavengers received pledges of sympathy from other workers, but they also collided with carters from municipal '*gow khanas*' whose carts could not be hired out for waste removal during the strikes. On the other hand, 'street urchins' – probably homeless youth – helped at their pickets and heaped garbage along with them on tram lines to derail tramcars at Wellington Square.[104] It is interesting that scavengers turned the instruments of their daily labour into weapons of struggle: throwing pots of excreta, heaping refuse. Class identities and solidarities were strong but not always stable.

Let me end this with a paradox. 1928 was a very busy year for labour activism in Bengal. But for jute mill and railway workshop workers, there was an immediate threat of retrenchment, rationalization, and drastic changes in working hours and shifts. Scavengers, in contrast, faced no similar threat to their employment terms, nor was there a decline in real wages. In fact prices of food had begun to go down. What, then, activated the dormant sense of the basic injustice of their existence at this precise moment? What made them go on strike repeatedly against tremendous odds? For scavengers were forbidden to down tools without due notice under several regulations. They could not really hope to save their jobs when strikes ended.

Was it simply their obedience to another set of authority, to educated middle-class union leaders? It is true that the union leaders, especially the WPP, intently worked on bringing about a general strike wave. But, as we saw, the scavengers' autonomy in decision-making was quite evident, and workers do not face dismissal, starvation and intimidation unless they themselves decide on strike action.

What union leaders provided to scavengers was not really a new or sudden revelation of their real conditions. Scavengers knew that themselves. But they brought them the world, their presence as middle-class, upper-caste persons who were so far inaccessible, in their opening up of public spaces and attention to workers, in their insistence that workers of the world supported them and were doing what they were doing. It was both an affirmation of their working-class identity, now translated as a source of strength as scavengers watched what they could do to the city; and also, perhaps – taking a cue from Rancière – an exit from the trap that was their work.[105] It was a new identity as citizens in the city and in the world that had shunned them.

For those two weeks, they were no longer scavengers – Doms and Haris; they were a new and different people – people on strike. Strikes were not, in the immediate instance, so much conjugated from a wage–price nexus, nor from caste or class problems, even though these did constitute the larger horizon of their conditions and experiences. They were, above all, both an intimation of equality and a transient yet palpable actualization of the promise.

Epilogue

The story does not end with colonial times, independence and the constitutional prohibition of untouchability – the Protection of Civil Rights Act, 1955, or The Scheduled Castes and Scheduled Tribes Act (Prevention of Atrocities) of 1989. Nor does it end with legal injunctions against manual scavenging which led to the Employment of Manual Scavengers and Constuction of Dry Latrines (Prohibition) Act of 1993 which sought to abolish manual scavenging. Let me end with a somewhat long postscript. Right now, an all-India consolidation of scavengers, the *Safai Karamchari Andolan*, is demanding legal termination of manual scavenging. Dry latrines cleaned by human hands continue even today, even in institutions and buildings owned by state and Union governments. The Union Ministry of Railways is especially culpable as the open discharge system in trains makes it imperative that excreta be picked up and removed by hand. Many municipalities continue to maintain dry latrines. In 2002, the Supreme Court directed all states to file affidavits on manual scavenging, after a public interest litigation was filed by the *Safai Karamchari Andolan*. The Uttar Pradesh government and the Railways Ministry admitted to its use, but most states denied it. Photographic records, preserved in the archives of the *Safai Karamchari Andolan*, however, contradict this. Since 2004, the Union Ministry of Housing and Urban Poverty Alleviation has been supervising the elimination of dry latrines. It seems that whereas the number of manual scavengers in the country was nearly 13,00,000 a decade back, currently it has come down to 3,00,000, predominantly as a result of deliberate avoidance of such work, conversion of dry latrines into pour flush toilets and governmental rehabilitation of scavengers as sweepers. But elimination of dry latrines does not entirely end manual scavenging. A recent report indicates that in poorer areas of many Indian towns and cities, they are relaced with *bahao* latrines which flow out into open drainage, from which sludge and excreta have to be manually removed by municipal workers with the most rudimentary tools.

Though the National Advisory Council promised far-reaching reforms in cleaning operations in October 2010, the system of manual removal continues under great health hazards, physical risks and degradation. Scavengers are employed from Dalit castes and among the listed names within this reserved category, we still find mention of Doms and Haris. Other Dalit castes look down upon them and often they pass themselves off to others as sweepers and not scavengers, indicating the persistence of hierarchies among Dalits themselves. Bezwada Wilson, who leads the *Safai Karamchari Andolan*, says that his parents advised him to call himself a boy from the sweeper caste when he was sent off to study in Andhra Pradesh, away from his native town of Kolar in Karnataka. As a boy, he was not told that his parents were manual scavengers. When he discovered it and pleaded with them to give it up, he was met with a numbing fatalism: they were fated to do this. He now leads a movement that asks scavengers to boycott this work and to find other employment. It also asks for the abolition of dry latrines. The change in the nature of their occupation would presumably lead on to an upward mobility in caste terms as well, thus combining social and physical relief. While the current state of scavenging operations reveals striking continuities with past practices, it also indicates a new departure: an abandonment of the work itself, rather than an increase in wages and facilities.[106]

In 2011, the Delhi High Court, responding to a public interest litigation appeal, directed the Delhi Jal Board to ensure the safety of sewage workers and to pay compensation to families if a worker died of inhaling poisonous gases while clearing manholes: something that was a major issue in 1928. The Board appealed to the Supreme Court against the order. In a landmark verdict, the Supreme Court dismissed the appeal and, in the strongest language, upbraided courts and the public for spending their time to defend rich criminals while they had no time for workers who do work that nobody else would do.[107]

Notes and References

1 These strikes are briefly referred to in Tanika Sarkar, *Bengal 1928–1934: The Politics of Protest*, New Delhi: Oxford University Press, 1987.

2 *Calcutta Municipal Gazette*, Imperial Silver Jubilee Commemoration Volume, Calcutta, 1935: 105.

3 Subhash Mukhopadhyay, *Tanaporener Maajhkhaane*, Kolkata: Ananda Publishers, 1994: 63–64. I owe this reference to Shri Sushil Ghosh.

4 John McGuire, *The Making of a Colonial Mind: A Quantitative Study of the Bhadralok in Calcutta, 1856–1888*, Monographs in South Asia series, Canberra: Australian National University, 1983: 10–11.

5 For a study of Bengal communists, see Gautam Chattopadhyay, *Communism and Bengal's Freedom Movement*, Bombay: People's Publishing House, 1970.

6 For a general account of such labour leaders, see Manju Chattopadhyay, *The Trail Blazing Women Trade Unionists of India*, New Delhi: All India Trade Union Congress, 1995.

7 I am grateful to Anna Sailer for bringing this to my attention from her research in the Special Branch archives in Calcutta.

8 Manju Chattopadyay, 'Kolkatai Dhangar Dharmaghat Ebong Prabhabati Dasgupta o Sakina Begum', in Gautam Chattopadhyay (ed.), *Itihas Anusandhan*, Vol. 2, Calcutta: K.P. Bagchi & Co., 1982.

10 Interview with Prabhabati Dasgupta, Oral History Section, Nehru Memorial Museum and Library, New Delhi, 24 April 1968.

11 *Forward*, 26 June 1928.

12 For a political biography of the early life of Muzaffar Ahmad, see Suchetana Chattopadhyay, *An Early Communist: Muzaffar Ahmad in Calcutta 1913–1929*, New Delhi: Tulika Books, 2011.

13 *Forward*, 26 June 1928.

14 See Kris Manjapra, *M.N. Roy: Marxism and Colonial Cosmopolitanism*, New Delhi: Routledge, 2010.

15 Intelligence Branch, File No 448/28, Confidential No 606/50-25, Intelligence Branch [IB] Archives, Kolkata; Progressive Report on Scavengers' Union, Dacca, 2 February 1928, IB Archives, Kolkata.

16 Intelligence Branch, Weekly Report, 8/1/29 – Part I–V, Extracts from week ending 21/1/29 and week ending 12/12/28, IB Archives, Kolkata.

[17] Intelligence Branch, Confidential No. 606/50-25 – District Intelligence Branch, Mymensingh, 2 February 1929, IB Archives, Kolkata.

[18] Report of Ahmad's speech, *Meerut Conspiracy Case Papers* [*MCCP*], P 193–40 (T), P.C. Joshi Archive of Contemporary History, Jawaharlal Nehru University, New Delhi.

[19] This assertion is one of the pillars of his seminal work. See Dipesh Chakrabarty, *Rethinking Working Class History: Bengal 1890–1940*, New Delhi: Oxford University Press, 1989.

[20] H.F.J.T. Maguire, *Report on the Census of Calcutta*, Calcutta: Bengal Secretariat Press, 1891: 198–99.

[21] L.S.S. O'Malley (ed.), *Report on the Census of India*, Vol. 6, part 2, Calcutta: Bengal Secretariat Press, 1913: 88–89.

[22] A.E. Porter (ed.), *Report on the Census of India*, Vol. VI, parts 1 and 2, Central Public Branch, West Bengal State Archives, Kolkata, 1933: 112.

[23] H.H. Risley, *The Tribes and Castes of Bengal: Ethnographic Glossary*, first edition, Calcutta: Bengal Secretariat Press, 1891; reprint, Calcutta: Firma K.L. Mukhopadhyay, 1981, Vol. 2: 91.

[24] Ibid.: 240–52.

[25] A Bengali proverb, which refers to the power of love that can conquer social inhibitions, goes thus: 'When you lose your heart, it does not matter if the beloved is a Hadi or a Dom.' It implies that only love makes you stoop so low.

[26] S.W. Goode, *Municipal Calcutta: Its Institutions in Their Origins and Growth*, Edinburgh: Calcutta Corporation Publication, 1916: 168.

[27] *Amrita Bazar Patrika*, 27 June 1928.

[28] Samaresh Bose, *Jug Jug Jiye*, Calcutta: Ananda Publishers, 1985: 291–92.

[29] Rabindranath Tagore, *Char Adhyay*, 1934; *Rabindra Upanyas Sangraha*, Calcutta: Kamini Prakashan, 2002: 1294.

[30] *The Statesman*, 6 March and 26 June 1928.

[31] I owe this reference to Ishan Mukhopadhyay who works on wartime Calcutta.

[32] This is the central argument in Nandini Gooptu, *The Politics of the Urban Poor in Early Twentieth Century India*, Cambridge: Cambridge University Press, 2001.

[33] The standard dictionary meaning of the word denotes 'non-Aryan inhabitants of the Vindhya mountain areas, a caste which is also known as barabarians'. Haricharan Bandyopadhyay (ed.), *Bangiya Shabdakosh*, first edition, 1933–34; reprint, New Delhi: Sahitya Akademi, 1966, Vol. 1: 1155.

[34] Subol Chandra Mitra (ed.), *Saral Bangla Abhidhan*, Calcutta: New Bengal Press, 1909: 1280.

[35] For a detailed study of Madras sewage and scavengers, see Vidhya Raveendranathan, 'Constructing the Scavenger: Caste and Labour in Colonial South India 1860–1940', unpublished M.Phil. thesis, University of Delhi, Delhi, 2011; for a study of Delhi scavengers, see Vijay Prashad, *Untouchable Freedom: A Social History of a Dalit Community*, New Delhi: Oxford University Press, 2000.

[36] Goode, *Municipal Calcutta*: 1–13.

[37] Cited in C.C. Chatterjee (comp.), *Calcutta Drainage Works: A Brief History*, Calcutta: Corporation Press, 1921: 1.

[38] Maurice Daunton (ed.), *The Cambridge Urban History of Britain*, Vol. III, Cambridge: Cambridge University Press, 2000: 316.

[39] *Calcutta Municipal Gazette*, 1935: 98.

[40] Abstract of the Report of the Health Officer of Calcutta, 1878, *Parliamentary Papers, East India: Statement Exhibiting the Moral and Material Progress and Condition of India, 1878–79*, No. 15, 1880, India Office, British Library: 89.

[41] Goode, *Municipal Calcutta*: 31–39.

[42] See, for instance, weekly excerpts from Bengali newspapers like *Soma Prakash*,

Sambad Bhaskar, *Samaj Darpan*, *Bharat Shangshakarak, Samachar Chandrika* and *Banga Hitaishi*, in *Reports on Native Newspapers*, Bengal, 1976–78.

43 *Calcutta Municipal Gazette*, 1935: 105.

44 Intelligence Branch, File No 80C/27 – part 11, Leaflet of 26 September, Howrah-Bali election poster of 1926, IB Archives, Kolkata.

45 *The Times of India*, 23 July 1928.

46 Memorandum of the Army Sanitary Commission on the Report of the Calcutta Municipality for 1878, cited in *Parliamentary Papers, East India (Progress) Statement of the Moral and Material Progress of India, 1878–79,* No. 15, 1880, India Office, British Library: 180.

47 From Florence Nightingale, 30 August 1889: Marquis of Lansdowne, Correspondence with Persons in England, 1888–89, Private Papers Collection, *Lansdowne Papers*, No. 88, National Archives of India, New Delhi.

48 Rabindranath Tagore, *Jibansmriti*, *Rabindra Rachanabali*, Vol. 10, Centenary Edition, Calcutta: Visvabharati Publication and Saraswati Press, 1961: 12.

49 Bengal Act of 1932, Government of West Bengal, Legislative Department, *The West Bengal Code*, second edition, Vol. 4: *Bengal Acts, 1920–35*, Calcutta: West Bengal Government Press, 1964: 413.

50 *Calcutta Municipal Gazette*, 1935: 99–105.

51 We find a very account for Delhi scavengers in Prashad, *Untouchable Freedom*: 3–6.

52 Chatterjee (comp.), *Calcutta Drainage Works*.

53 Goode, *Municipal Calcutta*: 151–63.

54 Ibid.

55 *Report of the Royal Commission on Labour in India*, London: His Majesty's Stationery Office, 1931: 17–18.

56 Goode, *Municipal Calcutta*, 162–72.

57 Memorandum of the Army Sanitary Commission, 1878, in *Parliamentary Papers, East India, 1878–79*, India Office, British Library: 176–80.

58 Ibid.

59 Prosecution Exhibits, P 545–48 (10), *MCCP*.

60 *East India Papers: Accounts and Papers, 1900*, British Library: 191.

61 Ibid.

62 *Census of India, 1911*, Vol. VI, part 1, Report by L.S.S. O'Malley, Calcutta: Bengal Secretariat Book Depot, 1913: 5.

63 Memorandum of the Army Sanitary Commission, 1878, in *Parliamentary Papers, East India, 1878–79*, India Office, British Library: 90–178.

64 *Report of the Royal Labour Commission on Labour*: 17–18.

65 *The Statesman*, on 26 June 1928, recalled the three-day stoppage of work in May 1924 during the organized strike of 1928.

66 Prosecution Exhibits, P 545–48 (10), *MCCP.*

67 Ahmad's speech on 20 May 1928, Bengal and Bihar Speeches, P 1926 (1) (T), *MCCP*.

68 A.C. Bannerjee's motion at the meeting, reported in *Forward*, 14 March 1928.

69 *Census of India, 1911*, Vol. VI, part 1, Report by L.S.S. O'Malley: 15–72.

70 Ibid., Table XV – Occupations, part D: 88–116.

71 A.E. Porter (ed.), *Report on the Census of India*, Vol. VI, parts 1 and 2, Central Public Branch, West Bengal State Archives, 1933: 12. The Calcutta sections were compiled by Prafulla Chandra Sen of the Bengal Civil Service in collaboration with the Corporation, although the Corporation was highly inefficient in providing information.

72 See Amiya K. Sen, *Hindu Revivalism in Bengal, 1872–1905: Some Essays in Interpretation*, New Delhi: Oxford University Press, 1993: 218–36; also Ramakanta Chakravarti, *Vaisnavism in Bengal: 1486–1900*, Calcutta: Sanskrit Pustak Bhandar, 1985: 396–98.

73 Kenneth McPherson, *The Muslim Microcosm: Calcutta, 1918 to 1935*, Wiesbaden: Franz Steiner Verlag, 1974: 92.

74 Ibid.: 82–97.

75 Intelligence Branch, Weekly Reports on the Political Situation in Bengal, week ending 22 February 1928, IB Archives, Kolkata.

76 *The Statesman*, 26 June 1928.

77 Speeches of Ahmad and Goswami, 4 and 8 March 1928, P 1925–26 (T), *MCCP*; also Prosecution Exhibits, P 1–56–a, list of articles seized from Prabhabati, including her letter to Bengal Trade Union Federation of 7 March 1928 and to All India Trade Union Federation on the same day.

78 *Forward*, 1, 2, 3, 4, 28 February 1928.

79 *Ganavani*, 27 September 1929.

80 Jackson's letter to Viceroy Irwin, 8 April 1929, Letter 314 A, *Halifax Collection*, India Office, British Library.

81 Prosecution Exhibits, P 1–56–a of 1928, *MCCP*.

82 *Forward*, 8 March 1928.

83 Muzaffar Ahmad, *Myself and the Communist Party of India, 1920–1929*, Vol. 2, Calcutta: National Book Agency, 1970: 27.

84 Intelligence Branch, Weekly Reports on the Political and Labour Situation in Bengal, week ending 22 February 1928, IB Archives, Kolkata.

85 Ibid., week ending 23 May 1928.

86 Patrick Joyce, *Visions of the People: Industrial England and the Question of Class, 1840–1914*, Cambridge: Cambridge University Press, 1991: 329–35.

87 Intelligence Branch, No 846 PSD, GOB, Political Department, Political Branch, West Bengal State Archives, Kolkata.

88 Intelligence Branch, File No. 357–28 of 1928 and File No 427/28 of 1928, IB Archives, Kolkata.

89 P 1925–6 (T), *MCCP*.

90 Chief Executive Officer's speech in Corporation, *Forward*, 14 March 1928.

91 Bengal and Bihar Speeches, P 1926 (1) (T), *MCCP*.

92 Ibid.

93 Letter of Prabhabati, 7 March 1928, P 28–29, Prosecution Exhibits, P 1–56, *MCCP*.

94 Intelligence Branch, Report on the Political Situation and Labour Unrest, week ending 14 March 1928, IB Archives, Kolkata.

95 Sarkar, *Bengal 1928–1934*, Chapter 1.

96 This is evident from issues of *Ananda Bazar Patrika, The Statesman* and *Forward* for those days. All urged the Corporation to negotiate and save the city from a total breakdown of sanitary health.

97 Intelligence Branch, Weekly Reports on the Political Situation and Labour Problems, week ending 7 and 14 March 1928, IB Archives, Kolkata.

98 Prosecution Exhibits, P 545–48 (10), *MCCP*.

99 *Forward*, 9 March 1928.

100 *The Statesman*, 26 July 1928.

101 Bengal and Bihar Speeches, P 1926 (1) (T), *MCCP*.

102 *Forward*, 12 April, 29 June, 30 June, 5 July, 6 July 1928.

103 Intelligence Branch, Weekly Reports on the Political Situation and Labour Problems, week ending 7 and 14 July, IB Archives, Kolkata.

104 *Ananda Bazar Patrika*, 6 March 1928.

105 Jacques Rancière, *The Nights of Labour: The Workers' Dream in Nineteenth Century France,* translated by John Drury, Philadelphia: Temple Press, 1989: 19–21.

106 Vidya Subramaniam, 'Throwing Off the Yoke of Manual Scavenging', *The Hindu*, Wednesday, 27 October 2010.

107 *The Hindu*, Friday, 15 July 2011.

'Various Paths Are Today Opened'

The Bengal Jute Mill Strike of 1929 as a Historical Event

Anna Sailer

In April 1929, a programmatic article was published in a Bengali paper called *Swadeshi Bazar*, about an imminent workers' struggle and its possibilities.[1] The author explained the contemporary situation as follows:

> Various paths are today opened before the workers of the nation. The workers, according to their own capacity, must each pick out a path and travel along it. . . . A struggle must be carried on with the opposing power from various directions. . . . At the present moment new workers are being bewildered at the sight of different ways and different parties. The worker must first choose his path, and thereafter choose the party.[2]

The article appeared in the middle of an intense phase of workers' militancy in Bengal, especially in Calcutta and its surrounding industrial areas. Between 1928 and 1929, many industries and labour regimes witnessed significant upsurges of industrial action, for instance among railway workers in Lillooah, oil workers in Budge-Budge and scavengers in Calcutta.[3] Among these upsurges was the unprecedented militancy of jute mill workers, who embarked on the first general strike in their industry's history just a few months after the publication of this article.

In the course of this strike, about 240,000 workers left their workplaces in a brief period of less than two months. The first protests started in the north of Calcutta, after an increase in the hours of work instituted by the mills of the Indian Jute Mills' Association (IJMA). Led by the Bengal Jute Workers' Union (BJWU), the strike soon affected the entire jute mill belt of Bengal. Faced with the threatening upsurge of workers, the government intervened and pushed for an end to the strike. A settlement mediated by the government of Bengal was soon arrived at, by which the IJMA was forced to agree to the demands posed by the BJWU on behalf of the workers.[4]

When analysing the history of this strike, we have a choice between two temporal perspectives. On the one hand, we could locate it within larger developments whose 'beginning' and 'end' were independent of the strike itself. The strike would then be an element of an already determined, larger process of change. On the other hand, we could analyse the general strike as *an event*, emerging at a particular moment in time. We then would have to

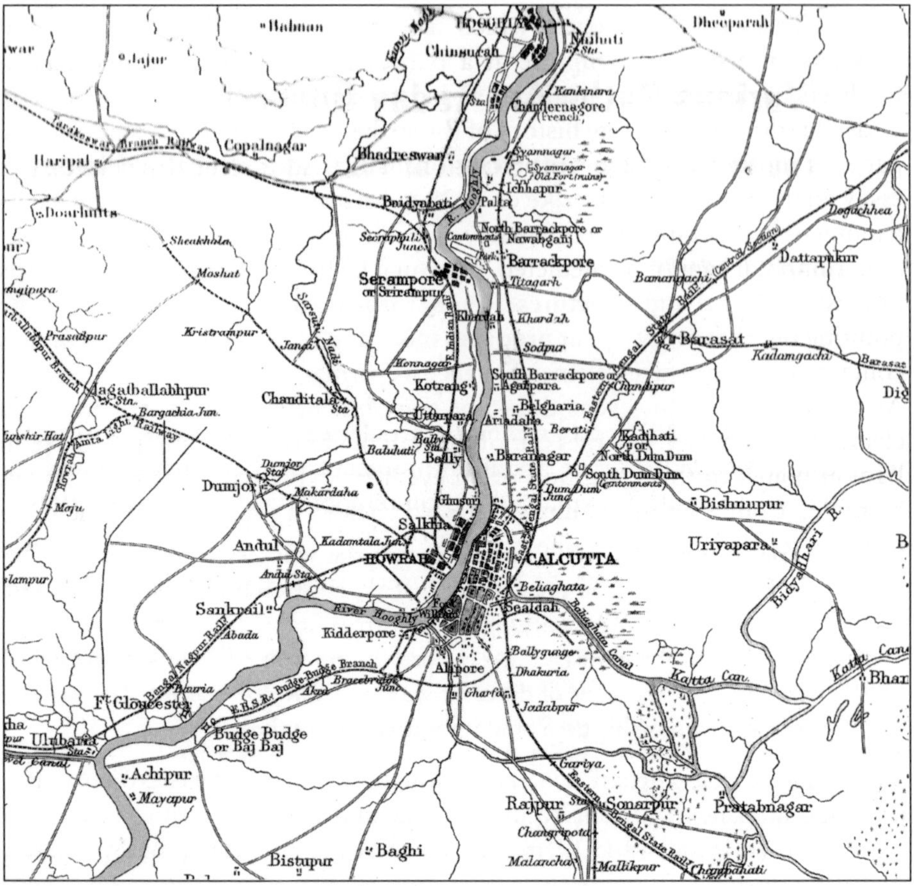

MAP 1 From *Imperial Gazetteer of India Atlas*, 1931

focus on the possibilities and paths, but also the contradictions and tensions, that were disclosed as the strike evolved. In this perspective, the general strike would also appear as a part – or rather a fragment – of an ongoing process of change, but this process would rather be approached through ruptures of the very change we seek to understand.[5]

For the first approach, several studies can be mentioned which have analysed the history of the strike through the lens of larger developments. The history of the strike here is a part of narratives about the development or transformation of workers' politics and labour conflicts, especially in the interwar years. The event seems, in several of these accounts, overshadowed and marginalized in its significance by the periods preceding and succeeding it: the 1920s, when nationalist and socialist trade unions entered the stage in the jute mill industry; and the 1930s, when communist trade unions became increasingly important in the politics of the jute workers.[6] Even in those rare accounts which deal solely with the general strike, the analysis is embedded within frameworks structured by long-term developments. In this respect they too sideline the role of the event.[7]

The second approach, which would lead us to analyse the general strike as an event, as a rupture at a particular moment in history, has so far been neglected. This neglect has led to serious problems, not only in understanding the concrete history of the strike, but also in understanding the patterns and shifts of the larger process of change. Addressing this neglect, this essay analyses the general strike of 1929 as an *event*. It considers an event as a moment that entails something new and can thus be described as a surprise. Accordingly, it cannot be predicted, nor can it be fully understood on the basis of existing norms and structures. Reinhardt Koselleck has expressed this by pointing out that every 'event produces more and at the same time less than is contained in its pre-given elements: hence its permanently surprising novelty'.[8] At the same time, an event does not exist independently of its 'pre-given elements' but, rather, emerges out of them. It might thus be anticipated. Alain Badiou points to this condition of an event by explaining that it 'is always extracted from a situation, always related back to a singular multiplicity, to its state, to the language connected to it'.[9]

Some implications of these observations can be illustrated by considering the *Swadeshi Bazar* article quoted above. In April 1929, the advent of an event could be anticipated since this was a time in the midst of unprecedented workers' struggles which (at least) the author of the article experienced as a moment full of possibilities – a moment that was part of an emerging process of change. At the same time, this was a time in the midst of repression of the labour movement. By March 1929 several strikes had been defeated and several labour leaders had been arrested in the context of the Meerut Conspiracy Case. The programmatic anticipation of an event at this particular moment thus also bears an element of attempting to prevent the defeat of the emerging possibilities. Besides expressing anticipation, the author could not predict the impending struggle (in the jute mill industry or elsewhere) since the actual shape the event took, its scale and its impact, had the character of an event – or a surprise. The author, in his statement, could therefore only express particular hopes and expectations regarding an event that he anticipated to be emerging in his present. This event, as hoped, would reopen possibilities and enable new trajectories, and therefore a path towards a 'future revolution'.

Considering the general strike of 1929 as an event in the sense explained above, the present essay analyses how the strike emerged and evolved, the shape it took in its various stages, and the possibilities embedded in these moments. At the same time, the essay argues that this event was to some degree unfinished. Through this analysis, it problematizes certain binaries and concepts by focusing on the tensions and conflicts through which the emergence of the strike was shaped in a dialectical process.

The argument develops around two conflictual yet mutually constitutive axes. First, the emergence of various possibilities, trajectories and anticipations which shaped and reshaped the event are considered. The strike in this respect was constantly emerging, realizing the *general* character of the event on different levels and with differing anticipations. This first axis, however, was also determined by various attempts to close off various possibilities and to control the unfolding of particular trajectories. It can be seen as a constant process of opening and closing of possibilities, as well as of shaping and reshaping of trajectories. This axis accordingly determines a field – or, to use Alain Badiou's term, an 'evental site' – in which the event could unfold.[10]

The second axis concerns interconnections, as well as tensions and conflicts, between various actors, taking place on various levels of the strike. These interconnections and tensions shifted in the course of the event, shaped by and at the same time shaping the particular dynamics of the general strike. Particular conflicts could become visible at different moments of the event, or tensions could evolve into serious conflicts. Both these were a part of the process of shaping and reshaping the event. While the first axis provides the site for the event, the second axis indicates its unfolding dynamics.

These two axes outline the basic dialectical tension through which the event constantly emerged and re-emerged, and through which it evolved in particular ways. This dialectical process, I argue, was disclosed most strongly in the tension between the strike's *representation* and its *movement*. I refer here not only to a tension between workers' agency and trade unionists' strategies, which has often been the focus of analyses of labour unrest in colonial India. Rather, in connecting this particular tension to a complex process evolving along two conflictual axes, I propose a wider conceptualization, especially when considering the question of the *representation* of the strike.

On the one hand, I use this concept to refer to the problem of the *presentation* of the event. An event, or a rupture, is never entirely and clearly presentable, as it breaks with the 'presentational logic' of the context it is extracted from.[11] In regard to general (and contemporary) expectations, on the other hand, a strike needed to have a clear and legally defined *political representation*, to be recognized as such. This *political representation*, further, had to be accepted by workers, by employers and by the colonial state. The *representation* of the strike, as a field between the problem of *presentation* of the event and the need for its *political representation*, thus mirrors the two axes referred to above. Accordingly, the *representation* moves between the constant emergence of possibilities and, at the same time, attempts to direct the trajectories of the event along particular lines.

Similarly, the strike's *movement* has to be understood in broader terms in order to analyse it as part of an event. With the movement of the strike, I refer to the *political movement* of workers and trade unionists, but also to the ceaseless *motions* of the event, shifting and changing the boundaries of the general strike continuously. While the first aspect seemed more or less clearly defined as a specific trade dispute, the latter aspect contained various paths and trajectories which were simultaneously emerging as possibilities of the event and enabling the general strike. These trajectories, assembled in the *movement* of the strike, were shaped by workers and trade unionists at various moments of the conflict, but they were also impaired by colonial authorities, managers, *sirdars* and moneylenders who tried to foreclose them.

The tension between the strike's *representation* and its *movement* was, as I argue, a central one from the beginning of the first strikes in July. When, for instance, the BJWU came to represent the general strike politically, the union also came to re-present the event, whose possibilities and scale were thus defined. The representation and definition of the strike, however, was not just 'presented' to workers, but also to labour activists, the colonial authorities and the colonial public, each trying to either participate or to countervail. Through the course of the event, this tension evolved into a serious conflict, which did not only affect the relationship between workers and trade unionists, but also emerged within the BJWU itself. This conflict was arguably brought to a point of rupture when the government of Bengal intervened towards the end of the strike. It was an important reason why the general strike was not as successful as usually assumed. Or why, as argued below, the event remained unfinished in 1929.

At the same time, this tension between representation and movement evolved also along spatial lines. While the strike was represented as a general upheaval of jute mill workers with a single political representation, none of the participants had a base in the entire jute mill belt. Various participants, trying to spread or to prevent the represented strike along differing routes, travelled through the industrial area around Calcutta, through different neighbourhoods and different districts, reaffirming and yet undermining the strike's representation. The jute mill belt of Bengal, usually seen as a fairly compact and dense industrial area, proved from this vantage point to be diffuse, far-flung and extremely hard to control.

I will follow the narrative of the event mainly chronologically. I will thus trace the emerging possibilities and closures, the tensions and conflicts, as they evolved, or rather, as they realized the unfolding event and as they were realized at the same time by this very rupture.[12] Considering the concrete emergence and development of the event, I have identified four phases in the strike, which are indicated here briefly and further illustrated below.

In the *first phase*, localized strikes broke out in the north of Calcutta. At the same time, the BJWU became involved in one of these strikes. The question of whether a general strike was to be supported at all was highly contested within the union. On 29 July new strikes broke out, also affecting mills in the direct neighbourhood of Calcutta, which I conceptualize as the *second phase* of the strike. While the BJWU tried to 'connect' these new strikes to the ones in the north of Calcutta, the 'unrest' of workers spread gradually into other mill towns and mill districts. The *third phase* began with the actual proclamation of the general strike on 6 August. On that day the general strike was politically defined; at the same time, the event transcended this very definition through the increasing militancy of workers. In the following days the strike spread rapidly, until a settlement was reached on 16 August. The *fourth phase* comprises the immediate aftermath of the strike's official closure. The strikes, which had been connected through the BJWU in earlier phases, were now localized again. In this respect the settlement was the end of the general strike, but it indicated only a gradual end of the movement which had sustained the event.

The General Setting for the Strike

The years 1928 and 1929 witnessed remarkable labour unrest in colonial Bengal, as well as in colonial India at large. These protests were sustained by a growth of working-class movements, as well as increasing importance of trade unions and labour organizations. Most of these struggles were supported or led by the communist Workers' and Peasants' Party (WPP). At the same time, these struggles were met with massive repression by the colonial authorities and by employers, which defeated several strikes and arrested labour leaders.[13] This repression was among the reasons that, by July 1929, a general strike of jute workers seemed possible as much as it seemed unlikely.

In 1928, the jute mill industry was an important centre of unrest in Bengal, especially in the southern parts of the mill belt. In March that year, the workers of the Ludlow Jute Mill in Bauria went on strike. They initially protested against the beating of a weaver, but eventually also came to (successfully) demand recognition of their union by the management.[14] In the same month, the workers of the Wellington Jute Mill in Rishra went on strike against the introduction of the single-shift system and demanding higher wages. When the mill managers decided to increase the hours of work to 60 hours a week, arguing that this would entail higher wages, the workers went out on strike again, this time against the increase in hours of work.[15] In July 1928, the workers of the Fort Gloster Jute Mills in Bauria went on strike, mainly against the introduction of the single-shift system. They stayed on strike for about six-and-a-half months but were finally defeated in January 1929. This was one of the longest and most militant strikes till then in the history of the jute mill industry. Shortly after the beginning of the strike a riot occurred, at which about 4,000 workers attacked European mill assistants and the manager, as well as the police force that was protecting manager and mill. The police, hopelessly outnumbered, fired at the crowds, injuring twenty-three workers. However, since the workers had cut through the telephone wires, reinforcements arrived only several hours later with a ferry.[16] The strike in the Fort Gloster Jute Mills also drew the attention of Jawaharlal Nehru and Subhas Chandra Bose, who visited the strikers in January 1929.[17] In the same month, the employees of the Clive Jute Mill in Garden Reach went on strike, after a conflict with the new manager over payment of wages.[18] At about the same time, workers of the Adamjee Jute Mill in Howrah went on strike demanding higher wages.[19]

Unrest among jute workers had thereby been rising since the second half of the 1920s, expressing itself in a growing number of strikes and lockouts.

This had become especially marked after a series of mills introduced the single-shift system of work, replacing the older, multiple-shift system. This change in the shift system was a part of attempts to rationalize the working process, and it resulted in large-scale dismissals throughout the jute belt.[20] For instance, the manager of the the Titagarh Jute Mill No. 2, which was still running on the multiple-shift system, explained in 1929: 'If you introduce the single-shift system in this district, you will be making 20,000 people idle at once.'[21]

At the same time, since 1928, there had been increased attempts by labour leaders to create a more general representation for jute workers in the jute mill belt, and the idea of a jute workers' strike had come up several times. There were also attempts to unify different unions in order to create a more general represenation of workers in the northern and the southern parts of the jute mill belt. The result of these attempts was the formation of the Bengal Jute Workers' Union (BJWU). This organization is usually supposed to have been more or less identical with the Bengal Jute Workers' Association (BJWA) from Bhatpara, in the north of Calcutta. New material from the Intelligence Bureau and especially the Special Branch of Police, however, suggests that the BJWU was rather a merger between the BJWA and the Chengail and Bauria Jute Workers' Unions from Howrah and Budge-Budge.[22]

The Bengal Jute Workers' Association had been founded in 1925 in Bhatpara by Kalidas Bhattacharya, a former jute mill clerk who later became a member of the communist Workers' and Peasants' Party.[23] The connection between the union and the communist movement was rather tenuous, however. The BJWA expanded its influence and opened up new branches in the north of Calcutta, largely on the eastern side of the river. It mainly supported workers in their everyday conflicts – for instance, it helped in claiming compensation, ran a school for workers' children and opened a recreation centre for workers. It also tried to open a cooperative credit society, in order to decrease the influence of moneylenders over workers.[24] Strikes were increasingly encouraged and supported by the end of the 1920s, also in order to expand the union's influence. In the case of the strikes in Rishra in 1928, the BJWA, which prior to this had a negligible presence in the area, opened a branch office and distributed food to the strikers.[25]

The Chengail and Bauria Jute Workers' Unions were founded in 1928, in the course of the strikes in the Fort Gloster and the Ludlow Jute Mills. They were led by the communists Kishori Lal Ghose and Radharaman Mitra, as well as by Bankim Mukharji, who was a member of the Indian National Congress with contacts to the communist movement. These unions worked together closely and were tightly connected to the WPP. They focused on organizing workers in particular struggles. Leaders like Radharaman Mitter and Bankim Mukharji often moved into the mill towns in order to support workers during their strikes, where they were joined by other labour leaders like Philip Spratt, who was a member of the Communist Party of Great Britain.[26] There were also connections between these new communist trade unions and the BJWA in Bhatpara. Kalidas Bhattacharya visited Bauria in 1928; Radharaman Mitter and Phillip Spratt came to the strike in Rishra in May that year.[27]

Around late 1928 or early 1929, the BJWA and the Chengail and Bauria Jute Workers' Unions 'amalgamated under a central organization called the Bengal Jute Workers' Union', due, according to a later police report, to the growing influence of communists in these unions and in the jute mill belt in general.[28] The new union was to be led by Kalidas Bhattarcharya, and its head office was opened in Calcutta.[29]

At about the same time, in November 1928, the IJMA decided to increase the hours of work in their mills from July 1929 – to 60 hours per week instead of 54 hours. The step was basically directed against the Indian-owned jute mills which had come up in the jute mill belt recently, and which had not joined the IJMA. The increase in hours of work, so the expectation, would create an overproduction and thus a fall in prices. The new mills, which had not yet built up enough reserves, would not be able to compensate for the loss in profits, while the older mills could survive a certain period of recession.[30]

The possibility of strike as a reaction to the increased hours of work was also debated. It does not seem, however, that this issue was of major concern or urgency to the managers, nor that a larger series of strikes was actually expected.[31] Much more debated was the question of how to implement the new hours of work. Several points were still undecided in July 1929. One decision that was taken, however, concerned the food allowance or *khoraki*. Payment of this allowance had already been discontinued in mills running on the single-shift system, and was now also to be stopped in mills running on the multiple-shift system.[32] It was also decided that piece workers, such as weavers, had to produce more pieces per week in order to receive payment of a bonus.[33] The change in bonus was not implemented in all the mills of the IJMA; in some mills the bonuses were raised or remained the same as before, while in others, computation of the bonus amount remained vague till the first weeks of July.[34]

While the jute industry had been an important centre of workers' unrest in 1928, it seemed unlikely to many contemporaries that there would be a larger series of strikes – or even a general strike – by July 1929, especially since most of the earlier strikes had been defeated. Another reason for scepticism was the low level of unionization among jute workers (even in comparison to the generally low levels of unionization among industrial workers in colonial India). In January 1929, Kalidas Bhattacharya explained this situation by pointing to the ignorance of jute workers, stating: 'Generally speaking, the bulk of the mill workers of jute mills or presses . . . are neither so expert nor so wide awake to their own interests as the operatives of railway, tramway, and other big workshops.'[35]

Apart from this image of jute workers as somewhat 'ignorant', a further reason for not anticipating a larger upsurge of workers in July was certainly the series of arrests made in connection with the Meerut Conspiracy

Case in March 1929. Several of the labour leaders who had organized the strikes in 1928 had been detained. Leading members of the BJWU were also arrested and the union's offices were searched. Kalidas Bhattacharya, who was supposed to lead the newly formed union, was sent to jail; so was Bankim Mukherjee.[36] The BJWU, which at that time was still in a process of formation, thus needed to find a new president and a new general secretary just a few months before the implementation of the new working time regulation.

In May 1929, Prabhabati Das Gupta was elected president of the BJWU. She was by then a well-known labour leader in Calcutta, especially after organizing and leading a big strike of city sweepers in 1928. She had worked with communist labour leaders during that strike, but was at the same time said to be politically independent. Ranajit Das Gupta has pointed out that she was, rather, a nationalist trade union leader with 'strong misgivings about the communists'.[37] She does not seem to have been active in the jute industry before, but because of her charisma and because she seemed able to combine different political approaches, her involvement in this situation was welcomed. Furthermore, her election as president of the BJWU was supported by Kalidas Bhattacharya.[38]

Kali Kumar Sen, who had been briefly active in the jute unions in Howrah and also worked with the BJWA, became the new general secretary.[39] He had been close to the new union from the beginning, and in March 1929, when the police searched the union office in Calcutta, they noted that he was even living in the office.[40] Like Prabhabati Das Gupta, Kali Sen was not a member of any party in 1929. But, in contrast to the union's president, he regarded himself a 'communist by conviction', as Suchetana Chattopadhyay has pointed out.[41] Kali Sen had joined left politics in the late 1920s, and in 1928 he became co-editor of the important socialist paper, *Ganabani*.[42] He was also connected to the paper *Swadeshi Bazar*, which had published the earlier quoted article about the 'Future Revolution'.[43]

At first, Prabhabati Das Gupta and, with her, the majority of the BJWU, did not endorse a strike against the increase in hours of work imposed by the IJMA. On 11 and 12 May 1929, a 'Labour Conference' was held at Jagatdal, with representatives of the BJWU, the moderate Kankinarah Labour Union (KLU), as well as some local 'labour leaders'. The 'majority of the speakers at this meeting were all in favour of an amicable settlement by discussion and against strike methods'.[44] At another meeting held on 14 July – when strike action had already begun in Baranagore and protests had started in Barrackpore – the speakers demanded a return to work and an amicable settlement. Bankim Mukherjee, who had in the meanwhile been released from jail, 'advocated continuance of the strike' but he was 'not listened to'.[45] Kali Sen, who does not seem to have attended this conference, not only advocated continuance of the strike but was already 'agitating' for its further spread.[46]

By July 1929, thus, a larger strike in the jute mill industry seemed just as possible – after an enormous wave of labour unrest, as it seemed unlikely – after the defeat of many strikes and a series of arrests. At the same time, the BJWU was still in a process of formation, led by two trade unionists who represented the different political directions of the new union while they themselves were not members of any party. They represented, in this respect, different political paths along which the BJWU could evolve, and which in July 1929 were conjoined in the same organization. This conflict between different sections of the BJWU, which is usually seen to have come up in the aftermath of the general strike, thus appears to have existed well before the strike began. As will be argued in more detail below, the conflict turned into a more or less open rivalry between the groups around Prabhabati Das Gupta and Kali Sen from the early phases of the strike, and, at the same time, played a crucial role in developing and shaping the particular dynamics of the event.

The Beginning of the Strikes

The general strike began with local confrontations in two areas of 24 Parganas, a district north of Calcutta. The BJWU came to be involved in one of these confrontations. The question of the precise and anticipated shape of the emerging conflict, however, was not resolved within the BJWU. Positions taken within the union ranged from advocacy of an amicable settlement to agitation for a general strike. When both factions of the BJWU tried to shape the direction of the emergent strikes in the industry, they also tried to define and control the possibilities of the emerging event. At the same time, however, the sudden burst of union activity in workers' neighbourhoods in this tense and conflictual situation opened up, or rather sharpened, the possibility that the strikes could actually spread within these neighbourhoods.

One week after the introduction of the new hours of work, on 5 July, workers of the Baranagore East and South Mills went on strike, demanding a return to the 54-hour week. The strike was at first carried out mainly by the weavers of the mills. When they resumed work on 8 July, the management dismissed several workers, and the mill workers went on strike again the next day. They now demanded reinstatement of the dismissed workers as well. Attempts by the management to reopen the mills failed, and the workers of the two mills – about 5,000 in number – stayed out till early September.[47] It seems that the unions were barely involved in these strikes. Prabhabati Das Gupta visited the mill town once during the strike, while other members of the BJWU were reported not to have come to Baranagore.[48]

Just when the weavers in Baranagore stopped work, strikes broke out in Jagatdal too, to the north of Baranagore. On 5 July workers of the Meghna Jute Mill went on strike, followed by the Alliance and Craig Jute Mills on 6 July and the Waverley Jute Mill on 13 July. Jagatdal was subsequently to become a major centre for the general strike. It also became the area where Prabhabati Das Gupta established herself and the BJWU as the representative of the protest most successfully. The unrest emanated from the weavers of these mills, whose grievances centred on the modes of wage calculation in the event of being compelled to work longer hours. It was at first a rather particular form of protest since the weavers 'simply left work after doing the usual 54 hours work and resumed work on the following Monday as usual'.[49] Other sections of the workforce were reported to have tried carrying on till closing time.[50]

The weavers of the four mills stopped work fully on 19 July and the mills had to be closed.[51] The BJWU did not yet endorse spreading the strike, and at a meeting on 20 July, it advised the workers to resume work but to produce less. Narendra Nath Chatterjee, a local lawyer who apparently had been called in by the workers themselves, supported this procedure.[52] The workers resumed work on 21 July and produced less, causing thereby a glut in yarn; the result was that the managers closed the mills fully on 23 July. After this lockout and escalation of the conflict, the majority of the BJWU seems to have supported the strikes in Jagatdal. Narendra Nath Chatterjee was working openly with the BJWU by now and he regularly spoke at meetings together with Prabhabati Das Gupta, thereby probably increasing her acceptance among the workers here.

The question of whether the strike was to be supported in these five mills in Jagatdal only, or whether a general strike was to be 'created', was not really resolved, however. With intensification of the conflict in Jagatdal after 19 July – possibly alongside intensification of the rivalry within the BJWU – Prabhabati Das Gupta increasingly supported a general strike against the IJMA. This strike was to be carried out mainly by struggles in the district of 24 Parganas in the north of Calcutta, with the sub-districts of Jagatdal and eventually Titagarh as the main centres. These areas employed the vast majority of jute workers and the bulk of jute goods was produced here.[53] At the same time, these were areas where the older BJWA had been active and had established itself among jute workers. The new BJWU could accordingly access a network of previous union activity, which provided an entry into the neighbourhoods of the jute mills here. This was the case in particular for Prabhabati Das Gupta, whose presidency of the new union had been approved of by Kalidas Bhattacharya, the president of the older BJWA. Her choice to centre the protest in these areas was probably also an attempt to keep control not just over the emerging strike, into which she was increasingly dragged, but also over the newly formed union whose president she had become.

Even in the early days of the strike the conflict within the union became visible with regard to the form of the strike and how the workers were to be approached. While trying to spread the struggle in particular ways, on 28 July, Prabhabati Das Gupta asked the strikers in Jagatdal to persuade the workers of the Anglo-India, Kankinarah and Reliance Mills to join the strike. At the same meeting, however, Bankim Mukherjee, who was apparently advocating a more general strike, spoke of 'of the advantages of joint action by 80 Mills and 2 or 3 lakh of workers'.[54] While Prabhabati Das Gupta and Bankim Mukherjee presented different statements about the kind of strike (or protest) they wanted the workers to embark on, Kali Sen actively supported a further spread of the strike throughout the jute mill belt and into all the mills of the IJMA. By the second half of July, he started touring particular mill towns in a car with 'two red flags in front and one big red flag wrapped at the back', trying to persuade workers to join the emerging general strike.[55]

Most of the people connected to the general secretary of the BJWU were described as 'known communists', and they were members of local unions around Calcutta or not affiliated to a union at all. Ram Logan Sha, for instance, was not a union representative. He had advocated a general strike at the Labour Conference in Jagatdal, jointly held by the BJWU and the KLU in May, when the vast majority at that conference had supported negotiations with the IJMA rather than strike action.[56] Moni Singh, also working with Kali Sen, was the secretary of the Metiaburuz Labour Union in Garden Reach. This union had originally been set up in order to organize the Bowreah cotton workers in 1928, and he had been able to establish himself among jute workers of the area as well. He too had advocated a general strike earlier.[57] Akhil Bandhu Bannerjee, another supporter of a general strike in the jute mill belt, was a member of the WPP and secretary of the Beliaghata Labour Union near Calcutta. He had already, on 14 July, held meetings in Beliaghata jointly with the local Khilafat Committee, trying to organize a large strike in the jute mill industry, citing the example of 'the Russian peasants and workers'.[58]

The group around Kali Sen seems to have focused its interventions in areas where it had connections to workers due to earlier strikes. On 25 July, for instance, Kali Sen and Moni Singh went to the Clive Jute Mills in Garden Reach. At the mill gate, the trade unionists explained to the workers the financial losses they would have to bear due to the increase in hours of work. They talked about strikes in Jagatdal and other places, pointing out that this was the workers' chance to join and win their struggles. After this visit to the Clive Jute Mill the group went to the Union South Jute Mill, in order to make similar speeches there.[59]

Parallel to this, the 'agitation' of the competing groups within the BJWU extended to Titagarh, which became, in the war-driven language of the Intelligence Bureau, the 'pivotal point of attack'.[60] On 24 July, Prabhabati Das Gupta visited Titagarh in order to talk to 'an up-country cloth-merchant in the local bazar' as well as to a certain Swami Rajrishi about 'the present situation in the jute mills', and to ask them 'whether any strike was possible'. Not much is known either about this merchant or about Swami Rajrishi, but about the latter it was said that he had some 'influence' over the workers in Titagarh. Right after the talk in the 'up-country' merchant's house, Prabhabati Das Gupta left the town. Briefly after she had left, the police noted the arrival of a motor car 'with a red flag hoisted on it' in Titagarh.[61] Kali Sen had come with a group of supporters to distribute leaflets, which were printed on red paper in the name of the BJWU but were said to have been composed by the union's general secretary.[62] The group tried to spread the strike to Titagarh before Prabhabati Das Gupta could establish herself there. Likewise, the union's president tried to establish alliances in the mill town before the communist groups within the BJWU could spread (and lead) the strike in Titagarh.

Kali Sen's success in Titagarh was initially quite limited. At a meeting held on 26 July in order to explain the situation in Jagatdal, only about '50 or 60 people attended'. A party with drums was sent around to announce the meeting, which attracted more attention to the group. But it also caused some turmoil since 'mill workers began to abuse the intending speakers and asked them to go away'. They accused the trade unionists of having betrayed the workers in Lillooah. Apparently in anticipation of the arguments of the visitors, some of the workers stated that they were not hungry and did not need the trade unionists' help. Similar interruptions went on 'in intervals right up to the end of the meeting'. In addition to this 'anti-propaganda', the meeting was disturbed by 'a diversion nearby in the shape of a Hindustani theatre', causing the attendance to thin even more.[63]

The next day, at 4 pm, Kali Sen's group organized another meeting in which Swami Rajrishi took part as well. It seems that there were now fewer conflicts with the audience; it is possible that the involvement of the Swami was an important factor in causing this change. The speakers at the meeting talked about the importance of forming a union 'for fighting with capitalists', who were living 'at the expense of the poor labourers'. It was further said that if 'all the 71 mills in Bengal could make a united stand then the authorities would surely have to come down and comply with them to act according to their dictation'.[64] Kali Sen underlined this statement by referring to the strike in Lillooah – a topic that had been raised by the workers the previous day. He said that this particular strike had failed only due to want of support 'from the brother labourers in other parts of Bengal'.[65] He pointed thereby to lack of solidarity, a failure of the workers and not the trade unionists.

Exactly one hour after this meeting, another meeting was organized in Titagarh, this time with Prabhabati Das Gupta, Bankim Mukharji and Swami Biswananda, among others, speaking. Probably in an attempt to increase the authority of the BJWU over the audience, a *sirdar* from the Emperor Jute Mills also addressed the workers in support of the strike. The arguments presented by the group around Prabhabati Das Gupta, in comparison with those put forward by the group around Kali Sen, were distinctly more moderate and even somewhat non-political. Presenting a strike as inevitable, they strongly invoked in its support a combination of the concepts of honour and solidarity, as well as strength and autonomy. Swami Rajrishi spoke here again. This time, however, he was 'found dead against' the strike. Further: 'He strongly protested against strike and left the meeting as soon as other speakers spoke in favour of it. He was later on found making anti-propaganda outside the meeting thoroughly condemning strike – the result being that the meeting got comparatively thinner.'[66]

There is no known reason for this sudden change of mind. It is however not unlikely that the arrival of different factions of the same union within the hour did not make a favourable impression on the Swami. It is also possible that there had been some pressure on him from within the neighbourhoods to not support the strike. The vast majority of the workers in Titagarh was still against any strike action, and perhaps even feared it. During the meeting, the workers again expressed their opinion through several interruptions, arguing that they 'had already heard, seen and experienced bitter results of the same'. Reacting to statements like these, first Bankim Mukharji and then Prabhabati Das Gupta pointed out

> that he was advocating strike knowing full well its bitter results and that his labourer brethren were too poor to meet the situation, but then did anybody ever hear that any man had died of starvation owing to any strike. No there was not a single instance. . . . Will not the authorities take advantage of the knowledge that you are not at all in a position to strike? To this Bankim got no direct answer, only there was a murmur among the audience and he tried to press home his point in the manner mentioned above. . . . She asked the audience why they were thinking from now how and on what they would live in case there is a strike. Supposing they were dismissed what would they do? To this some of the audience replied that all can not be dismissed at a time. One or two were dismissed if there were any dismissals at all and that in that case the other members of their respective families or even some of their fellow brothers might support them but this was not so in case of a strike.[67]

Despite the still prevalent mood against the strike and also the 'anti-propaganda' of Rajrishi, the group around Prabhabati Das Gupta was increasingly successful in addressing the workers in Titagarh. The next day, on 28 July, she held another meeting which was attended by a little more than 200 people. Among the speakers this time were also Narendra Nath Chatterjee and Ram Logan Sha, who by that time had joined the group around the union's president. All the speakers advocated a spread of the strike, to be led by the BJWU under Prabhabati Das Gupta.[68] The police also noticed the presence of 'respectable persons' from the locality at Prabhabati Das Gupta's meetings, which indicates that she was more successful in forging alliances in Titagarh.[69]

The strong focus of the 'agitation' on the industrial area around Jagatdal and Titagarh, and the increasing influence of Prabhabati Das Gupta's group on the workers did not yet result in a spread of the strike. In Jagatdal, where the weavers had started a protest against increased hours of work in early July, escalation of the conflict between workers and mill managers had rather led to an intensification of the conflict within the BJWU over the question of the strike and its anticipated shape. Prabhabati Das Gupta was therefore, in a way, dragged into supporting the (potentially spreading) strike by the failure of an amicable settlement in Jagatdal and by developments within the union itself.

In Titagarh, on the other hand, trade unionists of both factions had trouble gaining the trust of the workers. The encounters during the meetings turned, to some degree, into a conflict between solidarity and honour, which the trade unionists called for, and the collective memory of defeated strikes and the hardships the workers had to bear during these struggles, which everyday forms of solidarity could hardly sustain. Looking at earlier strikes in the jute mill belt and their regular features, it can be assumed that these hardships meant, among other things, wage losses, dismissals, clearing of coolie lines, cutting off of water supply and pressure on local grocers not to sell food to strikers.[70] Given, however, the increasing support for the trade unionists at the meetings – and also the fact that the mills in Titagarh eventually did join the strike – the conflict between the unionists and the workers should not be reduced to a conflict between moods of hope and despair. It should rather be understood in the context of an already growing atmosphere of militancy, within which the arguments of the trade unionists probably appealed to the workers. The rejection of the trade unionists by many workers may well have been caused by apprehensions that the strike demanded by the BJWU was an increasingly real possibility, and that the demand had real purchase in their own neighbourhoods. Apprehensions of strike action, then, polarized sentiments and positions among workers.

At the same time, the split in the BJWU – by which the president and the general secretary of the union would not even speak at the same meeting – was already obvious in this phase of the strike. In the president's group, what exactly a general strike meant and which areas it included remained vague. After the failure of an amicable settlement, notions of the anticipated strike ranged from a protest in Jagatdal to an anticipated deadlock in the mills of the IJMA. A certain uncertainty about what the 'general' of a general strike referred to, becomes apparent in this respect. Prabhabati Das Gupta, while remaining rather vague about the question in her public speeches, tried to combine the different tendencies around her, including people like Bankim Mukherjee and Narendra Nath Chatterjee within her faction. The group around Kali Sen, on the other hand, clearly supported a general strike of workers against the IJMA, and the trade unionists started touring various mill towns in the jute mill belt. Without stable support from local activists, however, it seems to have been very hard for them to gain the trust of the workers, especially after the largely defeated strikes of 1928.

In Jagatdal the conflict had thus evolved into a strike which increasingly seemed to bear the possibility of emerging into a larger struggle of jute workers, even though its anticipated scale was still unclear. This strike, however, had not so much emerged either from the union's *or* the workers' actions, as out of the interplay of the two within a larger context of conflicts. At the same time, the divergent reactions of workers in Titagarh indicated the anticipated *possibility* of a spreading strike, as well as of the collective memories of defeated strikes and hardships (which even included 'memories' of the defeated strike in Lillooah). The intensification of these conflicts within the union and within workers' neighbourhoods, and, on the other hand, the opening of possibilities and emergence of anticipations but also of fears, were the two interconnected and, at the same time, conflictual axes that provided an important context for the unfolding dynamics of the emerging general strike. The tension between 'various paths' constantly opened up by the movement, and, at the same time, various attempts to realize particular trajectories, disclose and also foreclose others, are not just crucial for understanding the emergence of the general strike, but also for understanding the particular ways in which the events unfolded.

The manner in which both groups *arrived* in Titagarh indicates a second dynamic: the different means of approaching workers that were exploited within the BJWU in this early phase. The group around Prabhabati Das Gupta seems at first to have tried to get in touch with potential mediators and locally influential persons, such as the 'up-country' cloth merchant and Swami Rajrishi. In a similar way, *sirdars* of other jute mills came to her meetings to address the workers in Titagarh and to increase her authority over the workers. The group around Kali Sen, on the other hand, went directly to the mill gates and into the neighbourhoods of these mills. But they too needed certain kinds of networks and the support of people who had already proved to the workers, at least to some degree, that they were not 'outsiders'. The routes along which they travelled through the jute mill belt were also directed by earlier strikes through which supporters of Kali Sen had established themselves in particular workers' neighbourhoods.

Despite these internal conflicts and rivalries over the representation of the strike, the BJWU presented itself in this phase – as also in later periods of the strike – as a joint union unitedly representing the jute mill workers. After all, both groups tried to establish the union's right to represent jute workers in general, even as they presented differing political approaches towards trade unionism – and thus towards workers – within the new union.

The Beginning of the General Strike

Between late July and early August, a potentially *general* strike seemed increasingly possible, while the struggle within the BJWU intensified with the emergence of new strikes. Prabhabati Das Gupta's representation of the struggle came to be increasingly accepted not just by the workers in Jagatdal and Titagarh, but also by the colonial authorities and the colonial public. This, however, also resulted in a further broadening of the meaning and scale of the *general* in the emerging strike: first, by workers, who appropriated the ongoing conflict in their own ways and along their own paths, while at the same time accepting the representation of their struggle by the BJWU; second, by the interaction of local labour activists and the colonial authorities, foremost the police, who tried to prevent the emergence of a general strike by increasingly intervening in workers' neighbourhoods. A certain tension between the emerging movement and its possibilities, and the struggle's representation through Prabhabati Das Gupta, was thus disclosed.

On 29 July, the North Union, Soorah and Beliaghata Jute Mills in Beliaghata went on strike, demanding higher wages.[71] Discontent, especially in connection with low wages, seems to have prevailed in Beliaghata for quite a while. The strike itself, however, was triggered by an assault on two 'boy workers' (possibly by an overseer) in the North Union Jute Mill on the morning of 29 July. After the incident, the workers left their workplace. Later

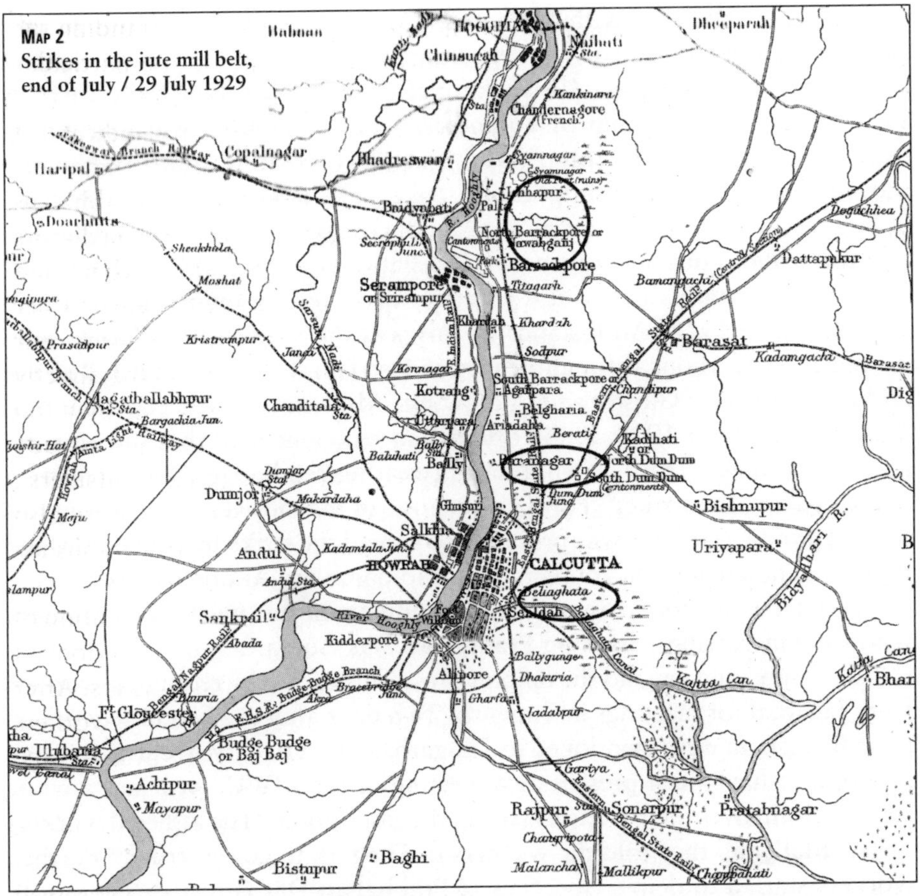

Map 2
Strikes in the jute mill belt, end of July / 29 July 1929

that day, the other two mills in the area joined the strike.[73] When workers of the North Union Jute Mill wanted to resume work on 2 August, a dispute arose between them and workers from the Beliaghata Jute Mill. They tried to prevent the early resumption of work by those workers who had brought them on strike, underlining the immense pressures created in the neighbourhoods over the question of solidarity during the strike. In the course of the dispute, brickbats were thrown, and, as the Special Branch reported, the 'gates of the mill were closed and even then some of the willing workers went to resume work by scaling over the wall'.[74] At a meeting on 4 August, Akhil Bandhu Bannerjee 'promised to try and bring out the workers of other Jute Mills if they would strike' – thereby promising also the possible emergence of a dispute within the whole jute industry.[75]

In the next couple of days, the strikes in Beliaghata and Jagatdal were presented by the BJWU as a joint strike for one common purpose – first by Kali Sen and his supporters, followed by Prabhabati Das Gupta and her group. The competing groups within the BJWU tried to generalize the conflict in the jute mill belt by recruiting strikers from Beliaghata and Jagatdal to 'agitate' in Titagarh. On 30 July, strikers from Beliaghata were mentioned for the first time as being present in Titagarh. They were wearing red badges on their arms or shoulders with the letters 'J.W.U.' – probably standing for Jute Workers Union – on them. The reporting officer noted: 'They were brought I am informed for propaganda work for strike and controlling the gatherings in meetings.'[76] The group of volunteers from Beliaghata was apparently called *Lal Paltan* (Red Army).[77] The practice of creating controlled spatial movements of workers in support of a strike seems not to have been common, at least in the north of Calcutta. Several police reports expressed surprise and confusion about this phenomenon.[78] Delegations of strikers to other workers are however reminiscent of the practices deployed by unions in the south of Calcutta in 1928. An instance of this was the strikers in Lillooah, who moved in processions through nearby industrial areas, and travelled to the strike-affected Fort Gloster and Ludlow Jute Mills, among other destinations. While in Bauria in 1928, Philip Spratt had recommended that the workers build up a 'union-army' of volunteers (wearing red badges) for supporting and spreading the strike.[79] For Kali Sen, one of the motives for applying this technique one year later was probably to spread the strike by connecting and thereby generalizing the conflicts that had come up. Another reason might have been to gain more trust and support among the jute workers in Titagarh, who were increasingly backing Prabhabati Das Gupta.

The group around the union's president reacted by recruiting workers from Jagatdal for meetings in Titagarh. Two days after the first time workers from Beliaghata were mentioned in Titagarh, at least twenty-five strikers were reported to have been present at a meeting of the BJWU, wearing 'a white strip of cloth' over their breasts bearing the inscription, 'The afflicted workers of Jagatdal', and they told the workers in Titagarh to go on strike.[80] Further, workers started to deliver speeches at Prabhabati Das Gupta's meetings. In contrast with the first phase of the strike, *sirdars* were not part of the meetings any more. On the contrary, people like Narendra Nath Chatterjee stated 'that within a year there would be no Sardars any more'.[81]

The increased activities of the Beliaghata group in Titagarh, and the prospect of a joint strike of workers in Jagatdal and Beliaghata, also had an influence on the speeches of Prabhabati Das Gupta and the BJWU. The strike, for one, was represented as more general, with a wide base of active support. At the same time, the strike's representation was increasingly centred on the person of Prabhabati Das Gupta as the undisputed leader of the movement. The speeches became more pressing, urging the workers to join the strike by practically insulting them, and by drawing further on concepts of honour and mutual support. Appeals to the honour of the workers were justified not only by referring to those workers who were already on strike, but also by insisting that the BJWU and especially Prabhabati Das Gupta should be supported – as the leader of the struggle and as '*mataji*'. For example, when Abdul Momin spoke first at the meeting on 30 July, he

> likened the audience to so many beasts or even worse than that. Even beasts have feelings and sympathy and love for their fellow brothers which are

> miserably wanting in the labourers at Titagarh. A few of those [who] were present, he said, promised to strike work and get others to strike positively . . . but they did not keep to their word. If they had a drop of human blood in them, if they had ever prided being men, they would never think of what they would do for their living in case of strike. . . . He failed to understand the conduct of the local mill workers, had they any heart? Any respect for their wives and their parents? Any love or responsibility regarding them and their children?[82]

The next speakers in that very meeting – after dwelling on the benefits of workers in England in contrast to the workers in India – explained the need for unity, especially now, when the hours of work had been increased without corresponding increases in wages. Ram Logan Sha told the workers

> that 'Mataji', the Lakshmi and saviour of Bengal (meaning Dr Das Gupta thereby) has taken a vow that she would not rest till all the mills in Bengal struck work. He requested the audience to respect their common mother and to keep her word, if they could not do that or thought it impossible they had better drowned themselves.[83]

He also told the workers that twenty-six mills were already on strike – clearly an exaggeration. Narendra Nath Chatterjee, speaking next, developed this point further, and generalized the support and solidarity for the jute workers even more, when he said 'that workers in England in one and all the mills had already struck work in sympathy with the workers here'.[84] He was probably referring to the cotton mill strike in Lancashire, which was happening parallel to the jute mill strike but was otherwise unconnected to it, and certainly did not affect all the mills in England.[85] Yet the image of a wide, even global support for a strike in Titagarh and Jagatdal seems to have been important, and was used in several speeches in order to persuade the workers of the strong basis and good chances for a successful (and short) struggle.

In comparison to the earlier phase of protests, attitudes towards the strike among the workers in Titagarh seem to have been more split by now. Police reporters mentioned that the 'majority of the labourers seemed to be against strike as yet', but at the same time cries like '*Majdur Dal ki Jai*' were shouted during the meetings from the audience.[86] The workers were reported as being 'somewhat impressed'.[87] In Titagarh, Prabhabati Das Gupta could increasingly present the BJWU and herself as the representative of a strong movement, and establish the general nature of the ongoing labour conflict in the jute mill belt (and beyond). It can however be argued that the strong representation, centred solely on the union's president, was also an attempt to retain control over the emerging movement. The notions of extensive, even global support for the struggle, almost solely led by Prabhabati Das Gupta, were thus not a call for a wider general strike, but rather an attempt to centralize the various possibilities and paths opened up through the movement, and thereby to maintain control over the meaning of what was *general* in the strike. The possibilities opened up by the emerging event thus seemed as wide as they seemed clearly defined. This probably was even more important after the group around Kali Sen managed to connect the strikes in Jagatdal and Beliaghata, thus also transcending the original reason for the conflict.

While the union's activities in Titagarh were crucial in connecting the otherwise local conflicts and providing an avenue for spreading a 'general' strike, the possibility and emergence of this event were simultaneously carried by the workers in Titagarh themselves. In contrast to the mills in Jagatdal, where 'up-county' weavers had first left their workplaces, in Titagarh it was 'madrassi' spinners of several mills who left their machines and started the strikes. This pointed to a peculiar discrepancy between the union's activities and workers' actual support. The 'agitation' of the BJWU's factions indicated, rather, an attempt to address 'up-country' mill workers. When trying to spread the strike to Titagarh, Prabhabati Das Gupta had first consulted an 'up-country' merchant in the local bazaar in order to get access to the workers' neighbourhoods. In the next couple of days, both factions of the BJWU addressed the workers through speeches and leaflets in Hindustani, Bengali and Urdu, but not in Tamil, Telugu or Oriya. The support growing in Titagarh for Prabhabati Das Gupta and for the strike, however, first emanated from 'madrassi' spinners. The 'up-country' weavers in Titagarh seem to have joined the strike actively only after it had started.[88]

It is not very clear how Prabhabati Das Gupta was able to establish herself more successfully among a group of workers whose language she did not speak. Nor is it clear why a strike which was started in Jagatdal by weavers was carried on in Titagarh by spinners. The workers themselves have not left any evidence that could provide an insight into the relations and pressures in their neighbourhoods. Police and newspaper reports, on the other hand, follow the event of the general strike along the routes chalked out and travelled by the major trade unionists, giving only vague indications of the ways in which workers responded to – and appropriated – the situation emerging in the jute mill belt. Prabhabati Das Gupta's claim to become the representative of the Titagarh strikes was paralleled by the workers' multiple responses to and appropriations of the strike. Thus the original strike in Jagatdal was extended, new paths opened up and new bases included in the conflict.

Parallel to the developments in Titagarh, the situation in Jagatdal became more intense, undermining the representation and scale of the strike even more clearly. Here, the workers themselves started to move around – at first within the mill towns, then between several mill areas within Jagatdal and finally in other districts as well. After the neighbourhoods, the streets around the mills and mill towns became contested spaces. In the next few days, 'bodies of strikers' were reported, and workers were seen 'admonishing men who crowded on the road, telling them to leave the road clear'.[89] There were repeated reports of picketing and attempts by workers to induce other mills to strike. Certain routes taken by the workers beyond the borders of the district were also indicated in the reports. Picketing workers from Jagatdal went to Titagarh, Kankinarah, to Champdani on the western side of the river and then on to Rishra. From Rishra, however, the picketing seems not to have moved on to Howrah, indicating a boundary between the northern and southern parts of the jute mill belt. Likewise, on the other side of the river, movements of picketing workers initiated in Jagatdal do not seem to have moved beyond Khardah (in the south of Titagarh).

Despite these limitations or boundaries, increased picketing of workers covered the major industrial areas in the northern parts of 24 Parganas as well as Hooghly district. The areas into which workers carried the strike were thus not congruent with those where either faction of the BJWU had been active. The situation in Jagatdal, in this respect, bore a certain resemblance to the situation in Titagarh, underlining a discrepancy between the union's representation and the ways in which the workers' struggles unfolded.

When faced with this situation, Prabhabati Das Gupta tried to direct and control the workers' movements. At a meeting in Jagatdal on 30 July, she suggested peaceful picketing of the four Anglo-India and Auckland Jute Mills.[90] On the next day, 31 July, however, massive picketing was reported at several jute mills in Jagatdal, Kankinarah and Titagarh, as well as in Champdani, which 'induced' the Alexandra Mills to go on strike.[91] The Alexandra Jute Mills seem to have been one of the earliest targets of picketing by strikers. As early as 24 July, *Liberty* had reported weavers from Jagatdal trying to reach these mills.[92]

As in Titagarh, so in Jagatdal, there is the question of why the workers' protest unfolded in these particular ways that were apparently not anticipated or controlled by either faction of the BJWU. One problem here is the silence of workers' voices in the sources. However, in the case of Jagatdal, another problem becomes apparent: uncertainty about the routes taken by the workers seems to have been a contemporary phenomenon already. This is especially the case with the perception of the event by the police. In various police reports the strike was increasingly understood to be led by the BJWU under Prabhabati Das Gupta. The workers' own actions, however, were either read through the assumption of a successful 'agitation' for the unrest and therefore as directed by trade unionists, or, when no 'leader' could be identified, by defining these actions as more or less irrational. From this perspective, the tension between the strike's representation and workers' agency was hard to identify or to comprehend. It seems as if the possibility of workers taking control over the direction of the strike, or extending its meaning and scale beyond the control of the union, was not within the horizon of expectation of the police. Interpreting these trajectories through a strict binary of 'agitation' and 'irrationality' thus served as a means of rejecting the sudden visibility of workers' agency in the jute mill belt. Denying the autonomy of the workers' actions, this mode or representation also reinforced the claim to political representation made by the union.

Considering, however, the routes actually taken by the workers, it seems that particular paths had been chosen – or also *not* chosen – by them.

For instance, there appears to have been an invisible boundary between the northern and southern parts of the jute mill belt, which the workers did not cross. Crossing the river appears to have been a path used even more commonly than the short overland route between the neighbouring mill towns of Jagatdal and Kankinarah. There was, moreover, the case of the Alexandra Jute Mills which were repeatedly a target of picketing by workers from Jagatdal for several days in a row.[93] These instances suggest that the paths along which picketing workers travelled were not random, but followed particular patterns.[94] Further, these patterns suggest certain sub-surface forms of organization among workers, connecting particular neighbourhoods in the jute mill belt.

While colonial observers struggled to define the spatial movement of workers, the anticipated and spreading unrest was at the same time confronted by a strong police force. On the eastern side of the river, this force was still reckoned to be 'adequate' for the situation.[95] Across the river, however, in Champdani and Rishra, the local authorities panicked when faced with the increasing physical movement of workers from beyond the river, as well as from within Champdani and Rishra. The problem for the police in comprehending and controlling the actual movement of workers here was increased by the weak infrastructure. Several reports complain about the lack of a telephone connection. A report of a meeting in Baidyabati mentions this problem accusingly by describing how a messenger had to be sent to Bhadreswar, 'a distance of about 3 miles to communicate the information' by phone. Even though the situation turned out to be peaceful, the complaint was underlined with the observation that it might have been very severe.[96] Since the railway system was not as closely knit as on the eastern side of the river, the police also needed to hire two buses from Serampore in order to transport forces in case of emergency.[97] Another problem here was the unclear presence of unions or individual labour leaders. It was not clear where the anticipated 'agitation' came from and several rumours were afloat of meetings and movements, eventually affecting an area between Champdani and Howrah.[98] The reaction to this tense yet hardly definable situation was immense police activity, aimed to prevent further spread of the strike. On 4 August, the police reports mention the following incidents:

> 8. Yesterday an information was received from the Deputy Commissioner, Special Branch, Calcutta, that a labour meeting would be held at Rishra and that several members of Peasants and Workers Party and some members of Bombay Labour Union would address the meeting but no meeting was actually held at Rishra.
> 9. From D.I.B., Howrah another information to the effect that strikers of this district [Champdani] would go in a body to attend the meeting at Howrah on the 3rd afternoon was received yesterday. But enquiries show no such body of men left the mill area.[99]

Similar reports abound – rumours are mentioned and various

meetings, but rarely is a concrete 'organizer' identified. Bankim Mukherjee, who was by now working with Kali Sen, briefly tried to establish a presence in Champdani – but without success.[100] He and Kali Sen were also prevented from 'agitating' the workers and local activists by their arrest on 1 August in Serampore.[101] They were at first denied bail, but were eventually released on 4 August.[102]

In Howrah, on the other hand, where the anticipated unrest roused anxiety among the police, local trade unionists tried to facilitate the strike. They were the ones who announced the meeting on 3 August to which 10,000 workers were expected to come from Champdani.[103] These local unions apparently tried to get the support of Kali Sen and Bankim Mukherjee (and thus also of the BJWU), but since both men had just been arrested, it is not really clear if they would have supported this initiative.

While the anticipated meeting in Howrah did not receive much attention from the workers themselves, it did from the police; it was also reported in the *Bengalee* with the question of whether there would be a general strike soon.[104] *The Times of India* wrote the next day, joining the expectation of a general strike: 'Although, at the moment of writing, only a small proportion of the mills are idle, strike fever as recently demonstrated, is an infectious disease difficult to isolate or circumscribe, once it appears in any part, however small, of a great industrial centre.'[105]

Thus, carried by the anticipation and expectations of various observers and participants who were trying either to prevent or support the unrest, the situation in the jute mill belt of Bengal became increasingly chaotic. Hope for support of their struggle, for instance, brought the picketing strikers from Jagatdal into various other mill districts; the spread of the strike to Beliaghata increased the activities of both factions within the BJWU; rumours and fears of a general strike triggered seemingly random police interventions in large parts of the jute mill belt; and anticipation of a general strike induced local labour activists, as in Howrah, to participate in the event. A general strike of jute workers became more and more of a possibility, strengthening Prabhabati Das Gupta's claim to represent it, but also undermining this very claim by constantly opening new perspectives and avenues for the strike.

On 3 August, Prabhabati Das Gupta called for a general strike in Jagatdal and Titagarh, to begin from 5 August.[106] A day later, the Metiaburuz Labour Union under Moni Singh followed suit and called for a general strike in the jute mill belt. This call was supported by Akhil Bandhu Bannerjee from Beliaghata.[107] Given that only one more mill had joined the strike in Jagatdal so far and none in Titagarh, and that, at the same time, the possible scale of the general strike had spread beyond the union president's control, Prabhabati Das Gupta's decision might seem somewhat surprising. Her reasons can better be understood by keeping in mind the recent (temporary) imprisonment of Kali Sen and Bankim Mukherjee – two of her main rivals in the union. In this respect, the call for a general strike seems to have been an attempt to settle the dispute over the political direction of the union at a time when her strongest opponents could not intervene. It also seems that the call for a general strike at this particular moment represented an attempt to regain control over the emerging movement by finally defining the scale and the meaning of the event whose representative she had become.

Meanwhile, Moulavi Latafat Hossain from the moderate KLU tried to intervene in the unfolding chain of events. At the Anglo-India Jute Mills, on 1 and 2 August, groups of weavers had temporarily left their workplaces, returning the same day. Moulavi Latafat Hossain, in an attempt to prevent the strike, arrived on the morning of 3 August at the mill gate with around 300 'loyal' weavers who were supposed to work in the mills. This intervention led to violent attempts by the workers to prevent the 'loyal' weavers from entering the mills.[108] The next day, when Moulavi Latafat Hossain again tried to prevent the strike from spreading, an angry 'mob' of mill workers attacked him. This led to massive intervention by the police in order to protect Hossain and to disperse the workers.[109] After this intervention by Hossain and the police, the workers at Anglo-India Jute Mills went on strike on 5 August. They were followed the same day by nearly all the mills in Jagatdal; and on 6 August, the mills in Titagarh, Kankinarah, Champdani and Rishra, as well as the Clive Jute Mill in Garden Reach, joined the general strike.[110]

Altogether, the emerging general strike in this period was characterized by three interrelated developments. First, due to the increasingly accepted political representation by the union and the increasing spread of unrest, the possibility of a general strike in the jute mill industry became suddenly very real by late July. Conflicts which would otherwise have been interpreted as local – such as the strikes in Jagatdal and in Beliaghata – could in this situation be connected with each other and thus be interpreted as united action. Workers, at the same time, appropriated the emerging event in their own ways. The police and local trade unionists tried to intervene in the ongoing event as well. The result was that due to the spread of the strike, and due to various events occurring simultaneously at different places (and carried out by different groups), the jute mill belt – usually seen as a small area – started to seem larger and much harder to control.

Second, while the wave of unrest was spreading and becoming more general, the movement was also being centralized under the leadership of Prabhabati Das Gupta, who was increasingly pitted against the IJMA as the principal representative of the workers' grievances. In a sense, she filled the need for a principal representative of the evolving movement, but equally, she emerged as a figure the colonial authorities could identify (and later negotiate) the strike with. As the strike wore on, both sides needed a figure who could legitimately 'speak for' workers' interests, both for purposes of agitation and of negotiation. As will become apparent at the end of this essay, this was a deeply ambiguous role.

Third, the centralization of the event under the leadership of Prabhabati Das Gupta also indicated an attempt to establish particular forms and trajectories of action as representation of the strike at large.

This representation was undermined, however, as support for the general strike grew among workers and as the event was consequently appropriated along various avenues. The question is not whether the union's authority *or* the workers' agency was crucial to the strike. It is precisely the tense interconnection between the two that is crucial for understanding the possibilities and dynamics of the event. While the union's actions enabled the connection of different strikes and general representation of the workers' grievances, this representation was simultaneously realized and undermined by the workers' appropriation of the event. In the process, the workers 'brought' the strike to areas where neither of the factions of the BJWU had been able to establish itself – the workers, thus, did not simply respond to the call for a general strike, but they enabled generalization of the event along a wider range of paths.

The General Strike

On 6 August, the BJWU under Prabhabati Das Gupta declared a general strike in the jute mill industry. By that day 120,000 jute workers had joined the strike (out of a labour force of about 350,000 workers).[111] Throughout the day, the union's president toured the northern part of 24

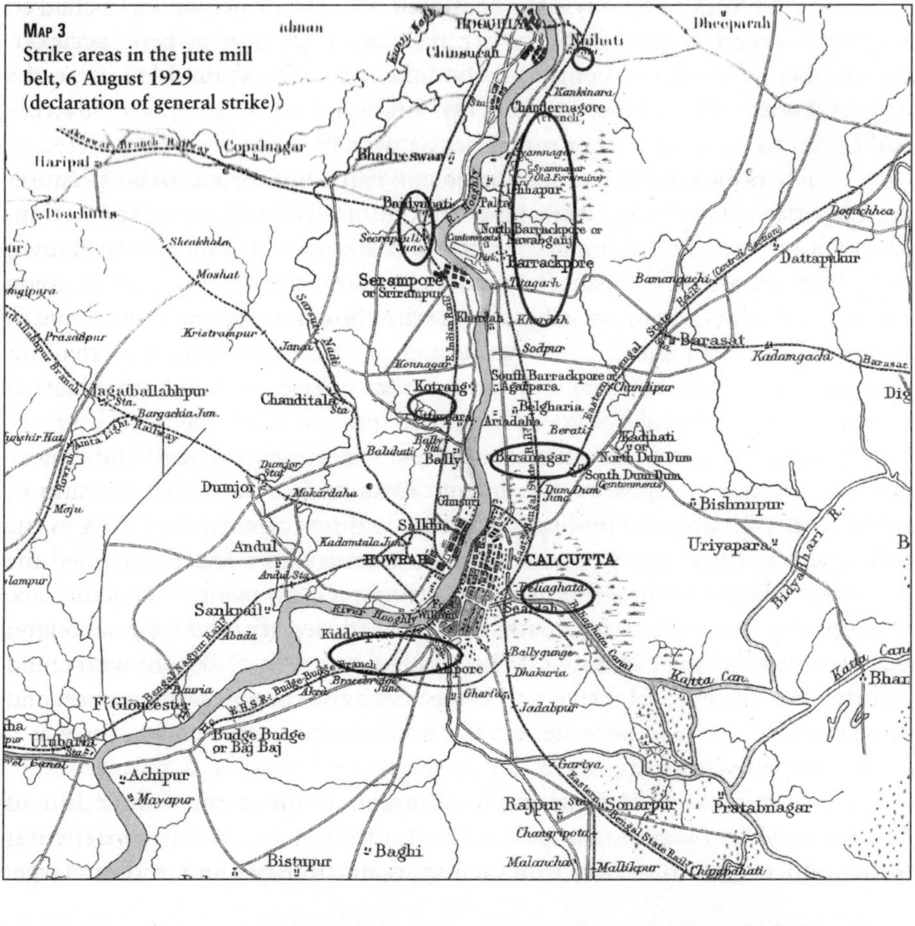

MAP 3 Strike areas in the jute mill belt, 6 August 1929 (declaration of general strike)

Parganas, announcing the strike and holding meetings.[112] A few days later, she explained the demands of the workers in an interview as follows: 'Strike pay, proportionate increment, commission rate and "khoraki" to mill workers in those mills where "khoraki" were not given and the formation of the committee to meet the grievances of the strikers.'[113] A return to the old bonuses, which had originally been demanded by the weavers in Jagatdal, was also an official demand of the general strike. However, neither the earlier demand of a return to the old hours of work, raised by workers in Jagatdal and also in Baranagore, nor the demand for increased wages as raised by workers in Beliaghata, was taken up by Prabhabati Das Gupta. The strikes which had started in the first two phases in various areas were now officially defined as a general strike in protest against the methods of implementation of new hours of work by the IJMA. The Association's decision to increase the hours of work was not officially questioned, nor were demands for higher wage rates (irrespective of hours of work) part of the general strike. At the same time, Prabhabati Das Gupta's definite leadership of the strike was settled, at least as a matter of formal representation.

While the general strike was being defined politically, the movement itself was already in the process of becoming more general and also more radical. In the following days, the spatial movement of people intensified as the strike spread rapidly. By 8 August, just four days after its proclamation, the number of workers reported to be 'idle' had almost doubled.[114] By 15 August, about 240,000 jute workers had left their workplaces, and the strike had begun to spread to other industries as well.[115]

The police reacted to the increasing spread of the strike with arrests and dispersals of meetings, while labour activists tried to direct the trajectories of the movement. The political meaning and the concrete aims of the *general* strike were increasingly pushed beyond the immediate industrial dispute, from various directions and at once. However, with the emergence and involvement of several different sites in the increasingly militant struggle, the situation also became muddled and chaotic, and the boundaries between an industrial dispute and a general social upheaval of jute workers became blurred. The 'general' was transcended in different directions through the event's representation as well as its movement. Thus Prabhabati Das Gupta, even as she finally became the undisputed leader and representative of the general strike, was neither able to control the constantly emerging movement nor direct the trajectories of either faction of the BJWU any longer. This tension, between the strike's disputed paths and its disputed representation, created a certain split between the two. When the government of Bengal intervened shortly after the general strike had begun, an agreement was found soon; at the same time, the split between movement and representation was finalized.

On 6 August, the same day as the general strike was proclaimed, a series of riots began in Naihati and Kankinarah, in the north of Jagatdal and Barrackpore. In Naihati, the police had noticed so far 'no attention from the agitators', and in nearby Kankinarah, their attempts had 'hitherto been repulsed by the workers'.[116] Reports about picketing workers from Jagatdal to Naihati were rare, suggesting a vague boundary between the far north of the jute mill belt and the early centres of the strike. On 5 August, however, the workers of the Nadia Jute Mills stopped work.[117] For the next day it was reported that picketing was expected in the nearby Gourepore Jute Mill, and that some police arrangements had been made but disturbance was not anticipated.[118]

When a group of strikers – about 500 in number, according to *Liberty* – arrived at the mill, a 'band of Kabulis and Peshwaris' appeared suddenly armed with knives and *lathis*, and asked the workers of the mill not to go on strike. The special correspondent of *Liberty*, while suggesting that 'some of them were drunk', mentioned 'that about a hundred Kabulis live near the Gourepore Mills and carry on the business of money lending among the operatives of the Mills'.[119] This second piece of information provides a clue as to why the Kabulis tried to interfere: the workers had to borrow money from them at various points of their lives in the mill towns, leaving them with debts to be paid, and the Kabulis therefore had an interest in preventing the workers from leaving their workplaces. The further events were reported as follows:

> The strikers who had assembled in front of the Mills at once demonstrated that they were only trying to persuade their fellow-workers to join the strike in a peaceful manner, and the Kabulis and Peshwaris had no business to interfere. At this, it is said, the Kabulis became enraged and suddenly whipped out big knives and attacked the strikers. As a result some of the strikers were seriously wounded.
>
> This news spread like wildfire and the workers of the Gourepore Jute Mill came out and joined the strike. Then they attacked the Kabulis who, it is reported, were assaulting them with knives and lathis. . . .
>
> Being outnumbered, the Kabulis and Peshwaris fled to their quarters. But the workers followed them with lathis in hand. There was then a free fight between the Kabulis and Peshwaris on the one side and the strikers and workers of the Gourepur Jute Mill on the other side. As a result, four men lost their lives, several were seriously wounded and a large number of people received injuries. The houses of the Kabulis, it is reported, were set fire to, their cycles and other belongings were destroyed and documents regarding business torn to pieces.[120]

Police arrived at the scene soon afterwards and brought the situation under control by arresting twenty Kabulis. Workers were only arrested two days later, when the police 'organized a raid on the coolie lines . . . to find out wounded participants in the Gourepore riot' and arrested about 100 'coolies'.[121] News of the riot, however, had spread instantly to Kankinarah, where the workers 'became infuriated and, it is said, began to attack the Kabulis residing there', causing three more deaths on the same day.[122]

On 7 August, closing of all the jute mills in Naihati and two mills in Kankinarah was reported, as well as posting of a strong police force in the region. Widespread panic among Kabulis and Peshwaris was further described:

> The Kabulis and Peshwaris are terror-stricken and many of them living at Bhatpara [nearby Kankinarah, A.S.] and the neighbourhood left for Calcutta, Hooghly and other places. The panic spread to Kanchrapara, a railway colony as well, and many Kabulis and Peshwaris who live there are also reported to have left the station out of fear.[123]

The opposite movement was also noticed: the Deputy Commissioner of Police (South) reported that some 'Kabuli money lenders . . . and others living in the jurisdication of Matyaburz (B.P.) [Metiaburuz] left for Naihati yesterday. It is rumoured that they had gone there to render help to their own caste people who are in trouble.'[124]

On the same day, 7 August, another riot occurred in connection with the planned funeral of the three dead Kabuli moneylenders. A crowd of workers tried to prevent the funeral, approaching the houses of the moneylenders in the morning. The Kabulis, it was reported, fled in fear to the nearby police station, around which, in the course of the day, more and more workers gathered. The following events were reported about this incident:

> The situation became menacing late in the afternoon, when the crowd of mill-hands had swollen to three thousand, all firmly resolved not to allow the funeral. The sardars being informed that they would be held responsible for the conduct of the operatives, attempted to persuade the mob to disperse.
>
> Addressing the rows of squatting men they argued that the Peshwaris were Moslems and that the dead man should not be refused a Moslem burial. The crowd shouted in return: 'These men are not our brothers. They killed our brothers.'
>
> The sardars replied that the Peshwaris at Kankinarah had nothing whatever to do with the fight at Naihati, but the crowd would not listen. Gradually, but without show of violence, they encircled the handful of police guarding the door of the house where the body lay.[125]

About half an hour later, the workers started throwing brickbats at the police and tried to enter the *thana*. Fortunately for the police, who were hopelessly outnumbered, armed reinforcements arrived at the scene just in time to disperse the workers. The dead Kabulis were buried that night under strong police escort. The next morning, about 500 policemen entered the Kankinarah coolie lines, arrested more than 230 jute workers and brought them to the police station in Jagatdal. On 8 August, 'thousands' of workers gathered and approached the police station in Jagatdal, apparently with the object of freeing the workers from Kankinarah who had been imprisoned. The police arrived again just in time to disperse the strikers.[126] Kali Sen came too, to try and calm the workers down and prevent them from further violence. For the rest of the day, crowds 'stayed on the roadway' which connected different mill districts in the north of Calcutta.[127]

These riots in Kankinarrah and Naihati started within the

neighbourhood where both the moneylenders and jute workers lived. At the same time, they took place beyond the immediate boundaries of the neighbourhood and different mill towns were actively involved. Again, also at the same time, they were part of the general strike, potentially affecting the entire jute mill belt. The spatial movements that both sustained and were generated by the riots travelled along routes unknown to observers in Calcutta and elsewhere, and were thus very hard to control. In a sense, the Kabulis seemed to join the already spreading physical movement of workers and trade unionists through the jute mill belt, each travelling along certain paths and yet each (foremost, the workers) breaking down the limited spaces allotted to them. In order to keep control over these 'movements', the police closed several ferries.[128] In the north of 24 Parganas, police buses, which came to be called the 'flying-police squad', started patrolling the industrial areas day and night, leaving the *thana* in tight intervals of thirty minutes.[129]

The events in Naihati and Kankinarah generated wide anxiety throughout the jute mill belt, for several reasons. In the reports of many newspapers, panic resonated about the fleeing Kabulis.[130] The moneylenders after all sustained workers – and not just jute mill workers – at various moments of their lives in industrial spaces. This very moment, during and after the riots, when moneylenders were fleeing, demonstrated the possibility of an even more momentous breakdown of social order in the areas inhabited by workers around Calcutta.

The impression of a sudden breakdown of social order was at the same time triggered by the actions of the workers themselves, who attacked Kabulis and the police against all rules of secular and sacred authority, and beyond the boundaries of districts. This situation, in which workers were repeatedly attacking social and colonial authorities, seemed not just dangerous but also incomprehensible to contemporary observers. This was even more the case since no 'outside-agitator' was at work and no *sirdar* could be identified – nor could either of them stop the violence of the workers when it was happening. The situation bears, in this respect, a certain resemblance to earlier phases of the event when workers started appropriating the emerging strike in particular ways and along particular routes.

At the same time, the strike of the jute workers had become general by now, while the involvement of moneylenders opened up the possibility of pushing the *general* even further. The scale of the conflict had suddenly increased, while its potential boundaries could only be anticipated. However, the organized militancy of an increasing yet undefined 'mass' of workers against several social and political boundaries at once closed the possibility of denying the fact of the workers' agency. Or else, the possibility emerged of several mechanisms of control over workers more generally collapsing – whether or not they themselves acted irrationally, and whether or not they were led by 'agitators' or *sirdars* at certain points of the struggle. The situation was thus not just incomprehensible, it was also unpredictable; it opened up several possibilities whose shape or trajectory could not be anticipated.

Another cause of fear triggered by the riots and by the militancy of workers towards the police was the temporary helplessness of the public authorities, which became obvious in that moment. The danger of the situation lay not only in the workers' opposition to the police in a single riot, but even more in their repeated and organized gatherings and attacks on the public authorities. Surprisingly, in the reports of the police little is to be found about the riots in Gourepore and Kankinarah, and some contemporary observers had already mentioned the missing information on the case.[131] The reasons for this lack of information can only be speculated upon. It is possible that the violent breakdown of social and public order during the riots caused some anxiety about similar flights or desertions, especially among the lower ranks of the police. Given that a *thana* like the one in Kankinarah was surrounded by thousands of workers and that the local police had to wait for reinforcements in case of riots, the situation probably seemed very dangerous. And when envisioning similar riots, for instance the one in Champdani where not even a telephone connection was working in order to call for reinforcements, there is likely to have been fear that policemen would join the flight or at least hesitate to do their duty. The situation made the large number of industrial workers in the area around Calcutta suddenly visible, while the routes along which various participants of the protest travelled through the jute mill belt became more and more blurred. As the unrest among workers grew and spread beyond different subdistricts and districts, the problem of not just identifying, but also of keeping track and controlling the different sites of the event, intensified.

In Jagatdal and Titagarh, on the other hand, the situation was largely quiet. The police even noted for Titagarh that the workers themselves helped to keep the roads clear of loitering men.[132] In the next days two-mile-long picketing lines were mentioned, connecting the early centres of the strike and the BJWU's activities.[133] At several meetings held by Prabhabati Das Gupta's group, workers were asked to not resume work. She herself does not seem to have appeared in public very often in this period, partially because of orders prohibiting her from addressing meetings.[134] Her role as sole representative of the movement had further developed, however, and she was by now called '*mataji*' regularly, at times even as 'Sakti personified'.[135] The content of speeches at union meetings changed considerably with the spread of the strike: the theme of global support for striking workers in the jute mill industry seems to have vanished, and the tone became more nationalistic and anti-British. The immediate experience of the struggle, with its increasing and potentially open-ended rupture of the social order, was thus led towards an anti-colonial and nationalist direction. 'Honour' and 'autonomy', for instance, still played an important role, but were now connected to political concepts such as 'injustice' and 'oppression', as well as 'freedom' and 'independence'. The element of 'honour' in the decision to fight against mill managers seemed less connected to solidarity with fellow-workers, but rather to the task of fighting against British oppression in order to re-gain honour. Consider, for instance, Jagannath Prasad, a member of the Barrackpore Congress Committee, who was reported to have spoken as follows on 11 August at a meeting of Prabhabati Das Gupta:

> [The English] have . . . nationalism and that is why they are progressing and ruling us. They never buy any goods which are not [from] their own country. . . . In this country clothes used to be so beautifully made that even the English used to praise their workmanship in England and now Indians have to remain naked if Manchester does not supply them. The English cut the hands of the Indian weavers when they came here and saw their skill. Now Indians are working in English jute mills as spinners and weavers. . . . He told the audience that if they wanted to be treated like men and wanted to live, it was for them also to find out means and act up to them and not to depend on anybody else.[136]

In speeches like these, the fight seemed to be directed less against the IJMA, and more against the colonial state and colonial capital. The original conflict was to some degree submerged within the larger project of nationalism by questioning not just the implementation of new hours of work in the jute mill industry, but colonial power at large. The (potential) political impact of the general strike was thus further strengthened, while the representation of the event was pushed beyond the industrial dispute and beyond the BJWU.

While the group around Prabhabati Das Gupta fought over the representation of the general strike mainly from the northern parts of 24 Parganas, the group around Kali Sen worked on spreading the strike to the south of Calcutta. As early as 3 August, a group connected to Kali Sen arrived at the Fort Gloster Jute Mills in Bauria. They could not, however, 'hold any meeting for want of audience'.[137] The next day a new meeting was announced with Kali Sen, Bankim Mukherjee and – as the rumour went – Philip Spratt's brother.[138] This announcement seems to have been quite successful and about 3,000 workers gathered that day. Of the announced speakers, however, only Bankim Mukherjee spoke. Talking about the struggle that was going on in the north of the jute mill belt, he said that 'they had included in their demands the case of Bauria for introduction [of the] double-shift system of work and he asked the workers to demand it from the manager when they would go to the mills the next day'.[139] It is most likely not true that workers in the north of Calcutta had officially taken up the demand of workers in Bauria – or rather, Prabhabati Das Gupta, who represented the strike there, would probably not have done that. After all, it was the communist faction of the BJWU which, in 1928, had established itself in these areas, while her followers had hardly been active in the south of Calcutta. It is possible that Bankim Mukherjee anticipated that once the strike was 'general', in the sense that it affected all parts of the jute mill belt at once, the defeated labour struggles of 1928 could be taken up again – this time successfully. This anticipation, however, was probably led by the assumption that once the strike spread to the south of Calcutta, representation of the general strike would broaden to also include the communist groups within the BJWU.

Meanwhile, the strike spread rapidly, eventually affecting all the mills in the northern parts of 24 Parganas, in Beliaghata and Garden Reach, and some mills in Hooghly. On 13 August, the Birla Jute Mill in Uluberia in the southern outskirts of the jute mill belt went on strike. The next day, the Shamgunj and Fort Gloster Jute Mill at Budge-Budge and Bauria started a partial strike. The movement now increasingly affected the south of Calcutta as well, even though this spread does not seem to have been prompted, in the main, by movements of workers from the northern parts.[140] A line between the north and the south of the jute mill belt appears to have been consolidated by the increased interference of the police and by the activities of the two trade union factions. At the same time, it seems that the BJWU, especially the group around Kali Sen, was important in providing the possibility of connecting the strikes. The physical presence of the same union made it possible for workers to take up the fight again within the general strike, after the defeated strikes of 1928. The struggle had in this respect changed from a political proclamation to the emergence of an actual general strike, involving the expectation that a strike backed by the solidarity of all jute workers could succeed.

Besides the regional spread, in this phase the strike began to involve other industries as well. After the riot in the Gourepore Jute Mill, workers at the nearby Paint Factory started sympathy strikes, eventually going on to demand higher wages.[141] On 14 August, the Britannia Engineering Works and a Rope Factory in Titagarh followed. Unrest was noted in Lillooah in the cotton mills and in the railway workshop. At the Bengal–Nagpur railway workshop in Kharagpur a parallel strike seemed possible, as well as in the railway colony of Kanchrapara in the north of Calcutta.[142] Unrest was noticed, too, among the oil workers in Budge-Budge, who formed their own union with the help of Subhas Chandra Bose. Further, rumours were afloat that the strike might spread to the sweepers of the municipality.[143] The possibility of the general strike expanding beyond the jute mill industry became increasingly real – triggering anticipation, hopes and fears about possible trajectories of the event, as well as attempts to accelerate or inhibit its dynamism. This situation bears some resemblance to the phases before the beginning of the general strike in the north of 24 Parganas, when the possibility of the event was emerging. At the same time, these anticipations, hopes and fears had also been shaped by the experience of workers' militancy in Kankinarah and Naihati, transcending the industrial dispute in several ways. The potentially emergent trajectories thus remained unpredictable and vague.

Faced with a general strike which spread constantly in multiple ways, the colonial authorities tried to intervene by mediating a settlement between the IJMA and the BJWU. The KLU was also eventually part of the negotiations since it was the only accepted union in the jute mill belt. As early as 9 August, the general strike was discussed at length in the Legislative Council with representatives of the IJMA.[144] The mill owners' association was however unwilling to recognize the conflict as a general strike, or even a trade dispute. They argued that the conflict had been caused by 'outside-intervention' and that the workers themselves had no genuine grievances.[145] Further, they denied any impact of the strike on the industry. On 13 August, only three days before a settlement was arrived at, the head of the IJMA claimed in an interview that 'the strike had not in the least affected the jute market and there would be no prospect of a settlement so long as the outside influence did not cease to work'.[146]

The public authorities, however, fearing further deterioration of law and order beyond their control, pressed for a settlement in order to end the conflict. On 14 August the IJMA made a last attempt to prevent negotiations, assuring the workers that:

(1) the wages paid shall be proportionate to the number of hours worked,
(2) Khoraki will be paid as at present
(3) there will be no victimization and
(4) maternity benefits will be extended.[147]

Negotiations began on 15 August, however, mediated by the government of Bengal, between the government's labour officer R.N. Gilchrist, the IJMA, the KLU and the BJWU represented by Prabhabati Das Gupta, which led to a settlement the next day.[148] Prabhabati Das Gupta was the only member invited from the BJWU. The rest of the union was excluded from the negotiations, and several trade unionists later expressed surprise that negotiations had taken place without their knowledge.[149] In this open-ended and still evolving situation, it seems that a rapid settlement provided Prabhabati Das Gupta with a possibility to escape the political pressures created by the government and the mill management, increasing political pressures within the union, as well as difficulties created by increasing loss of control over the strike's movement and its representation. Her presence at the negotiating table as the only representative of both the strike movement and the BJWU served to separate her from the general strike, and to place her in a situation that demanded compromise rather than continued struggle. This demonstrated the inner tensions between the general event and its centralized representation. It enabled the government to swiftly intervene at a moment when Prabhabati Das Gupta herself may have wanted to escape the struggles.

While the emergence of a general strike was clearly perceivable as a fait accompli in this phase, the process of emergence was far from complete. Throughout the jute mill belt various conflicts – within the union or within neighbourhoods – merged with the event; new sites and locations became part of the struggle; jute workers, other workers, moneylenders and also several labour activists joined the general strike. Within days the general strike of jute workers in the north of Calcutta evolved into a struggle affecting workers in all corners of the jute mill belt. While the strike spread in a way that was beyond the reach of Prabhabati Das Gupta, her role as leader of the union simultaneously contracted, even within the group around her. At the same time, Prabhabati Das Gupta's iconic role in the strike and her status as its representative was not directly contested but rather strengthened, even though the trajectories of this representation were disputed. The singular representation of the strike through Prabhabati Das Gupta and the BJWU provided the possibility of connecting various conflicts within the jute mill belt which otherwise would have come to be seen as local. In the case of workers such as those in Budge-Budge, these struggles might also otherwise have been interpreted as hopeless, occurring only a few months after their local strikes had been defeated. The political representation of the event through Prabhabati Das Gupta provided the possibility of connecting it to larger conflicts in colonial Bengal and in colonial India.

With the attempts on the part of the government to end the general strike soon after it had begun, the spreading movement, its practical leadership and its symbolic representation in the political arena (in the figure of the union president) were brought into even greater tension with one another than before. The relationship between the union and its president, as well as between the movement and its representation, thus evolved into an actual conflict. A settlement of the conflict in this situation, which seemed to enable the resolution of the general strike in the political arena, simultaneously implied a separation between the strike movement and its representation.

Apart from the tensions arising from the political representation of the general strike, the other constitutive element of this phase was the emergence of a distinct workers' movement beyond the issue of a pure industrial dispute. The strike became more and more general, addressing eventually labour regulation not only within the jute mills but also in other industries. At the same time, social relations within industrial towns as well as forms of resistance to state authority became increasingly part of the struggle. Mechanisms of solidarity were crucial for spreading the strike among workers, and so were attempts by various actors – such as the Kabuli moneylenders – to prevent this very solidarity. The massive presence, and helplessness at the same time, of public authorities pronounced the rupture of social peace in the jute mill belt. The spread of social upheaval beyond boundaries was sustained and intensified not only by emerging anticipations and possibilities, but also by the conflicts within the BJWU, the invisible routes of the labour force, and by the public authorities who were not able to control the movements.

The End of the General Strike and the Return of Localized Strike Movements

On 16 August, a settlement was arrived at. It was signed by Robert Laird for the IJMA, Moulavi Latafat Hossain for the KLU and Prabhabati Das Gupta for the BJWU. Work was planned to be resumed on Monday, 19 August. The settlement stated the following:

> The Committee of the Indian Jute Mills Association have agreed to recommend
> (i) The correct proportionate increase in total earnings for the extra hours involved in the change from 54 to 60 hours a week;
> (ii) Payment of khoraki on the same scale as before;

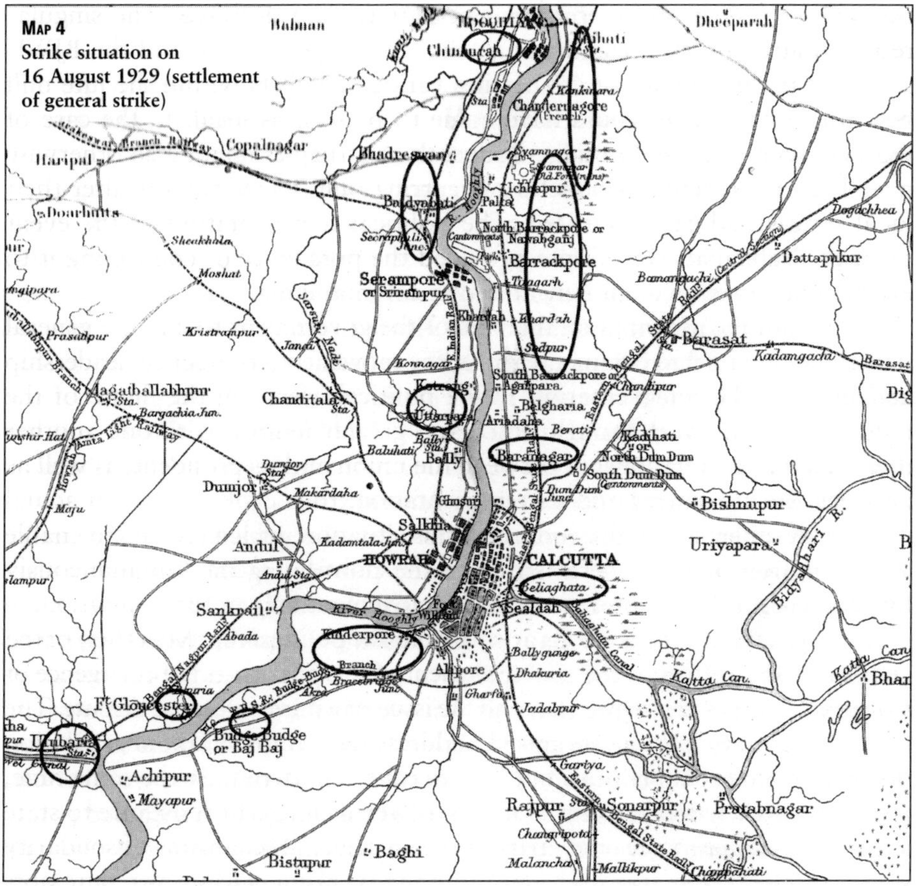

Map 4
Strike situation on 16 August 1929 (settlement of general strike)

(iii) The same scale of bonuses as the workers used to get before 1 July;
(iv) Provisions for maternity benefits and
(v) No victimization.[150]

This settlement is usually seen as a clear victory for the workers and the BJWU.[151] At one level it was indeed a real victory for the general strike movement. The IJMA had to agree to the main demands raised by the union on behalf of the workers. Also, for the first time in their history, they had been forced to accept collective responsibility for the labour conditions in their mills. The settlement was also a political victory for the BJWU. The government of Bengal, the IJMA and the KLU had to accept the new union, which was not registered, as a political force that represented workers' grievances in all their mills. They had to – as various newspapers pointed out – accept that the trade unionists of the BJWU were not just 'outside-agitators' but activists who cared for the workers and their genuine grievances, and were 'asked to speak for them'.[152] The settlement, which was favourable to the demands of the workers and the union, also spelt an end to the strike. Further development, and maybe even spread, of the strike would have disturbed the stability of the political compromise reached by negotiations between the unions, the management and the government.

The settlement, however, did not resolve the split between the general strike and its formal representation, but rather reinforced it. The end of the general strike thus posed more problems than it solved, considerably dwarfing the victory achieved through the agreement. These difficulties can be illustrated, first, by considering the provisions of the settlement. With the exception of the provision relating to the return to the old scale of bonuses, all the other points had already been offered by mill managers on 13 August. Workers and trade unionists alike had refused to accept that offer because they did not trust the mill managers, but also because it did not cover various demands raised by them at several moments during the event. A certain tension between the formal demands presented by Prabhabati Das Gupta and the demands raised by workers at the beginning of the strikes had already become apparent with the proclamation of the general strike.

Another set of discrepancies between the settlement of the strike and its movement becomes apparent when considering the demands raised by workers and the promises made by trade unionists in the course of the event itself. In the case of Bauria, for instance, Bankim Mukherjee had claimed that a return to the multiple-shift system had already been raised in the general strike, knowing that this was a central grievance of the workers here. A few days later he promised higher wages to the workers in Naihati 'for maintenance and education of children'.[153] In Metiaburuz, workers had posted their own demands on a signboard at the mill, which included points such as an increase in wages, strike pay, 'no man to be dismissed within one year', an eight-hour day and *khoraki*.[154] Such instances indicate that with the spread of the general strike, the demands raised by workers and by trade unionists shifted and to some degree expanded. New grievances had been raised in some mills, and new promises had been made by the union leaders. The demand for a proportionate increase in wages seems to have turned into a more general call for an increase in wages. New claims pertained to issues like curtailing dismissals of workers and longer holidays.[155]

The instability of the demands, on the one hand, undermined the political representation of the general strike through which the grievances of workers had already been established. On the other hand, the constant emergence of new demands was also an expression of the general strike as an unfolding event. Expanding the agenda of the general strike to accommodate the grievances of *all* jute workers was a condition for broadening the support for it, as local workforces were in turn offered the movement's combined support. Similarly, in the earlier phases of the strike, the workers in Beliaghata had joined the emerging general strike since it appeared that their struggle for an increase in wages was being fought for with the support of workers' solidarity throughout the jute mill belt.

At the same time, workers in the southern parts of the jute mill belt had joined the general strike not while it was emerging but when it was already happening. In this phase the general strike had, against all previous experiences, become a reality. Workers' solidarity across the jute mill belt was suddenly real, workers' agency was undeniably visible, and labour activists intervened and tried to direct it in various ways and at several places all at once. Conversely, the colonial authorities became more and more helpless, moneylenders were attacked, and managers could not induce workers to resume work. This moment of workers' strength, new and unexpected, even opened up the possibility that apparently lost causes could be won after all. Promises like those made by Bankim Mukherjee about reintroduction of the multiple-shift system and a general increase in wages, which otherwise might have been dismissed as impossible and thus not worth the suffering experienced during a strike, suddenly had a real purchase.

Thus, the emergence of new demands, especially *during* the general strike, was also an expression of the new possibilities that opened up, transcending the immediate experience of loss and suffering during strikes. Demands that otherwise would not have been expressed could be raised with the expectation of a short and successful struggle. And while a certain variety of emerging demands was already a condition for the event, the further emergence of new demands in the course of the event did not so much result in a random fragmentation of the general strike. Instead, a certain tendency can be identified in the development of these demands, and questions regarding wages, dismissals and holidays were raised by workers and promised by trade unionists in several parts of the jute mill belt at once.

A certain discrepancy is discernible between the demands raised during the strike and those formally propounded by the union leadership, which becomes even more apparent if we consider the actual provisions of the settlement of 16 August. Prabhabati Das Gupta, for instance, had raised the demand for payment of *khoraki* with respect to mills that were not paying it any longer. The respective provision of the settlement, however, only agreed to pay *khoraki* as before. In the supplement, it was further specified that *khoraki* would continue to be paid in mills which had already been paying it – which did not obviously meet any demand raised during the general strike.[156] Provision of maternity benefits, which was one of the concessions made by the IJMA, had probably come up in the process of the strike in interactions between workers and trade unionists.[157] At the same time, this point also reflects a certain trend in the jute mill industry at large. Since about 1923, welfare schemes for women workers had been gradually introduced in various mills, as an alternative to a legislative solution. As a result, as Samita Sen has pointed out, in the 1930s all mills had 'some sort of scheme in operation'.[158] The provisions regarding proportionate increase in wages, which the mill managers had offered in order to prevent negotiations with the BJWU, on the other hand, had already been rejected by workers and trade unionists alike. The third provision of the settlement, agreeing to return to the old scales of bonus payments, was the only real concession made by IJMA. This concession, however, only affected piece workers, and thus only a part of the workforce in the jute mill industry.

In the days after the official end of the general strike, discontent prevailed within the BJWU over the sudden settlement. Nine days after the agreement, on 25 August, Prabhabati Das Gupta was expelled from the union and Kali Sen became its new president. Prabhabati Das Gupta founded (or re-founded) the Bengal Jute Workers' Association, becoming its president.[159] This union, however, did not play an important role in future conflicts in the jute mill belt, in contrast to the BJWU.[160] The victory that Prabhabati Das Gupta had won by declaring the general strike and by becoming the accepted representative of the movement thus turned out to be pyrrhic. The communists within the union, though substantially weakened due to the Meerut Conspiracy Case arrests in March 1929, were able to not just re-establish and extend their influence in the jute mill belt, but also to direct the BJWU which had just organized and won the first general strike in the industry's history. At the same time, the split of the union immediately after the general strike also meant that controlling the implementation of the settlement became harder.

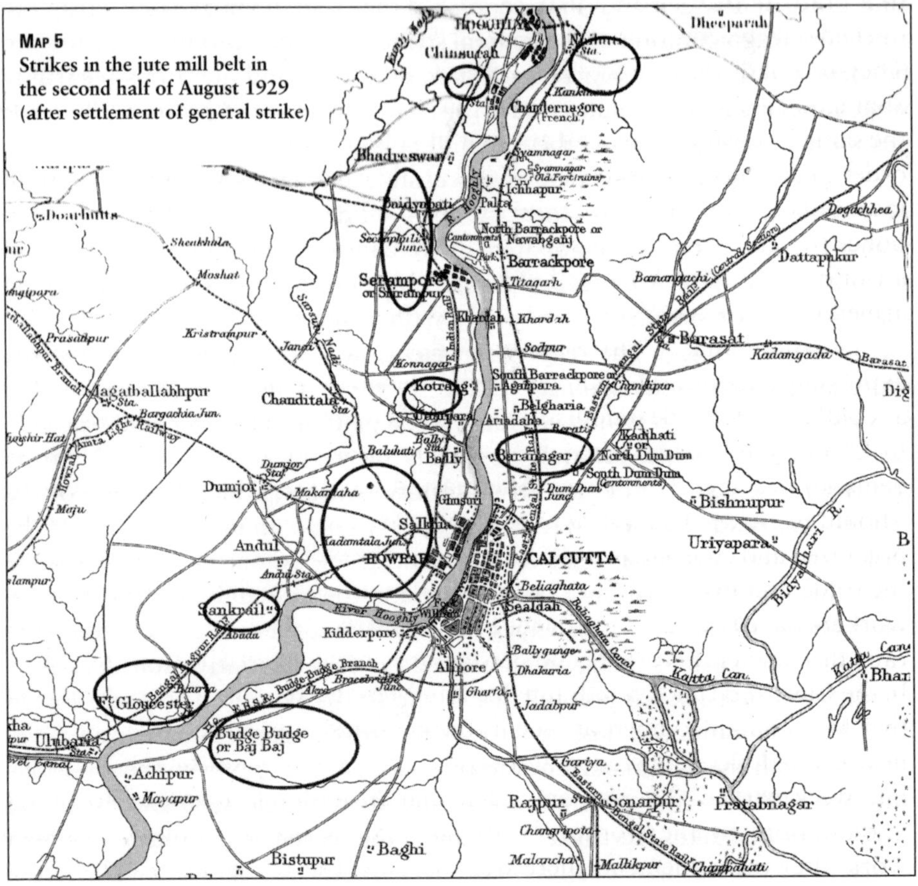

Map 5
Strikes in the jute mill belt in the second half of August 1929 (after settlement of general strike)

While the settlement and the official split of the BJWU indicated the political end of the general strike, it did not lead to an end of strikes in the jute mill belt. These strikes, however, were largely interpreted as isolated strikes by the general public, the colonial authorities, mill managers and trade unionists. The unrest in Howrah, Hooghly and 24 Parganas (now mainly in the southern parts of the district) was either treated as a misunderstanding of the terms of the settlement, or as sets of new strikes not connected to the general strike at all.[161]

The reasons for workers staying on strike, however, were more complex and diverse, and cannot be reduced to a 'misunderstanding'. In the early days after the settlement, one set of problems emanated from the difficulties of informing workers, local trade unionists as well as public authorities in various parts of the jute mill belt. The misunderstanding at the moment of the strike's end seems to have affected not the workers alone, but all the participants in various parts of the jute mill belt. On 18 August, for instance, at the Birla Jute Mill in the far south of 24 Parganas, a police officer reported that the workers were 'unaware of the general settlement'. He therefore had 'the vernacular newspaper read out by a young schoolboy and distributed a few spare copies', in order to inform them.[162] He then proceeded to a branch office of the BJWU in another part of Budge-Budge which had opened only recently and was apparently run by labour activists from Dhaka. They too had not heard of the general settlement and wanted to travel to Shamgunj, a bigger town in the area, in order to verify the information.[163] At the same time, in Jagatdal, an attempt by trade unionists to hold a meeting in order to inform the workers of the end of the strike raised the suspicion of the local police, who themselves had not been informed of the strike's end. The police therefore tried to disperse the meeting and this intervention triggered a riot by '10,000 mill-hands', which could only be quelled with the help of armed police forces.[164]

Another set of problems arose due to discontent with the settlement, expressing expectations that had been raised in the course of the event as well as conflicts with trade unionists who in a way represented these expectations. In Champdani, for instance, the workers asked Prabhabati Das Gupta to demand an increase in wages. She reacted by arguing that such a demand 'should be made after a year or so by which time the Union would be better organized and consolidated'.[165] In Titagarh, the workers' anger turned against the trade unionists and Ram Logan Sha 'could not explain in what way the workers have secured any benefit from the strike'. Only a 'heavy shower of rain' dispersed the workers and 'gave him a chance to escape molestation'.[166] In the Clive and Union South Jute Mills in Metiaburuz, the workers demanded that Moni Singh compensate them for one week of idleness since 'the terms now offered were concluded and notified at the mill gates by the Manager' one week earlier.[167] It was only luck that Moni Singh managed to escape 'molestation' by the workers.[168] In Jagatdal, where the workers resumed work after the settlement, there was discontent at the end of August when they received their pay tickets. Prabhabati Das Gupta, who came to Jagatdal, had difficulty in persuading the workers to resume work once again, and in convincing them that the problem was due to a belated implementation of the provisions, which take some time to adjust.[169]

Apart from reluctant resumption of work in mills affected by the general strike, strikes spread to new mills. In Howrah, where partial strikes had occurred only towards the end of the general strike, workers now went on full strike.[170] In Hooghly the strike spread further, to Champdani, Bhadreswar, Serampore and Rishra. In Budge-Budge, in the south of 24 Parganas, the strike not only spread gradually, but the strikers were also joined by oil workers in the municipality.[171] Many of these strikes did not last very long. In various instances workers stayed out till the second half of September, outlasting the end of the general strike by about a month.[172]

Contemporary observers as well as later scholars have interpreted these strikes after the actual general strike mainly as local conflicts triggered by a misunderstanding, namely, that workers who had not participated in the general strike believed that the terms of the settlement would not apply to them if they did not join the strike at this point.[173] This interpretation, however, cannot explain the scope of these strikes and the dynamics of the movement whose end had been proclaimed on 16 August. Rather, I argue, these strikes were largely part of the movement of the general strike which had in a way been *localized* again after its official end. The end of the BJWU's representation of the event thus did not immediately result in the end of the event itself, underlining again the complex relationship between the strike's representation and the workers' movement. The two sustained each other but were not congruent. The contemporary interpretation that these strikes were due to a misunderstanding by workers merely repeated a problematic assumption that had been noticeable, as we have seen, even in the earlier phases of the strike: that workers moved beyond the places allotted to them without representation, or, rather, that the leadership was seen to be somewhat irrational.

The struggles in the immediate aftermath of the general strike seemed at first to be rather sporadic, but they also appeared to sustain each other. In Hooghly, for instance, the strike had begun during the general strike – when it was already in the process of spreading in Rishra, Champdani, Bhadreswar and Telinipara. Similarly, in Howrah partial strikes had occurred in particular mills before the end of the general strike. In both cases the mills that had already joined the general strike were important centres for a further spread of the strike after its official end.[174]

Budge-Budge, where the main demand of the workers was an increase in wages and a return to the double-shift system of work, became a centre of the union's activities. As early as 2 August, the group around Kali Sen tried to spread the general strike here by distributing leaflets and opening a union office.[175] When the workers began to join the general strike about ten days later, they joined hands with the oil workers of the municipality. In the second half of August, the trade unionists repeatedly tried to prevent further spread of this joint struggle and pushed for resumption of work. In several meetings, the workers were addressed with arguments that turned the rhetoric used during the earlier phases of the event upside-down, pointing to the sufferings caused by the strike, but also presenting the strike itself as irrational and without much hope of success. On 23 August, in a meeting jointly held by Bankim Mukherjee and Prabhabati Das Gupta, the trade unionists explained to the workers as follows:

> He believed that [if] they can in a body hold out successfully, great results might come out of it but he seriously doubted if they were prepared to meet the consequences – the inevitable sufferings that must follow. Here the speaker was interrupted with all kinds of questions and remarks from the audience and some said that they were not prepared to listen to all such fine speeches with which they already grew tired. Then Dr Pravabhati Das Gupta rose to speak. She addressed doubt if the strikers really knew their own minds. . . . Pravabhati Das Gupta tried to bring home to the gathering that workers of the Jute Mills and Oil Companies stood on different grounds and their grievances were also different.[176]

Such attempts to stop the strike often ended with the audience shouting the speakers down, or with workers leaving the meeting *en masse*.[177] The jute workers in particular did not accept the argument that their struggle was different from that of the oil workers. They emphasized, on several occasions, the theme of their honour and the necessity of solidarity with the oil workers: they could not end the strike now that they had drawn the oil workers into a joint strike.[178] The patterns of solidarity among workers at such moments created a pressure to sustain the strike until it was successful. Despite the repeated attempts of the trade unionists to stop the strike and to separate the movements of oil and jute workers, the jute workers in Budge-Budge stayed out till the second half of September. By that time, conflicts within the workforce were increasing. In particular, 'up-country' workers were pushing for resumption of work since they could not sustain absence of work any longer.[179]

The situation that emerged after the formal end of the general strike seems to have evolved around the hopes generated by the solidarity and strength of the event. The general strike, sustained by the majority of workers in the jute mill belt, ended with the declaration of the settlement. The strike sustained by workers within their own localities, however, did not end automatically. The settlement seemed, from this vantage point, like an interruption of the emerging movement as well as an intervention in the patterns of workers' solidarity in the mill towns. The end of the general strike appeared an arbitrary decision in this respect. This situation also indicates the vulnerability of the workers who, at a moment of unprecedented strength and visibility, depended on trade unionists in Calcutta to represent their voice and to generalize the conflicts in the jute mill belt. While this underlined the ambiguity of the settlement that Prabhabati Das Gupta had signed in the name of all the jute workers, it also left the general strike unfinished to a substantial extent.

Most of the localized strikes in the aftermath of the general strike were defeated.[180] In a few cases the workers won, as for instance in the India Jute Mill in Hooghly or in the Belvedere Jute Mill in Howrah where workers received an increase in wages.[181] The situation in the jute mill belt seemed to indicate, however, that large sections of the workforce were dissatisfied with the settlement. As late as January 1930, a report of the Intelligence Bureau mentioned discontent among jute workers 'at several centres' in connection to the 1929 general strike.[182] But in the following months the Great Depression hit the jute industry massively, creating a new situation. The IJMA decreased the hours of work to 48 per week, wages and benefits were cut, and about 60,000 workers were summarily dismissed.[183] Managers enthusiastically described the 'plentiful supply of labour in the Bazaar', opening up numerous possibilities to replace workers for bad work or for causing trouble.[184] Thus the possibilities of a workers' struggle moving along several paths and trajectories, which prevailed during the strikes of 1928 and emerged forcefully during the general strike in 1929, were closed in 1930 for the time being.

Conclusion

Triggered by the increase in hours of work instituted by the IJMA in 1929, local strikes emerged in the north of Calcutta, which eventually involved the whole jute mill belt of Bengal in a general strike. This development was enabled by tense interactions of workers and trade unionists, and by the intervention of colonial and local authorities – each travelling along differing paths throughout the industrial suburbs of Calcutta. It was shaped by shifting conflicts and tensions, continuously opening up new meanings, possibilities and trajectories of the 'general' at a particular moment. Thus, while the general strike was happening, the shape of the strike's *generality* was constantly emerging, pushing its own boundaries in various directions at once.

In early July, when local strikes broke out in the north of Calcutta and the BJWU got involved in one of these conflicts, it was not clear whether the union was pressing for an amicable settlement or for a general strike. With the escalation of the conflict in Jagatdal and simultaneously increasing conflict within the BJWU, however, the whole union got involved in a potentially expanding strike. In the next couple of days, the two factions of the BJWU not only travelled through different parts of the jute mill belt, but also connected local strikes by sending delegations of workers from Beliaghata and Jagatdal to Titagarh. While the workers in Jagatdal had started the strike, the activities of both factions of the BJWU were crucial in opening up the *possibility* of a general strike.

This *possibility* became increasingly real towards the end of July. First, the possibility turned into a reality when it was appropriated by workers within their neighbourhoods and beyond. The basis of the potential strike was thus broadened and the 'unrest' travelled along new paths into areas where the BJWU had not been active. Second, as colonial authorities and moderate labour activists started to intervene in order to prevent a general strike, they revealed how close this potential event was to realization. In particular, the seemingly random interventions of the police, often guided by rumours and anticipations, accentuated the immediate danger of a general strike breaking out in the northern parts of the jute mill belt.

By early August, the possibility of a general strike had become a reality. The sudden interaction of various groups, driven by conflictual hopes, anticipations and fears, realized the emerging event. At the same time, it realized the claim of the BJWU – especially of the group around the union's president – to represent the general strike. While the spread of the strike along various paths and by various actors undermined the concrete representation of the BJWU, it also reinforced it by shaping the emergence of the general strike. Neither the protests by workers in Jagatdal nor the involvement of the BJWU at this moment started the general strike, strictly speaking. Rather, its *emergence* was initiated by opening up the possibility for a larger struggle, which was then shaped along various paths and with differing potential trajectories by workers and trade unionists, accompanied by interventions of the colonial authorities and of moderate labour activists. The possibility of a general strike, which had been opened up in early July, had thus by early August emerged into an imminent general strike, full of possibilities.

It was in this situation that Prabhabati Das Gupta proclaimed the general strike on 6 August, *while* repeated workers' militancy pushed its possibilities wide open. Thus the general strike became an actual event. Within a few days the strike spread into the south of the jute mill belt, spilled over into other industries, and opened the possibility of transcending the industrial dispute by turning into a more general social upheaval of workers. The immediate danger of the situation was that the conflict was not local any more; as part of a general strike, it *possibly* affected all jute workers and *potentially*, workers in general. This upheaval contingently spilled beyond the evental site and thus beyond the immediate dispute in question. This particular moment was also dangerous because it enforced the visibility of a potential emergence of a genuine workers' movement with increasingly political and specifically anti-colonial undertones, despite all its defeats in 1928 and early 1929. The moment, hence, was so dangerous not just because various paths had been opened before the workers, but because these paths had not been closed with the defeat of these movements and the arrest of their 'leaders'.

While the general strike was realized as an event and undermined the industrial dispute, the tense connection between the strike's representation and its movement was increasingly disrupted. The discrepancy between the political representation of the general strike through Prabhbati Das Gupta, on the one hand, and the creative possibilities of the movement, on the other, was growing for workers and trade unionists alike. When a settlement was arrived at between the IJMA, the moderate KLU and Prabhabati Das

Gupta of the BJWU, the connection between the strike's representation and its movement was fully torn, resulting in an ambiguous end to the general strike. The genuineness of workers' grievances throughout the jute mill belt was established with the settlement, as well as the right of jute workers to be represented by a trade union of their choice and on a general basis in a conflict with the IJMA. At the same time, the expectations that had been raised during the general strike and the possibilities that had emerged during the event were largely occluded in the settlement. While the strikes in the jute mill belt did not end with the settlement, the general strike did end with the withdrawal of the BJWU.

The result was that the general strike of 1929 was an unfinished event whose possibilities were neither realized nor fully closed. Only in 1930, when the Great Depression hit the jute mill industry leading to massive wage cuts and dismissals, did these paths seem to be closed – at least for the time being.

Notes and References

1 The paper *Swadeshi Bazar* was published by a group of (ex)terrorists – among them Bepinchandra Pal and Barindra Kumar Ghose, who had been key figures of the *Swadeshi* movement in Bengal. Kali Sen, who played a central role in the general strike in the jute mill industry in 1929, was also connected to the paper. Intelligence Bureau (henceforth IB), 28, 1928, West Bengal State Archives (henceforth WBSA).

2 'The Revolution of the Future' (translation), *Swadeshi Bazar*, 13 April 1929, IB, 387–28, 1928, WBSA.

3 Tanika Sarkar, *Bengal 1928–1934: The Politics of Protest*, Oxford: Oxford University Press, 1987: 49 ff.

4 See, among others, Nirban Basu, *The Working Class Movement. A Study of Jute Mills of Bengal 1937–1947*, Calcutta: K.P. Bagchi & Co., 1994: 61 ff; Subho Basu, *Does Class Matter? Colonial Capital and Workers' Resistance in Bengal, 1890–1937*, Oxford: Oxford University Press, 2004: 208 ff; Ranajit Das Gupta, *Labour and Working Class in Eastern India: Studies in Colonial History*, Calcutta: K.P. Bagchi & Co., 1994: 1 ff.

5 For further exploration of historical time and its *diachronic* and *synchronic* forms of analysis, read among others, Reinhardt Koselleck, 'Begriffsgeschichte und Sozialgeschichte', in R. Koselleck (ed.), *Vergangene Zukunft: Zur Semantik geschichtlicher Zeiten*, Frankfurt/Main: Suhrkamp, 1979: 124 ff.

6 See, among others, Nirban Basu, *The Working Class Movement*: 61 ff; Nirban Basu, 'Outside Leadership, Political Rivalries and Labour Mobilization: The Jute Belt of Bengal, 1919–1939', in Arjan de Hann and Samita Sen (eds), *A Case for Labour History: The Jute Industry in Eastern India*, Calcutta: K.P. Bagchi & Co., 1999: 114 ff; Subho Basu, *Does Class Matter?*: 208 ff; Amal Das, 'Outside Intervention in Jute Mill Strikes: Howrah, 1870–1930', in de Hann and Sen (eds), *A Case for Labour History*, 1999: 82 ff; Das Gupta, *Labour and Working Class*: 406 ff; Parimal Ghosh, *Colonialism, Class and a History of the Calcutta Jute Millhands, 1880–1930*, Hyderabad: Orient Longman, 2000: 236 ff.

7 Ranajit Das Gupta, *The Jute General Strike of 1929*, WPS 141 (90), Calcutta: Indian Institute of Management, 1990; Brij Kishore Sharma, 'Bengal Jute Mill Workers' General Strike of 1929', *Indica*, Vol. 44, 2007: 52 ff.

8 'Jedes Ereignis zeitigt mehr und zugleich weniger, als in seinen Vorgegebenheiten enthalten ist: daher seine jeweils überraschende Novität.' Reinhardt Koselleck, 'Begriffsgeschichte und Sozialgeschichte', in Reinhardt (ed.), *Vergangene Zukunft*,

1979: 151; for an English translation, see Reinhardt Koselleck, 'Representation, Event and Structure', in R. Koselleck (ed.), *Futures Past: On the Semantics of Historical Time*, New York: Columbia University Press, 2004: 110.

9 Alain Badiou, *Theoretical Writings*, London: Continuum, 2004: 98.

10 Ibid.: 98 ff.

11 Alain Badiou, *Logic of Worlds: Being and Event II*, London: Continuum, 2009: 79; also see Alain Badiou *Being and Event*, London: Continuum, 2005: 178 ff.

12 For further accounts on the connection between the narration and the analysis of events, see Koselleck, 'Darstellung, Ereignis und Struktur': 144 ff; Badiou, *Being and Event*: 178.

13 Tanika Sarkar, *Bengal 1928–1934*: 49 ff.

14 Das Gupta, *Labour and Working Class*: 450.

15 Superintendent of Police, Hooghly, 20 March 1929, IB, 303–I/26, WBSA.

16 District Magistrate, Howrah, 18 July 1928, L/PJ/6/1963, File 2796, India Office Records, British Library (henceforth BL).

17 Das Gupta, *Labour and Working Class*: 452 ff.

18 *Forward*, 9, 10 and 11 January 1929; *Times of India*, 11 and 22 1929.

19 *Times of India*, 16 March 1929.

20 A.M. Misra, '"Business Culture" and Entrepreneurship in British India, 1860–1950', *Modern Asian Studies*, 34 (2), 2000: 339; Tanika Sarkar (1987), *Bengal 1928–1934*: 49.

21 *Report of the Royal Commission on Labour in India* (Whitley Commission), Evidence, Vol. V, part 1, London: His Majesty's Stationery Office, 1931: 76.

22 Bengal Jute Workers Union, 1935, Special Branch of the Police, Calcutta, SW/521–A/35, WBSA.

23 Das Gupta, *Labour and Working Class*: 434.

24 Narendra Nath Mukerji, P.W. 19, *Meerut Communist Conspiracy Case Papers* (*MCCP*), 1929, Nehru Memorial Museum and Library, New Delhi.

25 Superintendent of Police, Hooghly, 20 March 1929, IB, 303–I/26, WBSA.

26 Das Gupta, *Labour and Working Class*: 452 ff.

27 Ibid.: 456; Report of DIB Officer, Hooghly, 19 February 1929, IB, 448/28, WBSA.

28 Bengal Jute Workers Union, 1935, Special Branch of the Police, Calcutta: SW/521–A/35, WBSA.

29 Subho Basu, *Does Class Matter?*: 209.

30 Gordon T. Stewart, *Jute and Empire: The Calcutta Jute Wallahs and the Landscapes of Empire*, Manchester: Manchester University Press, 1998: 99 ff.

31 Letter from P. Thomas to E. Benthal, 14 November 1928, Benthall Papers, Box 1, File 2, Centre of South Asian Studies, University of Cambridge.

32 Urs Olbrecht, *Bengalens Fluch und Segen: Die indische Juteindustrie in spät- und nachkolonialer Zeit*, Stuttgart: Steiner, 2000: 100 f.

33 Ibid.

34 For example, in the Gourepore Jute Mills in Naihati, the bonus was raised with the increase in hours of work. In the Clive Jute Mill in Metiaburuz, among others, the new working hours had been announced but not implemented when the strike started. *Liberty*, 23 July and 4 September 1929.

35 *Forward*, 13 January 1929.

36 Subho Basu, *Does Class Matter?*: 209.

37 Das Gupta, *The Jute General Strike*: 14.

38 Ibid.: 10.

39 Ibid.

40 S.N. Chatterjee, P.W. 9, *MCCP*.

41 Suchetana Chattopadhyay, *An Early Communist: Muzaffar Ahmad in Calcutta 1913–1929*, New Delhi: Tulika Books, 2011: 153.

42 Ibid.: 201.

43 Bengal Intelligence Branch, *The Politico-Criminal 'Who's Who' of the Bengal Presidency, 1930*, Calcutta: Bengal Government Press, 1930: 16.

44 R.W. Bell, Superintendent of Police, 24 Parganas, 1 August 1929, IB, 25/–29, WBSA.

45 Ibid.

46 Parimal Ghosh, 'A History of a Colonial Working Class, India 1850–1946', in Binay Bhushan Chaudhuri (ed.), *Economic History of India from Eighteenth to Twentieth Century*, New Delhi: Centre for Studies in Civilizations, 2000: 684.

47 R.W. Bell, Superintendent of Police, 24 Parganas, 1 August 1929, IB, 25/–29, WBSA; also see *Statesman*, 13 July 1929.

48 Daily report on the Labour situation for 24 Parganas district, 11 August 1929, IB, 25/–29, WBSA.

49 R.W. Bell, Superintendent of Police, 24 Parganas, 1 August 1929, IB, 25/–29, WBSA.

50 *Statesman*, 7 July 1929.

51 R.W. Bell, Superintendent of Police, 24 Parganas, 1 August 1929, IB, 25/–29, WBSA.

52 Ibid.

53 When, for example, considering the numbers of jute workers according to districts in 1928, this uneven distribution of the workforce becomes obvious: 200,365 jute workers were reported to be employed in the district of 24 Parganas, 71,991 in Howrah and 59,543 workers in the jute mills of the district of Hooghly. Cf. Annual Report of the Working of the Indian Factories Act in Bengal and Assam, 1928.

54 Report of ADIB Officer, 28 July 1929, IB, 25/–29, WBSA.

55 Report of Watcher ASI, 25 July 1929, IB, 25/–29, WBSA.

56 R.W. Bell, Superintendent of Police, 24 Parganas, 1 August 1929, IB, 25/–29, WBSA.

57 Report of DIB Officer, 24 Parganas, 31 July 1929, IB, 25/–29, WBSA; Das Gupta, *Labour and Working Class*: 465.

58 Extract from IB Weekly Report, 24 July 1929, IB, 25/–29, WBSA.

59 Report of Watcher ASI, 25 July 1929, IB, 25/–29, WBSA.

60 Extract from IB Weekly Report, 7 August 1929, IB, 25/–29, WBSA.

61 Report of ADIB Officer, 26 July 1929, IB, 25/–29, WBSA.

62 R.W. Bell, Superintendent of Police, 24 Parganas, 1 August 1929, IB, 25/–29, WBSA.

63 Report of ADIB Officer, 26 July 1929, IB, 25/–29, WBSA.

64 Ibid.

65 Ibid.

66 Report of DIB Officer, 28 July 1929, IB, 25/–29, WBSA.

67 Ibid.

68 Report of ADIB Officer, 29 July 1929, IB, 25/–29, WBSA.

69 Report of DIB Officer, 31 July 1929, IB, 25/–29, WBSA.

70 Das Gupta, *Labour and Working Class*: 423 ff.

71 *Times of India*, 31 July 1929.

73 *Times of India*, 30 July 1929.

74 Special Branch Office, 2 August 1929, IB, 25/–29, WBSA.

75 Extract from IB Weekly Report, 7 August 1929, IB, 25/–29, WBSA.

76 Report of ADIB Officer, 31 July 1929, IB, 25/–29, WBSA.

77 Extract from IB Weekly Report, 14 August 1929, IB, 25/–29, WBSA.

78 R.W. Bell, Superintendent of Police, 24 Parganas, 1 August 1929, IB, 25/–29, WBSA.

80 Ashutosh Mahapatra, P.W. 27, *MCCP*.

80 W.H. Bemrose, Assistant Superintendant of Police, Barrackpore, 2 August 1929, IB, 25/–29, WBSA.

81 Report of ADIB Officer, 31 July 1929, IB, 25/–29, WBSA.

82 R.W. Bell, Superintendent of Police, 24 Parganas, 1 August 1929, IB, 25/–29, WBSA.

83 Ibid.

84 Ibid.

85 *Statesman*, 18 August 1929.
86 Ibid.
87 E.S. Jones, for Superintendent of Police, 24 Parganas, 2 August 1929, IB, 25/–29, WBSA.
88 Director's Minute Books – Shamnuggur Jute Factory, Vol. 22, 11 March 1930, MS 86 1/1/19, Dundee University Archives.
89 R.W. Bell, Superintendent of Police, 24 Parganas, 1 August 1929, IB, 25/–29, WBSA.
90 Ibid.
91 *Times of India*, 1 August 1929; Copy No. 6418, 6 August 1929, IB, 25/–29, WBSA.
92 *Liberty*, 24 July 1929.
93 R.W. Bell, Superintendent of Police, 24 Parganas, 1 August 1929, IB, 25/–29, WBSA.
94 This impression of particular patterns or paths of picketing workers could be further extended by pointing to continuities and discontinuities when considering the second general strike in 1937. In this case, the boundary between the northern and southern parts of the jute mill belt proved to be important again, while the crossing of the river seems to have lost importance to some degree. In Titagarh, however, the strike was started by 'madrassi' spinners in both general strikes. At the same time, the Auckland Jute Mill was one of the last mills in Barrackpore to join the general strikes of 1929 as well as 1937. In the first case, the mill joined the strike after an intervention by *sirdars* from surrounding mills. In the latter case, the mill had to join the strike after a 'mob' of strikers attacked the factory. See Private official letters from Calcutta, 29 October 1936 to 6 May 1937, March–April 1937, MS86/V/7/3/, Dundee University Archives; Strike Report for 6 August 1929, IB, 25/–29, WBSA; *Times of India,* 4 May 1937.
95 R.W. Bell, Superintendent of Police, 24 Parganas, 1 August 1929, IB, 25/–29, WBSA.
96 T. Meerza, Hooghly Police Office, 6 August 1929, IB, 25/–29, WBSA.
97 Ibid.
98 Ibid.; see also Extract from IB Weekly Report, 14 August 1929, IB, 25/–29, WBSA.
99 T. Meerza, Hooghly Police Office, 4 August 1929, IB, 25/–29, WBSA.
100 E.W. Duckfield, Superintendent of Police, Howrah, 5 August 1929, IB, 25/–29, WBSA.
101 Ibid.
102 T. Meerza, Hooghly Police Office, 4 August 1929, IB, 25/–29, WBSA.
103 Ibid.
104 *Bengalee*, 4 August 1929.
105 *Times of India*, 5 August 1929.
106 E.S. Jones, for Superintendent of Police, 24 Parganas, 4 August 1929, IB, 25/–29, WBSA.
107 Extracts form IB Weekly Reports, 7 August 1929, IB, 25/–29, WBSA.
108 W.H. Bemrose, Strike Report for 3 August 1929, IB, 25/–29, WBSA.
109 Extracts from IB Weekly Reports, 7 August 1929, IB, 25/–29, WBSA.
110 Ibid.
111 Daily Report on the Labour Situation in the 24 Parganas District for 5 and 6 August 1929, IB, 25/–29, WBSA; *Statesman*, 6 August 1929.
112 *Liberty*, 6 August 1929; *Statesman*, 6 August 1929.
113 *Liberty*, 14 August 1929.
114 *Times of India*, 8 August 1929; *Statesman*, 8 August 1929.
115 *Times of India*, 15 August 1929.
116 Extract from IB Weekly Report, 7 August 1929, IB, 25/–29, WBSA.
117 W.H. Bemrose, Assistant Superintendent of Police, Barrackpore, 6 August 1929, IB, 25/–29, WBSA.
118 Ibid.; *Liberty*, 4 September 1929.
119 *Liberty*, 7 August 1929.
120 Ibid.

121 Ibid.
122 Ibid.
123 *Liberty*, 8 August 1929.
124 B.N. Bannerjee, Deputy Commissioner of Police, South, 8 August 1929, IB, 25/–29, WBSA.
125 *Statesman*, 8 August 1929.
126 *Liberty*, 9 August 1929.
127 *Statesman*, 9 August 1929.
128 T. Meerza, Hooghly Police Office, 7 August 1929, IB, 25/–29, WBSA.
129 *Statesman*, 8 August 1929.
130 *Liberty*, 8 August 1929; *Times of India*, 8 and 9 August 1929; *Statesman*, 8 and 10 August 1929.
131 Extracts from IB Weekly Reports, 7 August 1929, IB, 25/–29, WBSA; E.S. Jones, for Superintendent of Police, 24 Parganas, 8 August 1929, IB, 25/–29, WBSA.
132 Strike Report for 6 August 1929, IB, 25/–29, WBSA.
133 *Statesman*, 7 August 1929.
134 T. Meerza, Hooghly Police Office, 13 August 1929, IB, 25/–29, WBSA.
135 Report of DIB officer, 11 August 1929, IB, 25/–29, WBSA.
136 Ibid.
137 Report of Labour Situation in Howrah, No. 4, 5 August 1929, IB, 25/–29, WBSA.
138 Ibid.
139 Ibid.
140 Reports on Labour Situation in 24 Parganas, 15 August 1929, IB, 25/–29, WBSA; Labour Situation in the Jute mills of Howrah, 15 August 1929, IB, 25/–29, WBSA.
141 Daily Report on the Labour Situation in the 24 Parganas, 15 August 1929, IB, 25/–29, WBSA.
142 Extract from IB Weekly Report, 14 August 1929, IB, 25/–29, WBSA.
143 Extract from Report on Labour Situation of 24 Parganas District, 22 August 1929.
144 *Statesman*, 10 August 1929.
145 Ibid.
146 *Times of India*, 13 August 1929.
147 *Statesman*, 14 August 1929.
148 *Liberty*, 17 August 1929; *Statesman*, 17 August 1929.
149 Das Gupta, *The Jute General Strike*: 12.
150 *Liberty*, 17 August 1929.
151 See, among others, Nirban Basu, *The Working Class Movement*: 61 ff; Subho Basu, *Does Class Matter?*: 208 ff; Das Gupta, *Labour and Working Class*: 1 ff.
152 *Liberty*, 17 August 1929.
153 Daily Report on the Labour Situation of 24 Parganas District, 14 August 1929, IB, 25/–29, WBSA.
154 Extracts from the Report of Deputy Superintendent of Police, 12 August 1929, IB, 25/–29, WBSA.
155 *Liberty*, 8 August 1929; Daily Report on the Labour Situation of 24 Parganas District, 13 August 1929, IB, 25/–29, WBSA.
156 *Liberty*, 17 August 1929.
157 *Statesman*, 8 August 1929.
158 Samita Sen, *Women and Labour in Late Colonial India: The Bengal Jute Industry*, Cambridge: Cambridge University Press, 1999: 168.
159 Reports on Strike in and about Calcutta, 22 August 1929, IB, 25/–29, WBSA; Kali Sen, 20 March 1930, IB, 25/–29, WBSA; Subho Basu, *Does Class Matter?*: 214 f.
160 Das Gupta, *The Jute General Strike*: 15.
161 *Liberty*, 20 August 1929.

162 Daily Report on the Labour Situation of 24 Parganas District, 18 August 1929, IB, 25/–29, WBSA.

163 Ibid.

164 Ibid.

165 T. Meerza, Camp Champdani, 20 August 1929, IB, 25/–29, WBSA.

166 Daily Report on the Labour Situation of 24 Parganas District, 19 August 1929, IB, 25/–29, WBSA.

167 Ibid.

168 Ibid.

169 Daily Report on the Labour Situation of 24 Parganas District, 31 August 1929, IB, 25/–29, WBSA.

170 Extract from IB Weekly Report, 14 August 1929, IB, 25/–29, WBSA.

171 Summary Report of the proceedings of the Strikers meeting at Budge-Budge, 21 August 1929, IB, 25/–29, WBSA.

172 Daily Report on the Labour Situation of 24 Parganas district for 28 August 1929, IB, 25/–29, WBSA; Daily Report about Strike in and about Calcutta on 3 September 1929, IB, 25/–29, WBSA; *Liberty*, 8 and 12 September 1929.

173 *Liberty*, 4 September 1929.

174 T. Meerza, Camp Champdani, 21 August 1929, IB, 25/–29, WBSA; Extract from IB Weekly Labour Report, 21 August 1929, IB, 25/–29, WBSA.

175 Daily report on the Labour situation in 24 Parganas district, 2 August 1929, IB, 25/–29, WBSA.

176 Summary Report of the Strikers' Meeting at Ram Chandra Aweshi – Rice Mills, Budge-Budge, 23 August 1929, IB, 25/–29, WBSA.

177 Daily Report on the Labour Situation of 24 Parganas District, 26 August 1929, IB, 25/–29, WBSA.

178 Summary of Report on Proceedings at Budge-Budge, 25 August 1929, IB, 25/–29, WBSA.

179 *Amrita Bazar Patrika*, 1 September 1929.

180 Daily Report about Strike in and about Calcutta, 27 August 1929, IB, 25/–29, WBSA.

181 Ibid.

182 Extract from IB Weekly Report, 9 January 1930, IB, 25/–29, WBSA.

183 Arjan de Haan, *Unsettled Settlers: Migrant Workers and Industrial Capitalism in Calcutta*, Hilversum: Verloren, 1994: 26.

184 Managers' Reports to the Directors, Titaghur Jute Company Limited No. 1 Mill, 1931, MS 86/V/8/2/3, Dundee University Archives.

The Making of a 'Genuine Trade Unionist'

An Introduction to Bashir Ahmed Bakhtiar's Memoirs

Ahmad Azhar

Bashir Ahmed Bakhtiar would have liked to be remembered as a 'genuine' trade unionist. He does not unequivocally list the defining characteristics of this idealized type; however, in presenting his archetypal 'genuine' trade unionists, he cites the examples of J.B. Miller and M.A. Khan, contrasting them with communists like Sohan Singh Josh.[1] From the latter he gained 'theoretical knowledge' only, whereas, by implication, the former were able to teach him the 'practicalities' of organizing trade unions. While these 'genuine' trade unionists remained steadfast in the cause of labour, political 'leaders' would 'talk about both peasants and labourers, but in reality, would devote very little time to labour'.[2] So a 'genuine' trade unionist, to bring these strands together, would be skilled in and committed, above all, to organized union politics; any political affiliations would be secondary, although tactical alliances could be made and unmade if and when necessary. His account in fact gives us an unusually rich understanding of how, within the field-of-force of plebeian politics in late colonial Amritsar, the politics of labour was intertwined with various other political currents, indicating that he was not under any illusions as to the impossibility of effecting a clear demarcation. There is thus a tension in Bakhtiar's account between the desire to create an autonomous domain of institutionalized labour politics, and the acknowledgement that class-based political activity, in so far as it helped to develop a 'political consciousness', was necessary to build a labour movement.[3] In what follows, we will critically approach his conception of what constitutes 'genuine' trade unionism, arguing that the term 'professional' approximates best to his conception of 'genuine' – for any discussion of the memoirs should engage with the terms on which Bakhtiar wanted to be judged by posterity. These after all shaped the memoirs, which represent, first and foremost, an attempt to reflect on his legacy.

Bashir Ahmed Bakhtiar's influence on 'professional' trade unionism stretches from the mid-1930s, when he was instrumental in setting up the Amritsar Labour Federation, to the late 1960s, when he spearheaded working-class protests against General Ayub's faltering regime. It would be difficult to argue that it has waned in Pakistan since his death; in fact it helped stifle murmurings of discontent, and the consecration of Bakhtiar's legend is complete by now. An adequate appraisal of Bakhtiar's legacy cannot be based simply on the impressive institutional and organizational network he left behind, the most visible marker of which is the national web of 'Bakhtiar Labour Halls' that provides the concrete spaces around which working-class politics of Pakistan today organizes itself. What is the value of Bakhtiar's name? Is it the name that imbues these spaces with legitimacy and serves as the link to a rich tradition of trade unionism, in sharp contrast to the moribund state of organized labour politics in the present? Or do the unbundled stacks of his autobiography, gathering dust in a corner of the Labour Hall in Lahore, speak the truth of his relevance today?

The first edition of these memoirs came out in February 1970. This was a period when, emboldened by the progressive rhetoric of Bhutto's Pakistan People's Party (PPP), radical elements within the labour movement were reasserting themselves after a long hiatus. Massive street protests in Lahore during March 1969 by organized public sector unions, foremost among which were the Hydroelectric Central Labour Union under Bakhtiar's leadership and the Railway Union under Mirza Ibrahim, fed into a broad-based popular movement that eventually forced Ayub Khan to resign. The conditions created by Bhutto's rise in national politics appear as essential enabling factors for this upsurge, just as his ascent seems unlikely without the support shown by trade unions.[4]

The years between 1968 and 1972 were marked by unprecedented labour militancy; Bhutto's use of revolutionary rhetoric had contributed towards raising the pitch of working-class protest. Workers were further encouraged by the initial inability of the state to mount a concerted counter-assault, and resorted to *gherao* and *jalao* tactics to get their demands met. By February 1972, however, the government had formulated a policy, conveyed in unambiguous terms by Bhutto through the warning that henceforth 'the strength of the street will be met by the strength of the state'.[5] The subsequent clampdown on labour confirmed that this was no mere bluff. As in 1930s Amritsar, the very elements that helped shape the revolutionary zeal of workers into coherent demands ended up having to step in and control the resulting situation. In this regard the PPP in 1972 seems similarly placed to the Communist Party described in Bakhtiar's account. The parallel, however, can easily be overstretched, since the Communist Party never had recourse to state power or enjoyed a popular mandate the way Zulfikar Bhutto's PPP did in the early 1970s.

The field of labour politics, quiescent for decades, had suddenly been reinvigorated in the radically charged political climate of the late 1960s. This presented not only opportunities, but also threats; with the emergence of a new leadership from the rank and file, established trade unionists like Bakhtiar were wary of losing influence.[6] Arguably it was this fear, as much as the reluctant acceptance of its inevitability, that prompted the writing of these memoirs. Bakhtiar concedes as much when he concludes by saying that 'the next generations would probably think that those people [i.e. the previous generation of trade unionists] were incapable and did not know how to do their work'.[7] The reason behind writing the memoirs was therefore 'to recount the trials and tribulations faced by pioneers of the trade union movement'. Implicit in this, of course, is the claim to be counted amongst these pioneers, which explains why the narrative weaves together the highly personal and the political. In this way the text, inadvertently, deviates at points from the stylized political narratives of trade unionists and party members.

It should be clarified that in republishing these memoirs we are not particularly burdened with concerns regarding Bakhtiar's relevance, or irrelevance, to contemporary working-class politics in Pakistan. On the other hand, the purpose is also not simply to make the text available to an undefined audience that is not versed in Urdu. We suggest that through these memoirs, considered in contradistinction to a mainstay of labour historians of colonial India, namely, official sources as typified by intelligence reports, a very different set of questions emerges. The following discussion does not attempt a systematic deconstruction of the text but simply aims at highlighting specific themes, particularly those that tend to frame debates between historians of labour movements in colonial India. Some of these are still contentious; about others there could be a premature consensus.

The sparse use of memoirs in historical writings on South Asian labour tends to be concentrated at the uppermost echelons of formal trade union politics. These top posts were staffed from the educated middle-class or elite strata of society, and therefore Bakhtiar's plebeian background offers a fresh perspective; all the more so because Bakhtiar does not shy away from touching upon details that could be construed as 'personal'. Referring to memoirs of communist leaders, Sumit Sarkar laments the fact that these tend to be marred by a problematic 'separation of the political from the personal'.[8] Perhaps communists' recollections tend to be especially guarded in this respect; and while one could speculate at length on the reasons behind such reticence, the reader will be quick to appreciate the openness of Bakhtiar's retelling, where the personal and the political sometimes blend into each other.

Bakhtiar's narrative, due to its self-reflexivity, opens up very different perspectives from which to explore the institutionalization of labour politics and the birth of a labour bureaucracy (if not aristocracy). The attention to detail in descriptions of various strikes, particularly picketing, unburdens the confrontation between the forces of capital and labour of all abstractions, and we are able to see this struggle play itself out through the clash between bodies and batons, will and hunger, pride and shame. Bakhtiar's descriptions enable us to imagine a city in ferment, a living social conurbation, and its underlying structures; in this sense it compares with the best urban histories.

The text is rich with such images, and it would be inadequate to simply say that these enrich the picture one can create from traditional sources, like intelligence reports. We suggest and try to demonstrate that for our research, which tries to grasp the field-of-force of labour politics in colonial India, official sources alone are not sufficient. Take, for instance, the Intelligence Department reports, which disaggregate and abstract before reassembling certain elements according to the administrative logic underpinning the process. These memoirs, on the other hand, reconnect precisely those links that were severed, as we shall see. What emerges is a much more dynamic world of labour politics, shaped through the interactions between *babus*, *babas* and *dadas*. Different unofficial sources can be used to this end, including, for instance, Yashpal's novel titled *Dada Comrade*.[9]

Details that can at times appear superfluous to the cause of moving the narrative forward in fact comprise the distinguishing aspect of these memoirs; the story being told here is deeply personal even when it appears not to be, which precludes the possibility of simply abstracting impersonal facts relevant to the course of the labour movement. The making of Bakhtiar the *babu* holds the key to understanding the making of the labour movement.

Bashir Ahmed Bakhtiar's autobiographical account of the labour movement as it developed in late colonial Amritsar comprises a rare kind of source material for labour historians. First of all, the mere fact of Bakhtiar's plebeian social background distinguishes the memoirs from that body of literature – written by the intelligentsia in the Communist Party and other elite sympathizers of the labour movement (for instance progressive writers) – which has traditionally been a mainstay of historians of South Asian labour history. Of course this observation is more a reflection of the dearth of such material than a critique of the misplaced emphases of South Asian labour historiography. Their absence can partly be explained by the simple fact that men of Bakhtiar's station seldom crossed the threshold of literacy. Bakhtiar rose through the ranks, occupying all possible tiers in the labour hierarchy: from a casual labourer to a small-time local organizer, to the president of national labour federations. The different snapshots from various vantage points that we get of this individual career can be linked up so as to grasp the processes behind the formation of a labour bureaucracy; the transition, in other words, from a *mazdur* to a *babu*.

Unlikely Beginnings: *Khilafat* and the Roots of Radical Plebeian Politics

The memoirs present at best an ambiguous picture of Bakhtiar's social background. The trajectory he follows to the world of proletarian labour might be seen as much as the consequence of wider processes of social dislocation as an act of will; the former is hinted at, but the latter aspect of course is emphasized in the autobiography. Readers cannot help but be impressed by the initiative shown by Bakhtiar in negotiating his given circumstances to carve out a niche in the world of labour politics as it emerged in post-war colonial Punjab. We are cursorily informed that his father was a government servant and there is one other reference to him drawing pension from the *sarkar* (state); there are no more hints about his ancestry except when it is tied up with the narrative of his transformation.[10] In short, if one must make such a classification, Bakhtiar came from the ranks of a middling rural landholding class that was increasingly being pushed, as a result of economic dislocations, to take up supplementary wage employment. Although the tenants were challenging the legal claims of the landed gentry, ostensibly at least, traditional codes of deference were followed: being a *pathan* or a *syed* still carried some weight in the rural milieu Bakhtiar grew up in. Arguably, this background might help in understanding Bakhtiar's fierce sense of pride and heightened sensitivity to perceived insults. His social background, combined with the fact that although literate, Bakhtiar never made it to college, puts him in a demographic that was increasingly being pushed to proletarianization. Such men would not have been atypical in the ranks of footloose labour descending on cities in search of work during those decades.

Therefore, as the consequence of a complex mix of economic forces and personal reasons, Bakhtiar ended up in Lahore, where he was swept away by the popular current of anti-colonial agitations. The Khilafat and Congress Non-Cooperation movements shaped the political consciousness of an entire generation which was coming into its own in the post-war years, and plebeian social groups were mobilized on an unprecedented scale and through novel means. Historical scholarship has generally recognized that like most mass movements, the campaign for the Khilafat was based on a complex of motivations, some widely shared and others that would have been in opposition to each other. The movement did mobilize, for instance, the Muslim aristocracy as well as poor artisans, religious zealots and godless communists; no segment of the Muslim population of South Asia was entirely untouched. Its overlap with the Congress Non-Cooperation movement translated into an interesting admixture of popular plebeian forms of protest cutting across communities. Mirza Ibrahim, for instance, reminiscing about his 'political awakening', hearkens back to the days when as a child he would go on *prabhat pheris* (a form of procession with roots in Sikh religious culture) in the form of a *toli* to wake people up for *fajr* prayers (morning prayers at the break of dawn).[11]

None of these groups approached the movement without peculiar life experiences and pre-existing beliefs influencing that approach; this much, however, is purely axiomatic, a limitation that can arguably be transcended through source material of the kind presented here. Bakhtiar's retrospective transposition of the Khilafat movement and instances of racism at the arsenal, painstakingly detailed, describe an instance of how quotidian workplace experiences of racial discrimination substantiated the competing discourses of anti-colonialism, just as these discourses provided the template for arranging these experiences in politically meaningful ways.[12]

One offshoot of the Khilafat movement, which would prove to be crucial to the development of the communist movement in India, was the decision of some Muslims to migrate *en masse* to Afghanistan. Fazal Elahi Qurban and Sufi Ghulam Muhammad Turk, the latter mentioned by Bakhtiar as a founder of the Hijrat movement, were instrumental in shaping the labour movement in Punjab. They represent the *muhajirs* who, in unforeseen consequence of their religiously inspired migration, linked up with international communist networks and, after spending time in Moscow and Tashkent, returned to India to become active participants in radical working-class politics.[13] However, this was not the only instance of expatriate Indians forming radical international networks with the purpose of effecting revolutionary change in India; the Ghadr Party formed by Sikhs based in San Francisco was the first such organization.

Dadas, Babas and Punjab's Diverse Revolutionary Heritage

Bakhtiar's experiences led him, for some time, towards revolutionary terrorism based on the conviction that the British could only be turned out through violent means. Bakhtiar does not give us too many details about his activities as a member of revolutionary terrorist groups. He refers to an abortive plan to join the Pathans of the North-Western Province (NWP) and hints at being a part of other revolutionary networks. That was when he still believed in violence as the means to defeat British imperialism. Like many, however, disillusioned with these tactics as a means to bring about a revolution, he abandoned them, pledging instead to devote his life to the cause of building a labour movement. It is hard to be exact with the precise timing of this disillusionment, but it can be inferred from his account that it happened around 1929, which would situate him within the wider exodus that followed Bhagat Singh's trial.

The break could hardly have been complete, or clean. The progressive writer Yashpal, who would have been associated with the Hindustan Socialist Republican Army roughly around this time, in his novel *Dada Comrade,* explores this theme. The protagonist Harish, a *krantikari* (revolutionary), becomes convinced that the real path to revolution is through mass struggle, and to that end he immerses himself in the working-class politics of Lahore. The novel dwells at length on the inner conflicts that precipitated this ideological break and, importantly, transcended it. Bakhtiar and Yashpal, to varying degrees, along with countless others who abandoned this path, must have shared the anxieties of Harish. We will not conjecture on this further since Bakhtiar does not at all introspect on this. In the novel Harish's old comrades, including his mentor Dada, the respected older revolutionary and leader of the group, set out to kill him for betraying the cause. Ultimately, however, Dada comes around to Harish's point of view and helps him in prolonging a strike by providing cash, which, unbeknownst to Harish, he had stolen through dacoity. The strike is successful as a consequence but Harish is ultimately hanged, being caught in possession of the money and thereby charged with murder and dacoity. The cash, it can be argued, represents the tainted bond between *reformed* revolutionaries and their old comrades – a connection that was always ridden with tensions arising from unresolved debates on moral issues surrounding the question of revolutionary terrorism.

The strike in question could have been in Amritsar instead of Lahore, and Bakhtiar could have been leading it. There are clear indications that the links with revolutionary networks were never completely severed. After all the revolutionary Ghadr Party was bankrolling the Kirti Party, the Kisan Sabhas and the Naujawan Bharat Sabha, which, according to Bakhtiar's account, 'set the foundation of a strong labour movement in Amritsar'. The Akali leader Tara Singh provided the venue for the first Workers' and Peasants' Conference. When Bakhtiar fell sick, his comrades with links to the Ghadr Party sent him to a *gurdwara* to recuperate. *Gurdwaras* feature again as venues for organizing strike meetings. Bakhtiar is quick to acknowledge that the success of the strike at Model Woollen Mills was only made possible because a *gurdwara* provided free food to the strikers.[14] Perhaps we can see a convergence between Yashpal's fictional representation of the relationship and Bakhtiar's experience of it: the '*karha prashad*' (offerings of food by devotees) at the *gurdwara*, as a fortuitous intervention, sustained Bakhtiar just as the stolen cash in Yashpal's narrative fed the strike.

As late as in 1946, Fazal Elahi Qurban, the ex-*muhajir*, communist trade unionist who worked closely with Bakhtiar till the outbreak of the Second World War, was travelling to San Francisco to get financial support from the Ghadrites.[15] This was also the period when Baba Gurmukh Singh was appointed the treasurer of the Communist Party of India (CPI), leading intelligence agencies to report this as a move on the part of 'Bombay CPI communists to secure control over Ghadr Party financial assistance from abroad'.[16] The support of the Ghadr Party, accommodating of very diverse political causes at it was, remained conditional, however, on the *babas*' consent. *Babas* were the ones who had been incarcerated for their revolutionary activities in 1914–15. Revered as '*zinda shaheed*' (living martyrs) *babas*, this core group served as the trusted gatekeepers for expatriate funds funnelled through the Ghadr Party. The *babas*, not unlike Bakhtiar, were men of action, indulgent towards 'theorizing' but committed to and driven by, above all, pragmatism. After their release, beginning in the 1930s, these *babas* increasingly threw their support behind communist activities and particularly the Kirti Party, which included people like Sohan Singh Josh with whom Bakhtiar collaborated closely. Many more links could be drawn to illustrate the point that there was never a fine line dividing the worlds of revolutionary terrorism and labour politics; there was movement of funds and people from one to the other, and in fact, sometimes the success of particular strikes would be dependent on these links. In becoming a trade union *babu*, Bakhtiar, not unlike Harish, had not made a clean break with the *babas* or the *dadas*.

These connections can also be pieced together through intelligence reports, but the reports are structured in a way that tends to obscure them. The strict demarcation into discrete sections dealing with 'Labour', 'Revolutionary terrorism', 'Communalism', etc., does not allow us to see the links, for instance, between the Ghadr Party and labour disputes. It is when we penetrate to the level of concrete, localized struggles, like the strike descriptions we get from Bakhtiar, that the intimate relations of interdependence between these ideological repertoires and institutional structures confront us. The text forces us to face the question of how these various currents, apparently irreconcilable at an ideological level, came together in particular moments.

At the level of ideology and tactics, the Naujawan Bharat Sabha, particularly Bhagat Singh's faction, perhaps came closest to the politics of the *babas*. In so far as Bhagat Singh, in terms of his success in generating a groundswell of public sympathy through his actions, was able to elevate 'propaganda by the deed to the status of a tool serving mass organization, as opposed to merely a substitute for it', Maia Ramnath argues, he can be seen as 'the culmination of a synthesis that the Ghadr Party had embodied in both ideological substance and tactical approach'.[17] The ideological thread connecting the Naujawan Bharat Sabha and the Kirti Party to 'anarchistic and republican democratic movements',[18] signifying their libertarian leanings as opposed to the CPI orthodoxy's thrust on discipline, needs to be picked up to explain the long-standing dispute between the various left formations.

Sohan Singh Josh, in his memoirs eulogizing Bhagat Singh and other revolutionaries, remembers noticing portraits of Kropotkin and Bakunin at the secret hideout of Bhagat Singh.[19] He points out how some of the earliest editions of the *Kirti* magazine (1928) carried a series of articles by Bhagat Singh on the history of anarchism where he quoted Kropotkin and Vaillant, among other anarchist ideologues. A decade later Sukhdev Raj, who had been a member of the Naujawan Bharat Sabha and the Hindustan Socialist Republican Army, wrote an article titled 'Anarchist Gandhi' in *Baaghi* (November 1939), edited by Yashpal, arguing that Gandhi was the world's most committed anarchist and that his ideology was identical to Bakunin's, except that while the former spoke in material terms, Gandhi's approach was spiritual.[20] The disentanglement of communism from anarchism was not a simple matter of supplanting one theory with another – at least not for those on whom 'the Ghadr Party ideology of armed struggle and Ghadar heroes' unprecedented sacrifices had a firm hold'.[21] Still, it was inevitable and took the form of a drawn-out process without reaching closure, its ripples clearly visible on the surface of the labour movement.

For many, this period was one of transition from dalliance with revolutionary terrorism to immersion in working-class politics; but ideological, tactical and moral debates transcended this rupture. The observation that *muhajirs* and old Ghadrites were instrumental in shaping the labour movement of colonial Punjab leads to the investigation of apparently contradictory, yet overlapping, ideological repertoires. Communism might have trampled the corpse of anarchism to attain a hegemonic status in the radical political scene of 1930s Punjab, but the ghosts of Kropotkin and Bakunin continued to haunt it. The presence of the *zinda shaheed babas*, combining in their persons an inextinguishable revolutionary spirit with unwavering commitment to progressive principles, which they shared with the communists, meant that they served as the glue holding together the fractious coalition of Kirtis and communists.

As historians we have, in the shape of such memoirs, magazines like *Baaghi* and works of fiction like Yashpal's novels, the materials at hand to begin to reckon with these inner tensions within communism – in a way that contemporary communists would and perhaps could not. The distinction between revolutionary and reactionary politics is after all potentially misleading if the respective categories are reduced to their dominant tendencies, without sufficient appraisal of counter-currents within and how these created a certain permeability of the boundary between the two. It is important to remember that the communists by and large did not contest the labelling of these tendencies as revolutionary, or try to claim the title for themselves.

The point of the above discussion is that during the 1930s, divergent ideological tendencies were coming together under the '*laal jhanda*' (red flag), which in itself represented the most widely shared element drawn from the repertoire of communist symbolism. The question we want to ask is how the 'language of communism' was able to bring together these various ideological tendencies and acquire the hegemonic status as a vehicle for popular protest in the 1930s. It can be argued as well that the ideologies were not reconciled but simply had to resort to a common language which, over time, had come to resonate with the working classes. The communists might have introduced the use of the red flag, but it was only effective because of the meanings workers attached to it over time; the communists were not alone in shaping and, more importantly, articulating the ideological horizons of the working classes and therefore, as far as the workers were concerned, they did not have a natural monopoly over it. Long before communists had any influence on the working-class movement, workers were dyeing white flags red with their blood.[22] Bakthiar could after all proudly appropriate the red flag as his personal standard when leading the general strike which the communists had refused to support.[23] The red flag could be taken as both a distillation of the revolutionary idea and the channel for expressing popular instinct; the two roles could converge but did not have to. Not all battles waged under the red flag had revolution as the expected outcome; the most vituperative of struggles could and did end in ostensible displays of paternalism. Workers seemed to shift easily, and instantly, from shouting revolutionary slogans like 'Long live revolution' during industrial action to hailing their employer by chanting 'Long live Lala Kedar Nath' when returning to their work after a successful strike settlement.[24]

Bakhtiar identifies ideological differences coming to a head with the outbreak of the Second World War as the main reason for the rift in the labour movement. We are suggesting that the 'language of communism' emerged from and helped conceal such contradictions; what we have in the late 1930s is not just a consequence of the immediate political context, but also a delayed fracturing from within, along ideological fault lines that had been concealed effectively while the underlying tensions had remained unresolved. The tension within the movement between radical and reformist tendencies, between the tactical and the ideological, can be seen even, or arguably most clearly, during moments of confrontation. The important point, however, is to appreciate how these contradictory pressures did not *naturally* flow from clear-cut ideological commitments. As we shall observe in the next section, the communists in a given context could decide to curb workers' militant struggles led by the 'reformist' group. Of course the question of 'leadership' itself is a vexed one; from Bakhtiar's various strike descriptions, what emerges is a picture of a form of popular politics that was not dependent on centralized top–down leadership, as shown by the spontaneous creation, from the ground up, of creative organizational models. However, reactionary impulses in the form of religious ideologies, easily rebuffed in the 1930s (see the chapter on the strike at Punjab Rubber Works[25]), were arguably only able to split the labour movement along communal lines *after* the rift within the organized labour movement. How did this rift alter the nature of alliances made in the course of concrete struggles on the ground when, for instance, Bakhtiar's Amritsar Labour Federation joined M.N. Roy's Indian Federation of Labour, which, he was quick to point out, was *apolitical* and comprised of 'only' trade unionists?

Between the Red Flag and Red Tape: Communism, Trade Unionism and Workers' Militancy

Bakhtiar is very particular about having a separate category for 'trade unionists' whenever he is classifying the various players in the labour movement. The people he refers to as 'genuine trade unionists' conjures to mind the image of the *babu*, a controversial category, which, we argue, if properly contextualized, can be revealing of the structures of hierarchy within organized labour politics. People like Dewan Chaman Lal, M.A. Khan and M.A. Ghani, whom he cites as exemplars of genuine trade unionism, were all respectable, middle-class, highly educated, professional trade unionists. Bakhtiar did not share this social background with them, but it is clear that he did emulate them, in matters not only of formal trade union politics but also in terms of their mannerisms and dress. Even when he was just starting out with his informally organized union of construction labourers, he points out how these labourers would refer to him as *babu*; he certainly took this seriously enough to make sure that when representing them to the employer, he would wear a clean set of clothes.[26] With regard to his habitus, though not the same as the people he idealized, he was still different from the *mazdoors* he worked alongside. This limited cultural capital, combined with his charisma, were attributes that served him well in establishing himself as a leader; these same qualities convinced the *babus* that in Bakhtiar they had someone that they could do business with.

Even during his brief stint in jail the other inmates began referring to him as *master ji*, a sign of respect and deference.[27] That he mentions these instances probably says something about how they mattered to his perceptions of self. On the other hand we have someone like Mirza Ibrahim, who did not attempt to assume the appearance of a *babu*, but was just as popular with the workers and a very successful trade union leader. In a video interview recorded shortly before he died, when asked about his association with Faiz and other progressive intellectuals, Mirza responded that he could never really be one of them owing to his social background. In what is a particularly poignant reminder of the cultural differences that acted as an invisible barrier between comrades from vastly differing class backgrounds, Mirza said: 'I had the habit of chewing *paan* [betel leaf] and spitting it out . . . these people did not like it . . . they laughed at me.'[28] At another point, in another interview, Mirza pointed out how he had to suffer much more than his 'intellectual' comrades, whom he refers to as '*laat sahab de puttar*', or spoilt brats. Reflecting on the differential treatment he got at the hands of the authorities, he said, 'my class background didn't help either, I belong to a *bemaalik kisan gharana* [landless agricultural household] and [was] a *mazdur* in the railways'. These differences did not preclude the possibility of working together, and Mirza was quick to point out that he respected these individuals 'who betrayed *their own* class interests'. Of course, even in this statement there is a clear identification of intellectuals in terms of their class. Obviously, Mirza's relationship with these *babus* was more fraught with tension than Bakhtiar's, who seems to have had an easier time blending in.

The pictures interspersed, in what appears to be a random distribution, throughout the text can be used in the form of a slide show, and they would capture beautifully this transition. The illustration on the cover is a superimposition of a smaller picture of a rather smartly dressed Bakhtiar occupying the podium, in suit and tie and a fez, on a picture of *mazdoors* sitting huddled together on the floor and listening in what appears to be rapt attention. The pictures with other trade unionists, appearing at random intervals in the text, invariably conjure up the figure of the *babu*. That is only half the story though; the persona of Bakhtiar as the suave *babu* has to be reconciled with the person who goes around Amritsar on the back of a camel, rallying workers with his bugle; someone who stays on the picket line, shoulder to shoulder with his comrades, even at hearing the news of his child's death.[29] In the Bakhtiar Labour Hall in Lahore there is a picture of Bakhtiar on the back of an elephant, surrounded by a jubilant crowd of workers gathered to celebrate their victory in a strike. Khursheed Ahmed Khan is seated beside him. When queried about why they went to the trouble of getting that elephant, Khursheed replied blankly that it was the workers who had arranged it as a sign of respect.[30] In this case I was seeing the picture, plain and clear, as a vulgar example of a clear hierarchy between the workers and their representatives, but missing the proverbial elephant in the room: the everyday acts that consciously and demonstratively levelled these hierarchies, which in turn led to the workers creating new ones on their own terms. That is how Bakhtiar was different from the *babus* he meant to emulate. He straddled the world of the *babu* and the *mazdoor* with an ease that was both astounding and of considerable political value.

So can we proceed from that and argue that Bakhtiar's memoirs are unique in that they offer an insider's account? The argument could be made and it would be partly true, but it would be more useful to consider this distinction of outsider–insider itself first. Employers and the government frequently used this argument to discredit middle-class representatives of labour, casting them as *babus* usurping the right of the 'actual toiling and turmoiling classes' to represent themselves.[31] The response was invariably defensive, arguing not against the validity of drawing this distinction but how it would dissolve as labour came into its own. In his oral evidence to the Indian Franchise Committee (1933), M.A. Ghani, president of the Punjab Labour Board, responded that the labour movement was in its infancy and the workers, being illiterate, required people 'like me to come to their rescue'. The Committee followed this up with the suggestion that this could lead to interested parties exploiting labour for their own political or communal agenda. Ghani replied: 'nobody can exploit labour. They are shrewd enough to know who is their best representative and who will advocate their cause best. Therefore they may be trusted to elect their sympathizer whether he be a barrister or anybody else.' He ended by reiterating that 'in every movement you will find barristers and Vakils . . . and the labour movement is no exception'.[32] The Committee was not entirely off the mark since the reforms of 1935, particularly the introduction of labour seats, gave greater incentive to aforementioned barristers like M.A. Ghani and Dewan Chaman Lal to enter the field of labour politics. In doing so, however, they needed to tap into existing networks of mobilization and gather the support of local leaders like Bakhtiar, who was more than willing to oblige, since for him it opened up 'a large, vast field . . . which included Muslim Leaguers, trade unionists, farmers, workers, Communists, Socialists and Congress members'.[33] The Committee, and arguably the *babus*, underestimated the potential of this sea of 'toiling and turmoiling' workers to throw up representatives who aspired to join, and possibly supplant, the *babus* in professional trade unionism.

It is interesting to note that Ghani, in his testimony to the Franchise Committee, argued for elections to the labour seats to be through trade unions. He was not alone in this demand. Established 'labourists' were invariably in favour of this and the state, after much debate, accepted this principle. The implications of this for the growth of trade unionism and the direction it took in corresponding to the new legal framework regulating the process are yet to be appreciated and systematically explored by historians of labour.[34] However, even now we may argue with some confidence that the act of unionization became an end in itself for the labourists. Consider, for instance, the staggering list of unions that Bakhtiar's Amritsar Labour Federation helped set up. The impetus for such indiscriminate unionization arguably can be seen as originating in a response to state policy; labour politics at this point were brought into the realm of constitutional politics, which opened up, at the same time, an avenue towards internal bureaucratization that was chosen by many trade unions in subsequent decades, especially if they wished to be vertically integrated into national federations. Bakhtiar served as general secretary of the All-India Postmen R.M.S. and Lower Grade Staff Union in the mid-1940s, and later, in Pakistan, as president of the Hydroelectric Central Labour Union. Thus we see the beginnings of a drive towards bureaucratization from within the trade union movement. Ideological and even political considerations would now have to contend with the bureaucratic impulse, which, operative as it would have been on the reformist as well as radical trends within the trade union movement, holds the key to explaining the points of convergence and disagreement between these opposed ideologies.

Bakhtiar gives a very interesting description of how 'labour' became another site of elite power politics between the Unionist Party and the Congress. In the particular instance he mentions that the support of the Unionist Party was grudgingly elicited since the workers were sympathetic to Congress and saw this as a ploy of the Unionist Party to upstage it. The intelligence report dealing with the strike expressed delight at what it prematurely saw as a 'passing of the initiative from the hands of the extremists to the hands of the moderate politicians'.[35] Impossible terms were presented to the Unionist Party but, incredibly, they came through. They were able to do this purely through intimidation; in this rare instance, the state's *goondaism* was deployed on the side of labour.[36] Bakhtiar's thick descriptions of specific strikes, particularly the details dealing with picketing, show another, more common side of the extralegal/illegal forms of coercion employed by the state in labour disputes. Unprovoked and indiscriminate *lathi* (baton) charges at picketers, arrests without trial on made-up charges, prolonged periods of detention, torture, etc., were just some of the tools available to the state in its exercise of *goondaism*. If Bakhtiar frequently fell back on tactics that did not strictly belong within the ambit of constitutional trade unionism, it must be remembered that the Unionist Party initiated him into these methods early in his career. In the wars of attrition that these strikes became, the *dadagiri* of the state, in a highly uneven match, was pitted against the support of local strongmen like Bijli Pehelwaan. This reiterates the observation, now accepted as common sense amongst historians of labour, that without recourse to neighbourhood structures of support, involving the local *dadas*, these strikes would have been impossible to sustain.

Strikes are exceptional moments in which the state's collusion with capital is brought into sharp relief. Bakhtiar, however, broke down the legal and institutional framework designed to regulate industrial relations in order to show how the *law* itself was complicit in the quotidian forms of exploitation of labour. He pointed out how the Factories Act contained within it the necessary loopholes for employers to nullify its stated intent. Complaints would be directed to the Additional Inspectors, but they had to consult with the Chief Inspector of Factories in order to carry out an investigation. This time-lag would rule out the possibility of surprise inspections, since the employer would be forewarned and ensure that no overtime work would be exacted on the day of inspection. The flaws of this system were pointed out repeatedly and various improvements suggested by the representatives of labour, and occasionally even by those charged with working it. The state, however, was content with making the minimum concessions it felt necessary to maintain the façade of legality. The barrister *babus* of course continued to work within this flawed legal framework, which, largely discredited though it might have been in the eyes of workers, was nonetheless recognized as a crucial, and sometimes the only available, site of struggle. The ability of the *babus* to negotiate this terrain was their expertise and the justification for their credentials as trade unionists. However, barring a few exceptions when the law could be made to work in favour of the workers, victories were earned through concrete struggles on the street. To wage such battles the *babus* needed to include in their ranks people like Bakhtiar – people who had painstakingly earned the respect of the workers, and were willing to barter that for gaining the privilege of access to the *babu* circuits of professional trade unionism. The consolidation of a labour bureaucracy as a distinct layer was dependent on the formation of this *babu* class from within the rank and file. The success of Bakhtiar's unionization drive, culminating in the formation of the Amritsar Labour Federation, at some level reflects the desire, shared by *babus* and the rank-and-file leaders, to move beyond agitational politics into more stable, constitutional modes of trade unionism; the North Western Railway Union, the largest and most organized union, is held up as the ideal, and it most likely served as the template.

Bakhtiar gives us descriptions of his tactics to mobilize workers; not all of these are original. Many in fact were inspired by J.B. Miller, to whom, along with M.A. Khan, he dedicated his memoirs. Miller and Khan organized the North Western Railway Association and pulled off the massive railway strike of 1920; a strike that lasted over three months and at its peak, involved tens of thousands of railway workers of all grades. Between themselves, Miller and Khan embodied, respectively, the 'radical' and 'conservative' tendencies of the trade union movement. Miller was the self-proclaimed 'General' of his army of the poor; the claim was not exaggerated for by all indications, the workers acted like obedient foot soldiers. So, while Miller was out there rallying the troops in his highly original and flamboyant style, Khan was involved in backdoor negotiations with political parties and the railway management. This division of labour meant that the workers surrendered to the charisma of Miller, who in turn depended on Khan's negotiations at the top to come through. In the figure of Bakhtiar, however, we witness an unusual confluence of these functions; perhaps he can be seen as the logical outcome of a mode of trade union politics that necessitated this two-pronged strategy. Being in this position, however, meant being subject to contradictory pressures; Bakhtiar's account of the All-India Postmen R.M.S. and Lower Grade Staff Union strike reveals the tensions of being situated between these two worlds.

The spread of the postmen's strike had stretched the strike committee thin, but while Bakhtiar, from his top–down perspective, grasped the impossibility of maintaining the strike, there was great pressure from below to keep it going. The strike committee, desperate to end the strike and at the same time afraid of being seen to have capitulated, transferred the responsibility for a settlement to Sardar Patel. Whether Bakhtiar perceived this as a betrayal, we cannot know for sure; certainly, the matter-of-fact style in which he narrates this story leads us to believe that he saw it as a natural response, dictated by the fundamentally different imperatives he faced in his position as the secretary of a national trade union. There was, of course, never any inevitability as to where Bakhtiar ended up. However, his personal trajectory was part of a broader tendency within the field of labour politics. The earlier emphasis of the communists as well as the 'trade union *babus*' to bring together the working classes – reflected in Bakhtiar's indiscriminate drive to organize dozens of unions, cutting across what would later emerge as the 'formal'–'informal' distinction – was to be replaced by a focus on 'formal', state-sector unions.[37]

The split between communists and Royists translated into a fierce competition between the All-India Trade Union Congress and the Indian Federation of Labour to mark out their turf; the policy now was to 'capture' key national trade unions. The biggest gain the communists had to show for following this policy was when, after a protracted struggle, they managed to displace the Royist union under M.A. Khan with Mirza Ibrahim's union in 1946.[38] In Amritsar, however, they were routed and lost control of the Amritsar Labour Federation. The communists, at least until the strike wave of 1946 when they once again interested themselves in localized labour disturbances, seem to have extricated themselves from the project of reaching out to non-industrial, informal labour during the late 1930s and early 1940s, leaving the field open to Royists and Congress Socialists, among others.

Already, in the general strike of 1937, tensions could be seen within the leadership of the Amritsar Labour Federation, with Bakhtiar blaming Sohan Singh Josh and Feroze ud Din Mansoor for striking a compromise with the Amritsar Textile Manufacturers' Association. These conflicts would dramatically come out in the open soon. The general textile mill strike of 1938, which the communists within the Amritsar Labour Federation opposed and Bakhtiar supported, was indicative of this impending split and the resulting turf wars. Besides signifying a clear personal victory for Bakhtiar, this tussle showed that it was only a matter of time before the tensions within the movement would crystallize in the form of two distinct factions. The attitude of the communists towards the general strike of 1938 already showed an emerging tendency towards restraining labour militancy, which arguably was part of a developing logic that viewed strikes not initiated or managed by them as victories for rival factions. In being seen as opposing such a popular strike, it is easy to see how the communists would have been discredited. Intelligence reports too identified this as a turning point when they noted that 'this is the first victory won by the mill owners in the labour disputes that have been going on in Amritsar now for some considerable time'.[39] Being on the wrong side of popular strikes became a regular occurrence with the declaration that the war was a 'people's war'. Bakhtiar blames the split on ideological differences, while his account demonstrates how, within the context of factional rivalries, narrow political and personal agendas of the various players were instrumental in determining the shape of concrete struggles on the ground. Ideology loses its value as an adequate explanation for the vicissitudes of the labour movement when confronted with the immediate exigencies introduced by a crude logic of 'balance of power'; the explanation lies as much in the red flag as in red tape. Bakhtiar's account provides a fresh perspective that allows us to link the ideological dimension of the labour movement to its concrete organizational structures in a non-teleological manner.

The memoirs open up a world of labour politics shared between, and shaped indelibly by, the *babas*, *dadas* and *babus*. However, even apart from its value as a rare source for the reconstruction of 'subaltern politics', the memoirs are an excellent chronicle of contemporary plebeian society, especially when it comes to recording the conditions of Amritsar's working classes and providing insight into the prevailing structures of labour relations. One only has to consider Bakhtiar's description of how he got his first job as a carpenter to realize how such source material can help shed light on the unwritten codes that governed the world of labour. We find out that the customary method of recruitment as a carpenter was through the *raj tarkhan* and not through the head *mistri*; bypassing the former was a breach of custom and carried repercussions.[40] Or, consider the detailed description of conditions in the weaving industry. One might also choose to simply allow oneself to be led by Bakhtiar along the streets of Amritsar. Whichever route one chooses, the memoirs will likely open up a refreshingly different perspective.

Notes and References

1 See Bashir Ahmed Bakhtiar, *The Labour Movement and Me*, English translation of the Urdu original, edited by Ahmad Azhar, first published in this volume: Ravi Ahuja (ed.), *Working Lives and Worker Militancy: The Politics of Labour in Colonial India*, New Delhi: Tulika Books, 2013: 287.

2 Ibid.: 286.

3 Ibid.: 296–97.

4 For an overview of post-partition development of the labour movement, see Rashid Amjad and Khalid Mahmud, *Industrial Relations and the Political Process in Pakistan*, No. 73, Geneva: International Institute for Labour Studies, 1982. Khalid Mahmud's thesis, 'Trade Unionism in Pakistan' (1958), submitted at the Department of Political Science, University of the Punjab, Lahore, gives a more detailed account of the organizational splits within the trade union movement in the immediate post-partition period.

5 Kamran Asdar Ali (2005), 'Strength of the Street Meets the Strength of the State', *International Journal of Middle East Studies*, 37 (1): 83–107.
6 Khalid Mahmud, *Pakistan main Mazdur Tehreek*, Lahore, 1983.
7 Bakhtiar, *The Labour Movement*: 327.
8 Abani Lahiri, 'Introduction', *Postwar Revolt of the Rural Poor in Bengal: Memoirs of a Communist Activist*, Calcutta: Seagull Books, 1990: xlii.
9 Yashpal, *Dada Kamareda*, in *Yashpal Rachanavali*, Vol. I: *Upanyasa*, Allahabad: Lokabharati Prakasana, 2007.
10 Bakhtiar, *The Labour Movement*: 279–80.
11 Video recording of interview recorded in the late 1990s (private archive of author).
12 Influential published life narratives that exemplified how personal experiences of racist discrimination triggered a process of political awakening had been circulating for decades (when Bakhtiar's memoirs were published). We do not know, of course, what Bhaktiar had read before he wrote his own memoirs, but it cannot be assumed that the narrative structure, 'personal experience to political consciousness', emerged in his mind independent of established patterns of how a political life story was to be properly presented.
13 For a detailed account of the Hijrat movement, see Naeem Qureshi, 'The Ulama of British India and the Hijrat of 1920', *Modern Asian Studies*, Vol. 13, 1979: 41–59.
14 Bakhtiar, *The Labour Movement*: 306.
15 Intelligence file on Fazal Elahi Qurban, IOR/L/PJ/12/299: 59–60, Oriental and India Office Collection (henceforth OIOC), British Library (henceforth BL).
16 Summary of Communist and other subversive activities, for the fortnight ending the 30 April 1946, Secret Punjab Police Abstracts of Intelligence, National Archives of Pakistan, 1946.
17 Maia Ramnath, *Haj to Utopia: How the Ghadar Movement Charted Global Radicalism and Attempted to Overthrow the British Empire*, Berkeley/Los Angeles/London: University of California Press, 2011.
18 Ibid.: 162–63.
19 Sohan Singh Josh, *My Meetings with Bhagat Singh and on Other Early Revolutionaries*, New Delhi: Communist Party of India, 1976: 18.
20 *Baaghi*, November 1939, Urdu monthly (private archive of Ahmed Salim).
21 Josh, *My Meetings*: 52.
22 'Flag Dyed in Blood: Railway Strike a Demonstration in Lahore Services', *The Times of India*, 1 June 1925.
23 Bakhtiar, *The Labour Movement*: 324.
24 Ibid.: 306.
25 Ibid.: 310–14.
26 Ibid.: 282.
27 Ibid.: 318.
28 Video recording of interview with Mirza Ibrahim (personal archive of author).
29 Bakhtiar, *The Labour Movement*: 325.
30 Interview with Khursheed Ahmed Khan at Lahore, December 2011.
31 Oral evidence of M.A. Ghani: 47–56, Indian Delimitation Committee, Punjab Oral Evidence (uncorrected proof), published as *Evidence*, Vol. V, IOR/Q/IDC/20, OIOC, BL.
32 Ibid.
33 Bakhtiar, *The Labour Movement*: 287.
34 Note on delimitation of constitutencies for the Delimitation Committee's deliberations on assigning Labour seats through Trade union constituencies, V/27/261/20, OIOC, BL.
35 Governor's situation reports, Punjab Governor to Governor-General, May 1937, IOR/L/PJ/5/238, OIOC, BL; Secret Punjab Police Abstracts of Intelligence in the

National Archives of Pakistan contain fortnightly reports that have a section devoted to 'Labour'. These touch upon all the strikes mentioned in Bakhtiar's memoirs.

[36] Bakhtiar, *The Labour Movement*: 287–89. For the official version, see also Governor's situation reports, Punjab Governor to Governor-General, May 1973, L/PJ/5/238 f, OIOC, BL.

[37] See Report of the Lahore District of the Communist Party of India, June 1946, Reference Code CRER/GS/Box 2/33, Modern Records Centre, Coventry. The inordinate focus on the organized sector, particularly the North Western Railway Union, is representative of this bias.

[38] Ibid.; also *People's War* of Sunday, 19 May 1946, which celebrates the ouster of the 'Royist unions'.

[39] Governor's situation reports, Punjab Governor to Governor-General, First half of June, 1938, L/PJ/5/238, OIOC, BL.

[40] Bakhtiar, *The Labour Movement*: 280.

The Labour Movement and Me

Bashir Ahmed Bakhtiar

(edited by Ahmad Azhar)

These memoirs of Bashir Ahmed Bakhtiar were originally written in Urdu, edited by Khurshid Ahmad of the Pakistan Hydroelectric Central Labour Union, and published in 1970 by Asian Art Press, Lahore; they have been reprinted severally since. A rough translation into English was prepared by Tooba Akhtar, and revised and edited by Ahmad Azhar. This translation is published in the present volume for the first time. Explanatory comments by the editor are indicated by squared brackets.

The cover of the original Urdu edition of Bashir Ahmed Bakhtiar's memoirs

Dedicated to
Mr. M. A. Khan and Mr. J. B. Miller

In their name
Who were from the founders of the Labour Movement in India

Foreword

Friends interested in the labour movement have been insisting for a while that I pen down my experiences in the form of a book. I also feel that this demand is not unfair because it is important to educate the labourers of today in the history of the labour movement in this region, so that they can appreciate the difficulties and problems their predecessors had to overcome. At that time raising a voice for labour's rights was not an easy task. As soon as one would step into this field, one had to face the wrath of British colonialism, which required immense courage. Foreign rulers and their local intermediaries would offer maximum protection to employers, whereas the helpless labourers were not even allowed to complain. Those who dared to raise a voice for this oppressed class were blamed for this 'crime', and vengefully subjected to extremely humiliating and torturous punishment.

Bashir Ahmed Bakhtiar addressing workers at Lahore during the historic procession of 18 March 1969

The labour movement grew despite all this because the people running it had the courage and forbearance to endure suffering for the cause.

This book, *The Labour Movement and Me*, is a collection of a few of my memories culled from the period between 1924 to the creation of Pakistan. God willing, I will elaborate upon the developments occurring post-partition in my second book. I have not mentioned my political activities in this book as I am writing a separate book on that theme.

Bashir Ahmed Bakhtiar
25 November 1969

My Story

I was born on 4th April 1909 in Ferozepur Cantonment. My father was a government servant. When I came of age, I was enrolled in Ferozepur's Anjuman High School. After school hours, my parents would send me to a religious scholar to recite the Holy Quran. I highly disliked studying at two places every day, but my parents' pressure left me no choice. I finished the Holy Quran in approximately two years. Now I had time to play after school. My father disapproved of how I was spending my spare time, so he started sending me to a workshop to learn carpentry. This was completely

Bashir Ahmed Bakhtiar when he entered the field of labour politics (1924)

against my nature, so after getting off from school I would spend my time just roaming about. I would get a beating every time my father learnt about my absence from the workshop. This cycle went on for a while until I finally declared that I would either study or learn carpentry. Consequently, I was sent to Lahore to learn carpentry at the Mayo School of Arts. Here I had to work with small tools to carve intricate floral patterns on wooden blocks. I did not like this work, and with four other like-minded boys, I started to bunk school. We formed a group and would skip school together. We would attend Congress and Khilafat movement rallies, and sometimes go for fishing at the Raavi River or pick fruits from gardens.

I was very impressed by the Congress and Khilafat movements, which instilled in me a hatred for the British; this feeling grew more intense with the passage of time. Congress wanted to expel the British through non-violent means, but I had a different viewpoint. I thought that the British should be kicked out of India by force. In 1924 this passion took me to Bannu, where my wish was to collect the *Waziri* Pathans and create an army in order to wage war against the British. This dream of mine was never realized because of a few reasons. Firstly, I was not yet used to bearing hardships, and secondly, the people there did not understand my language. After a while I realized how impossible success there would be, and therefore I postponed my plans and returned to Ferozepur.

After returning to Ferozepur, I kept thinking of ways to expel the British from India. This was the time when Kamal Pasha and Anwar Pasha, representatives of the Turkish people, were engaged in freeing Turkey from British subjugation, and their selfless struggle had become the stuff of folklore in India. The sympathies of the Muslims of the subcontinent were with the Turkish people and were often passionately expressed. I, along with my companions, was overcome by the same zeal, and we would come out on the streets and bazaars in the form of *tolis* to sing this popular anthem of the time.

Ronde Samarna de baal bewa ho gayeian maawan
Ghazi Mustama Kamal teriyan duur bulaiyan

[The children of Smyrna cry, the mothers have been widowed
Our hero Mustafa Kamal may no harm come to you]

In those days activities of the All-India Congress were at a high, and although I was not a member, I once again started attending rallies. During that time I befriended a boy called Bankay Laal whose father was a very poor man and grazed cattle to earn a living. Bankay and I would spend many afternoons thinking about the problem of expelling the British from the country. After a while, Bankay Laal got employed in the Ferozepur Arsenal as a store keeper, where all ranks of the management were staffed with British soldiers. At this time British colonial power was at its peak, and in the eyes of the British, the Indian labourers were no better than animals.

Bankay Laal suggested that I should get employed at the Arsenal and witness with my own eyes the harsh treatment meted out to Indian labourers by their British overseers. Therefore, in 1924, I became a carpenter in the Arsenal where I received a daily wage of 14 annas.

I started observing the situation in the Arsenal. I saw that every morning, at the time of entry into the Arsenal, everybody except the officers was searched under the supervision of lower-ranked British officers, and that these officers adopted an extremely disdainful attitude towards the workers. The employees entered from the outside in a line and they would be searched by the *khalasis* (guards). However in the evening the situation was different; after work the British officers would count the number of workers. The workers had to sit in rows of four, and anyone even marginally out of line would be kicked and abused by the white men. After the counting, the workers had to form two lines and exit through the main door of the Arsenal. Everyone would hold their shoes in one hand and their turban, cap or food tins in the other. Then the search would commence. First, two guards would stand on either side of the two lines and thoroughly search every passing worker. In front of them, two guards sitting on either side would repeat the process. At the door a three feet high bar was suspended so that the workers had to jump over it to leave and, in the process, anything that might have been concealed between their thighs would fall out.

Outside the gate there were two more guards who, under the supervision of a white sergeant, would ransack the workers' shoes, turbans and other things. If, after this intense search, any worker still appeared suspicious to the white sergeant, he would be ordered into the 'tent'. This 'tent' was pitched outside the main gate, and one sergeant and several guards would be present in it in groups of two. Here every suspicious worker would be completely stripped in the name of a routine search. All this was not only limited to the main gate; the random searches and the three feet high bar were present outside the gate of every department inside the Arsenal.

Bankay and I would meet secretly even in the Arsenal to discuss the various injustices of the British, and try to think of ways to get rid of them, but to no avail. Slowly, we included more people in these discussions. The one thing that united us was our wish to cast out the British from India; and the anxiety about finding a solution to this problem contributed to our increasing hatred for the British.

At Ferozepur Arsenal

After taking in the situation at the Arsenal, I realized that the wage given to workers here was grossly inadequate. I convinced the workers at my workshop to demand an increase in pay. After a discussion, an application was drafted demanding a raise in our wages; but other than me, no one was willing to sign the application or take it to the officer in charge of the workshop. In the end, I decided to take the application to the Captain in charge. In those days it was impossible for a worker to go up to the British

Captain; besides, there were guards assigned at every gate inside the Arsenal so that no worker could go from one department to another. However, my colleagues found a way around that. Smoking was prohibited inside the Arsenal, so the guards used to chew tobacco instead. We bought some tobacco and kept it in the workshop, and my companions started distributing it to the guards daily. This bribe worked and the guards agreed to let me go to the Captain without any hindrance. After deliberating for many days, I finally entered his room with the application. The British Captain's name was Sandy; he was built like an ox and was an extremely sadistic person. He was shocked at suddenly finding me in his room; it was hard for him to imagine that someone would be brash enough to barge into his room without seeking permission. He cursed me in English and asked me who I was and what I was doing there. Meanwhile his head clerk also entered the room, took the application from my hand and read it aloud. On hearing the demand for an increase in wages, the Captain jumped up in anger, swore and said: 'You say your wages are inadequate. Indian dogs! We'll pay you peanuts for your work.' As he said this, he kicked and shoved me out of his room. This news spread like wild fire throughout the Arsenal and I gained immense respect in the workshop for my actions. People from all departments of the Arsenal would surreptitiously try to get a glimpse of me or meet me.

Many days passed and all the workers who had secretly joined Bankay Laal and me kept wondering how our circumstances could be improved. Meanwhile, a newly arrived British man was appointed the foreman of our workshop. Every day he would make rounds of the workshop, and beat any worker found lazing around or talking. He became notorious for his strict attitude. Consequently, my companions and I decided that a solution had be found. After discussion, it was decided that one day when the foreman came, someone would throw a blanket on him and I would beat him up. However, despite deliberating for many days, no worker was willing to be the one to throw the blanket, and so I decided to proceed without any help. One day I sat with a bamboo stick and waited for the foreman to abuse or beat a worker, but unusually, he did not do either of these things that day. After walking around for a while, he came over to where I was waiting with a bamboo stick and asked me why I was not working. I boldly replied that I chose not to and picked up the bamboo. He realized that I was up to something; before I could do anything, he grabbed me by my throat and, being much stronger, overpowered me, despite my best efforts to break free. Meanwhile a hue and cry broke out because the workers knew that today Bakhtiar was going to beat up the foreman. Soon a few of the Arsenal guards came and after completely overpowering me, took me to the same Captain who had already beaten me over the demand for a raise in wages. He immediately made my gate pass and had me thrown out of the Arsenal. A few days later I was informed at my house that I had been fired and could never work at any Arsenal ever again.

After that the workers came to my house and congratulated me for my courage. Now Bankay Laal and I started thinking of some way to make bombs and collect ammunition so that we could kill the British and force them out of the country. We made many pans and to execute them, we travelled to many cities. However, this is a long story that I will elaborate upon in another book.

Realization of Life's Goal

In 1929 I had to go to my ancestral village, Kot Badal Khan, which is situated in Jullundur District. Badal Khan, one of my ancestors, had populated this village, and its ownership had also been under our family's name. But now all the village *mazaras* [landless tenants] had attained the status of *adna malik* [secondary landowners], and we were simply *aala malik* [primary landowners]. Our financial situation had worsened too. Despite that, every time we Pathans sat in the village tribunal court, only the Syeds and the Rajputs were allowed to sit beside us. Recently, the court had ruled that Badal Khan's heirs had exclusive claims over the land in the village, and that all the land would be under their sole ownership. Everyone in the village became our enemy because they rejected our superiority. Consequently, they formed a secret organization against us; the secretary of the organization was the village accountant and he started collecting two paisas per rupee with interest as donation. Since I was actively trying to establish my family's authority, I was also at the receiving end of the villagers' retaliation. False cases started getting registered against me. For example, if an old man's tooth or a man's arm was broken, the case would be registered against me. These cases would be heard in the court of District Phillour, which was twelve miles away from the village, hence resulting in wastage of time and money. This situation became extremely worrisome for my father; one day he blamed me for being extremely lazy, at which I got upset and left for Lahore in protest.

After coming to Lahore, I soon ran out of money. Therefore I went to Amritsar in search of employment. I had only ten annas on me when I left Lahore and after spending six annas on the bus fare, I was left with only four annas. When I reached Amritsar, I found work as a carpenter on a construction site at Eid Gah Nai Abadi, under Munshi Abdul Qayyum's supervision. At that time, I was a thin, lean young boy. I did not even have my own tools, but the head *mistri* did me a favour by hiring me nonetheless. When I was asked to come to work in the morning, the carpenters who were already working there took offence as normally the *raj tarkhan* [roughly translatable to jobber] would only hire people from his own party. In retaliation, they immediately assigned me the hardest task. I spent my entire first day chiselling big wooden slabs, and ended up with boils on my hands and aching fingers. I decided that I would not return to work the next day. In the evening I went to the owner and asked him for my wages. He gave me four annas, promising to give the rest on Sunday since labourers were normally paid on Sundays. So I had to return to work the following day and continue doing the same hard work. By the end of the day, my boils ruptured and I started bleeding. I cannot describe the pain that I was in. I was also in extreme mental anguish at that time; sometimes I considered quitting the job, but then the thought of starvation would keep me going.

I could not sleep that night; first, because my hands were aching terribly, and second, because I kept thinking how hard it was for labourers to earn a living and how they were still considered inferior. I began to realize that those claiming superiority on the basis of landlordship, ownership or caste were extremely naïve. The people who really deserved respect were those who worked hard, and sacrificed their blood and sweat to provide for their families.

Before this, the British had been my only enemy and my sole wish was to expel them from the country, but now the direction of my thoughts changed. I now had a new mission. I decided to never go back to Kot Badal Khan and to dedicate my entire life to fighting for the rights of labour.

The next morning, when I went to work, I was a completely changed man. I now knew what my life's purpose was. I would go to work every morning and return in the evening, but my mind was preoccupied with thoughts of how to accomplish this monumental task.

First Demand

Till then the labour movement was non-existent in the country; neither was there any literature on the matter in the Urdu language which could have helped me in uniting labourers and establishing a labour movement. There were only two organizations in the entire country: the Railway Workers' Union and the Postmen's Union. But their agendas were limited, so much so that they did not even have any communication between them. They could not therefore be considered part of a broader labour movement. In those days, the maximum that workers could do in protest was to leave work; the absence of a union ensured that there could be no proper negotiations with the employer, and eventually, after futile talks, the workers would have to go back to work. I was worried since I did not have any established model to follow, and for a while, I could not achieve anything worth mentioning. However, I did not give up. I eventually gathered the construction workers in Amritsar and formed a small union, which was named the *Amarti* [Construction] Committee and had only *mazdoors* [unskilled casual labourers] as its members. Carpenters, ironsmiths and masons were not made members. Our first demand was that we should no longer be referred to as *mazdoors* but should be called *jamadaars* instead. This demand was based on the personal opinion I had formed after my experience of working in construction: that people should not be respected on the basis of their being Pathans, Syeds, Rajputs, Mughals, etc. [different castes] simply because they were born into these families; instead, respect should be allotted to those who earned it through their hard work. In fact I believed that these Pathans, Rajputs and Mughals had come from foreign countries with their armies and plundered India – some had captured lands while others collected gold and silver – and hence become landlords and wealthy people. Now my companions and I would work all day, and at night we visited the labourers' *deras* [shared residences for single male workers] and tried to win them over to our side. Most labourers were usually Hindus from the Kangra District and they failed to understand what benefit they could gain from this. Only a few workers, who were called Rajputs, were interested in this project of being called *jamadaars*. We kept demanding this for a long time, but without any success. This was quite disappointing for us. However we would call each other *jamadaar*, and other carpenters, ironsmiths and masons who worked with us would also call us that. But in the rest of the city, labourers were called just that. Therefore, the Construction Committee could not come alive. It neither had any donation or fee, nor did it require any forms. In 1930 we called a meeting of the important members of the Construction Committee and a lot of workers from Amritsar participated in it. We decided that labourers who had been laid off by their employers should be given work again and their outstanding dues would also be demanded. The Committee did not have any president or secretary, nor did it have any specific rules and regulations. I did most of the work and people often called me '*Babu*'. We would hold our meetings at the *deras*. What would happen is that one smart worker would rent a big room or hall under his name at a cost of about four or five rupees per month. Then he would allow other workers of his choice to stay with him and split the rent equally amongst everyone. In each of these residences there would be at least ten workers, and in some there would even be as many as forty. These workers usually came from outside the city and had left their wives and children behind. They would sleep on the floor as neither could they fit that many charpoys in a room, nor could they afford them. In winter, they would light a fire inside and sit around sharing their stories and smoking coconut *hookah* [pipe] till late. The smoke would blacken the walls and create cobwebs all over the ceiling. There were no shower, kitchen or bathroom attached to these rooms, and if there happened to be one, it would be in a very dirty condition. At night, they would light lamps made of round cigarette boxes and filled with kerosene oil. However, these would be lit only at times of special need. Why was this so? Because a labourer earned a daily wage of only six annas and he was not able to find work for more than ten or fifteen days per month.

Beginning of Success

Our new programme soon attracted the labourers and as our Committee's sphere of influence grew, the *Amarti* Committee and I became more famous in labour circles. We would call meetings on a rotating basis at different *deras*. Wherever we convened, the residents would arrange for tobacco and water for the guests and would also light candles and lamps. Whichever worker was removed from his job without being paid his wages would come to me to report the situation. I would then immediately take leave, dress up in clean clothes, take six or seven unemployed workers with me, and go to claim the man's wages. I would go and ask in a loud voice: 'Who has your money?' He would point at the person concerned, saying that he has kept his money. Meanwhile people would start gathering around us, asking what the argument was about. In such situations, we would receive the money eighty per cent of the time: firstly, because the money would not be a large amount, about six annas for a couple of days or maximum a week; and secondly, because these people knew in their hearts that they were deliberately committing an injustice. Based on this, the *Amarti* Committee and I became increasingly famous in Amritsar. On the other hand, my own income kept decreasing as I would take leave from work to recover the labourers' due wages, and would spend at least ten to fifteen days a month doing this. No sort of commission was ever taken for these services. My companions and I were extremely happy to be finally doing some good for the labourers. Before this, employers would normally keep the workers' money since they did not have a way of claiming it. The contractors were mostly Hindus and they habitually found ways of confiscating the workers' wages. They would cite excuses such as 'you were idle', 'you came late', 'you were smoking' or 'you went to urinate and returned late', etc., and use these to fire the workers from their job. They would say, 'take your outstanding wages some other day', and the worker would keep going to them every day until he got frustrated and found some other work, helplessly giving up his past earnings. At that time there was no law or any government official in the country that could get the labourers their rights. The labourers did not have enough courage to go to civil courts; there was also no organization for the workers that could get them their wages. When our *Amarti* Committee filled this void we became very popular and our meetings started to attract a large number of people. So much so, we started to hold our meetings at Amritsar's famous Gol Bagh at night.

The days kept passing and the year 1932 arrived. Nothing worth mentioning happened during this time. You can evaluate the *Amarti* Committee's stature and how weak my colleagues and I were, from the following incident. One day, as I was passing by a market inside Ram Bagh Gate, I saw a Pathan loan shark mistreating a lean, thin man. His teeth were bleeding. I stopped the Pathan and asked him to come to the police station with me. Bystanders also came to my aid. We grabbed hold of the Pathan and took him to the Ram Bagh police guard. The Pathan and the man stood outside while I went in. I asked the sub-inspector to punish the Pathan as he had badly injured the thin man; I told him that I had brought them both. The sub-inspector asked me who I was and what I did. I told him that I was a carpenter and a worker of the *Amarti* Committee. At this, he called a constable and said, 'Take this man to the other room and give him a massage' ['massage' here refers to a beating]. Upon asking him my fault, he swore at me, started hitting me and said: 'What business is it of yours to apprehend someone and bring him here? For your own well-being, get out of here and never do this again.' I was surprised at being made out to be a criminal when I had just been trying to help an innocent man. I was terrified and silently left the police station; I did not breathe a word of this to anyone for a long time. My confidence plummeted and I was worried for a long time because of this. Here I want to clarify that I had never encountered the police before this. This was the first time I felt fear. Before this I had never been so frightened, not even when I was fighting the British at the Ferozepur Arsenal.

Workers' and Peasants' (*Mazdoor–Kisan*) Conference

Till 1932 we did a lot of work among the labourers but could not give the organization a definitive form. In the beginning of 1933, I saw a poster on the walls of Amritsar city announcing a Workers' and Peasants' conference soon to be held at the *putli ghar* [weaving factory]. I wondered who these people were since I was under the impression that I was the only one working with labourers. The next evening I went to the office of the organizers of the conference, which was situated at Katrah Sher Singh Kehna. At the office, Sohan Singh Josh, Mohammad Tufail Khadr Captain, Bashir Ahmed Sehrai, Nisar Ahmed, Abdul Ghaffoor Taish, Hakeem Sikandar Khizar and Feroz-ud-Din Mansoor were present. I told them that I worked with the labourers of Amritsar and a carpenter myself, and that I would like to be one of the conference organizers. They looked at me with surprise and suspicion as I said all this. After listening to me they asked me to wait outside the room. After a long discussion about God knows what, they called me back in. They then asked me in detail about the labourers I worked with, when I started working, where I lived and what my father's occupation was. After that, they assigned Comrade Mohammad Tufail Khadr Captain the task of verifying these details. I took him to several *addas* [workers' hangouts] and introduced him to my various operatives. After an investigation lasting for three days, he was satisfied and informed his party that 'Bakhtiar will be beneficial for us.' And so I was inducted into the reception committee of the conference and started working with them. Truth be told, I had done more work with labourers than all the people arranging the conference, and compared to them, I had a lot more influence; but despite all that, they did not trust me. They would never include me in their discussions and I was often made to sit at the foot of the stairs to the office with instructions to not let anyone up. I later found out that they were Communists, and that even after the investigation they were afraid I might be an agent sent by the CID.

The preparations for the conference were going ahead full steam. New posters were being published which requested farmers and labourers of the entire world to unite. About three months were spent preparing for the conference. The most difficult task was to arrange for a place. We had to keep changing the venue because as soon as we announced one, that area's police would come and harass the owner of the place and make him sign a written agreement that he would not let us use his land for the conference.

Therefore, the dates for the conference were changed many times until finally, Master Tara Singh, who was the biggest leader of the Akali Party, gave us permission to hold the conference at his mansion, which was near the Khalsa College in Amritsar. Thus, the first Workers' and Peasants' conference was held in February 1933, headed by Dr Saif-ud-Din Kitchlew. On this occasion, the ceremonial waving of the red flag with the sickle and hammer was executed by Comrade Sohan Singh Josh, and all the workers present sang the following song:

> *Lehnde charhde utar dakhan jhanda laal jhulawan ge*
> *Phansi de takhte te charh ke geet aise de gaawan ge*
> *Sadiya lothan da aeh khapan is di shaan acheeri aye*
> *Maar farate jida yeh udada man wich bhare daleri aye*
> *Daro na daulatmandan koloon mano na roub ameeran de*
> *Shahenshayan nu jar tu pat diyo kholo paaj wazeeran de*
> *Siron nange haan taan ki hoya asi cho-tarfe dhawan ge*
> *Dharti keh samundar te wi jhanda laal jhulawan ge*
>
> [Getting off, getting on, north or south, we'll wave the red flag
> We'll sing its praise going to the gallows
> Its grandeur is beyond compare
> When it flies fluttering, it fills the heart with courage
> Don't be afraid of the wealthy, don't bow to the authority of the rich
> Rip out the kings from their roots, rob the ministers of their ranks
> What if we are bare-headed, we'll attack from all four sides,
> Let alone the land, we'll wave the red flag even on the seas.]

This conference was the first of its nature and I consider it the key to laying the foundation of the labour movement from Peshawar to Delhi. It is true that before this there were some labour unions operating, for example, the NWR Workers' Union, which in 1919 organized the first strike in Saharanpur and for a second time in 1925 on the North Western Railway, and was led by J.B. Miller Irish [popularly referred to as such due to his Irish roots] and M.A. Khan. The second one was the Punjab Miners' Union, which was formed in 1931 in Khewra and was led by M.A. Ghani. The third was the Postmen's Union whose leader, Munshi Willayat Ali, was also a postman. Similarly, there was the Punjab Government Printing Press Workers' Union. But these unions had no links with each other. The people who ran them did not do so with the aim of forming a strong and unified labour movement in the entire country; rather, their only goal was to alleviate the sufferings of the workers in their respective departments. However, there was a vision behind this labour conference that was brought by Comrade Sohan Singh Josh and his companions from prison, where they were held due to their involvement in the Meerut Conspiracy Case. Their mission was to bring about a revolution by uniting the labourers and farmers of the entire country, and to form a government led by these labourers and farmers.

Although this dream was never realized, one benefit of this conference was that labour now had the idea of uniting on one platform, and the various labour parties started to familiarize and associate with each other. That is why I consider this conference the beginning of the labour movement. The conference only lasted a day and only about a hundred workers participated in it. This was because on the day the conference opened, the roads leading to the venue were lined with armed police; and the word spread that there would be firing at the conference. Besides this, the workers coming to participate were threatened with various means to stop them from coming since the resolutions passed at the conference were all against the government, industrialists and landlords. The resolutions were as follows:

(1) Labourers and peasants should not get recruited in the army because all battles are fought to strengthen monarchy and especially British imperialism, and the labourers and farmers gain no benefits from them.
(2) Landlordism and feudalism should be completely abolished and the land should be distributed amongst the farmers.
(3) Fazal Ilahi Qurban, Ahsaan Ilahi and Abdul Waris, who were prisoners of the state and were being held at Muzaffargarh Jail, should be released. (Fazal Ilahi Qurban and Abdul Waris had visited Russia before their detainment.)
(4) Labourer's wage should be at least 30 rupees per month.
(5) All loans should be completely cancelled.

The conference was attended by Congress Party members Dr Saif-ud-Din Kitchlew, Hakeem Sikandar Khizar, Bawa Hakam Singh, Pundit Amarnath Vidyalankar, Master Sanpur Nanand and Bal Kishan Hali; from the Communist Party, Sohan Singh Josh, Abdul Ghafoor Taish, Feroz-ud-din Mansoor, Comrade Muhammad Tufail, Karam Singh Man Bar-at-law and Narain Singh Sindhu, who organized a 'hunger march' in America and was subsequently kicked out of the country; from the Socialist Party, Bashir Ahmed Sehrai, Muhammad Tufail Khadr Captain, Gaurbaksh Rai Bakshi and Nisar Ahmed; from the Kirti Kisan Party, Ram Muhammad Singh; and various other political leaders.

During and after this conference, I got the opportunity to meet many political leaders, which only intensified my hatred for the colonial government. I was hopeful that these leaders would work with me in the cause of labour, but, I must sadly write, this did not happen. After the conference none of these people, except for Sufi Ghulam Mohammad Turk, who was in jail at the time of the conference, and Abdul Ghafoor Taish, joined me in the labour movement. Turk and Taish did some work, but they could give very little time. The rest of the people either worked in the Congress or were focused on peasants and students. I sometimes attended peasant conferences as well. At that time these people worked more in villages as compared to cities, and mostly with students, and later even formed peasants' committees. I worked with them from 1933 to 1935 but without much progress for the labour movement. Therefore, I was always upset with these leaders as they would talk about both peasants and labourers, but in reality, would devote very little time to labour.

The 'Real' Method

In 1935 the British government decided to introduce reforms in India, as a consequence of which elections were to be held in all the provincial assemblies of India. One day, Dewan Chaman Lal Bar-at-law, along with M.A. Majid of the Meerut Conspiracy Case, J.B. Miller and M.A. Khan, who was the leader of the railway workers and founder of the labour movement, came from Lahore to see me in Amritsar. They informed me that Dewan Chaman Lal, who I had often met before regarding the labour movement, wanted to stand for elections from Amritsar, Dhariwal and Jalandhar on the labour seat. I was asked to help him and the benefit to me would be that I would be able to strengthen my movement with his money once Dewan Chaman Lal won the election. After discussing this with my companions, including Sufi Ghulam Muhammad Turk and Abdul Ghafoor Taish, we decided that we should take advantage of this opportunity. So we promised to help and rented an office in Hall Bazaar, Amritsar, the same day. After a few days M.A. Khan came, along with Railway's Chaudhry Umar Din and Khwaja Muhammad Hussain, and said that they would also help us with the election work. I had never met these two gentlemen before.

During the election work, I got the opportunity to visit those factories of Amritsar, Jalandhar and Gurdaspur that were registered under the Factories Act, because for the labour seat, the votes of these workers had to be entered in a list. The elections took place, Dewan Chaman Lal became a member of the Assembly, and I gained the benefit of individually meeting the labourers of Bannu district. Before this, due to the companionship of Sohan Singh Josh and his group, I had gained theoretical knowledge but had no awareness about the practicalities. But now I understood the real method of running a labour movement as I was in contact with Dewan Chaman Lal, M.A. Khan and J.B. Miller; these gentlemen were genuine trade unionists. In addition, I had also become familiar with factory labourers. Now I had a large, vast field in front of me and I also had good companions who included Muslim Leaguers, trade unionists, farmers, workers, Communists, Socialists and Congress members. Therefore, as compared to before, I started working with a lot more energy and vigour.

First Union

The first proper union that I created was the Narain Swadeshi Mill Workers' Union. It was situated at Chheharta in Amritsar and had approximately 500 workers. They were given no holiday in the entire week and had to work twelve hours a day without any overtime wages. After forming the union, we demanded that the labourers should work eight hours a day, receive a holiday with pay on Sundays, and receive at least thirty rupees a month as salary. The factory was the sole property of Sardar Narain Singh. When he learned about the union, whose secretary Jagat Ram Datt worked as a tailor there, he dismissed Jagat Ram Datt and other members of the union and refused to accept their demands. At this, a strike was declared at the factory. About 400 workers participated in the strike while around 100 continued to go to work. To stop those who were going to work, we started picketing against them under the supervision of the strike committee. The factory's owner called the police which came in large numbers. For the first two or three days, the picketing was peaceful and had no effect on workers who were going to work. However, such few workers could not do the entire work. Despite that, coal was burnt in the boilers to produce smoke from the chimneys and some machines were operated to put on a show. Alongside, fresh recruitment also began. The people working were delivered food from outside on time and all items of necessity were supplied to them inside the factory. We thought the strike could be successful only if the food supply to the factory was stopped. From the next day, the workers involved in the picketing started appealing to the workers taking food inside the factory to not do so, with the effect that the food could not be delivered. The next day, around eleven o'clock, when the strikers stopped the food from being taken in, a fight broke out. At this, the police engaged in violence and started a *lathi* [baton] charge, injuring many workers. The labourers retaliated in anger against the police, and many policemen and labourers were seriously injured in this conflict. Many constables' uniforms were torn; at this additional police, led by S.P. Durant, reached there and an intense *lathi* charge ensued. After this, thirty workers including myself were arrested and sent to jail under Sections 392 and 448, and a case of robbery was registered against us. In those days, Sir Sikandar Hayat Khan had taken over the ministry in Punjab and his Unionist Party had a majority in the Assembly. In competition with him was the Indian National Congress whose members occupied the opposition benches. Elections had taken place recently, and all political parties had made many promises to the public. After the news of our arrest was published in bold headlines, with many newspapers writing editorials about how labour was being persecuted under Sikandar Hayat's ministry, these parties started taking issues in their own hands to achieve their political goals. The Congress wanted to use our strike and the violence against us for propaganda against the Unionist Party, and the Unionist group wanted to solve our case and take the credit.

Therefore, on one side, Congress took up the strike issue and managed to become popular by distributing food and money as charity, while on the other, the Unionist Party appointed Nawab Shahnawaz Mamdot, Mir Maqbool, Begum Shahnawaz and Moulvi Ghulam Mohiuddin Kasoori to gain influence among us. They all came to me in jail and through their parties, proposed to arrange an agreement for us with the owner of Narain

Swadeshi Mills and to get our demands accepted. At this, the thirty-five of us held a meeting and decided that since the Unionist Party favoured the British, we would not use their power to solve our problem and that therefore, we should make our agreement through the Congress. After our decision, Nawab Mamdot came to me in jail again to try to convince me to let his party mediate the agreement but, as before, I rejected it. Meanwhile, Congress arranged for lawyers to fight our case and tried for bail, but without any success. The Unionist Party had a hand in our request for bail being rejected since they could not stand to see the Congress win this round. A few of the labourers got worried at not being able to get bail and tried to force us to work with the Unionist Party. Therefore we presented extremely harsh conditions with the motive that the Unionist Party would fail at achieving them. The conditions were as follows:

(1) The owner of Narain Swadeshi Mills, Sardar Narain Singh, who is the sole owner of the factory and lives inside the factory should shift his residence to the city and should stop visiting the factory altogether. Instead, he should appoint his son, Sardar Gurdial Singh, as Director or hire a manager to supervise the factory.
(2) Jagat Ram Datt and all other workers who were dismissed should be reinstated.
(3) No worker should be punished for the strike.
(4) The government should withdraw the cases against all the workers.
(5) Labourers should not be made to work for more than eight hours.
(6) The overtime wages should be doubled.
(7) The wages should be increased by twenty-five percent.

We thought that the first and fourth demand would not be accepted under any circumstances; but three days after presenting these conditions, we were informed that all the demands had been accepted. As far as the first condition was concerned, the Unionist government threatened Sardar Narain Singh that if he refused to accept it, the government would release the workers and provide no assistance to him. Consequently, the factory's owner accepted all the demands. We were all released from prison and the government withdrew the cases against us. The labourers held a grand celebration at Chheharta, Amritsar; those released from prison were greeted with garlands in a rally in which workers from many other mills participated. At a meeting held after the rally it was decided that the workers would return to work from the next day. The next morning, I, along with the other workers, went to the factory in the form of a rally. Precisely as we were entering the gate of the factory a truck full of Sardar Narain Singh's belongings was leaving. This fact cannot be denied, that our success would not have been possible without the Unionist Party, especially Begum Shahnawaz, Mir Maqbool and Nawab Shahnawaz Mamdot's efforts. However, the party's real motive was not to help us but to make the Congress look inferior. The Unionists thought that could win our sympathy and support by doing more for us than the Congress, and hence diminish the Congress' prestige. However, that never happened. The Congress Party's goal was to expel the British from the country, and any sensible and politically conscious individual in the country wished the same. In comparison, the Unionist Party not only supported the British but was also its creation.

My confidence was raised by this first complete and unprecedented victory, and I felt that if a handful of labourers could unite and make a factory owner give up his property, then the dream of forming a workers' and peasants' government and kicking the British out of the country could also be realized.

A Union in Every Factory

I increased the pace of my activities even more. Henceforth, I worked very hard and created a labour union in every factory. I was living in Amritsar and the factory area was situated in Chheharta, at a distance of approximately five miles from the city. I did not own a cycle or any other means of transport. The fare from Amritsar to Chheharta was only one anna but I could not afford even that because my situation was fast deteriorating. I was earning a living by working as a carpenter on construction sites. In the beginning, I would spend one week every month doing the organization's work but as these activities increased, I gave up work to do union tasks for two to three weeks every month. Therefore, my income kept decreasing as there was no question of getting money for union-related work since none of the unions took donations from any member. Although, in every union, one anna or two paisas was fixed as the monthly fees, its collection was never enforced because in the beginning neither did we have an office, nor did we pay anyone a salary.

After achieving success in the Narain Swadeshi Mills battle, the list of unions I created is as follows:

(1) Narain Swadeshi Mills Workers Union, Chheharta, Amritsar.
(2) New India Embroidery Mills Employees' Union, Chheharta, Amritsar.
(3) Lals Limited Steel and Metal Works Labour Union, Chheharta, Amritsar.
(4) Upper India Metal Works Labour Union, Cheharta, Amritsar.
(5) Surgical Dressing Manufacturing Company Labour Union, Chheharta, Amritsar.
(6) H. R. Gramophone Workers Union, Chheharta, Amritsar.
(7) Mahabir Hosiery and Textile Mills Labour Union, Chheharta, Amritsar.
(8) Indian Woollen Mills Labour Union, Chheharta, Amritsar.
(9) Amritsar Rayon and Silk Mills Labour Union, G.T. Road, Amritsar.
(10) Shambhunath Chemical Industries Labour Union, G.T. Road, Amritsar.

(11) Batala Moulders Union (Batala City). (This union included workers of fifty factories spread all over Batala.)
(12) Sawitri Textile Mills Labour Union, behind Ghee Mandi Gate, Amritsar.
(13) Mohra Textiles Mills Workers Union, Old Jail House, Amritsar.
(14) Model Woollen and Silk Mills Labour Union, Makool Sar, Amritsar.
(15) Amritsar Metal Works Labour Union, G. T. Road, Amritsar.
(16) Amritsar Distillery Company Limited Labour Union, Amritsar.
(17) Jhul Labour Union, Amritsar. (This union included workers who made hessian sacks and '*jhul*', which was put over animals.)
(18) Wagi Union Amritsar. (All the cow and buffalo herders of Amritsar were included in this.)
(19) Garhwalia Labour Union, Amritsar. (This was a union of people who worked in houses and shops. They came to work from Garhwal, and hence were called 'Ghurh walay'.)
(20) Til Cut Labour Union, Amritsar. (Amritsar was a market hub for sesame, from where it was supplied to all of India. Therefore, it had a lot of small factories where sesame was ground and cleaned. This was a union of those factories.)
(21) Zari Dozan Union, Amritsar. (Amritsar had 50–60 small factories that made cloth adornments like stars; there were a few workers in each. This was their union.)
(22) Warq Sazaan Union Amritsar. (Amritsar was a market for gold and silver lamellas from where it would be supplied all over India. There were a few small factories that were involved in this. Their workers combined to make one industrial union.)
(23) Bankeshwar Cotton Mills Labour Union, Putli Ghar, Amritsar. (Before me, Bashir Ahmed Sehrai had also worked in this factory and a strike was also held because of which Bashir Ahmad Sehrai, Nisar Ahmad, Muhammad Tufail and various other workers were jailed. But they had not created a formal union.)
(24) Cloth Hawkers Union, Amritsar.
(25) Bahishti Union, Amritsar.
(26) Municipal Workshop Labour Union, Amritsar.
(27) Central Workshop Labour Union, Amritsar. (Central Workshop was a government-owned factory and about 2,000 people worked in it.)
(28) Punjab Rubber Works Labour Union, Amritsar.
(29) Amritsar Labour Federation, Amritsar. (Almost all of Amritsar's labour unions were affiliated to this.)
(30) Pawa Kharadia Union, Amritsar. (Charpoy legs were sent from Amritsar to all of Punjab and NWFP, and their small-scale factories were spread all over Amritsar. All their workers united to form this industrial union.)
(31) Central Government Saddle Works Employees Union, Amritsar.

(The central government had created this factory in Amritsar to make leather goods for the army. This was its workers' union).

(32) Bharat Cloth Manufacturing Company Labour Union, Amritsar.

(33) O.C.M. and East India Carpet Factory Labour Union, Amritsar. (This company was formed by some Britishers of the East India Company. This was a union of its workers.)

(34) Shop Assistant Union, Amritsar. (This union included those accountants who worked in shops.)

(35) Chabeel Das Industry Labour Union, Weerkah.

(36) Tandoor Workers Union, Amritsar. (This union included all the workers who made bread at hotels, shops or '*tandoor*' ovens.)

(37) Cinema Operators Union, Amritsar.

(38) Punjab Motor Drivers and Cleaners Union Amritsar. (This union included all the drivers and cleaners of Punjab's buses, lorries and trucks. I was its general secretary, Muhammad Abdullah its vice-president and M.A. Khan was its president.)

(39) Anjuman Baykaraan-e-Punjab, Lahore. (I, along with Sitaram Bharti, founded this organization. It was based in Lahore and in those days, unemployment had reached unprecedented levels. Our demand was that the government should provide an unemployment allowance to the unemployed and create jobs for them. Sitaram and I visited all the cities of Punjab in this regard but most of the activities took place in Lahore. Here we would also hold conferences and conduct rallies. Once, late Maulana Zafar Ali Khan published a poem about us on the first page of *Zamindar*:

Executive Committee of the Hydroelectric Central Labour Union (Simla).
Front row, right to left: Chaudhry Niaz Ali, K.N. Nanda, Bashir Ahmed Bakhtiar (president), R.L. Bashir, H.U. Mirza, Sardar Daula Singh. *Back row, right to left*: K.C. Mehta, Muhammad Ibrahim, C.L. Sakuha, Sheikh Abdul Rahim, Muhammad Rafiq, Jaswant Rai, Sheikh Bashir Ahmad, Bashir Ahmad

Aa pohanche bhai aa pohanche
Pet ke bhooke aa pohanche.
[They have arrived, they have arrived,
Those with empty stomachs have arrived.]

(40) Barsati Nala (Rain Gutter) Labour Union, Amritsar. (This was a union of those who worked in the gutters near and around Amritsar.)
(41) Construction Workers' Committee, Amritsar. (This committee included carpenters, ironsmiths, masons, etc. It was created by Mistry Zia-ud-Din and me.)
(42) Amritsar Sweepers Union, Amritsar. (Allah Rakha Chaman and I created this union, and because of the strike initiated by this union, I was jailed.)
(43) Jawala Flour Mills Labour Union, Amritsar.
(44) Bhargava Glass Factory, Putli Ghar, Amritsar.
(45) Punjab Hydroelectric Central Labour Union.
(46) Punjab Hydroelectric Sub Union.
(The last two were unions of the government's power sector workers. Members of the Central Union were groundsmen, line men, bus drivers, fitters, coolies, etc., and members of the Sub Union were the superintendents, test inspectors and various senior subordinate members. Their geographic spread extended from Jugandarnagar to Lyallpur, Qasur and Ferozepur.)
(47) All-India Postmen, R.M.S. and Lower Grade Staff Union. (I became a part of this organization, which was older, in 1942. I was selected as the president of its Amritsar district union the same year. In 1943, I was made the general secretary of the union for the Punjab province and vice-president of the all-India Union. The All-India Postmen R.M.S. and Lower Grade Staff conference was held in Amritsar in 1945 and I was made its chairman. I was a member of the strike committee which held a strike that extended all over India in 1946.)

Besides these, I created many other organizations and hence kept working towards strengthening the labour union.

Amritsar Labour Federation

Amritsar Labour Federation, which has been mentioned before, was the result of cooperation between labour unions of more than 70 factories. Its president was Dewan Chaman Lal Bar-at-law, MLA, Punjab and its senior vice-president was Sufi Ghulam Muhammad Turk, who was one of the founders of the *Hijrat* movement and had worked against the British in Afghanistan. Abdul Ghafoor Taish was the junior vice-president, who was a clerk at the Municipal Committee in Amritsar. I was nominated as the general secretary. The secretary was Jagat Ram Datt with Harchan Singh and Rakhi Kishan as joint secretaries. The treasurer's post was awarded to Gopal Das Sehgal, a friend of Dewan Chaman Lal who, although a businessman, had worked with complete honesty and loyalty among the labourers. Miss Mumtaz Shahnawaz also joined this Federation after returning from Europe, and for two-and-a-half years she worked as a dedicated member. She would come from Lahore to Amritsar by train and after working all day, would return to Lahore in the evening, bearing the travel expenses herself.

Miss Mumtaz Shahnawaz was given the position of chief organizer in the Federation. She gave excellent speeches, would educate the workers regarding organizing unions and would also tell us a lot about European labour unions. After working for almost four years, she resigned because of ideological differences.

Workers from various factories of Amritsar taking out a procession, organized by the Amritsar Labour Federation, through a bazaar in Amritsar.

Amritsar Labour Federation is what gave birth to the labour movement. This Federation was formed soon after the country's general election and according to its mandate, various small and large-scale strikes were orchestrated for different purposes. Amritsar still has a branch of this organization, however, it is not the same as before.

Study Circle

In 1936, study circles were formed to create awareness among workers regarding the labour movement. At that time, labourers had no idea why or how a labour movement is run. Therefore, study circles created in the industrial areas of Amritsar educated the workers about labour movements. I would choose workers to be part of the study circle, giving preference to the secretary, president and other post holders of various labour unions.

In the beginning, Faiz Ahmed Faiz, Professor Mohib from MAO College, Ramesh Chandar Jai Gopal M.A. and the Punjab Finance Commissioner's son Danial Latifi, would teach the labourers. After a while, Madam Mumtaz Shahnawaz, who had obtained her education in Britain, took the educational responsibilities in her hands. Every morning, she would come from Lahore to Amritsar via train and after working all day, would return to Lahore in the evening, bearing all the travelling expenses herself. Other than this, Madam Mumtaz Shahnawaz also worked as an organizer for the Amritsar Labour Federation for two and a half years.

The study circle proved to be very beneficial. The workers of various unions gained an understanding of labour movements because of it; it also created a political conscience amongst them. Due to this, they were much better equipped to perform their organizational responsibilities.

Indian Federation of Labour

After World War II started in 1939, the labour movement in India was split in two sections. One section continued to be affiliated with the Indian Trade Union Congress and the other founded the Indian Federation of Labour. This separation was caused by the differences in opinion amongst the various leaders regarding the Second World War.

At that time, the labour movement in the subcontinent included, other than trade unionists, communists, socialists, Congress Party members, American Ghadar Party workers, who were called the Kirti Kisan Party in India, and companions of M.N. Roy who were called Royists. All of them worked in the Indian Trade Union Congress at that time. When World War II broke out, the Indian National Congress began the Non-Cooperation movement against Britain and preached to the Indian people against recruitment into the British army. Communists, socialists and some trade unionists agreed with this verdict of the Congress: since the war was being fought to protect imperialism/colonialism, the Indian people should not participate in it. However, M.N. Roy disagreed and announced that since Hitler was a dictator, he was sure to attack socialist Russia and hence this was a people's war. His prediction turned out to be true later on as Germany, after capturing various European countries, went on to attack Russia. Consequently, Russia, Britain and America united, and Germany, Japan and Italy were no match for the Allies. When Germany attacked Russia, the socialists and communists, who were being held at Deoli camp, declared the war a 'people's war', on the basis of which the British government released them.

Because of the ideological differences resulting from international developments, M.N. Roy organized a convention of like-minded labour leaders at Delhi in 1941. At this convention, it was decided that an organization separate from the Indian Trade Union Congress should be formed. Therefore, an organization was established by the name of Indian Federation

Seated, right to left: Bashir Ahmed Bakhtiar, J.B. Miller.
Standing, right to left: Satar Shah, Ashrah Ali Shah, Sheikh Muhammad Ashraf

of Labour. Jamnadas Mehta, who was a member of the Central Assembly at the time, was selected as the Federation's president. The general secretary was M.N. Roy, the vice president was M.A. Khan, and the secretaries of finance were A.K. Mukherji and Mrs. Ellen Roy. The advisors and executive mentors were M.A. Khateeb, Khwaja Muhammad Hussain, Umar Din, Mr Munkar, Rajni Mukarjee, Mr Mathur, J.B. Miller and myself – Bashir Ahmed Bakhtiar. The second conference of the Federation was held at Mochi Gate in Lahore in 1942; here the demand for an inflation allowance was raised for the first time and was accepted by the government.

From 1941 to 1947, M.A. Khan, J.B. Miller, M.A. Khateeb, Chaudhary Umar Din, Khwaja Muhammad Hussain, Sufi Ghulam Muhammad Turk and I worked in the Indian Federation of Labour. In 1948, after the creation of Pakistan, a conference of the Federation's workers was called in Karachi, at which the name of the Federation was changed to the Pakistan Federation of Labour; M.A. Khan was selected as its first president and M.A. Khateeb as its first general secretary. I was chosen as an executive member.

In 1948, there were only two federations in Pakistan. One was the Pakistan Federation of Labour with M.A. Khan as president, M.A. Khateeb as general secretary and I, Bashir Ahmed Bakhtiar, along with Chaudhary Umar Din and Khwaja Muhammad Hussain, as executive members. All the people in it were apolitical and only trade unionists. The second federation, called the Mazdoor Federation, had Fazal Ilahi Qurban as its leader. Its members included extremist socialists and communists. At that time, except for these two, there were no other federations in Pakistan.

The Weavers' Plight

After starting work at Chheharta, Amritsar, I also began union work at the *khadi* factories in Amritsar. Having heard about the strikes at Narain Swadeshi Mills and New India Embroidery Mills, Ferozuddin, also known as Dr Jalal Puri, and Sultan, also known as Kulu Weaver, who worked at handmade *khadi* factories, came to me from the city and suggested that I form a union in these factories as well. There were about 50,000 workers in these factories in Amritsar alone, and they were facing numerous problems, some of which are listed below:

(1) The Factories Act was not being followed at all.
(2) A labourer was normally made to work from twelve to fourteen hours without any pay for overtime.
(3) No compensation was given in case of an accident.
(4) Two paisas were cut from the salary or wage of every worker in the name of [*dharam*?] account.
(5) If a worker's weekly wage was six rupees and one anna or six rupees and fifteen annas, he would only be paid rupees six, meaning that any paisas or annas would not be given to him.
(6) The wages for cloth were paid per yard, which would normally be

according to the following principle. Twenty to thirty tablet for shirts would get seven annas per yard, and 64/2 and 64/3 tablet for coats would get one anna per yard as wages. One weaver, after working for twelve to fourteen hours a day, could make twenty or thirty yards of shirts and eight or nine yards of coats in a day.

(7) Weavers were only paid per yard. Any knots above the yard mark were not compensated for.

(8) If there was even a slight mark in the entire batch, the worker's wages would be cut for the whole batch. Often in the name of compensation for the loss, the worker would not be paid for his work.

(9) The cloth made in the factory would be loaded on the heads of the labourers, to be carried to the shops. The workers were paid no additional money for this.

(10) The wages of the *mehtars* who were hired to clean the factories were paid from the labourers' salaries.

(11) Weavers had to live inside the factories and were not even allowed to leave at night. They were not given rooms or houses in the factories but instead a veranda was made on a portion of the roof for them to stay in winters, and in summers, they would sleep on the open roof. Their entire luggage would also be on this veranda. Their luggage would normally be old and dilapidated beds and flour canisters. The only clothes they owned would be the ones on their back.

Why were the labourers treated like this? There were reasons for it. Firstly, there were few laws for the welfare of labourers. At that time, there were only the Factories Act and Trade Union Act and there was no department for their implementation. For all of Punjab, there was one Chief Inspector of Factories under the Director of Industries, Punjab, whose office was in Lahore. There were four superintendents of industries who held the position of Additional Factories Inspector. However, they did not have the power to inspect a factory without getting written permission from the Chief Inspector of Factories fifteen days prior to the inspection. Consequently, any time they received a complaint of misdemeanour towards workers or a request from workers against any injustice in the factory, they could not inspect the factory on the same day; instead, they would first have to write to the Chief Inspector of Factories to grant them permission for inspection. The Chief Inspector would give permission and select a date, and the inspection could be carried out only on that fixed date. Why was it like this? Because the Chief Inspector of Factories at the time was a Britisher, Mr W. Abel, and it was infamously known that he took a monthly bribe from the factory owners in return for the guarantee that he would not let them be fined according to the Factories Act. When he gave permission for inspection to the Additional Inspector of Factories, he would also alert the respective factory owner so that he could shut the factory on time that day and not force overtime work. Hence, the factory owners avoided any problem. Normally, the Additional Inspectors also received bribes from them. At that time, there was no labour department for the provinces. The labour department was formed in 1952 in Pakistan, after a resolution was passed to create it at one of the labour conferences in Punjab. The Chief Minister of Punjab at the time, Mian Mumtaz Daultana, created the labour department and Shehzada Alamgir was appointed the first Labour Commissioner. The first Punjab tripartite labour conference was held on 3 and 4 May 1952 in Lahore. Syed Ali Hussain Shah Gardazi was the Minister of Labour at the time. At his request, the Chief Minister of Punjab, Mian Mumtaz Muhammad Khan Daultana, inaugurated this conference.

My Initial Method

The procedure I would follow in the initial days of the labour movement was that I would plan a meeting, then make the posters or advertisements for the meeting, carry the bundle of posters on my shoulders with a bucket of glue in one hand to the working-class neighbourhoods at two, three in the morning, and put thc posters on the walls. During daytime, I would go everywhere in a *tonga* (horse-drawn carriage) with a drum and announce the meeting by the beat of the drum. At night I would carry carpets, tables and chairs on my shoulders, and transport them to the venue of the meeting. At the meeting I would deliver the speeches and afterwards would carry the equipment back to the office, sometimes with the help of other workers who had attended the meeting.

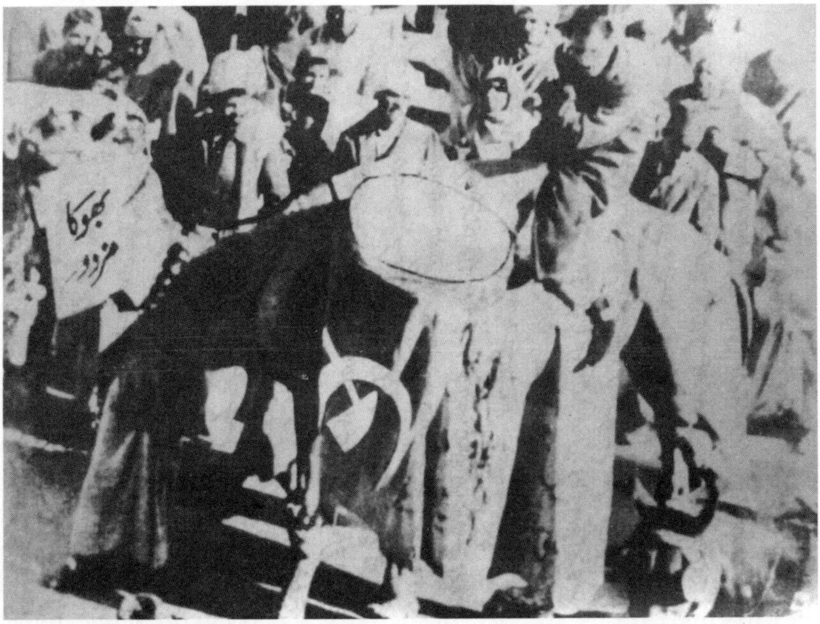

Bashir Ahmed Bakhtiar rallying workers while astride a camel; the placard says: 'hungry labourer' (*bhookha mazdoor*)

I had found a new way to draw peoples' attention to me. I would take a large red sheet with a sickle and hammer sign on it, along with the labour demands, and drape it on a camel. On either side of the camel's neck, I would hang large pieces of cardboard with the words '*bhookha mazdoor*' [hungry labourer] written on them. Then I would tie the drum on the camel and ride it into factory area and would start beating the drum. Workers and the general populace would gather in droves to watch this new sight. Then, while sitting on the camel, I would give speeches for half an hour. This way I would travel to ten or twenty places a day and address rallies while sitting on the camel. These speeches were normally against the government and factory owners, and the people would listen to them patiently.

I was constantly preoccupied with the affairs of the labour movement and got very little leisure time to earn my own living. My situation was hence worse than the labourers I was fighting this battle for. My family's financial situation was also bad in those days. I would normally bring spearmint, pomegranate grain, salt, spices, flour and wood, and my wife, child and I would eat just bread with a *chutney* [a kind of sauce]. Milk, cooking oil, pulses and meat were for rare occasions. This was a time when my activities had gained such momentum that to maintain peace and order, the government was forced to place a police guard constantly in Amritsar's industrial area of Chheharta. Whichever factory I went to, the workers would give me milk, tea and fruits out of respect. But I would never accept these things, and would simply eat some gram and drink water from street taps. Even if I got thirsty in the factory I would never drink water from the factory taps.

There were no beds in my house. In the summer we would make do with the charpoy but in winters that was impossible. Therefore, Fazal Din, who was a laid-off labourer and worked with me, would be instructed to collect dry grass from the market which the shopkeepers took out of boxes and throw away. We would spread this grass in the rooms. We owned only one blanket. At night my wife, son, later on my daughter and I would all lie on the grass and cover ourselves sideways with this blanket. That condition used to be so strange: if I straightened my legs, they would stick out of the blanket and I would wake up because of the cold, and would have to curl my legs again so that I could go to sleep. This situation continued for about five years. It changed after five years because a landlord, Sardar Gurbaksh Singh, decided to stand for the Lyallpur Municipal Committee elections. Our party decided that some workers from Lahore and Amritsar should go and help him. So Sufi Ghulam Muhammad Turk, Abdul Ghafoor Taish, Harchan Singh, Fazal Ilahi Qurban and I, along with some other workers, went to Lyallpur and started working for Sardar Gurbaksh Singh. There the workers held a meeting and decided that a blanket and thick bedding should be procured for Bakhtiar. This is how my household got an additional blanket and bedding, and winter nights became tolerable.

Once, I fell seriously ill. The doctors were of the opinion that because of poor diet my intestines had been damaged, and I needed complete rest and a good diet. At this the party held a meeting in which Comrade Karam Singh Maan Bar-at-law, Sufi Ghulam Muhammad Turk, Abdul Ghafoor Taish, Comrade Sohan Singh Josh and various other top leaders participated, and decided that I should be sent to Gulmarg, Kashmir, for a month. A grant of twenty rupees was allotted for this purpose. This amount covered the travelling costs. A letter was written to the *mahant* of the *gurdwara* at Gulmarg to arrange for my residence in the *gurdwara*, and to provide me with good food donated at the *gurdwara*. Therefore, for about a month I lived at the *gurdwara* in Gulmarg, Kashmir and ate their '*karha parshaad*', due to which my health improved and I returned to Amritsar and resumed work with renewed vigour. At a difficult time, my companions and the *gurdwara*'s food came to my rescue; otherwise my situation was so bad that it would have been impossible to arrange for medicine and food to improve my health.

Strike: At Model Woollen and Silk Mills

To get the existence of the labour movement acknowledged, it was important to organize many strikes successively. In order to attain this objective, I orchestrated thousands of strikes between 1935 and 1947, many of which were on a very large scale. A few of these major strikes are worth mentioning and their details will follow.

Model Woollen Mills, Amritsar, was the property of two brothers, Lala Kedar Nath and Lala Amar Nath. Around 300 labourers worked in this factory. Three strikes were held here for various reasons and each of them was fairly long.

The first union was created in this factory in 1936 with Sardar Teja Singh as its first general secretary. We faced many problems in the creation of this union. There was no holiday the entire week in the factory and even the working hours were not fixed. The work would start before sunrise and the factory would shut only after sunset. Because of this, approaching the workers and holding a meeting with them was extremely difficult. After a lot of reflection, what I started doing was that after sunset I would go stand at a slight distance outside the factory's gate and when the workers were leaving for the day I would ask them: 'What are your wages? Why are you not given a holiday on Sunday? Why are you fined so much money?' Then I would advise them to form a union so that a solution to their problems could be found through unity. However, at that time the workers knew nothing about labour unions and hence would ignore what I was saying, and there would be no result. Then I started talking to the workers on their way to work before sunrise and I would ask them questions regarding their difficulties at work, as follows:

(1) There were no holidays in the week.
(2) The labourers were made to work for twelve to thirteen hours every day, and were paid for only eight hours.
(3) There was no compensation for overtime work.
(4) The wages were very low.
(5) If even a small portion of cloth got damaged in the making, the worker was not paid for the entire yard. Sometimes the entire cost of the thread and colours etc. of the cloth were cut from the labourer's wage even though the factory owner kept it.

After three to four months of hard work, I finally managed to unite some like-minded workers and formed a union, which was named the 'Model Woollen and Silk Mills Labour Union', and its officials were selected in the dark of the night at a *gurdwara*. Later, we would hold our labour meetings at the same *gurdwara*. Sardar Teja Singh, who also worked as a weaver at the factory, was nominated as the union's secretary. A delegation of three people was formed including Sardar Teja Singh, and was assigned the responsibility of presenting the union's demands to Lala Kedar Nath. Therefore, the next day this delegation went to Lala Kedar Nath and Amar Nath in the factory office, and told them that they were union representatives and had been selected by the factory workers to present the demands of the labourers. Lala Kedar Nath got angry and asked Teja Singh: 'Who are you to take on the task of representation?' Teja Singh replied that he was the secretary of the Model Woollen and Silk Mills Labour Union. At this Kedar Nath said: 'We are the owners of the mill, how can you be the secretary of our mill?' Teja Singh replied that he was the union's and not the factory's secretary. Kedar Nath cursed and said he did not recognize any union in his factory, and with that he called a *chaprasi* and told him to kick Teja Singh and the others out of the office. Hence, they got kicked out of the factory.

They came straight to the Amritsar Labour Federation's office where I was waiting for them. I asked them what had happened: 'Was there any good news?' Teja Singh replied sadly that they had got the reward for making a union: 'We all got fired from our jobs and also faced humiliation.' I comforted them and said that we would hold a meeting at night to decide the next step. That evening, after sunset, the workers of Model Mills started coming to the Labour Federation's office because they had all found out that their representatives had been thrown out of the mill. The meeting continued for a long time into the night, and all the workers took an oath that if Teja Singh and the other representatives did not get their jobs back, none of them would go back to work. Sufi Ghulam Mohammad Turk and I were assigned the task of meeting with Lala Kedar Nath the next morning and getting the union officials their jobs back.

Accordingly, the next day we went to the factory and met with Lala Kedar Nath and Amar Nath. I informed them that I was the general secretary of the Amritsar Labour Federation and Sufi was the vice president.

We said that we had come to get the union officials their jobs back. Secondly, they should accept the union of their mill's workers. At that time there was no law regarding the acceptance of unions. The two brothers were extremely angry; they said that they did not recognize any Labour Federation or union and kicked us out. All the factory workers had their eyes on us; some were standing outside the door to overhear our conversation and were reporting it back to all the workers. After getting out we informed the workers that there would be a meeting at the *gurdwara*'s pond that night. Therefore, that night a meeting was held at the *gurdwara* where candles were lit to provide light. In the meeting it was decided that a strike be declared in the morning and all the workers were asked to take an oath to adhere to this decision. However, the mill owners found out about the proposed strike and they started going to the labourers' houses at night. The *mistris* were given money, and they were coaxed and bribed in various ways to go to work. Consequently, the next day, about half the workers went to work while the other half went on strike. The factory kept functioning and the owners called in a heavy police force and positioned them all around the factory. We were extremely disappointed that our members had failed to respect their oath. At night a meeting was held of the workers who were striking. It was decided that the next morning we would picket outside the factory gate. According to the plan, picketing began the next morning. The workers going inside were pleaded with to not do so, but to no effect; two days were spent like this. For these two days the police did not behave badly.

On the third day we found out that Lala Kedar Nath had bribed the policemen because early in the morning, all of them were seen smoking good quality cigarettes and they kept getting tea and pastries from the factory. That day the police was harsh. The sub-inspector ordered that the picketers should stand at least ten feet away from the factory's gate and they were not allowed to talk to the workers going inside. That day many labourers went to work because, on the one hand, the police was being strict, and on the other, the factory owners were bribing the workers in various ways and persuading them to go back to work. That night we decided in a meeting that our current method would not lead to the strike's success and so we should change it. We should stop following police orders and picket near the factory's gate. Therefore, from the fourth day, we started to follow this plan. At this, the police became angry and started pushing the picketers away from the gate; but the picketers kept returning to the same spot. One police constable became extremely angry; this constable, Shahbaz Khan with a big moustache and ID number 222, pushed a picketer and started kicking him. When the other picketers saw that a fellow-picketer was being beaten, they all descended upon the constable. They beat him up, so much so that his uniform tore. In the meanwhile, the in-charge sub-inspector reached the spot and gave orders for a *lathi* charge. When the baton charge started, even those labourers who had just been watching initially got provoked and they started pelting the police with stones. At this, police from the *kotwali* was sent for and a *lathi* charge took place again, which injured many labourers. The injured labourers were brought to the office of the Amritsar Labour Federation. After their injuries were bandaged there, they lay down on bullock carts and a rally was taken out in the major bazaars of Amritsar. At the end of the rally, a meeting was held in Jallianwala Bagh, in which thousands of workers from Amritsar city and Chheharta participated. Speeches were made against the police and the factory owners. Other workers, besides those belonging to the Model Woollen Mills, offered their services for picketing, and it was decided that from the next day the picketing would become more severe. Next morning, hundreds of workers arrived at the factory gates for picketing. The beating of the previous day had made the workers more sympathetic towards their companions; so, from among those who were going to work previously, only a handful continued to do so. Labour throughout the city was more spirited. The police sub-inspector and constables responsible for the previous day's wrongdoing had been replaced by new officers. Now the attitude of the police had softened.

After these disturbances a meeting of the Amritsar Textiles Manufacturers' Association was held. Dewan Chand Mehra was the secretary of the Association. At the meeting, Lala Kedar Nath said that since he could not take on the union and the Federation, he would accept the union's demands. However, the other members decided that the labour movement should be nipped in the bud; otherwise it would create problems for all the factories. Therefore, according to our information, all the factories collected about one lakh rupees to make the strike unsuccessful and also decided that, irrespective of which factory he was from, any labourer found picketing would not only be fired from his job, but also no other factory owner would hire him again. This order was printed and notices were put up in all the factories. On the other hand, the Amritsar Labour Federation started holding meetings every day at Jallianwala Bagh where the current situation would be analysed and new plans formulated. When the news spread that the factory owners had united, the labourers became even more passionate in their resolve to retaliate forcefully and unite against the factory owners; they figured that if the capitalists could unite, so could they. It was decided that from the next day onwards, a group of workers from different factories would picket outside the gate of Model Woollen and Silk Mills, and even if one worker was fired from his job all the workers of that factory would resign in protest. After this decision, a meeting was held every night at Jallianwala Bagh where workers from a factory would put down their names for picketing the next day and they would start picketing the next morning. This way the factory shut down completely. Later, when some supervisors started sneaking into the factory at night to do work, the picketing continued through the night. Therefore, workers from different factories would picket every day. Two factory owners fired workers who were involved in picketing, at which all the workers of the respective factories quit their work as had previously been decided; hence those two factories shut down.

The meetings at Jallianwala Bagh continued with thousands of increasingly enthusiastic labourers participating in them. What acted as a catalyst was the realization that if the industrialists could unite against labour, the latter could do the same. Hundreds of workers would present themselves for picketing every day. The selected workers would go to their factory owners a day in advance and demand their balance dues, since the following day they would picket and hence be fired according to the industrialists' agreement. At the same time, the other workers of the factory would also demand their balance payments and the factory would shut down the same day. Now that factories which had nothing to do with the conflict started suffering losses, their Association was forced to take back its decision. This was a huge success for the labour movement. Labour gained more confidence after having witnessed the result of unity. The number of labourers attending the Jallianwala Bagh meetings started increasing. Now a factory's workers would go for picketing every day and would not be fired as a consequence, since the factory owners no longer had an objection to their activities. Labour gained encouragement and the belief that the industrialists could do nothing in the face of a strong labour movement. The picketing continued for thirty-two days. Even though the factory had shut down in the initial days, the day and night picketing continued so that Lala Kedar Nath could not take the cloth already made and supply it to the dealers.

The dealers had a conditional agreement with the factory owners that if they did not receive the order on time, the owners would have to pay compensation. That is why we did not let the cloth leave the factory so that Lala Kedar Nath would have to pay a heavy compensation. We received complete information regarding the orders from the factory clerks. Lala Kedar Nath became extremely worried because, firstly, the factory was closed, and secondly, the season for selling the ready goods was ending. He and his brother, Amar Nath, tried very hard to enter the factory, but the picketing was so strong that they could not succeed. Only the watchmen were allowed to enter; the owners or their relatives were not allowed to do so. Finally, one day, they sent their two sisters to the factory to retrieve some money and papers, and the first night they succeeded to some extent; but that night we approached Atma Devi and Bibi Kartar Kaur who worked in the Akali movement, and after explaining the entire situation, asked for their help. The next morning, they took a faction of Akali women to the factory gate. This day too, Lala Kedar Nath's sisters came and attempted to enter the factory, but the group of women interfered. At first they were asked nicely but soon the situation degenerated into a brawl, at which Lala's sisters panicked and went back; thus this attempt also failed.

Lala Kedar Nath was completely discouraged, but the Association kept pressurizing him to stand firm and finish the labour movement. Lala Kedar Nath became distrustful of these people as they were the same who had withdrawn their decision against the picketing labourers. He now understood that the other industrialists wanted to make him the scapegoat while running their own factories comfortably. Therefore, one day, Lala Kedar Nath and his brother Amar Nath suddenly came to the Amritsar Labour Federation's office. They put the factory keys in front of me, begged for forgiveness, and said that they would hire secretary Teja Singh and the other workers if only we would let the factory operate again. It was decided then that the factory would reopen the next day and all the labourers would go back to work. At night, a grand meeting was held at Jallianwala Bagh, where the success of the strike was announced. The next morning, all the workers gathered in front of the Amritsar Labour Federation's office and

Sister Kartar Kaur and Sister Atma Devi picketing in front of Model Woollen and Silk Mills

proceeded to the Model Woollen and Silk Mills in the form of a rally. Teja Singh was right in front, with me and Sufi Muhammad on his right and left. Every labourer was wearing a garland. Throughout, everyone chanted slogans of 'Long live revolution', 'Long live labour unity' and 'Long live Amritsar Labour Federation'. Lala Kedar Nath Singh was waiting at the factory's gate to welcome us. Here I gave a speech in which I said that our battle was one of principle, which is now over. We did not have a personal argument with the factory owners. The principle has been accepted, and now all the labourers should work hard and improve their performance. After this, the labourers entered the factory, chanting slogans of 'Long live labour unity' and 'Long live Lala Kedar Nath', and started work.

It is important to mention here that the union and the Federation had no funds which could be used to help the labourers who had been fired for the strike. The unemployed labourers got lentils and bread from the Sikh *gurdwara*, Baba Tal, which was nearby. That can also be termed as one of the reasons of the success. Another reason was that the police violence created unimaginable passion in the labourers, because of which not only did the workers, who had earlier given in to the factory owners' sweet talk, leave work, but the entire city's labour stood shoulder to shoulder as well. In this strike, leaders of the Indian National Congress, Hakeem Sikandar Khizar, Pundit Amar Nath Vidyalankar and Dr Sanath Ram Seth, also greatly assisted us.

Strike: At Daulat Ram Weaving Factory

Daulat Ram Weaving Factory was at Tokrian Wala (Basket Makers) Market in Amritsar. There was only handmade *khadi* at this factory. The strike at Model Woollen and Silk Mills had just finished when the issue of wages came up here. I tried to explain to the factory owner, Lala Daulat Ram, that fighting with labour would not be beneficial for him. I urged him to look at Lala Kedar Nath and Amar Nath's example, and how they had to bend to labour's wish after suffering a loss of millions of rupees. Therefore, he should not let the issue exacerbate and should increase the workers' wages immediately. Lala Daulat Ram replied that Lala Kedar Nath may have given in to labour's will and accepted the union, but he would neither accept the union nor give in to the demands, no matter what we did. At this, we decided to call a strike. Lala Daulat Ram gave money to some of the labourers and convinced them to join his side; he arranged for their boarding and lodging inside the factory. On the other hand, we started picketing outside the factory. One of the factory's weavers, Nawab Din, would recite excellent poems. He wrote poems about the persecution in the factory and recited them outside the factory's gate at which a large crowd would gather; it was a festive atmosphere. Every morning, the picketing labourers would gather outside the Amritsar Labour Federation's office and go to the factory in the form of a rally while reciting poems. After picketing all day, they would return also as a rally, reciting poems throughout. Those who were working in the factory against the union's decision would stay inside all day and would leave the premises at night only after the picketers had left. There was no effect on the factory after a week's picketing. Therefore, we decided to picket at night as well. Now we formed two groups of picketers, one to picket during the day and the other at night. The day and night picketing had continued only for three days when Lala Ram had to shut down the factory. He put a lock on the factory's gate with a notice which said that the factory had permanently shut down. The picketing continued for two, three days after the lockdown, but it was useless since neither the factory owner nor any of his workers came to the factory now.

Our efforts seemed to have been in vain and I was worried because I had been comforting the labourers for many days now by saying that if they continued the picketing the factory owner would have to give in to them. But now, after seeing the lock on the gate, the workers started losing hope and they questioned me regarding the next step. After a lot of reflection, I devised a plan and presented it to the labourers. Everyone agreed with my suggestion. The plan was to find out the address of Daulat Ram's son-in-law, to whom his daughter had recently been married, and picket outside his house. Therefore, one day at ten in the morning, we reached the house of Daulat Ram's son-in-law carrying a drum and red flags which said 'Oppressed workers of Daulat Ram's factory', etc. At that time, there were no men in the house, only women. We started shouting slogans of 'Death to Lala Daulat Ram', 'Death to those who suck the blood of labourers' and 'Long live revolution'. After shouting the slogans we started blowing the bugle, at which hundreds of passers-by gathered and the women climbed on to the roofs of their houses to witness the situation. The bugle would be blown for ten to fifteen minutes, after which poems would be recited against the factory owner. After short intervals, I would stand on a stool and give a speech.

> Brothers and sisters! Lala Daulat Ram, whose daughter's house is in front of us, is sitting on the labourers' wages. The luxurious lifestyle that he enjoys is all because of the sweat and blood of the workers. We have brought our complaints to the brothers and sisters of this neighbourhood. You should speak to Lala Daulat Ram's daughter and ask her to talk to her father to stop this oppression and give these poor labourers their wages.

This had a very positive effect. All the women who used to socialize with Daulat Ram's daughter went to her house, and all those who were against her started talking against the entire family in groups: that the father had given so much gold, silver and clothes at the wedding and it was all from the labourers' exploitation; these people are not rich, but are in fact thieves and robbers, etc. Women would ask the mother-in-law whether or not it was true that the girl's father had run away with the labourers' money. The daughter was extremely worried because she did not know how to respond to these accusations. Her in-laws too were worried and embarrassed because she was causing them humiliation. In about four hours, the news spread in all of Amritsar that labourers were picketing outside Lala Ram's daughter and son-in-law's house because he had run away with their money. The news of this entire situation reached Daulat Ram's son-in-law and he immediately went to Lalaji and brought him to the house. As soon as he reached, Lalaji put the factory's keys in front of me and said, 'Go run the factory, I accept all the labour demands.' At this, we started chanting slogans of 'Long live labour unity', 'Long live revolution' and 'Long live Lala Daulat Ram'. We reached the factory while shouting these slogans and started work.

It is worth mentioning that during the strike, a police squad would be with us every day but it never interfered in our affairs. Even when we started picketing outside Lala Daulat Ram's son-in-law's house instead of the factory, they did not interfere. The reason was that labour was now organized and the police had seen the result of the baton charge outside Model Woollen and Silk Mills during the picketing.

General Strike: At the Textile Mills of Amritsar

In 1937, the Amritsar Labour Federation, with myself as general secretary, Dewan Chaman Bar-at-law as president and Sufi Ghulam Muhammad Turk as vice-president, orchestrated a general strike to increase the labourers' wages. This strike continued for one month and fourteen days; labour from about 120 small and large factories participated in it. The largest factory among these was Bankeshwar Cotton Mills with about 2,000 workers. Collectively, more than 30,000 labourers participated in this strike. During the strike, there was daily picketing in front of approximately 50 factories. Amongst the picketers, about 500 workers, including myself, were arrested and sentenced to different jails for punishment. Some were sent to Amritsar Jail, some to Gurdaspur Jail and about 300, including myself, were sent to Lahore Central Jail. After two months everyone except me was released. During this strike, labour did not use any violence and remained completely peaceful. For the labour involved in the strike, which included Hindus, Sikhs, Muslims and Christians, there was free food distribution at Jallianwala Bagh where separate food was cooked for Hindus and Sikhs, and Muslims and Christians. Every day, about fourteen bags of flour and two *degs* [cauldrons] of lentils would be cooked. This food was distributed till the last day of the strike. Neither the Amritsar Labour Federation nor any of the unions had any funds, so the people provided the flour, lentil and cash for the food. For this *langar* [can be compared to a soup kitchen] Amritsar's Bijli Pehalwan ['*pehelwan*' is the term for wrestlers who would have managed their own *akharas*; neighbourhood strongmen fluctuating between the role of local gangsters; and community patrons] gave two sacks of flour and one ton of lentil every day from the start to the finish. All the Hindu industrialists of the city went to him and said that the Muslims are trying to ruin us by striking, so do not help them; Pehalwan did not listen to anyone and said that he had promised to provide help.

On the day of my arrest during this strike, there was violence. I had gone to the gate of Amritsar Rayon and Silk factory to check the picketing arrangement when the police superintendent, Mr Durant, came with many constables to arrest me. The workers started shouting slogans after seeing the police, at which the superintendent gave orders for a 'baton charge'. The labourers who numbered in the hundreds started throwing stones in retaliation. The superintendent told me to ask them to stop. He made me stand on top of a police lorry and give a brief speech in which I asked the workers to stop the violence since it was against our principles. At this, the retaliation stopped immediately. Then the police arrested me and several other picketers.

After my arrest, the picketing and rallies continued with force for a few days. The police stopped registering cases and instead, implemented the following plan. They would arrest the labourers in the evening, load them on buses and leave them in a deserted area twenty or thirty miles away from the city. The labourers would have no money for food or transport fare to travel back. Helpless, they would go to a nearby village, beg for food and return home after two or three days.

The movement became weak after my arrest. Sufi Ghulam Muhammad Turk, Sohan Singh Josh, Comrade Feroz-ud-Din Mansoor and Pundit Amar Nath Vidyalankar, who later became governor of southern Punjab in the Congress ministry, struck a compromise with the Amritsar Textile Manufacturer's Association, but it did not serve the purpose of the strike. There was no increase in the labourers' wages. The only decision was that the labourers released from jail would be hired back for work and no one would be punished for going on strike. However, those with serious allegations against them would be screened. A committee was formed for screening which included representatives from the Amritsar Labour Federation and the Textile Manufacturers' Association. However, this committee did not execute its responsibilities properly and did not implement the aforementioned agreement fully. Consequently, many of the labourers did not get their jobs back.

Strike: At Punjab Rubber Works

The Muslim shoe sellers of Amritsar and Jalandhar had come together and opened a boot-making factory at Weerkah District in Amritsar by the name of Punjab Rubber Works Limited. The factory was created in competition with Bata and it only made canvas boots at that time, but there were plans to produce all kinds of leather boots. The factory's managing director was Haji Abdur Raheem Jalandhari and about 300 people worked in it. We had created a union in this factory before it had even started running, while the machines were still being installed. It was called the Punjab Rubber Works Labour Union. The union's officials were selected through a general meeting, but I had to do all the work as they were new and unfamiliar with the labour movement. Initially, the factory owner made no objection to the union's activities. However, when the union started making demands, Haji Abdul Raheem became alert and started objecting to the labourers coming to me and my visiting them in the factory. At that time, I would conduct two or three meetings a week in front of the factory's main gate. The labourers used to work for ten to twelve hours a day. Even though according to the law they had to be paid twice their wages for any work they did beyond eight hours, this was not implemented; and the general wage was also very low. They would only get twelve annas for making a dozen canvas shoes. In such a situation, even the best of workers was not able to make more than a rupee a day even after working for twelve to fourteen hours. They would work twenty-four days a month at best, because, along with a weekly holiday, there would also be one or two festivals a month. Sometimes, however, if there was a lot of work, the labourers would be made to work on Sundays as well, and would then get twenty-eight or twenty-nine working days a month. However, the workers' health was suffering because of the constant overtime work. That was the reason why almost all the workers had become union members. Their demand was that the wages should be increased so that the labourers could earn one rupee after working eight hours. The union officials met the managing director once or twice during the month in this regard, but with no result.

One day, I heard that the union officials had been bought by the managing director and the union had been broken, and preparations were underway to celebrate a day of deliverance. Therefore, Sufi Ghulam Muhammad Turk and I went to Weerkah, which was a distance of three miles from Amritsar. We saw a notice posted on the factory gate, which had the signatures of the union's president and secretary. The notice said that they had dissolved the union because there was no need of one in their area. The Quran says that Muslims should not fight other Muslims and a verse of the Holy Quran was also printed. It was also written that since the managing director had decided to increase the labourers' wages, there was no longer an argument and hence the union was broken. The next day, the day of deliverance would be celebrated and the factory owner would treat the labourers to a feast. Sufi Ghulam Muhammad and I stayed outside the factory till the working hours were over. When the labourers started coming out, the union officials kept telling them to not listen to us and go straight to their homes. However I started a meeting, which, save for a few, all the workers attended. I tried to explain to them that the factory owner was not their friend. He uses the verses of the Holy Quran for his own ulterior motive and he will extract hundreds of rupees for the rice he will feed you. 'We are telling you beforehand that in a few days, you will be surrounded by problems and will then realize the need of a union. We will not shut our doors to you even then; instead the Labour Federation will always be ready to offer help.' The next day, inside the factory, the managing director said his Friday prayers with the labourers, and many sermons were given in which it was constantly repeated that Muslims are all brothers and hence should not fight with each other. On the other hand, *pulao* [a rice dish], sweet rice and chicken *qorma* [gravy] were served. There was a huge celebration that day and in the midst of the grand feast, labourers lost track of the reality that there was a difference between them and the factory owners.

Many days passed after the day of deliverance and for two months no major event occurred. However, after a while, the ex-secretary and president were fired on the basis of a similar excuse. They did not come to us out of embarrassment, but we found out that they were found guilty because they pointed out the factory owner's mistakes out of their old habits. The managing director, Haji Abdur Rahim, could not stand the fact that the workers were questioning him and asking for additional money for overtime. After a few days, cutbacks began and the wages were also reduced by two annas per dozen. The workers were shocked when these hardships kept increasing; finally, one day, a delegation of labourers of Punjab Rubber Works came to our factory and asked for forgiveness for their mistake. They invited Sufi Ghulam Muhammad and me to attend a meeting outside the factory's gate. We accepted their request and set a date for the meeting. The meeting was held at the designated date, and it was decided that a strike would be conducted and continued until all the demands were accepted. At that time, there was no law in the country on the basis of which labour could not strike. The next day, a strike was declared according to plan and a list of demands were sent to the managing director along with a request for a union delegation to meet him. When the union's representative took demands to Haji Abdul Rahim, he refused to meet him. The same evening, another meeting was held in which all the workers participated enthusiastically. They were determined about their decision to not resume work until all their demands had been met. It was decided that a rally be organized the following morning. A rally was taken out the next day which started from the factory's gate, and went from Weerkah all the way to Amritsar passing all the major markets in Amritsar, especially Katrah Jameel Singh, where the shops of all the shareholders of Punjab Rubber Works were situated. Various poems were recited in the rally, one of which was as follows:

Uth jaag zara mazdoora
Uth jaag zara mazdoora
Tera reh gya kaam adhoora
Tera reh gya kaam adhoora
Zordaar da dekhein chala
Bharda mool na tera hala
But sarmayadari wala
Kar de chura chura
Uth jaag zara mazdoora
Apne kaam sawareen aape
Jay tu aye qaul da poora
Uth jaag zara mazdoora

Motiyan dhadhiyan waale yaara
Sanu bara satande ne
Kha kha maal ghareeban wala
Kohlu bande jaande ne
Nit building nawi tyaar howe
Kehnde ghaate pained jaante ne
Uth jag mazdoora dhar ragra
Mit jaye zulm da sab jhagra
Aye Bakhtiar da ragra aye
Jira mita dainda sab jhagra aye

[Wake up oh labourer, wake up oh labourer
Your work is yet incomplete, your work is yet incomplete
See the ways of the powerful, they don't give a damn about your condition
Break into bits the idol of capitalism
Wake up oh labourer
Make right your things yourself if you're a man of your word
Wake up oh laborer
The mighty, my fellows, tease us a lot
Eating up the poor's riches, they're becoming fat
Every day they construct a new building and then they say 'we're incurring losses'
Wake up oh labourer and struggle, finish the fight against tyranny
This is Bakhtiar's remedy, that will remove all conflicts!]

Other than this, at every town square and market, after going short distances, I would stand on a stool and make a speech explaining the entire situation to the people, and also informing them that Haji Abdur Rehman was a very dishonest man. His beard and prayers were only for demonstration. He sucks the poor labourers' blood by confiscating their hard-earned money. First he gives labour *pulao* and sweet rice to eat, and now he is making them pay several rupees for each grain. Thus every day a rally would be taken out, speeches would be made, poems would be recited and slogans chanted:

Inqilab zindabad!
Mazdoor ittihad zindabad!
Haji Abdul Rahim murdabad!
Sarmayadari ka bera gharq!
Mazdooron ke mutalbaat poore karo!

[Long live revolution!
Long live labour unity!
Death to Haji Abdur Rahim!
Down with capitalism!
Fulfil labour's demands!]

This continued for a week. The factory remained shut with the police on guard. We did not try to meet Haji Abdur Rahim, and he did not call us. The shareholders of Punjab Rubber Works whose shops were in Katrah Jameel Singh, and who would witness our rallies and hear our speeches, poems and slogans, decided to meet Sufi Ghulam Muhammad Turk, myself and Haji Abdur Rehman in order to reach a settlement. They called Turk and me and said that they have tried to talk to and explain to Haji Abdur Rahim that he should reach a decision with labour, but 'he is not in favour of running the factory because he is afraid of the labour union and scared by the mere mention of our names'. Therefore, they suggested that Haji should be called 'so that we can assure him that we will neither go towards the factory, nor make a union. All the labour demands will be accepted.' If we did not reassure him, the factory would be shut down for good and the labourers would be unemployed. This was the first factory owned by Muslims in Amritsar and the only organization in competition with Bata in all of India. So many people were employed here that we should prevent it from closing down.

We thought that we should agree as this way, the labourers' demands would be accepted and the factory would start functioning again. Then, after a while, we could make a union again. Consequently, we accepted this condition. The next day, all the shareholders gathered and called Haji, Turk and myself to their meeting. The active workers of this meeting were Mairaj ud-din, from the General Boot House, Haji Muhammad Ameen from the Ameen Boot House, Abdul Hafeez and Abdul Hameed. When Haji Abdur Rehman arrived, he was extremely angry and was not ready to have a word with us. He said that he would not run the factory under any circumstances and would leave Amritsar because people had spread immense hatred against him. 'People point fingers at me and whisper amongst themselves, no matter which market I go to.' He said he got nervous and looked at them as if he was a thief. Secondly, he was against the labour union. At this, I tried to assure him that we would not go towards the factory or try to make a union, on the condition that he accepted the labourers' demands. All the shareholders also tried to convince him by saying that now Bakhtiar and Turk would not do anything to him and would not form a union, as long as he just accepted the demands. The meeting continued for three or four hours; at the end of which, Haji Abdur Rehman got up, said the following and left:

> Kill Bakhtiar and Sufi and cut them into pieces, burn those pieces to ashes and spread these ashes on two mountains. When the wind blows, these ashes will fly. A union will be formed in every factory where even a particle of those ashes will land. I refuse to believe that they will not form a union in my factory.

Hence the meeting proved to be in vain. The factory was shut down for good and its machinery was sold off. Haji Abdur Rehman left Amritsar and went to Jalandhar. Punjab Rubber Works' name was erased from existence forever, and a capitalist's extreme stubbornness became the cause for an industrial organization's destruction.

Nationwide Strike at the Postal Department

The biggest strike was by the All India Postmen R.M.S. and Lower Grade Staff Union. This strike began in 1946 and continued, simultaneously, from Peshawar to Bombay, Madras, Calcutta, Bihar and Delhi to Simla for twenty-six days. Post office employees from eleven of India's provinces participated in it. The government declared the strike illegal but did not dismiss any employee or punish anyone. Some people were fired from their jobs only in Peshawar but I, accompanied by the union's treasurer, Muhammad Shareef Postman, and Punjab and NWFP's general secretary, Pundit Kishan Chand, went to Peshawar and got the workers their jobs back. After twenty-six days the strike committee and the director-general of the Postal Department, Krishna Prasad, finally met in Bombay and reached a compromise to put an end to the strike.

The most important aspect of this strike was that after spreading to Bombay, United Province, Central Province, Bengal, Simla, Delhi, Punjab, North-West Frontier Province, etc., its constituency became fairly vast, as a result of which the strike committee's difficulties also increased. Therefore, we were forced to end the strike and think of alternate ways of getting the demands accepted. At the same time, it was not easy to end the strike without fulfilment of the demands since the strike had spread across all of India and was especially strong in Bombay. Other than the postmen and the lower grade staff, approximately two lakh people, including textile mills' labour, tram employees and college students, had also gone on strike in sympathy.

After many deliberations, we, the members of the strike committee, decided to go to Qaid-e-Azam Mohammad Ali Jinnah, who was living in Bombay in those days, request him to take the matter of the strike in his hands, and announce that even though the struggle for the demands would be continued, the strike must come to an end. Qaid-e-Azam told us to leave all the related documents, and that he would inform us in two days as to whether or not he could take the responsibility of ending the strike and getting the demands approved. We did not see our purpose being satisfied by this reply and hence we went to Mahatma Gandhi and said that we had come for his blessings. We told him that the employees were in immense difficulty; their salary was insufficient. He prayed for them. Then we requested him to take control of the strike. He said that he could not do it himself; however, he could ask Sardar Patel to do our work. He telephoned Sardar Patel and said that he was sending some union representatives to him for his help. Therefore, we went to Sardar Patel. He heard our story, took the situation in his hands and announced that the strike should be put to an end.

When this announcement was broadcast on the radio, the striking workers came to our Bombay office with sticks and attacked it. They started cursing us, saying we had joined forces with the government and deceived labour. We explained to them with immense difficulty that the decision to end the strike was taken by Sardar Patel, and if we did not agree with him the Congress would turn against us and therefore we were forced to listen to him. At this, the crowds turned towards Sardar Patel's house and started chanting slogans of 'Death to Sardar Patel!' outside his house, and throwing stones at it. Consequently, the police interfered and dispersed the crowd with great difficulty. After that, Pandit Jawaharlal Nehru released a statement in the newspapers and said that if the strikers do not end the strike, the Congress would provide no assistance to them. Along with this, he gave directions to the Speaker of Bombay Assembly, Mangal Das Pakwasa, to call the director-general of the Postal Department, Krishna Prasad, to Bombay and bring about a compromise with the strikers. Therefore, the director-general was called to Bombay and a compromise was reached. It was decided that firstly, the government would appoint a pay commission which would analyse the salaries of all the employees of the Central Government and present its recommendations to the government. Till the time the recommendations were implemented, all the employees would be given a good conduct pay of ten rupees per month.

First Time in Jail

I was sent to jail four times because of the labour movement, but the hardships of imprisonment could not stop me. Every single time the four walls of the jail became a hotbed for my activities and I kept becoming the axis of strange incidents; a few are written below for the knowledge of the next generations of labourers.

The first time I was sent to jail was on 4 May 1936. This arrest was during the strike at Narain Swadeshi Mills, Chheharta, Amritsar. This was the second big labour strike in Amritsar. Before this, a similar strike had occurred at Bankeshwar Cotton Mill, Putli Ghar, in 1932, during which Bashir Sehrai, Nisar Ahmed and many labourers had been arrested. On 4 May 1936, at three in the afternoon, the police arrested me and thirty-six other labourers because of the strike and sent us to Amritsar Jail. However, we were sentenced according to Section 392/448 of the Indian Act alleging a robbery. This was my first experience of spending time in jail.

In those days, the '*roti* parade' was practised in jail, during which the prisoners were made to sit in one line and food distributed amongst them. The first day, the bell rang at six in the evening for the '*roti* parade'. All the prisoners slowly started moving in one direction. My companions and I were in jail for the first time, and we had no idea why the bell had been rung and what we were supposed to do. Secondly, many of my companions had been injured because of the police's 'baton charge'. Someone would be sitting on one corner and the other would be lying somewhere else, gasping in pain. It was true that we felt extremely harassed at being in jail for the first time. My condition was no better. My head was spinning and panic gripped my heart, but I let nobody see my condition and kept consoling my companions.

As the bell rang, I saw the '*Jamadar* prisoners', some of whom were wearing black and others yellow uniforms; they were carrying leather belts and saying, in a stream of filthy curses, 'Let's go for the parade'. These '*Jamadar* prisoners' were called 'good conduct prisoners' in prison parlance, on the basis of their joining the administration in beating up and harassing the other prisoners. In return for these services, they were made officers amongst the prisoners, and were given yellow and black uniforms. Other than cursing, they would also hit the prisoners with their leather belts. It looked as if they were shepherding goats. On seeing this, we started going where all the other prisoners were headed.

On that day, there were 500 prisoners in jail; the maximum capacity of the jail was only 350 prisoners. The prisoners sat in two lines, and my companions and I also sat down in one of them. The yellow and black uniform-clad *Jamadars* were ordering the prisoners to straighten the lines and now, along with the abuses, they were also kicking the prisoners: 'Move forward', 'Sit straight'. Each prisoner had two '*batian*' each. A '*bati*' was a bowl-like dish of ten or eleven inches diameter. Each prisoner would get two pieces of bread (*roti*) in one, and gravy in the other *bati*. We did not have any utensils, but soon a *Jamadar* gave each of us a steel *bati*. The *batis*' condition was such that they looked as if they had never been used but instead had been picked up from a pile of filth; a thick layer of rust covered them and they were emanating a very foul smell. We later found out that all these *batian* were also used for urine and stool in the toilet. The two *rotis* we got were completely uncooked and the gravy looked like fodder given to cattle: it had only water and was cooked without salt, spice or oil. According to the law, designated amounts of oil, salt, onion, tamarind, etc., were supposed to be put in the 'vegetables'. But the jail officers would unlawfully sell these things and keep the money. When our turn came, we took the bread in our hands because the *bati* was unusable. When the gravy which had an excess of water was put on the bread, the bread, being raw, disintegrated and the gravy fell down. Some of my companions took the gravy in their hands only. None of us could eat when we began because firstly, the bread, made out of flour and mixed with mud, was raw, and the gravy was completely tasteless and bland. Many of my friends became teary-eyed. I was worried myself but when I saw my companions' condition, I became even more so. Even then I hid my nervousness and assured my friends that very soon we would correct these conditions and that there was no need to worry.

That evening, none of us ate anything. We threw away the bread and gravy, and after the '*roti* parade', went with the other prisoners to drink water from the taps. In the meantime, the bell rang again and the *Jamadars* started shoving people into the cells while hitting them with leather belts and abusing them, and locked their doors.

Each barrack and room had brick slabs for the prisoners to sleep on; they were called '*khadian*'. Each slab was 6 feet long, 2.5 feet wide and 2 feet high; one man slept on each. Because of the large number of prisoners, my companions and I could not even get these slabs, and we had to spend the night on the floor without any blanket or bedding. Because of the injuries sustained during the 'baton charge', intense hunger and lack of a bed, we spent the night wide awake. Before the sun rose, the black and yellow uniform-clad *Jamadars* opened the cell doors, woke up the ones asleep with a barrage of abuses and ordered them to get out.

There was no toilet inside the cell, only two bricks that lay near the sleeping and sitting place. Whether it was day or night, if any prisoner felt the need to relieve himself he would have to do so on the bricks in front of everyone. There was no question of a curtain. The neighbouring prisoners were asked to turn their faces to the other side and that would be the only screen. There was an extremely foul smell in the cells because of the filth. Outside the cells, there were only fifteen toilets for 500 prisoners, but even these were without any cover. When the prisoners were let out of their cells, most would head directly towards the toilets, but because of the limited capacity, would be forced to wait for hours in line. The first morning we faced a similar situation, which was extremely difficult to bear. This increased our worries. Some friends got so worried that they became ready to ask for forgiveness. But even then I kept comforting them, although I too was extremely worried and kept thinking of possible solutions to these problems.

Then, I started analysing the different kinds of prisoners in the jail. I found that there was a Malli gang of dacoits, whose members were involved in crimes of murder and robbery. The second was dacoit Kartar Singh's party. There was one Akali Jatha Dar (group leader) whose name I cannot remember. He, along with his group, had snatched Amritsar's Darbar Sahab keys from the British when the British government, because of their displeasure with the Akali movement, had kicked the Akalis out and locked up the Darbar Sahib. Jatha Dar's height was, without exaggeration, at least six-and-a-half feet and his entire body was covered with hair. He was a very grand and brave person, and was kept alone in a separate '*kothi*'. '*Kothi*' was the name given to a small room in the prison where a dangerous criminal or a prisoner about to be hanged was kept in isolation.

Within a week, I was able to meet and get acquainted with all of them. Jatha Dar started calling me 'Master Jee' and slowly everyone started referring to me by that name. All the prisoners of the jail were fed up with the bread made from a mixture of flour, mud and salt, and the vegetable gravy without oil or spice, which they had to eat almost daily. Only once a week would we get lentils, in which there would be more water than lentil grains. Despite this, the days the prisoners got pulses would cause more jubilation to them than *Eid*.

I convinced Malli, Jatha Dar and Kartar Singh to demand from the jail authorities that the prisoners be treated like human beings and not animals. Consequently, it was left to me to formulate a plan and the rest of the people would support me in whatever it might be. I started spending day and night reflecting on this, thinking of one programme or the other, but due to my lack of experience with regard to the jail, it was difficult to reach a final decision. Finally, one day I decided that we should openly fight the jail authorities. If all of the 500 prisoners united, there should be no reason for us to not get our demands accepted. I informed Jatha Dar, Kartar Singh and Malli of my decision to openly fight the authorities, and they agreed. It was decided that the fight should begin when all the prisoners were together in one place. For this, the morning *roti* parade was considered most appropriate. Hence it was decided that in the morning, when everyone collects for the *roti* parade, and the jail workers and the *Jamadar* prisoners start distributing food, they should be attacked suddenly. I was assigned the responsibility of getting on the second floor of the prison and declaring war, at which Malli and Kartar Singh's people would get up and attack the guards and *Jamadar* prisoners. At night, selected companions were secretly informed of the plan.

In the morning when the *roti* parade began and all the prisoners sat in straight lines, I got up on the second floor of the jail and, just as the distribution of food began, started addressing the prisoners in a loud voice.

> My imprisoned brothers!
> You are being given this filthy food; bread made out of flour and mud and stew cooked without salt, spice or oil, which is the food for animals, and you silently keep eating it. Had you ever eaten such food outside the jail? At home, you would break the dishes if your wives put even slightly less salt in your food and would curse your lovely wives. Today, you are being treated worse than dogs. Why are you afraid and why do you silently bear this terrible diet and degrading treatment? Some of you are to get hung. Some have to spend a lifetime, some ten years and some five years in imprisonment. If you raise your voice against this persecution, the jail officers can do you no harm. Get up, be brave and tell these spawns of hell that we may have committed crimes, but we are still human and we should be treated like human beings.

As I finished the speech, Malli and Kartar Singh moved forward, knocked over the gravy pots and started throwing the bread around. After this, all the prisoners got up from the lines and started chanting slogans of 'Long Live Revolution', 'Long Live Prisoner Unity' and 'Death to Daroga Jail'. Prisoners who had already received food threw it away, and everyone started hitting the jail guards, constables and *Jamadar* prisoners. Within the blink of an eye, these jail officials and prisoners became merged into one crowd and the guards started blowing their whistles. The jail norm was that if the prisoners started fighting or someone ran away, any employee who discovered that would start blowing his whistle. Any guard, inside or outside the jail, upon hearing the whistle was supposed to pick up his stick and start a baton charge without any investigation, to spread fear amongst the prisoners. Consequently, as soon as the whistles blew, all the guards standing outside came in and started assaulting the prisoners. The prisoners retaliated with the metallic *batian* but the guards seemed stronger because they had sticks; the prisoners seemed helpless in front of them. In front of the rooms on the second floor of the jail, where I was standing, there was a balcony and a railing in front of that. There was wood on its top and bottom but in between there were 1/8 inch thick, 1.5 inch wide and 4 feet long metallic wires. When I saw my companions weakening under the onslaught of the *lathis*, quickly, with the help of some other prisoners, I broke the railing and started throwing the metallic wires to the prisoners downstairs. As soon as they got their hands on it, the prisoners started attacking the guards with full force. After this, we soon gained control of the field, and the guards and *Jamadar* prisoners ran out. A few days after this incident all the metallic wires of the railings in the jail were taken down and replaced with wooden blocks.

That day the prisoners neither ate anything nor did any work. Many prisoners had got seriously injured during the fight. One Sikh prisoner had a broken arm and leg, along with fourteen wounds on his body caused by the sticks. I remember, after peace was made, when I visited my friends in the jail hospital accompanied by Jatha Dar, this Sikh prisoner's condition was so bad that he couldn't even move. When I asked him about his health, he slowly opened one of his eyes and said: 'Master, how are you? Do you have any injuries?' I replied saying that I was completely fine and asked him how he was doing. He looked at me with a smile and said, 'Thank God you are okay; no worries about me.'

In the evening, when the time came to lock the prisoners back in their cells, the jailer, who was a Sikh, sent a message to me saying that he was ready to accept our demands and that we should go talk to him. I got Malli, Kartar Singh, Jatha Dar and other ringleaders together and gave them the jailer's message, and suggested that we go to him. Jatha Dar, who had been in jail many times before, said on the basis of his experience: 'Master ji, these jail officers should not be trusted, they will deceive us, we should not go to them.' I replied to Jatha Dar: 'Then the question is, how will this argument be resolved?' At this he replied that he had only given his opinion; he would accept any decision I made but would not go to the jailer. A lot of time was spent to convince Jatha Dar to go to the jailer, but because he deeply hated the jail officers and the British government, and would rather bear the difficulty than have it go away by begging for a compromise in front of the jailer, Jatha Dar remained steadfast in his decision like a brave general. Finally, it was decided that I would go to the jailer with ten men and would call Jatha Dar if the need arose. We decided upon the following demands:

(1) A committee, comprising of five prisoners, should be formed which would look after the food distribution. The food would be cooked under this committee's supervision.
(2) The flour mixed with mud, currently used in the jail, should no

longer be used. Instead, new flour should be purchased from the market in the morning.
(3) Urns for drinking water should be kept in all the cells and rooms.
(4) Covered toilets should be made in all the cells.
(5) Some of the jail guards who were called warders should be suspended because they had carried out an intense baton charge on the prisoners.
(6) Some of the black and yellow uniform clad *Jamadar* prisoners should also be removed from their posts and made normal prisoners again, and locked up in *kothis* because of their extremely harsh treatment of the prisoners.
(7) Shower taps should be installed in the jail.

My companions and I took these demands to the jailer after sunset. The Sikh jailer was being extremely accommodating; he was nervous and worried because all the cells and *kothis* of the jail were unlocked and the prisoners were roaming about freely in the jail. This was extremely objectionable according to the regulations of the jail, and its responsibility fell upon the jailer. The jailer took off his turban, placed it in front of us, joined his hands and said: 'I will accept whatever you say. Instruct the prisoners to go back to their cells so that the guards can put up the locks. If the jail isn't locked, I will be dismissed from my job. I have little kids, have mercy on me.' I felt great pity for his condition. I said that if he agreed with us we would also listen to him, and that if he accepted our demands then he should give it to us in writing. The jailer said that it would be difficult for him to give it to us in writing, but he promised that our problems would be solved according to our demands. The debate with the jailer regarding a written promise continued for a long time. Finally, we sent for Jatha Dar. He came after a while and when we told him that the jailer was hesitating in making a written promise to us, he said: 'Master ji, I told you earlier that these jail people are cheats. It doesn't matter even if he gave it in writing because eventually he will deny it.' After a lot of deliberation it was decided that the jailer's behaviour in the morning should be observed and no final decision should be taken at the moment. At this the jailer begged and pleaded that the prisoners be sent back to their cells so that the guards could lock them up, and the metal wires used in the fight be returned to him. However, we refused to accept these conditions. We decided that the prisoners would be sent back to their cells but no locks would be put, and the metal wires would not be given to the jailer. A final decision would be taken based upon the jailer's behaviour the next day.

During the time we were busy in dialogue with the jailer, the prisoners, in different groups, were enjoying their freedom. Some were singing songs, while others were having discussions about the event. The entire internal system of the jail was now in our hands because all the prisoners were organized. After returning from the jailer's room, we directed the prisoners to go back to their cells but not to let anyone lock them. All the prisoners went back to their respective cells and that night, no cell was locked. In the morning, when the bell rang, the prisoner count was complete.

First thing the next morning, the jailer asked me for five names for supervision of the food and its distribution. Therefore, I formed a five-member committee and sent the names to him. The jailer made them inspect the bread and the gravy and they informed us that the food was okay. That day, the bread was made from flour brought from the market and was decently cooked. Although the contents of the gravy were the same, it was cooked with appropriate amounts of salt, spices, onion and mustard oil. That day, water urns were also kept in all the cells. The yellow and black uniform clad *Jamadar* prisoners we had pointed out were locked in their cells and their uniforms had been removed. The jailer told us that other demands would also be met soon.

The five-member committee inspected the food at night as well. The food was good. The second and third day also passed well. However, on the third night, when all the cells were closed and locked and darkness had set in, some *Jamadar* prisoners, who had now become sympathetic to us,

Bashir Ahmed Bakhtiar in 1936, on his release from jail

informed me that Kartar Singh's cell door was open, and that he and his party men were drinking alcohol. The jailer had sent them roasted chicken and now our power had been divided in two. I was extremely worried after hearing this because it was clear to me that the jailer had made this move to create a division amongst us to get his revenge. The gates were shut at that time and we could not meet each other. However, I sent a report of this critical incident to Jatha Dar and Malli Sahab via the sympathetic *Jamadar* prisoners.

The next morning when the *roti* parade began, Kartar Singh and his group did not come to it. We found out that they were all together in one cell, drinking alcohol, and eating and roasting meat. The same day, many of the prisoners who were considered members of our party were transferred from Amritsar Jail to jails in other cities. This way, our strength was countered and the prison once again came under the jailer's rule.

Jatha Dar was right: prison officers are cheats and should never be trusted.

At Central Jail, Lahore

By 1938 we had formed unions in almost all the industries and factories in Amritsar. The process of awakening was on the rise amongst labour, and the labour movement was gaining momentum. At this point, I had an idea: to further the movement, we should display the strength of labour in the form of a general strike, in which labour from all the industries and factories should participate.

Bashir Ahmed Bakhtiar leading a May Day procession (1938) on horseback

Sufi Ghulam Muhammad Turk, Malik Fazal Ilahi Qurban and Abdur Ghafoor Taish did not agree with this idea; they thought a strike on such a grand scale could not be successful without a lot of finances. Therefore, a general meeting was held at Jallianwala Bagh to take a poll. Labour from almost all the factories in Amritsar participated in this poll. That night, Jallianwala Bagh was packed with labourers. The meeting was attended by at least 40,000 labourers. At the beginning of the meeting, the general secretary of the Amritsar Labour Federation enlightened everyone about the purpose of the meeting and informed labour of the need for a strike. Comrade Fazal Ilahi Qurban and Sufi Ghulam Muhammad Turk gave speeches against the strike. Voting was conducted after the speeches; approximately 10 per cent of the votes were in favour of the strike and the rest were against it. However, I was not ready to change my stance because I believed that at this point the strike would be extremely profitable for the labour movement.

Therefore, I stood up again on the stage with determination and announced in a confident tone that I had heard everyone's decision. 'Now, my decision is that the strike will take place.' I demanded to know who opposed it. Silence set in the meeting. I reiterated, 'The strike will take place, is there anybody who opposes it? If so, raise your hand.' But not a single hand was raised. Thus the decision was made in favour of the strike. The meeting ended. All the workers were immediately instructed to gather in the office. At two in the morning, a meeting of the workers was conducted in the office and they were sent off with directions regarding the next morning's plan. At that time, the total amount of money we had was six annas, but I was confident even then.

The following day, about 50 factories in the city were completely shut down and about the same number were on partial strike. To strike completely in the factories that were partially operating, we started picketing outside their gates. Feroz-ud-Din, aka Dr Jalal Puria, and Sultan Ahmed Kulu were appointed in charge of picketing. I established my headquarters at Jallianwala Bagh and also started free food distribution there for the labourers. There was separate food for Muslims, where all the cooks were Muslim. Hindus and Sikhs had separate food too, and its responsibility was given to Hindu and Sikh women who did their jobs efficiently. Every day, about 10,000 labourers would eat here. For this food distribution, the important people of the city would daily send flour, lentils and rice. I remember that Bijli Pehalwan had accepted the responsibility of sending one ton of lentils and two sacks of flour every day until the strike continued. Therefore, for approximately a month, Pehalwan's servant would bring one ton of lentils and two sacks of flour daily. Similarly, many charitable gentlemen of Amritsar would send flour and lentils. We collected so much stock that daily 10,000 people ate during the day and the same number ate at night from our distribution. It is a long story as to how we were spending hundreds of rupees daily and who was bringing this money, when, at the time of the announcement of the strike, we only had six annas!

Some industrialists, because of the fear of picketing, would shut their factories during the day and run them at night. When we found out, we arranged for picketing at night as well. Meanwhile, a heavy contingent of police was called from Gurdaspur District to Amritsar. The picketing was being carried out day and night outside several factories, and the police was stationed outside each factory for protection. The labourers would picket in the presence of the police and nothing would be said to them. It was to the credit and fortitude of the British government of the time that they had given such freedom to labour, because of which no arrests were made for quite a while. The police were instructed to not interfere in the activities of labour as long as they were peaceful. Every day, labour rallies would be taken out and meetings would be held, but the police did not lay a hand on them.

Those days, I used to wear a red shirt and white pants, and a sword would hang by my waist. Ten volunteers, similarly clad in red shirts and white pants and carrying a sword in their hands, would accompany me day and night for my safety. When I would go somewhere, a volunteer carrying the red sickle and hammer flag would walk in front of me.

For a while during the strike nothing unpleasant happened, but after a few days, fights broke out. One evening, as I was supervising the picketing outside Amritsar Rayon and Silk Mills, vans filled with police officers and constables arrived suddenly. As soon as the vans stopped, the police jumped out and started a baton charge on the labourers. A police captain grabbed my hand and some constables surrounded me. After making about 200 labourers get into the vans, the police captain, Durant, made me sit in his car with him. When the arrests started, the labourers, with full gusto, started getting into the buses. When a bus filled up, the labourers would cling to its outside at which the police would push them down. That evening, approximately 300 labourers were arrested in the city. The captain took me to the police station headquarters and put me in lock-up. The next morning, we were presented in front of Magistrate Muhammad Shafi of District 30. After cursory proceedings, he sentenced all of us to two months of imprisonment and sent us to Lahore Central Jail. The series of arrests continued on the second and third day. Some labourers were sent to Amritsar Jail and some to Gurdaspur Jail. When these jails were filled to their capacity, the police started loading their vans with labourers and abandoning them forty miles away from the city.

After spending two months in Lahore Central Jail, when the time of our release arrived, all my companions were released but I was held back. Upon inquiry, I found out that my sentence was for a longer time. Later, after being released, when I came to Amritsar and asked Magistrate Muhammad Shafi, he said that he had been instructed by Magistrate MacDonald to not let me out at the time, and hence my sentence had been extended.

I did not face any special difficulty in Lahore Central Jail because, firstly, the 300 of us were prisoners of the same group, and secondly, after the previous experience of Amritsar Jail, I knew how to deal with prison officers. However, we would hold daily meetings to see if anyone was facing any difficulties. Then I would meet the jailer who was in charge of our premises and get the problem solved. At one such meeting, one of our companions, Mairaj-ud-Din, who was a weaver and was called Mairaj-ud-Din 'Teetran Wala' because of his pet '*teeters*' (partridges), presented a demand that since they did not find the Lahore water suitable, they should either be provided water from Amritsar or be moved to Amritsar jail. All of us laughed heartily at this demand. During this strike, the people who did notable work were Nizam-ud-Din aka Chahoota Jalal Poorya, Feroz-ud-Din aka Doctor, and Muhammad Sadiq aka [Sadqa?] Jalal Poorya.

The officers at Lahore Central Jail tried their best to make the prisoners beg for clemency but not one of the labourers agreed to do that. During imprisonment, the wedding date arrived for one of the labourers. His father drafted an apology letter and sent it inside the jail so that he could sign it and get released. He brought the apology letter to me and asked for advice. I said that he should postpone the wedding date if possible, because if he apologized the labour movement would be humiliated. At this, he sent a clear reply to his father and did not apologize. Consequently, his engagement broke off. Another labourer received news of the death of his only son, along with a message to ask for forgiveness and return home. When he asked me, I reminded him that during the previous strike, when we were picketing, I too had received news of my son's death. But instead of leaving and going home, I had stayed, out of fear that my absence would lead to a conflict between the labourers and the police. I had instead sent Ghulam Muhammad Haripuria, Ahmed Bin Haripuria and twenty or thirty other labourers with instructions to bury the departed. I did not even go to see my late son's face. He affirmed this by saying that he was one of the twenty or thirty people who had buried my son. Therefore, he took control of his emotions and replied to his family that he would never apologize and only return after completing his term in jail. And so, he completed his entire sentence.

The other prisoners in the jail also greatly respected me. When the old prisoners, especially Sikh prisoners, went out to work in the fields, they would bring me back green chillies and onions as gifts, hiding them in their turbans or clothing. At that time, such items were considered great blessings inside the prison. I would use some of the onions and green chillies myself and distribute the rest amongst the other labourer prisoners.

Third Arrest

On 14 June 1939, around five o clock in the afternoon, I was in my house at Sharif Pura, Amritsar when there was a knock on my door. I peeked downstairs to see who it was, to find a head constable from CID, dressed in white clothes, standing at my door. When I asked him for the purpose of his visit, he said: 'Come downstairs; the head officer has sent you greetings and called you to the station.' I put on my clothes and went downstairs to find a different situation. A police inspector and some uniformed constables, who had been hiding around my house, suddenly appeared and surrounded me. They told me that I was being arrested but for what crime, they never specified. The sub-inspector took me along and started walking, while some constables walked in front and some behind.

At about a quarter to six in the evening, I was locked up in the Amritsar city police station. Till ten o'clock, none of the police officers even spoke to me. After ten, a sub-inspector opened the gate and said, 'I've been ordered to take you out of this cell and take you to the jail. The officers think this room is too small and infested with the smell of urine etc.' It was true because the prisoners were forced to urinate or defecate inside. But I said that it did not matter; there was no question of good or bad smell if I am in captivity already, and I should stay there. But the sub-inspector did not agree and said he had orders. A prison van was outside the station. I was made to sit in it. In the shadow of the night, the van passed through Hall Market and headed towards the court, which was located at a distance of approximately two miles from the city. At one place, the van stopped and I was made to get out. It was pitch black outside. The place I had been brought to was the Civil Lines Station. I asked a station constable why I had been brought here when I had been told that I was being taken to the jail. He said he did not know and locked me up in the station. I was confused and surprised as to why I had been locked up first at Kotwali Station and now at Civil Lines Station. It turned eleven in the midst of these thoughts. In the darkness of the cell, the caravan of my thoughts was trying to find some destination.

Around 11.30, I heard the sounds of a motorcycle and a car stopping; then I heard a foreigner's strident voice. He asked the constable, 'Where is that dog we sent to you?' Then I heard the noise of heavy boots moving towards the cell. After a few moments, the cell door opened. Two British officers, one of whom was Inspector Takredi and the other S.S.P. Durant, were standing there with the station constable. The constable was ordered to leave as soon as the door opened. After he left, Inspector Takredi, who was a Britisher of strong build and medium height, and who was wearing army boots, entered the cell and said: 'O, you dog! You have greatly annoyed us.' While saying this, he forcefully kicked my ankles with his pointed boots and started slapping and punching my face. I fell to the ground because of the injuries, while the inspector continued kicking, punching and slapping me; so much so, I fainted. When I regained consciousness, the constable was pouring water in my mouth and Inspector Takredi and S.S.P. Durant were sitting on chairs outside the cell. Upon my waking up, both entered the cell. Durant said that I had greatly annoyed them and so the government directive was that I should leave Amritsar, for otherwise I would be executed. I said that I was neither a thief nor a crook, and the only thing I say is that labour's condition is extremely bad. Even after shedding their blood and sweat, they neither get a fulfilling meal nor clothes to cover their bodies – and saying that was not a crime. 'Bastard! Dog! Your father was sustained on this government's resources; he was given a pension by the state. You have used this government's resources. You have to follow the government's wishes', S.S.P. Durant yelled in a rude tone. I replied: 'I'm not committing a crime. Trying to get labourers remuneration for their hard work is not opposition of the government and the law."

Takredi grabbed my throat, thrust my head against the floor and harshly said that I would have to obey his commands. He then said, 'Write with your nose that you will not work for the labour movement and will not organize any more strikes.' I said again, 'I do not commit any crime.' At that Durant said, 'This dog will not agree like this – use the second method.' Takredi started punching, slapping and kicking me again, because of which two of my upper teeth broke and I was covered in blood. I was so badly injured that I could not withstand the pain and lost consciousness. When I regained consciousness again, I was lying on the floor. Darkness ruled inside and outside the cell. Durant and Takredi had left. The cell door was locked and a guard was keeping watch outside. My teeth and one of my ribs were broken. My ears, nose and face were swollen. Every part of my body was convulsed in pain. I lay on the floor in this condition, without any bedding or blanket, in the dead of the night. Half the night had passed. The *batis* and blankets had been taken out of the cell. Gasping in pain, I asked the guard for water and requested a blanket, but the only reply he gave was that he was not allowed to talk to me. I felt no one but God Almighty was with me. I prayed: 'God, keep me steadfast; you know I have not committed a crime.'

One thing that kept bothering me at that time was that forthcoming generations would have no knowledge of those who had worked in the early days of the labour movement and the kind of circumstances they had to deal with. The next generations would probably think that those people were incapable and did not know how to do their work.